The Economics of Being Poor

B

The Economics of Being Poor

THEODORE W. SCHULTZ

BLACKWELL
Oxford UK & Cambridge USA

First published 1993

Blackwell Publishers
238 Main Street, Suite 501
Cambridge, Massachusetts 02142
USA

108 Cowley Road
Oxford OX4 1JF
UK

Library of Congress Cataloging-in-Publication Data

Schultz, Theodore William, 1902–
    The economics of being poor / Theodore W. Schultz.
        p.   cm.
    Includes bibliographical references and index.
    ISBN 1–55786–320–2
    1. Poor.   2. Rural poor   3. Human capital   4. Poor – United
    States.   5. Rural poor – United States   I. Title.
    HC79.P6S335   1993
    330'.08'6942–dc20   92–27436   CIP

British Library Cataloguing in Publication Data

A CIP catalogue record for this book is available from
the British Library.

Typeset in 10 on 12 pt Sabon
by TecSet Ltd, Wallington, Surrey

This book is printed on acid-free paper

Contents

Acknowledgments

In selecting and organizing the collection of papers for this book, I benefited a great deal from the rich editorial experience in economics of Elizabeth Johnson. Margaret Schultz turned to the library to check sources. She also spotted ambiguities and awkward statements. My long time secretary, highly skilled Kathy Glover, stayed abreast of the on-going revisions and saw to it that "permissions to publish" and the introductory parts came in hand.

Theodore W. Schultz

1

Introduction

In spite of the fact that most people throughout the world are poor, the economics of being poor is not a well developed part of economics. Unless we can show that economics matters in explaining what poor people do as they eke out a living and how some manage to improve their economic lot, the title of this volume would be presumptuous.

In general it is easier to identify people who are poor than it is to bring relevant parts of economics to bear on their circumstances.

1   Identifying People Who Are Poor

I have not focused on particular individuals or on particular families. My endeavor has been to identify communities and states where nearly all of the people are poor.

The cost of food relative to personal income is a strong identifying indicator. Where half and more of real income is required to acquire food, most people are very poor. It is helpful to think of these communities and states as *high food drain* economic entities. People who live in communities or states where 20 percent and even less of the real income is spent on food are in general not poor people.

Data pertaining to food and income have become widely available. There are also many excellent studies specializing in food consumption and in the economics of households.

Life span is another important indicator in identifying poor people. In communities or states where life expectancy at birth ranges between 30 and 40 years, most people are very poor. Information, including data and specialized studies in health, nutrition, and life span, has become abundant.

A third strong identifying attribute of being poor is a low level of skills and knowledge. Skills and knowledge are major components of human capital. Human capital studies serve as useful guides to approaches to reduce the extent to which people are poor. Where there is little human capital there is only hard manual work and poverty, except for those who have some income from property. A novelist's words are often most telling as in Faulkner's *Intruder in the Dust* in his early morning scene of a poor, solitary cultivator at work in a field: the man without skills and knowledge leaning terrifically against nothing.

2 Where is the Economics in Being Poor?

It could be concealed in historical economics. If so, modern economists are not inclined to search history for it. History is a rich source of economic puzzles.

One of the odd intellectual twists that prevailed in England between 1660 and 1775 was the *Utility of Poverty Doctrine*. The puzzle is what could have distorted the thinking of so wide an array of enlightened individuals including Thomas Mun, Arthur Young, John Law, William Pettey, and even David Hume, on this issue?[1]

It followed logically from their belief in the utility of poverty that real wages of the laboring classes must be held low. One way of doing this, so it was argued, was to increase the price of necessities. When corn becomes plentiful, measures should be taken to subsidize its export. There should be a tax on consumption. Access of the poor to amusement, including strolling players, should be curtailed. Consumption of tea on the part of the poor was viewed as an evil. Charity was thought to be the nursery of idleness.

This puzzle is a warning that there are intellectual twists that originate out of the way the economy is organized.

Where people are poor, the meagerness of production (the source of real income) is not a consequence of indolence or of a lack of thrift. It is not because of some quirk in the preferences of poor people. Instead, it is a matter of costs and returns. The marginal returns to labor, land, and to reproducible capital are very low. The sparse family income of people, here under consideration, is not a consequence of a lack in the economic efficiency in allocating the resources that are in the domain of these poor people.

An important part of the *economics* of being poor rests on the hypothesis that there are comparatively few significant inefficiencies in the allocation of the factors of production in long established communities where most people are poor.[2]

3 The Economic Efficiency Hypothesis

There exists a large class of communities consisting of poor people who have been engaged in the same economic activities for generations. It is widely held that these people save and invest too little of their income, and that they do not respond to prices or to other normal economic incentives.

What is overlooked is the fact that for them neither consumption nor production provides any new opportunities. These people know from long experience the production possibilities of the resources in their domain, their own work abilities, and the arts of production available to them. They have one basic attribute in common: these poor people for years have not experienced any significant changes in the state of the art. They exist in a stationary state. People in this class continue year after year to engage in production activities using the same techniques of production and bringing the same skills to bear. It is for this important class of poor people that there are few significant inefficiencies in their allocation of resources in their domain.

While at Iowa State College in the thirties, I began to see that new biological materials were becoming "substitutes" for land and that the stranglehold that land held on the supply of food was being relaxed.[3] It also became clear to me that advances in the sciences could not explain all of the gains in productivity. At the University of Chicago, from the early forties on, I began to search for a more complete explanation and I came to see the role of the acquired abilities of human agents as a major source of the unexplained gains in productivity. These acquired abilities were obviously not free. Scarce resources were being allocated to acquire these abilities; thus the analytical stage was set for investment in man.

To deal with investment in man the traditional concept of capital had to be extended to make room for human capital. I was perplexed by the omission of human capital in the economic growth models that dominated the literature of economics. I noted at that time some of the reasons why economists were shy in coming to grips with human capital. Although I was aware that there were several distinguished economists who had looked upon human abilities as capital – Adam Smith, H. von Thunen, and notably Irving Fisher, I did not know then that others also had perceived the economic importance of the advances in knowledge and of improvements in the "quality" of the labor force. I was unduly critical of a particular view of Alfred Marshall, namely that it was neither appropriate nor practical to apply the concept of capital to human beings as he had expressed in his objections to Fisher's approach. Human beings were incontestably capital from an abstract and mathematical point of view as Marshall saw the issue, but human capital had no practical meaning because it was out of touch with the marketplace. But it has been pointed out by others, since I first called attention to this view of Marshall, that Marshall saw the relevance of investment in human beings in several parts of his work. With respect to knowledge also, Marshall anticipated much of what is now becoming clear in economics; for example, his dictum that "Knowledge is our most powerful engine of production."

Frank Knight, so I discovered, in what I now consider to be one of his classic papers, "Diminishing Returns to Investment" (*Journal of Political Economy*, 1944), perceived clearly and cogently both the improvements in the "quality" of the labor force and the economic contributions from the advances in the sciences and their effects on the rate of returns to investment.

Once I saw the pervasive role of human capital in a modern economy, I also began to see the inadequacies of the traditional concept of capital. The traditional concept went down the road of capital homogeneity thus avoiding the all-inclusive concept of capital with its vast heterogeneity. Human capital is of many different forms, and it renders many different consumer and producer services. If it were possible analytically to aggregate all of the different forms of human capital in a modern economy, it would exceed by a wide margin all nonhuman capital. The thrust of my studies has been primarily to clarify the investment processes and opportunities that provide the incentive to invest in human capital. I consider mainly formal education and organized research. The investment approach, however, opens for analysis a wide array of different forms of investment in people with many new vistas.

In a modernizing economy there are opportunities to invest in on-the-job learning, in searching for economic information, in migration, and in engaging in activities that contribute to health. All of these have received considerable attention analytically. A particular class of human capital consisting of investment in children may hold the key to a better theory of population.

In my presidential address to the American Economic Association (1960), I ventured to present a comprehensive view of *Investment in Human Capital* based on my research during the late 1940s and 1950s, especially during 1956–57 as a fellow of the Center of Behavioral Sciences. The second paper in Part Two indicates where I had arrived in my thinking and research when I wrote my presidential paper.

By 1967 major advances had been achieved in analyzing the economics of technical change, treating it as a new form of capital. The economic importance of advances in technology was established and the validity and usefulness of the rates of return approach, along with the empirical findings, had become important. The time had come for a critique on the state of concepts, theories, and the new empirical evidence.

The primary objective of this volume is to bring economics to bear on the actions of people who are poor. How can this objective be achieved? A more general approach, and conceivably a more rewarding one, would be to identify and explain real advances in economic knowledge.

Most of what is written by economists consists of endeavors to weed out bad economics. It could be that these endeavors are the ultimate source of good economics. Adam Smith devoted over 200 pages of his *Wealth of Nations* to show that a mercantile system is bad economics. Another possibility is that an important part in the advances of economics is induced by *economic changes*. Schumpeter devoted an entire book to the origins of the changes that give rise to economic development.

The first paper in Part Three on institutions is marked by John R. Commons who was my mentor on institutional economics as I did my graduate work. Would that economics could have been blessed by a marriage of Irving Fisher's all-inclusive concept of capital and John R. Commons' *Legal Foundations of Capitalism!*

The rise of the value of human time makes new demands on institutions. Particular political and legal institutions are especially subject to these demands. Lags occur in adjusting to these demands. These lags are the source of important public policy problems. Economic theory is a necessary tool in clarifying and resolving these problems.

I dealt with institutions that render services to the economy. It is a concept of institutions which took me into the domain of political economy. My list of activities included: (1) those that reduce transaction costs, (2) those that influence the allocation of risk among the factors of production (contracts, share tenancy, cooperatives, corporations, insurance, public social security programs), (3) those that provide the linkage between functional and personal income streams (property, inheritance laws, seniority, and other rights of labor), and (4) those that establish the framework for the production and distribution of public goods or services (highways, airports, schools, agricultural experiment stations).

In closing the paper on institutions I noted that when the economic value of human agents is rising we are in the realm of new and better opportunities. The range of private and social choice is enlarged. It is, indeed, an optimistic set of circumstances that all too few people of the world enjoy. But even so, this favorable type of economic change is not without its institutional stresses and strains. Since we can specify and identify these institutional lags we can also analyze the benefits in terms of the efficiency and welfare that could be had by reducing these lags. Meanwhile, it is not simply a matter of catching up, because there are strong reasons for believing that the economic value of man will continue to rise.

Where economic modernization has been achieved, the value of human time is high. Human fertility is not as simplistic as Malthus envisioned it and the Ricardian law of land rent has lost its economic sting. The rise in wages relative to that of rent is indeed a fundamental economic change for the better.

Many women are demanding a better deal. More human capital is being embodied in women, adding to their skills and enhancing their productivity and efficiency in the home and in the labor market. There are lags in adjusting the household, the family, and the labor market to these developments. The bargaining position of women is strong and it is increasing.

In low income communities, children are in an important sense the *poor man's capital*. They do household and farm work. They provide some old age insurance for their parents. Investment in children is in many ways akin to trees that are grown for their beauty and fruit. Children are an important part of the standard of living of most families. People want their own children and they proceed to bear and rear them. The advances in economic knowledge pertaining to children continue to be impressive.

4 Summary

To identify people who are poor we have three strong indicators: where half or more of personal income goes for food, where the life span is down to between 30 and 40 years, or where the level of skills and knowledge is low – people in general are poor.

History is rich with economic puzzles. But the economics of being poor is not one of the strong parts of economics. The Utility of Poverty Doctrine was bad economics. It is also bad economics to attribute the lot of poor communities to indolence, to a lack of thrift, or to a lack of economic efficiency in allocating their resources.

This volume, the first of two, is mainly devoted to the economics of acquiring skills and knowledge, to investment in the quality of the population and to the increasing economic importance of *Human Capital*.

As the value of human time rises and personal incomes increase, parents choose to have fewer children and spend more to enhance the acquired abilities of each child. The rise in value of human time also sets the stage for a population equilibrium. Consumption requires time. It cannot exceed 24 hours during any day. An upper limit occurs long before so many hours are devoted to consumption. Diminishing returns in consumption may then prevail over diminishing returns in production.

Economics matters in comprehending the nature and significance of more rewarding sources of income. New forms of capital that augment income matter greatly. The significance of human capital is strongly evident in accounting for the increase in the share of personal income derived from work (wages, self employment, and entrepreneurial activities), and in declines in the share of income from property. Much harder to observe is the tendency toward less inequality in the distribution of personal income. There is much to be said on behalf of pondering the measurements, explanations, and implications present in the last paper in Part III below.

Notes and References

1 Edgar S. Furniss, *The Position of Laborers in a System of Nationalism* (Houghton Mifflin, Boston, 1920), chapter 6.
2 Theodore W. Schultz, *Transforming Traditional Agriculture* (Yale University Press, New Haven, Conn., 1964), chapter 3.
3 Here I draw on part of my Preface to *Investment in Human Capital* (The Free Press of Macmillan Co., New York, 1971).

Part I
Most People Are Poor

Part I

Most People Are Poor

1

Nobel Lecture: The Economics of Being Poor[*]

Most of the people in the world are poor, so if we knew the economics of being poor we would know much of the economics that really matters. Most of the world's poor people earn their living from agriculture, so if we knew the economics of agriculture we would know much of the economics of being poor.

People who are rich find it hard to understand the behavior of poor people. Economists are no exception, for they, too, find it difficult to comprehend the preferences and scarcity constraints that determine the choices that poor people make. We all know that most of the world's people are poor, that they earn a pittance for their labor, that half and more of their meager income is spent on food, and they reside predominantly in low-income countries, and that most of them are earning their livelihood in agriculture. What many economists fail to understand is that poor people are no less concerned about improving their lot and that of their children than rich people are.

What we have learned in recent decades about the economics of agriculture will appear to most reasonably well-informed people to be paradoxical. We have learned that agriculture in many low-income countries has the potential economic capacity to produce enough food for the still growing population and in so doing can improve significantly the income and welfare of poor people. The decisive factors of production in improving the welfare of poor people are not space, energy, and cropland; the decisive factor is the improvement in population quality.

[*]Delivered in Stockholm, Sweden on December 8, 1979, and first published in *Journal of Political Economy*, 88, No. 4 (1979), 639–51. (© 1979 by the Nobel Foundation). Reproduced by permission of University of Chicago Press. I am indebted to Gary S. Becker, A. C. Harberger, D. Gale Johnson, and T. Paul Schultz for helpful suggestions on the first draft of this paper. My debt to Milton Friedman is especially large for his painstaking expositional comments. I am also indebted to my wife, Esther Schultz, for her insistence that what I thought was stated clearly was not clear enough.

In discussing these propositions, I shall first identify two intellectual mistakes that have marred the work of many economists. I shall then point out that most observers overrate the economic importance of land and greatly underrate the importance of the quality of human agents. Last, I shall present measurements of the increases in population quality that low-income countries are currently achieving.

Much of what I have learned about these propositions I owe to the research of predoctoral and postdoctoral students, to subsequent studies during their professional careers, and to my academic colleagues. In recent decades their work has produced a veritable explosion in the understanding of the economics of human capital, with special reference to the economics of research, the responses of farmers to new profitable production techniques, the connection between production and welfare, and the economics of the family.

1   Mistakes by Economists

This branch of economics has suffered from several intellectual mistakes. The major mistake has been the presumption that standard economic theory is inadequate for understanding low-income countries and that a separate economic theory is needed. Models developed for this purpose were widely acclaimed until it became evident that they were at best intellectual curiosities. The reaction of some economists was to turn to cultural and social explanations for the alleged poor economic performance of low-income countries. Quite understandably, cultural and behavioral scholars are uneasy about this use of their studies. Fortunately, the intellectual tide has begun to turn. Increasing numbers of economists have come to realize that standard economic theory is just as applicable to the scarcity problems that confront low-income countries as to the corresponding problems of high-income countries.

A second mistake is the neglect of economic history. Classical economics was developed when most people in western Europe were very poor, barely scratching out subsistence from the poor soils they tilled, being condemned to a short life span. As a result, early economists dealt with conditions that were similar to those that prevail in low-income countries today. In Ricardo's day about half of the family income of laborers in England went for food. So it is today in many low-income countries. Marshall (1920)[1] tells us that ". . . English labourers' weekly wages were often less than the price of a half bushel of good wheat" at the time Ricardo published his classic work. The weekly wage of the plowman in India is currently somewhat less than the price of two bushels of wheat.[2]

In India many people live under the Ricardian shadow. Understanding the experience and achievements of poor people over the ages can contribute much to understanding the problems and possibilities of low-income countries today. That kind of understanding is far more important than the most detailed and exact knowledge about the surface of the earth, ecology, or of tomorrow's technology.

Historical perception is also lacking with respect to population. We extrapolate global statistics and are horrified by our interpretation of them, mainly that poor people breed like lemmings headed toward their own destruction. Yet that is not what happened looking back at our own social and economic history when people were poor. It is equally false with respect to population growth in today's poor countries.

2   Land is Overrated

A widely held view – the natural earth view – is that there is a virtually fixed land area suitable for growing food and a supply of energy for tilling the land that is being depleted. According to this view, it is impossible to continue to produce enough food for the growing world population. An alternative view – the social-economic view – is that man has the ability and intelligence to lessen his dependence on cropland, on traditional agriculture, and on depleting sources of energy and can reduce the real costs of producing food for the growing world population. By means of research we discover substitutes for cropland, which Ricardo could not have anticipated, and as incomes rise parents reveal a preference for fewer children, substituting quality for quantity of children, which Malthus could not have foreseen. It is ironic that economics, long labeled the dismal science, is capable of showing that the bleak natural earth view for food is not compatible with economic history, that history demonstrates that we can augment resources by advances in knowledge. I agree with Margaret Mead: "The future of mankind is open ended." Mankind's future is not foreordained by space, energy, and cropland. It will be determined by the intelligent evolution of humanity.

Differences in the productivity of the soils are not a useful variable to explain why people are poor in long-settled parts of the world. People have been poor for ages both on the Deccan Plateau where the productivity of the rain fed soils is low and on the highly productive soils of south India. In Africa, people on the unproductive soils of the southern fringes of the Sahara, on the somewhat more productive soils on the steep slopes of the Rift landform, and on the highly productive alluvial lands along and at the mouth of the Nile all have one thing in common: they are very poor. Similarly, the much publicized differences in land-population ratio throughout the low-income countries do not produce comparable differences in poorness. What matter most in the case of farmland are the incentives and associated opportunities that farm people have to augment the effective supply of land by means of investments that include the contributions of agricultural research and the improvement of human skills.

A fundamental proposition documented by much recent research is that an integral part of the modernization of the economies of high-and low-income countries is *the decline in the economic importance of farmland and a rise in that of human capital – skills and knowledge.*

Despite economic history, scratch an economist and you will find that his ideas about land are still, as a rule, those of Ricardo. But Ricardo's concept of land, "the original and indestructible powers of the soil," is no longer adequate, if ever it was. The share of national income that accrues as land rent and the associated social and political importance of landlords have declined markedly over time in high-income countries, and they are also declining in low-income countries. Why is Ricardian Rent losing its economic sting? There are two primary reasons: First, the modernization of agriculture has over time transformed raw land into a vastly more productive resource than it was in its natural state, and second, agricultural research has provided substitutes for cropland. With some local exceptions, the original soils of Europe were poor in quality. They are today highly productive. The original soils of Finland were less productive than the nearby western parts of the Soviet Union, yet today the croplands of Finland are superior. Japanese croplands were originally much inferior to those of northern India; they are greatly superior today. Some part of these changes, both in high- and low-income countries, is the consequence of agricultural research, including the research em-bodied in purchased agricultural inputs. There are new substitutes for cropland (call it land augmentation if you so prefer). The substitution process is well illustrated by corn. The corn acreage harvested in the United States in 1979 was 33 million acres less than in 1932. Yet the 7.76 billion bushels produced in 1979 was three times the amount produced in 1932.

3   The Quality of Human Agents is Underrated

While land per se is not a critical factor in being poor, the human agent is: investment in improving population quality can significantly enhance the economic prospects and the welfare of poor people. Child care, home and work experience, the acquisition of information and skills through schooling and in other ways consisting primarily of investment in health and schooling can improve population quality. Such investments in low-income countries have, as I shall show, been successful in improving the economic prospects wherever they have not been dissipated by political instability. Poor people in low-income countries are not prisoners of an ironclad poverty equilibrium that economics is unable to break. There are no overwhelming forces that nullify all economic improvements, causing poor people to abandon the economic struggle. It is now well documented that in agriculture poor people do respond to better opportunities.

The expectations of human agents in agriculture – farm laborers and farm entrepreneurs who both work and allocate resources – are shaped by new opportunities and by the incentives to which they respond. These incentives are explicit in the prices that farmers receive for their products and in the prices they pay for producer and consumer goods and services that they purchase. These incentives are greatly distorted in many low-income countries.[3] The effect of these government-induced distortions is to reduce the economic contribution that agriculture is capable of making.

The "reason" why governments tend to introduce distortions that discriminate against agriculture is that internal politics generally favor the urban population at the expense of rural people, despite the much greater size of the rural population. The political influence of urban consumers and industry enables them to exact cheap food at the expense of the vast number of poor rural people. This discrimination against agriculture is rationalized on the grounds that agriculture is inherently backward and that its economic contribution is of little importance despite the occasional "Green Revolution." The lowly cultivator is viewed as indifferent to economic incentives because it is presumed that he is strongly committed to his traditional ways of cultivation. Rapid industrialization is viewed as the key to economic progress. Policy is designed to give top priority to industry, which includes keeping food grains cheap. It is regrettable but true that this doctrine is still supported by some donor agencies and rationalized by some economists in high-income countries.

4 Entrepreneurs

Farmers the world over, in dealing with costs, returns, and risks, are calculating economic agents. Within their small, individual, allocative domain they are fine-tuning entrepreneurs, tuning so subtly that many experts fail to recognize how efficient they are. I first presented an analysis of this entrepreneurial behavior in *Transforming Traditional Agriculture*.[4] Although farmers differ for reasons of schooling, health, and experience in their ability to perceive, to interpret, and to take appropriate action in responding to new information, they provide an essential human resource which is entrepreneurship.[5] On most farms there is a second enterprise, the household. Women are also entrepreneurs in allocating their own time and in using farm products and purchased goods in household production.[6] This allocative ability is supplied by millions of men and women on small-scale producing units; agriculture is in general a highly decentralized sector of the economy. Where governments have taken over this function in farming they have prevented this entrepreneurial talent from being used, and these governments have been unsuccessful in providing an effective allocative substitute capable of modernizing agriculture. The allocative roles of farmers and of farm women are important, and their economic opportunities really matter.[7]

Entrepreneurship is also essential in research. All research is a venturesome business. It entails allocating scarce resources. It requires organization. Someone must decide how to allocate the limited resources available for research, given the existing state of knowledge. The very essence of research is that it is a dynamic venture into the unknown or partially known. Funds, organizations, and competent scientists are necessary. They are not sufficient. Research entrepreneurship is required, be it by scientists or by others engaged in the research sector of the economy.[8]

5   Inevitability of Disequilibria

The transformation of agriculture into an increasingly more productive state, a process that is commonly referred to as "modernization," entails all manner of adjustments in farming as better opportunities become available. I have shown that the value of the ability to deal with disequilibria is high in a dynamic economy.[9]

Such *disequilibria are inevitable.* They cannot be eliminated by law, by public policy, and surely not by rhetoric. Governments cannot perform efficiently the function of farm entrepreneurs.

Future historians will no doubt be puzzled by the extent to which economic incentives were impaired during recent decades. The dominant intellectual view is antagonistic to agricultural incentives, and the prevailing economic policies deprecate the function of producer incentives. For lack of incentives the unrealized economic potential of agriculture in many low-income countries is large.[10] Technical possibilities have become increasingly more favorable, but the economic incentives that are required for farmers in these countries to realize this potential are in disarray, either because the relevant information is lacking or because the prices and costs they face have been distorted. For want of profitable incentives, farmers have not made the necessary investments, including the purchase of superior inputs. Interventions by governments are currently the major cause of the lack of optimum economic incentives.

6 Achievements in Population Quality

I now turn to measurable gains in the quality of both farm and nonfarm people.[11] Quality in this context consists of various forms of human capital. I have argued elsewhere[12] that, while a strong case can be made for using a rigorous definition of human capital, it will be subject to the same ambiguities that continue to plague capital theory in general and the capital concept in economic growth models in particular. Capital is two-faced, and what these two faces tell us about economic growth, which is a dynamic process, are, as a rule, inconsistent stories. It must be so because the cost story is a tale about sunk investments, and the other story pertains to the discounted value of the stream of services that such capital renders, which changes with the shifting sands of growth. But worse still is the capital homogeneity assumption underlying capital theory and the aggregation of capital in growth models. As Hicks has taught us,[13] the capital homogeneity assumption is the disaster of capital theory. This assumption is demonstrably inappropriate in analyzing the dynamics of economic growth that is afloat on capital inequalities because of the differences in the rates of return, whether the capital aggregation is in terms of factor costs or in terms of the discounted value of the lifetime services of its many parts. Nor would a catalog of all existing growth models prove that these inequalities are equals. But why try to square the circle? If we were unable to observe these inequalities, we would have to invent them because *they are the mainspring of economic growth*. They are the mainspring because they are the compelling economic signals of growth. Thus, one of the essential parts of economic growth is concealed by such capital aggregation.

The value of additional human capital depends on the additional well-being that human beings derive from it. Human capital contributes to labor productivity and to entrepreneurial ability. This allocative ability is valuable in farm and nonfarm production, in household production, and in the time and other resources that students allocate to their education. It is also valuable in migration to better job opportunities and to better locations in which to live. It contributes importantly to satisfactions that are an integral part of current and future consumption.

My approach to population quality is to treat quality as a scarce resource, which implies that it has an economic value and that its acquisition entails a cost. In analyzing human behavior that determines the type and amount of quality that is acquired over time, the key is the relation between the returns from additional quality and the costs of acquiring it. When the returns exceed costs, the stock of population quality will be enhanced. This means that increases in the supply of any quality component are a response to a demand for it. It is a supply-demand approach to investment behaviour because all quality components are here treated as durable scarce resources that are useful over some period of time.

My hypothesis is that the returns to various quality components are increasing over time in many low-income countries; the rents that entrepeneurs derive from their allocative ability rise, as do the returns to child care, schooling, and improvements in health. Furthermore, the rates of return are enhanced by the reductions in the costs of acquiring most of these quality components. Over time the increases in the demand for quality, in children and on the part of adults in enhancing their own quality, reduce the demand for quantity; that is, quality and quantity are substitutes, and the reduction in demand for quantity favors having and rearing fewer children.[14] The movement toward quality contributes to the solution of the population "problem".

7   Investment in Health

Human capital theory treats everyone's state of health as a stock, that is, as health capital and its contribution as health services. Part of the quality of the initial stock is inherited and part is acquired. The stock depreciates over time and at an increasing rate in later life. Gross investment in human capital entails acquisition and maintenance costs. These investments include child care, nutrition, clothing, housing, medical services, and the use of one's own time. The flow of services that health capital renders consists of "healthy time" or "sickness-free time," which are inputs into work, consumption, and leisure activities.[15]

The improvements in health revealed by the longer life span of people in many low-income countries have undoubtedly been the most important advance in population quality. Since about 1950, life expectancy at birth has increased 40 percent or more in many of these countries. People of western Europe and North America never attained so large an increase in life expectancy in so short a period. The decline in mortality of infants and very young children is only part of this achievement. The mortality of older children, youths, and adults is also down.

Ram and Schultz[16] deal with the economics of these demographic developments in India. The results correspond to those in other low-income countries. In India from 1951 to 1971 life expectancy at birth of males increased by 43 percent and that of females by 41 percent. Life spans over the life cycle after age 10, 20, and on to age 60, for both males and females in 1971, were also decidedly longer than in 1951.

The favorable economic implications of these increases in life span are pervasive. Foremost are the satisfactions that people derive from longer life. While they are hard to measure, there is little room for doubt that the value of life expectancy is enhanced. Measurement, however, is not impossible. Usher[17] devised an ingenious extension of theory to determine the utility that people derive from increases in life expectancy. His empirical analysis indicates that the additional utility increasese substantially the value of personal income.

Longer life spans provide additional incentives to acquire more education as investments in future earnings. Parents invest more in their children. More on-the-job training becomes worthwhile. The additional health capital and the other forms of human capital tend to increase the productivity of workers. Longer life spans result in more years of participation in the labor force and bring about a reduction in "sick time." Better health and vitality of workers in turn lead to more productivity per man hour at work.

The Ram-Schultz study provides evidence on the gains in the productivity of agricultural labor in India, realized as a consequence of improvements in health. The most telling part of that evidence is the productivity effect of the "cycle" that has characterized the malaria program.

8   Investment in Education

Education accounts for much of the improvements in population quality. But reckoning the cost of schooling, the value of the work that young children do for their parents must be included. Even for the very young children during their first years of school, most parents forego (sacrifice) the value of the work that children perform.[18] Another distinctive attribute of schooling is the vintage effect by age over time. Starting from widespread illiteracy, as more schooling per child is achieved the older adults continue through life with little or no schooling, whereas the children on entering into adulthood are the beneficiaries.

The population of India grew about 50 percent between 1950–51 and 1970–71. School enrollment of children ages 6–14 rose over 200 percent. The rate of increase in secondary schools and universities was much higher.[19] Since schooling is primarily an investment, it is a serious error to treat all schooling outlays as current consumption. This error arises from the assumption that schooling is solely a consumer good. It is misleading to treat public expenditures on schooling as "welfare" expenditures and as a use of resources that has the effect of reducing "savings." The same error occurs in the case of expenditures on health, both on public and private account.

The expenditures on schooling including higher education are a substantial fraction of national income in many low-income countries. These expenditures are *large* relative to the conventional national accounting measures (concepts) of savings and investment. In India the proportion that the costs of schooling bear to national income, savings, and investments is not only large but has tended to increase substantially over time.[20]

9   The Highly Skilled

In assessing population quality, it is important not to overlook the increases in the stock of physicians, other medical personnel, engineers, administrators, accountants, and various classes of research scientists and technicians.[21]

The research capacity of a considerable number of low-income countries is impressive. There are specialized research institutes, research units within governmental departments, industrial sector research, and ongoing university research. The scientists and technicians engaged in these various research activities are university trained, some of them in universities abroad. The research areas include, among others, medicine, public health (control of communicable diseases and the delivery of health services), nutrition, industry, agriculture, and even some atomic energy research. I shall touch briefly on agricultural research, because I know it best and because it is well documented.

The founding and financing of the International Agricultural Research Centers is an institutional innovation of a high order. The entrepreneurship of the Rockefeller Foundation in cooperation with the government of Mexico first launched this type of venture. But these centers, good as they are, are not a substitute for national agricultural research enterprises. Suffice it to give the flavor of the remarkable increases in the number of agricultural scientists between 1959 and 1974 in 22 selected low-income countries. All told, the number of scientist man-years devoted to agricultural research in these 22 countries increased more than three times during this period. By 1974 there was a corps of over 13,000 scientists, ranging from 110 in the Ivory Coast to over 2,000 in India.[22] Indian agricultural research expenditures between 1950 and 1968 also more than tripled in real terms.

We come to the bottom line. In India this investment in agricultural research has produced excellent results. An analysis by states within India shows the rate of return has been approximately 40 percent, which is indeed high compared with the returns from most other investments to increase agricultural production.[23]

10   Concluding Remark

While there remains much that we do not know about the economics of being poor, our knowledge of the economic dynamics of low-income countries has advanced substantially in recent decades. We have learned that poor people are no less concerned about improving their lot and that of their children than those of us who have incomparably greater advantages. Nor are they any less competent in obtaining the maximum benefit from their limited resources. The central thrust of this lecture is that population quality and knowledge do matter. A goodly number of low-income countries have a positive record in improving population quality and in acquiring useful knowledge. These achievements imply favorable economic prospects, provided they are not dissipated by politics and governmental policies that discriminate against agriculture.

Even so, most of the people throughout the world continue to earn a pittance from their labor. Half or even more of their meager income is spent on food. Their life is harsh. Farmers in low-income countries do all they can to augment their production. What happens to these farmers is of no concern to the sun, or to the earth, or to the behavior of the monsoons and the winds that sweep the face of the earth. Farmers' crops are in constant danger of being devoured by insects and pests. Nature is host to thousands of species that are hostile to the endeavors of farmers, especially so in low-income countries. We in the high-income countries have forgotten the wisdom of Alfred Marshall when he wrote, "Knowledge is the most powerful engine of production; it enables us to subdue Nature and satisfy our wants" (1920).[24]

Notes and References

1 Alfred Marshall, *Principles of Economics*, 8th edn (Macmillan, New York, 1930).

2 Theodore W. Schultz, "On Economics, Agriculture and the Political Economy," in Theodore Dams and Kenneth E. Hunt (eds), *Decision-Making and Agriculture*, 16th International Conference of Agricultural Economists, Nairobi, Kenya (Alden, Oxford, 1977).

3 Theodore W. Schultz, "On Economics and Politics of Agriculture," in Theodore W. Schultz (ed.), *Distortions of Agricultural Incentives* (Indiana University Press, Bloomington, 1978).

4 Theodore W. Schultz, *Transforming Traditional Agriculture* (Yale University Press, New Haven, Conn., 1964).

5 See Finis Welch, "Education in Production," *Journal of Political Economy*, 78, No. 1 (1970), 35–9. See also Welch, "The Role of Investments in Human Capital and Agriculture," and Robert E. Evenson, "The Organization of Research to Improve Crops and Animals in Low Income Countries," both in Theodore W. Schultz (ed.), *Distortions of Agricultural Incentives*.

6 Theodore W. Schultz (ed.), *Economics of the Family: Marriage, Children and Human Capital* (University of Chicago Press, Chicago, Ill., 1974).

7 Schultz, "On Economics and Politics of Agriculture."

8 Theodore W. Schultz, "Concepts of Entrepreneurship and Agricultural Research," Kaldor Memorial Lecture (Iowa State University, Ames, 1979).

9 Theodore W. Schultz, "The Value of the Ability to Deal with Disequilibria," *Journal of Economic Literature*, 13 (Sept. 1975), 827–46.

10 D. Gale Johnson, "Food Production Potentials in Developing Countries: Will They Be Realized?," Bureau of Economic Studies Occasional Paper No. 1 (Macalester College, St. Paul, Minn., 1977); also, "International Prices and Trade in Reducing the Distortions of Incentives" in Theodore W. Schultz (ed.), *Distortions of Agricultural Incentives*.

11 Theodore W. Schultz, "Investment in Population Quality Throughout Low-Income Countries," in Philip M. Hauser (ed.), *World Population and Development: Challenges and Prospects* (Syracuse University Press, Syracuse, NY, 1979); also, "Reckoning the Economic Achievements and Prospects of Low-Income Countries," Snyder Memorial Lecture (Purdue University, West Lafayette, Ind, 1979).

12 Schultz (ed.), *Economics of the Family*.

13 John R. Hicks, *Capital and Growth* (Clarendon Press, Oxford, 1965).

14 Gary S. Becker and Nigel Tomes, "Child Endowments and the Quantity and Quality of Children," *Journal of Political Economy*, 84, No. 4, part 2 (1976), S143–S162. See also Mark R. Rosenzweig and Kenneth I. Wolpin, "Testing the Quantity-Quality Fertility Model: The Use of Twins as a Natural Experiment" (Yale University Economic Growth Centre, New Haven, Conn., 1978).

15 Michael Grossman, *The Demand for Health* (National Bureau of Economic

Research, Occasional Paper No. 119, Columbia University Press, New York, 1972); see also Alan Williams, "Health Science Planning," in Michael J. Artis and A. R. Nobay (eds), *Studies in Modern Economic Analysis* (Basil Blackwell, Edinburgh, 1977).

16   Rati Ram and Theodore W. Schultz, "Life Span, Health, Savings, and Productivity," *Economic Development and Cultural Change*, 27 (April 1979), 399–421.

17   Dan Usher, "An Imputation to the Measure of Economic Growth for Changes in Life Expectancy," in Milton Moss (ed.), *The Measurement of Economic and Social Performance* (Columbia University Press, New York, 1978).

18   Robert L. Shortlidge Jr., "A Social-Economic Model of School Attendance in Rural India," Dept. of Agricultural Economy Occasional Paper No. 86 (Cornell University, Ithaca, NY, 1976); Indra Makhija, "The Economic Contribution of Children and Its Effects on Fertility and Schooling; Rural India," PhD dissertation (University of Chicago, 1977); and Robert E. Evenson, "Fertility, Schooling and the Economic Contribution of Children in Rural India: An Econometric Analysis," *Econometrica* 45 (July 1977), 1065–79.

19   Government of India Planning Commission: *Draft Five Year Plan 1978–83* (Government of India Press, New Delhi, 1978).

20   See Ram and Schultz, "Life Span," pp. 410–12 and table 2.

21   Theodore W. Schultz, "The Value of Higher Education in Low Income Countries: An Economist's View" (International Institute of Education Planning, Paris, 1979).

22   James K. Boyce and Robert E. Evenson, *National and International Agricultural Research and Extension Programs* (Agricultural Development Council, New York, 1975).

23   Robert E. Evenson and Yoav Kislev, *Agricultural Research and Productivity* (Yale University Press, New Haven, Conn., 1975).

24   Marshall, *Principles of Economics.*

2

The Economics of Poverty in Low Income Countries*

Our language is more comprehensive than any theory. The welfare of human beings is more comprehensive than welfare theories. Alms, charity and gifts have meaning that reaches beyond economics. The age-old concept of being poor is more comprehensive than the now politicized concept of poverty. Theory and evidence enrich our understanding of the adverse circumstances of families and individuals who are poor. Judging from all that is said and being done to help the poor, it is difficult to bridge the gap between moral obligations calling for alms, charity, gift and presently for foreign aid and the economic requirements that will improve the lot of people who are poor.

Evidence that is reliable and relevant for the purpose at hand is hard to come by. We live in an age of population statistics with projections that are interpreted as horrendous. They tell us very little about families and human beings. We have become addicted to counting and publishing numbers. But we have all too little information about the preferences of people who are poor and how they manage to live in accordance with their preferences given the limitations of their resources and opportunities. Nevertheless, it may be useful to start with some of the available evidence.

I began my Nobel Lecture[1] by noting that most people in the world are poor and that most of the world's poor people earn their living from agriculture. As of 1980, 2.16 billion people lived in "low income" countries and most of them, namely 1.53 million were in agriculture. In countries where people are somewhat less poor, there were 1.2 billion and of these half a billion were in agriculture.[2] Thus, three-fourths of the people in the world live in poor countries and those who presumably earn their living from agriculture in these countries account for close to

*First Published in *Lo Sviluppo E'll Nuovo Nome Della Pace*, ed. Giovanni Galizzi. (By permission Franco Angeli, Milano, Italy, 1984.)

half of the world's people. There must be linkages between the lack of income from agricultural production and people being poor.

What is now known about the economics of agriculture will appear to most reasonably well-informed people to be paradoxical. Agriculture in countries where most of the world's poor people live has the potential economic capacity to produce enough food for the still growing populations and also to significantly improve the income and welfare of poor people. When it comes to agricultural production space, energy and cropland are overrated; *whereas improvements in health, schooling and advances in useful knowledge are underrated.*

The moral obligation to help families and individuals who are poor is supported by long standing social values in most societies. But there are few studies of the use and misuse of private charity and of public foreign aid. Experience since World War II indicates that a considerable part of foreign aid provided by the International Donor Community has not helped poor people; on the contrary, some of it has worsened the well-being of many poor farm people in low income countries. The main reasons for these adverse results are consequences of the politics of foreign aid and of the neglect of the economic requirements that are necessary in helping poor people improve their lot.

Estimates of the amounts of resources that low income countries are receiving from donors abroad are useful although they do not tell us what is, or is not, achieved in improving the lot of poor people.

Grants by private voluntary agencies in 1980 came to 2.3 billion dollars[3] a tidy sum. Over half of this amount, 1.3 billion,[4] came from the United States. In the early 1950s, my associates and I made an assessment of US public and private aid throughout Latin America. We found that per dollar of aid, private agencies contributed much more to improvements in health and schooling and to advances in useful knowledge than that contributed by the official aid of the US government.[5]

Foreign aid has become institutionalized as has the church and the philanthropy of foundation.[6] Since its management and its purposes have much in common, it is convenient to think of official aid agencies as the International Donor Community. Although budgets and staffs are large, it is difficult to get at the economic effects of this foreign aid. It is fair to say that the economics of foreign aid is concealed in many different boxes. There is a lot of talk about the design of these boxes, their dimensions, construction and whether they are big enough. Some critics fail to see that they are black boxes. Some contend that what they see is red, while other critics see them as a pale gray that is politically neutral.

The funds that are put into each of these boxes are known. These amounts are proxies of the apparent costs that are incurred. What is unknown is the true economic value of the activities that are supported by these funds. There are some general useful clues, notably in the Oecd Annual Reviews by John P. Lewis on *Development Co-operation*.[7]

Net official disbursements of aid worldwide are not trivial. In 1980, 33.46 billion dollars of such aid were distributed (Table 1.2.1). To be fascinated by these billions is a far cry from understanding what they do to families and individuals who are poor.

Table 1.2.1 Net official disbursements of aid in 1980

Net Disbursements	In Billions of Dollars
I. Bilateral	
DAC Countries	17.64
OPEC Countries	6.11
CMEA Countries	1.80
Other Countries	.20
Sub total	25.75
II. Multilateral agencies	7.71
Total	33.46

The 1980 disbursements of resources to low income countries that are classified as non-concessional came to 55.49 billion dollars (50.69 billion were bilateral and 4.8 billion multilateral). Some of these disbursements were in essence grants.

Richard Critchfield is one of the rare exceptions who has not been beholden in his studies to gross national and international statistics. Most rural people in Asia and Africa live in villages. He has gained important insights about the economic behavior and the preferences of these people who are by Western standards poor. Since the late 1960s, he has lived in 21 villages for months on end and in three of them for over a year. He also revisited many of them after the elapse of a decade and longer. The effects of village cultures has been high on his agenda. One of his major findings is the interaction between the adoption of science in agriculture and the adoption of science pertaining to family planning. His keen observations have a ring of optimism. His paper, "Science and the Villagers: The Last Sleeper Wakes", featured in *Foreign Affairs*, Fall, 1982, is decidedly rewarding.

My main concern is, what are the political and economic linkages between these large numbers of aid dollars and the close to one-half of the world's people who reside in low income countries and who earn their living in agriculture? Before turning to this question, there are several important issues to be considered.

1 Issues to Ponder

The economics of production and welfare of rural people has been on my agenda for over 50 years. I have spent much time investigating the economic circumstances of farm families in many low income countries, including both the Soviet Union and China. I have on each occasion spent time in the countryside to see and to talk with rural people, most of whom are indeed poor. I believe strongly that economics matter and that much can be learned from economic theory supported by evidence. For me it has been decidedly rewarding. Although I realize I am not professionally qualified to deal with the moral aspects of charity, they are too important to be put aside. Thus, I venture to comment on some moral objectives, the consequences of which in practice, especially when they become politicized, tend to have adverse effects on farm families in low income countries.

1 I assume that the primary moral objective of charity is to help families and individuals who are poor. Private charity, as I have already suggested, has a better record than official public aid (charity) that is being given to low income countries presumably to help poor people in these countries. Foreign official aid, however, in large measure, does not reach poor people in these countries; instead it tends to increase the control of the recipient governments, resulting in public controls that impair the freedom of choice and opportunities of the poor, especially so in the case of farm families. Surely these adverse consequences are inconsistent with the primary objective of charity.

2 The moral obligation that people in high-income countries have to help poor people in low-income countries is being misused and exploited by official donor agencies. In their endeavor to acquire more funds, they invent figures showing ever more malnutrition, the worsening of the availability of food, the increasing danger of famine and the decline in health using pictures of starving children and all manner of distorted stories with little regard to the fact that low-income countries in general have achieved a remarkable increase (40 to 50 percent) in life span during

recent decades. These pronouncements are clearly self-serving in exploiting the essence of our moral obligations.

3 More serious is the use that is being made of the moral issue pertaining to poverty to establish and support totalitarian regimes. Intellectuals, and others who are committed to totalitarian governments, during the late 1960s and most of the 1970s appealed to the presumed success of Chairman Mao's dictatorship in China as proof that his regime had solved the poverty problem by liquidating all families who owned land and by additional means that had equalized family incomes throughout China. We now know that millions of families in China became more, not less, poverty stricken, that millions of deaths occurred from famine[8] and that the average real income of rural families who make up most of the population is about half that of the city population. More ambiguous is the official foreign aid that has been given to support highly centralized governments in a considerable number of low income countries on the pretext that these governments would promote social reforms compatible with the moral objectives of people of countries that provide the funds to these countries. Tanzania is a prime example of how bad this approach can be in reducing the freedom of choice and welfare of rural people.

2   Economies of Agriculture and Welfare of Farm Families

Advances in production techniques are important, as I shall argue when I consider agricultural research; nevertheless, all too little consideration is paid to the distortions of the prices that farmers in many low income countries pay for what they buy and what they receive for their products. The adoption of superior techniques is seriously thwarted by these distortions. Donor agencies have long been indifferent to the adverse effects of these distortions of agricultural incentives on production and on farm family welfare.[9] The prevailing anti-market biases of many donor agencies account, in large measure, for this indifference. There is some recent evidence that a change for the better on this issue is underway. The *World Development Report 1982* of the World Bank, as D. Gale Johnson has noted in his review of it,[10] reveals a new understanding of markets, prices and of the requirements of economic efficiency in the allocation and use of resources for agricultural production. I quote from his review:

Knowing something of efforts within the staff of the World Bank to obtain appropriate consideration of the role of markets and prices in determining the outcome of the Bank's projects and loans. I wish to take this opportunity to salute those who made the effort. This report, and others such as *Accelerated Development in Sub-Saharan Africa: An Agenda for Action* (World Bank, 1981), reveals a striking shift in the dominant pattern of thought and analysis within the Bank's staff.

The cleaner economic thinking within the World Bank as it is revealed in its 1982 report, is also evident in US Aid. There is an emphasis on reducing the economic distortions that farmers face, on improving farmer's incentives to modernize agriculture, on investing in farm people, and in doing so, on lessening the exploitation of farm people in support of cheap food policies. The President of Egypt is informed on these critical policy issues. It does not follow that Egypt's internal repressive agricultural pricing policy is being significantly improved nor that the United States government is prepared to use the massive food aid going to Egypt to achieve this purpose.

An important clue to the dynamics of agriculture is revealed in the uneven performance of agriculture by countries. In the United States agriculture has produced large surpluses of food and feed grains. Stocks of these grains have become exceedingly large. The real market prices of grains are at record lows. The income that farm families derive from their agricultural activities has declined sharply.

An overview of agriculture throughout most of the world is about as follows. In China, agricultural economic policy has taken a favorable turn. But one must wait and see whether this progress in economic reforms will continue to prevail.[11] The countries in Asia – Taiwan, South Korea and to a considerable extent, India and Indonesia in terms of economic policies are, in general, doing what needs to be done to increase agricultural production and by so doing, are improving the welfare of farm families. Despite considerable political instability, a few countries in South America are presently doing moderately well; their exports of some major agricultural commodities are increasing. China aside for the time being, the centrally planned economies, except for Hungary, are in serious trouble.[12] There are two groups of countries in which the agriculture and food situation has gone from bad to worse. Most of the countries in Central (tropical) Africa are doing badly.[13] Egypt also has a very poor record. In my view, what the international donor community has been doing to assist these countries has been a series of failures. It is hard to see how charity can improve the sad state of agriculture and of the rest of the economy in these countries. Nigeria, and a few others, are cashing in on oil exports. Egypt is receiving massive food aid. Despite all this, the prospects are bad.

The other group consists of various countries in Central America that are being torn apart by internal conflict and warfare.

3   Economic Efficiency Matters

Let me stress once again that those who administer official charity in the form of foreign aid have long been blissfully indifferent to the lack of economic efficiency in low income countries. With some exceptions, agricultural scientists also fail to see that the pervasive economic inefficiency in low income countries is the predominant barrier to the effective adoption of high yielding crop varieties and of other contributions from the advances in agricultural research. Economists who are committed to elegant growth models are also, as a rule, silent on the important issue of economic efficiency.

The growth of an economy depends fundamentally on increases in the quantity and quality of resources and on economic efficiency. Correspondingly, the modernization of agriculture depends basically on the additional quantity and quality of agricultural inputs and on the economic efficiency of agriculture. High yielding crop varieties, fertilizer, insecticides, tractors, combines, experiment stations, and well trained agricultural scientists and related technical personnel are all more or less necessary, but they are not sufficient. Wherever the economic organization of agriculture is inefficient, production languishes even though the quantity and quality of the inputs are at hand along with a high order of technical services. In terms of the technical requirements that I have listed, agriculture in the Soviet Union should be highly productive. But it is not. The main reason why it fails is the inordinate economic inefficiency which is a consequence of economic organization of Soviet agriculture. Most of the donor agencies have not yet faced up to the critical importance of economic efficiency in agriculture.

Farmers the world over are not to blame for the officially imposed economic inefficiency that burdens agriculture. Farmers in their small private domain are calculating economic agents. In my *Transforming Traditional Agriculture*[14], I presented evidence that farmers in traditional agriculture are "poor but efficient" by the test of marginal costs and marginal returns. There is now much more evidence in support of this proposition. Thus, I contend that within low income countries, farmers are intelligent economic agents, poor as they are in terms of resources, and in living with the distortions of incentives that are imposed on them in the prices they receive and pay, and with their dependency on corrupt, inefficient governmental agencies as suppliers of fertilizer, insecticides and seeds and on marketing boards that have a monopoly as purchasing agents and, in some cases, enforced by mandated procurements.

Most governments in low-income countries seriously impair the economic efficiency of agriculture. Nor are other parts of the economy spared on this score. To some extent, but very slowly, governments learn from their economic mistakes. These economic inefficiencies are presently not as pervasive as they were two and three decades ago. At the extreme, they have been reduced somewhat in China but not in the Soviet Union. The situation on this issue throughout most of the countries of tropical Africa is, indeed, serious.

Donors of foreign aid do not deal with farmers although they make believe that they are primarily concerned about the production and welfare of the poorest of the poor. They talk equity and forget about economic efficiency. There is no way that farmers in low income countries can convey to these donors their economic priorities. Donors deal with the governments of these farmers and the economic distortions imposed on farmers are, more often than not, supported in part by donor funds.

Donors of foreign aid have provided an increasing share of the funds that support the International Agricultural Research Centers. The achievements during the 1970s of many of these Centers are not in doubt. By my last count, there are now 13 with a current total annual budget of about $150 million. They have an international dimension that owes much to the Rockefeller Foundation and the pioneering entrepreneurship of George Harrar in Mexico. These centers are supported by 35 donors. In recent years, the World Bank, the various regional banks and US AID have contributed substantial funds to support them. These centers are a decidedly worthwhile innovation.

I have, however, four concerns pertaining to these International Agricultural Research Centers.

1 They are not a substitute for on-going national agricultural experiment stations and laboratories.
2 They do not do and, therefore, are dependent upon basic agricultural research to be done elsewhere.
3 The central management, i.e. the allocation of funds to each of the centers, is becoming over-organized in the sense that too much of the time of the research personnel at the centers is spent on paper work justifying research.

4 The center located in Nigeria has concentrated on local food production and it has neglected the important non-food export commodities.
More generally, the emphasis that AID has placed on food production,
especially so throughout central Africa, has been a serious mistake in
view of the fact that the economic comparative advantage was, and
continues to be, in the larger gains to be had from the real growth in
their exports, primarily from cotton, rubber, and other tree crops.
Clearly, agricultural scientists have no comprehension of the economic
importance of the role of comparative advantage in production and
trade among nations. There is truth in the dictum, namely, "trade not
aid" In fact, foreign aid for research to promote only food crops in
tropical Africa is decidedly harmful to the economy.

When a sudden destruction of resources occurs, whether it is caused
by the vicissitudes of Nature or by war, foreign aid is, as it should be,
a humanitarian response.[15] US food and medical aid, when floods,
earthquakes, and serious droughts occur, deserves a high mark.

The Second World War devastated countries that received Marshall
Plan aid benefits. Much physical capital had been destroyed. The stock of
human capital was still first-rate. Marshall Plan aid helped rebuild and
restore the structures, equipment and inventories. The pay-off that
accrued to these countries was large. But the economic circumstances
that prevail in low income countries do not correspond to those that
existed in Europe following World War II. Low income countries, in
general, have meager stocks of human capital.

But what about sudden riches? Consider the economic disarray that
occurred in Nigeria, Venezuela, and Mexico, which was compounded by
sudden large revenue from the sales of oil. Mexico, for example, acquired
about $18 billion from oil during one year. Do large amounts of foreign
capital and foreign grants (aid) have corresponding adverse effects on the
economy of the recipient country? My view is that Tanzania and
Bangladesh experienced similar economic distortions in recent years
because of all manner of foreign aid. In this connection, we do well to
ponder the reasons for the remarkable growth of agricultural production
in Malaysia. Their high yielding rubber and palm varieties did not come
from us. Nor did we provide the funds to do the necessary research.
There are countries where low per capita income is not a necessary and
sufficient condition to receive foreign aid to achieve real agricultural
growth.

It is all too easy to forget the lesson we learned from our Point Four
agricultural aid throughout Latin America. As already noted, with the
help of a competent staff, supported by a large grant from the Ford

Foundation and sponsored by the National Planning Association, I had the opportunity during the early 1950s to assess the achievements of Point Four programs.[16] They failed mainly because Point Four was committed to building agricultural extension services and only belatedly learned that the necessary worthwhile agricultural research had not been done. In sharp contrast, the agricultural research of the Rockefeller Foundation in Mexico was on the right track. At the beginning of the 1950s the Ford Foundation joined the government of India in an expensive agricultural extension program. It, too, was premature. Neither the high yielding new wheats nor other worthwhile possibilities to increase production were as yet available.

Foreign aid to India did not produce the new high yielding wheat that contributed greatly to the wheat producing capacity of India. The profitability of the new wheat variety induced the formation of a large amount of additional physical capital for the production of wheat. None of this additional capital was provided by foreign aid or by the World Bank or by any other foreign entity, public or private.

US foreign aid and American leadership, notably that of Ralph W. Cummings, Frank Parker and others in Aid in Washington, and members of several US Land Grant Universities, assisted Indian political and academic leaders in establishing the agricultural universities in India, which stands as a major achievement of permanent value. It was not a short term undertaking. It entailed building a new institution for the long term.[17] But regrettably, foreign aid had failed to undertake corresponding enterprises throughout tropical Africa.

4   The Sad Case of Egyptian Agriculture

The United States is providing Egypt with massive amounts of aid. From information available to me, US Aid going to Egypt comes to about two billion dollars a year. It includes large amounts of agricultural products. Egypt meanwhile is a model of economic inefficiency with respect to her own agriculture. But why should Egypt not take advantage of cheap food aid? She is immune to the going international market prices of agricultural products. Under these circumstances, Egypt is pursuing a rational policy. With agricultural products at concessional prices from abroad, Egypt maintains her cheap food for consumers and awful low prices for farmers. What is sad is the raw deal that the poor Egyptian farmers are dealt.

The pervasive economic distortions that dominate the Egyptian agricultural economy cannot be corrected by reorganizing the ministry of agriculture, or by tinkering with controls and with this or that price. Nor will a first-rate biological research program designed to serve Egyptian agriculture and a well organized, competent, agricultural extension program, eliminate these economic distortions.[18]

5   A Summary of Key Issues

Private charity aside, which is relatively small and which seems to have a fairly good record, official charity (foreign aid) which is large is flawed for the following reasons.

1 Official foreign aid underrates the importance of health; education, and entrepreneurial ability, i.e., improvement over time in the acquired abilities of farm people from their investment in human capital.
2 In the United States, agricultural programs to improve the economic lot of US small farmers have been failures. Despite these failures Congress, in providing funds for aid, insists that AID see to it that low income countries do what we have been unable to do within the US.
3 The credibility of foreign aid is being impaired by pronouncements on the dire state and bad prospects, supported by heart-rending pictures, stories, and bad data on hunger, malnutrition, starvation, and a future beset with famines. The international donor agencies have seriously overplayed these self-serving pronouncements in their quest for funds.
4 A creditable analysis of the food situation throughout the world is basic in putting foreign aid on the right track.
5 The relationships among the official foreign aid donors of the high income countries are all too cozy. They do not criticize one another. Would that there were public debates and tensions on basic issues. I know of no public documents that deal critically with the foreign aid activities of others. For example, a competent analysis of the actual harm that has been done by the aid of the World Bank, of the International Monetary Fund, and of other multilateral and bilateral agencies to the economy of Tanzania, would be exceedingly instructive.
6 Official foreign aid agencies have a poor record in their endeavors to improve the economic lot of women in low income countries. There has been no lack of talk and papers with stress on social reforms. Taking the long view, what is long overdue is the establishment of

organized research centers that would do for household production activities what agricultural research does for the production activities of farmers. There is even a lack of simple equipment to break and remove the hard husk of sorghum that would eliminate the backbreaking work of so many women throughout Central Africa. Inasmuch as much of the work in agriculture in many countries of Africa is done by women, a part of agricultural research should be oriented to the activity of women.

Fortunately, advances in knowledge pertaining to birth control oriented to the requirements of parents in low-income countries is being supported despite the adverse political mood that presently prevails on this issue.

7 The state of knowledge about nutrition applicable to low-income countries is inadequate. The use of public funds via aid to establish in low-income countries organized nutrition research centers, staffed by competed scientists and social analysts, would over the long term produce a rate of return comparable to that derived from organized agricultural research.

8 The International Agricultural Research Centers are a first-rate investment. National agricultural research in a considerable number of low-income countries, however, is as yet not viably established. Foreign aid has a spotty record in this area. I would not advise low income countries to become dependent on foreign aid for this purpose because of the lack of continuity of aid.

9 The anti-market bias of most foreign aid agencies is harmful because it lends support to the economic inefficiency that governments of low-income countries impose on their farm people.

10 The economic value of the physical capital provided by foreign aid for structures, equipment and inventories, is overrated. The amounts are large, much of which is used wastefully, whereas funds for human capital are meager despite the fact that the contributions of additional schooling and improvements in health over the long term to production and welfare are as a rule impressively large.

6 Choices Pertaining to Foreign Aid

In making choices, it is necessary to distinguish between the economic activities that belong in the domain of markets and those that tend to fall into the public domain.

In large measure, worldwide experience supports the proposition that most organized agricultural research, agricultural extensions, primary schooling and some welfare activities fall within the public domain. All of these activities entail cost, none are short term undertakings; there are no quick fixes. They have long time dimensions and for that reason, to be done efficiently, they must be approached as long term investments. Foreign aid is seriously handicapped by short term budget authorizations. The short time dimension of foreign aid funding is decidedly inefficient.

The one notable exception is that of food and medical aid when sudden emergencies occur in low income countries.

The strong and persistent anti-market bias conceals the choice between trade and aid. For low-income countries better opportunities to trade are much more important than foreign aid.

There is also the choice of providing capital for structures, equipment and inventories on private accounts at market terms or on public accounts via foreign aid. The economic efficiency of foreign aid as a source of subsidized physical capital for these purposes is in general unduly wasteful.[19]

Most of the capital that is required for agricultural research, extension, primary schooling, and for some welfare programs is not to be had from private sources at market terms. The implication is that to the extent that foreign aid is in the business of providing capital to low income countries, its comparative advantage is precisely in the areas indicated and not in funding structures, equipment and inventories that dominate the formulation of physical capital.

In making choices, do not be misled by the clamor that the time has come to choose between *food versus feed*. It is a false dichotomy.

We do well to ponder why it is that countries that acquire sudden riches from oil exports experience serious economic troubles. Clearly, in the case of Nigeria and Mexico, oil and agriculture do not mix.

It is doubtful that US AID can succeed in resisting the political influence of agriculture groups and that of the Congress in once again using US foreign aid to engage in dumping large quantities of agricultural commodities by this means. The administrators of AID are well aware of the harm that such dumping would do to parts of agriculture in low-income countries.

The moral purposes of charity are badly served by much of official foreign aid wherever it increases the control of governments in low-income countries which impair the freedom of choice and the opportunities of poor farm families. These adverse consequences are inconsistent with the primary objectives of charity. The self-serving pronouncements of donor agencies exploit the essence of our moral obligations. Much more serious is the use that is being made of the moral issue pertaining to poverty to establish and support totalitarian regimes.

My basic position is that most of the poor people in the world are farm people, that farm people in low-income countries have very little political influence when it comes to improving their economic lot, and that foreign aid has all too long served the recipient governments and, in doing so, has in large measure failed farm people.[20]

Notes and References

1   See above, Part I, No. 1.
2   *World Development Report 1982*, published for the World Bank (Oxford University Press, 1982). Indicators beginning on p. 110.
3   *Development Co-operation, 1981* (OECD, Paris, November 1981), report by John P. Lewis, table A.1, p. 172.
4   Ibid., table 3.16, pp. 194–5.
5   *Technical Cooperation in Latin America: Recommendations for the Future* (National Planning Association, Washington DC, June 1956), pp. xii–192. See lists of reports issued, appearing on p. ii.
6   Here I draw in part on "A Critique of the Economics of US Foreign Aid," which I presented at a seminar at Colorado State University, Fort Collins, Colorado, December 10, 1982.
7   *Development Cooperation 1981*: the estimates that follow are from table A.1, p. 172.
8   On this issue of deaths from famine see the perceptive essay by A. Sen, "How is India doing," *New York Review*, December 16, 1982.
9   Theodore W. Schultz, *Distortions of Agricultural Incentives* (Indiana University Press, Bloomington, 1978), pp. vii–343.
10 D. Gale Johnson, *Population and Development Review* (Population Council, New York), 1982.
11 D. Gale Johnson, "Progress in Economic Reform in the People's Republic of China," *Agricultural Economic Paper*, No. 82:7 (University of Chicago, February 17, 1982).
12 Here again I turn to my colleague D. Gale Johnson. See his study, "Food and Agriculture of the Centrally Planned Economies: Implications for the World System" in *Essays in Contemporary Problems: Demand, Productivity and Population* (American Enterprise Institute, Washington DC, 1981), pp. 171–213.
13 Three competent studies are at hand on this part of Africa. Uma Lele, "Rural Africa: Modernisation, Equity and Long Term Development," *Science* (6 February 1981), 547–53; Robert H. Bates, *Markets and the States in Tropical Africa* (University of California Press, Berkeley, 1981); and *Accelerated Development on Sub-Saharan Africa: An Agenda for Action* (World Bank, 1981).
14 Theodore W. Schultz, *Transforming Traditional Agriculture* (Yale University Press, New Haven, Conn., 1964).
15 The humanitarian cocnept connotes human welfare and social reform. The moral concept as it pertains to charity for the purpose of this paper is not a

secular concept as is the humanitarian concept. The limitations of the humanitarian approach to poverty in low income countries is succinctly presented by D. Gale Johnson in *The World's Poor: Can They Hope for a Better Future? Perspective '83, The World Food Situation* (International Minerals and Chemical Corp., Northbrook, Ill., 1983), pp. 9–15.

16 The University of Chicago Press published most of our studies. The Basic Summary Report assessing the achievements of these Aid Programmes was published by the National Planning Association (Washington DC, 1956), p. 192.

17 Theodore W. Schultz, "The Production and Distribution of Agricultural Knowledge with Special Reference to India," in *Minerva*, XCX, No. 3 (Autumn, 1981), 502–9. See also Hadley Read, *Partners with India Building Agricultural Universities* (University of Illinois, 1974), p. 159.

18 It should be noted that Egypt's foreign earnings from petroleum exports increased from $US 300m in 1978 to 3,300m in 1981; during the same period, receipts from remittances rose from $1,800m to 3,300m, receipts from Suez Canal operation were up from $550m to 1,000m and from tourists, the receipts were $700m in 1978 and 900m in 1981.

19 Uma Lele, "Rural Africa."

20 For an extended analysis of the "Distortions by the International Donor Community," see Theodore W. Schultz, *Investing in People* (University of California Press, Berkeley, 1981), chapter 7.

3

Investing in Poor People*

Poverty, for want of a theory, is lost in economics notwithstanding all of the statistics that show the size distribution of personal income and the age, sex, and family composition of people with low income and with consumption below some standard. A vast catalogue of the attributes of poor people is at hand. But for all that, there is no integrated body of economic knowledge and no agenda of economic hypotheses to get at important economic questions about poverty. Although there are valuable empirical studies, there is no integrated analytical approach to determine the factors that account for the distribution of personal income and wealth. It would be a mistaken view, however, to blame those who have produced these statistics; for economists have not formulated a theory to guide the organization and analysis of facts pertaining to poverty. Although it is obvious that without theory statisticians founder, if blame we must, we should fault economists for not bringing poverty into the analytical realm of economics.

Nor was it always thus. Malthus theorized about the causes of poverty and from the type of population growth that he considered normal he derived his well-known dismal consequences.[1] Marx built a system which gave the fruits of progress to the owners of capital. Marshall's conception of enterprise implied progress with poverty diminishing; Pigou then complemented this with welfare programs. But modern economists have not found poverty to their analytical taste. There is a concern about the personal distribution of income. The elegant community welfare function has been fashionable; but its purpose is not to analyze poverty and it is obviously empty in specifying and identifying poverty. The conventional thing to do, of course, is to believe in a natural law which will cause poverty to disappear. What then remain in the affluent society are pockets of people who because of preferences or

*First published in *American Economic Review*, lv, no. 2 (May 1965), 510–20. Reproduced by permission of the American Economic Association. I am indebted to Harry G. Johnson, Herman P. Miller, and Eugene Smolensky for pointing out a number of omissions and ambiguities. Each made available to me a recent paper he had prepared on which I drew with profit.

circumstances have not been cleansed by progress! Little wonder then that poverty has a very small place in economics.

Meanwhile poverty has been placed on the political agenda. A war on poverty has been declared. Data showing the personal distribution of income were never more abundant as they are presently, and yet anyone who examines them critically is convinced that they are far from satisfactory in identifying the people who are really poor. Who are the poor? Why are they poor? What can best be done to improve their lot? These are questions that would seem to require economic analysis. But economic theory seems to be of little avail. It could, of course, be true that they are not economic questions, or that the economic components in poverty are trivial and of no importance. I am under no illusions that anyone can in one fell swoop formulate the required theory. It seems to me, however, that parts of the core of economics can be used and the contributions that they can make may not be trivial in adding to our knowledge of poverty.

My plan is, first, to consider two applications of "consumer" demand, then to present three hypotheses with respect to changes in the sources of income and the effects of these changes upon poverty, and lastly to call attention to some of the implications of this approach.

1   Two Applications of Demand Theory

In applying the concept of demand, I turn to the effects of rising per capita income upon demand in an attempt to determine why the so-called "poverty line" is rising, and also why more young people and more of the aged become consumer units with earnings that place them in the low-income class. Although it is obvious that the standard by which society judges the welfare of the poor has been rising over time, it is not obvious that this rising standard represents an increase in the demand for welfare services for the poor, and that this increase in demand as it is revealed by the social-political process is a function of the rise in per capita income which can be treated as an income elasticity.[2] The underlying observed behavior appears to be consistent with an income elasticity substantially less than unity. During the period between the mid-1930s and mid-1960s real income per family virtually doubled and the poverty line, measured in constant dollars, may have risen about one half.[3] I venture that the relevant income elasticity here, although it is gradually becoming less elastic as per capita income rises, is sufficiently stable to make useful and dependable projections.

The rise in per capita income also increases the demand for the convenience of smaller households where young people can move from their parental household and set up separate households of their own and older people can maintain their status as separate families longer than formerly.[4] The demand here also can be treated as a function of the rise in income. The economic logic here presumes that families prefer and can afford as their incomes rise to have their young people break away from the parental unit and establish their own homes at an earlier age than formerly. It also presumes that families prefer and can afford to maintain their old people as separate units longer than formerly before these aged members become an integral part of the household of their offspring. It has been widely observed that this process of subdivision creates and maintains additional consumer units which functionally earn relatively small incomes.[5] But what then is the welfare implication of the fact that some of these additional consumer units show statistically as poor? When treated as an increase in the demand resulting from the rise in income, the implication is that the subdivision which occurs for this reason represents a superior welfare position, notwithstanding the fact that we observe as a consequence more young and old people who are poor statistically in terms of earnings.[6]

But these two applications of the theory of demand will not tell us much about poverty. They call for no investigation of the sources of the rise in income, whereas these sources are, so it seems to me, the key to the economics of poverty. The history of poverty since the industrial revolution can usefully be divided into two parts: economic growth with no appreciable rise in per capita income and, then, with substantial increases in per capita income.[7] The latter is a comparatively recent development and it is for this type that we lack a theoretical scaffold. Classical theory meanwhile continues to be relevant in investigating poverty in an economy in which there is growth but no rise in per capita income. The magnificent dynamics of Malthus, Ricardo, James Mill, McCulloch, and Senior – the leading classicial economists – are based on a model in which earnings per laborer do not rise.[8] Our economy obviously is not of this type. The plain fact is that the earnings of labor are rising, that these additional earnings account for virtually all of the rise in per capita income, and that they are the primary factor in reducing poverty over time. Why are these earnings increasing? Why is labor's functional share of national income becoming larger? These questions as already noted have become relevant rather recently in our history. How then are we to approach the dynamics of our economy with a view of settling these questions?

Before turning to them let me mention some well-established differences among the sources of income and some specialized chains of economic logic to guide particular types of analysis in this field. We are accustomed to classifying the functional sources to show whether they are from wages and salaries, from property, or from self-employment which is as a rule a combination of the two. To these sources income transfers are then added in classifying the sources of personal income. Nor is all of it monetary income; for a part of it is in kind and in services that are as a rule consumed directly by those who have such sources. But these differences are less important for our purpose than are the differences with respect to price, marketability, and the time it takes to develop the various sources and to obtain income from them. With regard to economic logic, the movements of the different income streams, i.e. those from profits, property, and labor, associated with the business cycle, undoubtedly have their own internal logic.[9] So do the effects of the process of economic growth upon the income of different regions, industries, and occupations.[10] Then, too, we now have a theory with respect to consumer behavior for assaying the transitory and permanent components of different classes of income.[11] Without detracting from these achievements, they do not tell us why earnings are rising relative to other income and rising per worker. To cope adequately with these questions, we await a general theory that will integrate these specialized chains of economic logic and provide us with a comprehensive and consistent analytical framework for determining the functional and final distribution of personal income. As a first step, I shall present the following hypotheses.

2   Three Hypotheses

My purpose here is to classify and organize the different sources of income streams and then to show how they are related to the observed changes in poverty. I propose to use the concepts of supply and demand to determine the changes in the prices of the different sources of these income streams. Income streams can be given quantitative dimensions per unit of time; i.e., a one-dollar-per-year income stream. Except for income transfers, to obtain possession of an income stream it is necessary to acquire the source of that stream. These sources are valuable, and each income stream in this sense has a price. The price may be low or high. If a source of a one-dollar-per-year income stream can be acquired for $10, it presumably would be cheap; if it cost $25, it would be dear. Thus what we should do is to identify the different sources and then proceed to ascertain the price at which each of the respective sources can be acquired. The central economic problem then becomes one of explaining what determines the price of these income streams. In this approach, then, it is meaningful to apply the concepts of supply and demand.[12]

The underlying assumptions, which are quite conventional, are as follows: the sources of income streams are acquired at particular prices; these prices change over time, and people respond to changes in these prices subject to the restraints of the capital market, their preferences and capacity to save, the effects of taxes and subsidies, and of discrimination with respect to employment and investment. We can then postulate a dynamic process from which we can derive the following complementary hypotheses that pertain to the type of economic growth that we have had during recent decades:

1   The price of the sources of income streams that represent the acquired human capabilities of value in economic endeavor declined during this period relative to the price of material forms.
2   In responding to this change in the relative prices of these two sources of income the rate of investment in human sources rose during this period relative to that in material sources.
3   The increase in the investment in human sources relative to the investment in nonhuman sources has increased earnings relative to property income and the more equal distribution of investment in people has tended to equalize earnings among human agents.

These are testable hypotheses. They appear to win support from a number of new studies. The private rates of return to schooling support the first. My attempt to test the second, admittedly a very rough approximation of the increases in the latter two of these stocks, indicates for the period between 1929 and 1957 that the stock of reproducible tangible wealth increased at an annual rate of about 2 percent while that of education in the labor force rose at a rate of 4 percent, and that of on-the-job training of males in the labor force at over 5 percent.[13] The marked increase in the proportion of the labor force that has attended high school and college is one of the developments in support of the third hypothesis.[14]

But this is not the occasion to enter upon a survey of the studies that provide estimates to test these hypotheses. Instead, I want to explore the developments that have been altering the underlying supply and demand of the major sources of these income streams.

During a normal business cycle the supply does not change substantially. The demand, however, shifts back and forth considerably during recessions and booms, and as a consequence the income from corporate and from some other forms of property fluctuates more over the cycle than national income. The fluctuations in income from wages and salaries are largest for unskilled labor, for workers who are least specific in their training in terms of the labor requirement of employers, and for workers who have the least seniority, with the result that the inequality of the personal distribution of income decreases in years of prosperity and increases in years of depression.[15]

Over the long run, both the demand and supply are subject to shifts some of which are accumulative and become large over time. Among the factors that shift the demand for the sources of income streams in this context, three are of major importance:

1 The aggregate demand for goods and service. Theory here is better than the art of fiscal-monetary policy. The aggregate demand was obviously far from sufficient during the massive unemployment of the early 1930s. It was more nearly enough during the high employment of the mid-fifties. Since then there has been much slack. Idle plants and idle workers reduce the demand for the sources of income. Clearly poor people have much at stake in government policy that will maintain full employment.

2 The demand effects of the advance in knowledge. These effects are commonly   concealed   under   "technological   change."[16]   New knowledge that is useful in economic endeavor requires either new forms of material capital or new skills on the part of labor, or, what is true in general, both are required. This factor, so it appears, has increased the demand for high skills relative to low skills and for the productive services of labor (numbers and quality combined) relative to the productive services of old and new material things.

3 The demand effects and changes in restrictions "on the opportunity for individuals to participate in the productive process to the full extent of their potential."[17] What matters here is discrimination against Negroes with respect to jobs, against the aged poor who still are willing and able to do productive work but who are required to quit working, or work only part-time to be eligible for retirement and survivor payments, and against the participation of women in the labor force.

Turning next briefly to the long-run changes in the supply of the sources of income streams, these changes may be explored either in terms of adjustments to shifts in the demand or in terms of factors which play a fairly independent role. The adjustment process in which the demand and supply interact is the core of the economic behavior underlying the formulation of the second hypothesis here advanced. The major "independent" factors affecting the supply are as follows: research and development activities and dissemination of the resulting useful knowledge from these activities, the mobility (immobility) of particular sources, predominantly labor, in leaving declining industries and occupations, the amount and distribution of public investment in schooling and, closely related, the discrimination against Negroes, rural farm children, and others with respect to schooling.

Thus, the analytical task at hand might be to account for the observed decline in poverty, or alternatively to account for the poverty that remains. Although the latter has its appeal, for it is more direct, it may be less efficient because it is undoubtedly true that the first task is a prerequisite to doing the second. I shall therefore continue to concentrate on the first task.

Income from Property

By all accounts the functional share of income from property has been declining. The stock of tangible reproducible wealth has not increased at as high a rate as the acquired abilities of workers. Differences in the rates of return have favored investment in human capital. True, the relative decline in income from material wealth would undoubtedly have been somewhat less had the tax on corporate income remained at the pre-war level. Meanwhile, what has been happening to the personal distribution of wealth holdings? It is hard to believe that poor people have been acquiring a substantially large share of this wealth and that it is the source of the income that has brought about the observed decline in poverty. The stock of wealth represented by houses may be an exception, in the sense that it has been an attractive investment for many low-income families while the economy has been adjusting to the favorable tax treatment that home ownership has been receiving. But homes owned by families with less than $3,000 of income in 1962 had a mean value of only $3,750.[18] Any plausible increase in the net worth of low-income consumers since the mid-1930s could account for only a very small part of the decline in poverty.[19]

Income from Labor

Meanwhile, labor's functional share of national income has been rising. The demand for workers with high skills has been increasing at a higher rate than that for low skills. Thus, the incentive to increase skills has been strong and the supply of skills has been responding. People have been investing much more than formerly to increase their skills. But why has the demand for skills been shifting upward in this manner? In my judgment it has come about mainly as a consequence of the dynamic process in which skills along with new useful knowledge gradually have been increasing national income, and at the same time the resulting rise in per capita income of consumers has altered the mix of products and services demanded in such a way that the products and services requiring high skills have increased at a higher rate than that of those requiring low skills. Another factor of some importance in this process has undoubtedly been the increase in the demand for producer durables and services by the military establishment, which also has been increasing the demand for high skills.

3   Implications

The first and most general implication is that the observed large decline in poverty is primarily a consequence of increases in income from labor. It is not to be attributed to income from property. The real earnings of workers have been rising because the demand for high skills has been increasing relative to that for low skills and because workers have been acquiring the more valuable skills.

Another implication is that a substantial part of the remaining poverty is a consequence of a number of disequilibria. Although workers have been responding to the changes in the market for skills, the economy in this respect has been in substantial disequilibrium at many points. The reasons why this is so are fairly obvious; namely, unemployment, the adverse incidences of economic growth on some sectors, inadequate information, and a lack of opportunity to invest in acquiring the more valuable skills because of discrimination and the restraints on the capital market in providing funds for this purpose. Let me call attention to three of these disequilibria.

1   The market for the skills that are required in agriculture has been long depressed. Although the labor force devoted to farming has declined by one-half between 1940 and 1965, the market for these skills is still in serious disequilibrium. Older members of this labor force have had no real alternative but to settle for the depressed, salvage value of the skills they possess. In many farm areas the quality of elementary and secondary schooling has been and continues to be far below par[20] and thus the oncoming generation from these areas is ill-prepared to take advantage of the strong market in other parts of the economy for high skills. It

should also be said that the vast expenditures by the federal government on behalf of agriculture have not been used to raise the level of these skills; on the contrary, they have been used in ways that enhance the income from some classes of property and that worsen the personal distribution of income among farm families. Thus, it should not come as a surprise that although farm families are presently a very small faction of all US families, they account for much of the observed poverty[21] and that many of the families in urban areas who are below the poverty line have recently come from our farms.

2   The market for the skills of Negroes has also been long depressed and the poverty component here is large. This market has been intertwined with that of agriculture; and both on our farms and in our cities, there has been and continues to be much job discrimination. More important still is the low level of skills of Negroes, which is mainly a consequence of the history of discrimination against Negroes in schooling. Not only have Negroes obtained fewer years of schooling but the schooling has been of very low quality; it was especially so for the older Negroes in the labor force.

3   The South is burdened with much more poverty than other regions basically for three reasons: (1) it is more dependent upon agriculture than the rest of the United States (it accounted for over 45 percent of all US farms at the time the 1959 census of agriculture was taken); (2) the labor force in the South is more largely Negro than in the North and West and in terms of marketable skills the Negroes in the South are even worse off than the Negroes in other regions; and (3) relatively more of the whites in the labor force in the South have low skills than whites in other regions. In short, the South has been lagging seriously in providing people the opportunities to invest in acquiring the high skills for which the demand has been increasing at so rapid a rate, predominantly because of social, political, and economic discrimination adverse to poor people.

In conclusion, this paper is a modest proposal to provide a small room for poverty in the house that economists have built. To furnish it there are two handy demand pieces. Both go back to the preferences of people underlying their demand: one is for welfare which marks the poverty line, and the other is for consumer units which divide families. They give us two more attractive income elasticities to estimate and to converse about. A more useful piece is designed to explain the large decline in poverty. The concepts of supply and demand can be applied to determine the price of the different sources of income streams. Instructions are included for setting up the economic logic of our development during the recent past and for deriving from this logic three testable hypotheses.

Available tests are comforting. Thus, it would appear that there have been strong economic incentives to invest in human beings and such investments will explain most of the observed decline in poverty. The poverty that remains is to a large extent the result of such investment opportunities having been thwarted.

Notes and References

1 The Malthusian conception of the growth in population is by no means obsolete when one examines the upsurge in population in relation to the supply of food in many poor countries. See Theodore W. Schultz, "Economic Growth from Traditional Agriculture," in *Agricultural Sciences for the Developing Nations* (American Association for the Advancement of Science, Pub. No. 76, 1964). The monumental study by G. H. Slicher Van Bath, *The Agrarian History of Western Europe A.D. 500 to 1850* (St. Martin's Press, 1963), leaves little room for doubt that for ages past the growth in population and the expansion of agriculture were broadly related in the way that Malthus represented that relationship.

2 To visualize this process, it is helpful to use a conventional demand and supply diagram. Place the price of a standard unit of welfare service on the vertical scale and the quantity of such welfare services that will be provided per family for poor people on the horizontal scale. Assume for convenience that the supply curve is horizontal in the sense that the supply price remains constant. The demand curve of the usual slope is then drawn. The intercept will indicate the quantity of such welfare services per poor family that the social-political process will "vote for" at the price indicated by the intercept. Suppose now that the per capita income of the community rises and that the income elasticity of the demand for these welfare services is positive, the demand curve will as a consequence shift to the right and this means that the social-political process will vote for a larger quantity of these welfare services per poor family than formerly and that the quantity will be indicated by the new intercept. Meanwhile, of course, the development that produces the rise in per family income generally may increase the income of many families who were formerly poor, so much that even by the new higher standard they are no longer among the poor.

3 Eugene Smolensky, in "The Past and Present Poor," developed a concept of poverty which showed that when one took the poverty line in the mid 1960s to be $3,000, the poverty line in 1935 was in the neighborhood of $1,950, both expressed in 1959 dollars, thus by this measure the poverty line rose 55 percent since 1935. Real income per family between 1935–56 and 1963 rose from $3,343 to $6,613 in 1954 dollars; see *Survey of Current Business*, (Apr., 1964), table 13. Smolensky placed 37 percent of the families in poverty as of 1935 and 23 percent so situated in 1959. In the text of his

paper he refers to one-third and one-fifth as the appropriate estimates for the mid-1930s and mid-1960s. Herman P. Miller, in "Measurements for Alternative Concepts of Poverty" (American Statistical Association, Chicago, Illinois, Dec. 1964), presents cogent reasons for the rise in the poverty line and data to show the extent of the rise. He cites estimates of the cost of subsistence budgets made by Ruth Mack. According to the estimates, the percent of families with income below this budget were as follows:

	Contemporary Definition of Subsistence	1960 Definition of Subsistence
1935................................	28	47
1941................................	17	31
1950................................	13	26
1960................................	10	10

4   The studies by Dorothy S. Brady are especially relevant in this connection.
5   Between 1947 and 1960 the trend of family income of heads of families, ages 14–24 and 65 and over, has been declining relative to the income of all families. The following estimates of the median income of all families and the two age classes mentioned show this trend.

	1947		1960	
	In 1959 dollars	Relative	In 1959 dollars	Relative
All families............	3,957	100	5,547	100
Age 14–24.............	3,075	78	3,965	71
Age 65 and more...	2,398	61	2,862	52

Source: H. P. Miller, *Trends in Incomes of Families in the United States: 1947 to 1960* (Technical Paper No. 8, Bureau of Census, Washington, DC, 1963).

6   The consumption picture is of course substantially modified by income transfers, not only through public measures, but importantly by private income transfers to young people from their parents and to older people from their established offsprings.
7   For differences between these two parts and the movement from the first to the second in terms of sociological-economic evidence and in terms of agricultural-economic evidence, respectively, see Jean Fourastié, *The Causes of Wealth* (Free Press of Glencoe, 1960), translated by Theodore Caplow; and Slicher Van Bath, *The Agrarian History of Western Europe.*
8   See William J. Baumol, *Economic Dynamics* (Macmillan Co., 1951), Part I.
9   The income effects of changes in rate of unemployment have received much deserved attention. See, for example, Harry G. Johnson, "Poverty and Unemployment," (Nov. 1964, unpublished). In explaining the decline in poverty historically, this paper attributes more importance to this factor

than it would appear to warrant. See also Eugene Smolensky, "The Past and Present Poor." Robert J. Lampman's study, "The Low Income Population and Economic Growth" (Joint Economic Committee, 86th Congress, 1st session, Nov. 16, 1959), also treats unemployment. There are, of course, many more treatments.

10   My first attempt to treat poverty belongs here. See below, Part 1, No. 4, "Reflections on Poverty within Agriculture". See also "A Policy to Redistribute the Losses from Economic Progress," *Journal of Farm Economics* (Aug. 1961), also printed in *Labor Mobility and Population in Agriculture*, (Iowa State University Press, 1961).

11   Milton Friedman, *A Theory of the Consumption Function* (Princeton University Press, 1957).

12   In this paragraph I follow closely my *Transforming Traditional Agriculture* (Yale University Press, New Haven, Conn., 1964), chapter 5, pp. 74ff.

13   Theodore W. Schultz, "Reflections on the Investment in Man," *Journal of Political Economy*, Sup. (Oct. 1962), under the title "Investment in Human Beings," table 1, p. 6.

14   Between 1940 and 1959, for the labor force 18 to 64 years old, both sexes, the number that had completed four years of high school rose from 20 to 32 percent, and that had attended college from 13 to 19 percent of the total labor force. *Statistical Abstract of the United States 1960*, table 139, p. 109.

15   Entrepreneurial income aside, in a free enterprise economy there are two sources of income fluctuation that are very burdensome for many poor people. One is a consequence of the low price elasticity of the demand for farm products where there are wide year-to-year variations in production because of weather. The other arises from short-run inelastic supply of unskilled labor where the shifts in demand for such labor are large over the business cycle.

16   See Schultz, *Transforming Traditional Agriculture*, chapter 9.

17   I follow closely here Harry G. Johnson, "Poverty and Unemployment."

18   See "Survey of Financial Characteristics of Consumers," *Federal Reserve Bulletin* (Mar. 1964), Supp. table 2B.

19   The families with less than $3,000 of income in 1962 in the Federal Reserve "Survey" had a mean net worth of $18,875. Even if one were to assume that this net worth had doubled over recent decades for those at this real income level and one were to allow a 10 percent rate of return, it would account for only $444 of additional income.

20   See Theodore W. Schultz, "Underinvestment in the Quality of Schooling: The Rural Farm Areas," in *Increasing Understanding of Public Problems and Policies 1964*, Proceedings of the 14th National Agricultural Policy Conference, College Station, Texas, Sept. 15–17, 1964 (Farm Found., Chicago, Jan. 1965).

21   It should be noted, however, that the precise amount of poverty attributed to farm families is not as large as the widely used statistics appear to show. Wealth holdings are large relative to measured income. My estimate of the

average net asset position of farmers actually farming (3.48 million in 1963) was approximately $35,800 per farmer in 1963 (see below, Part 1, No. 5, "Our Welfare State and the Welfare of Farm People"). In the Federal Reserve "Survey", table 2, p. 293, the average net worth of the 2 million farm operators in this sample came to $43,973 on December 31, 1962. My colleague, Margaret Reid, has done yeoman work in directing attention to components of real income of farm operator families that are still not measured.

4

*Reflections on Poverty within Agriculture**

There is room for a lament on the state of beliefs held with regard to poverty within agriculture. The chronic problem of poverty in parts of agriculture is viewed by many as being mainly a private and personal affair of the families who are poor and as having no social roots or major social implications. There is also the belief, now firmly established among many industrial-urban people, that most farm people are poor most of the time. The lament becomes deep and mournful when one sees the formation of agricultural policy proceed as if all farm families were poor and when one observes the failure of agricultural programs to come to grips with the poverty that actually exists within American agriculture.

Poverty – the state of being in need – is an acceptable state socially; the poor have always been with us (and, of course, respectable; it is not an unknown academic state!). It is neglected in research about agriculture, since thinking on this issue is usually not received with favor; and it is ill conceived in the formulation of agricultural policy and misused in seeking public support for agricultural programs. Poverty within agriculture is acceptable, for it is looked upon as natural. It is "natural" (1) because, so it is believed, poor farmers gravitate to poor land, and there is much poor land in the United States; (2) because many farm people prefer to stay poor rather than make adequate effort to improve their lot; (3) because in farming, although people may be poor in dollars, they are nevertheless rich in those valuable appurtenances that go with being close to nature and living independently; and (4) because the Negro and the Mexican, of whom there are many in agriculture, are naturally poor. So run the mythology and folklore of our day, making poverty not only acceptable but necessary.

The neglect of the study of poverty within agriculture is understandable because the poor in agriculture are politically impotent. Although

* First published in *Journal of Political Economy*, *58*, No. 1 (Feb. 1950), 1–15. Reproduced by permission of University of Chicago Press.

political influence may gradually come to them, such influence is still in the distant future; and those who administer research are necessarily sensitive to the immediate political repercussions of such research. If they were inclined otherwise, they would do well to look back and reflect on the fate that befell the rural sociologists from the fire that was directed against the Bureau of Agricultural Economics, and on the frigidity of Congress toward proposals to help the poor in agriculture in the early 1940s. But this neglect runs deeper, for those who do research are not prone passively to accept political coercion curtailing their freedom of thought when they feel strongly on the issues at stake. The inference is that they do not believe that poverty in agriculture is an important social problem. This belief may exist because, for the most part, agricultural research workers have been trained in an intellectual climate that gives little emphasis to the strong, liberal, and humanitarian currents that have characterized our Western culture; because their research problems have not brought them into close contact with the poor in farming; and, probably most important of all, because they have been inclined to accept the prevailing folklore about poverty in agriculture. Thus, since thinking and ideas must precede social action to diminish poverty, it should surprise no one that the formation of policy with regard to poverty is ill conceived and misapplied.

1 Preliminary Considerations

To analyze the economic aspects of the poverty that has gradually become imbedded in agriculture, it is necessary to have some conception of economic development. The classical economists had a theory of economic growth and progress, which, however, as I shall show, does not have sufficient generality to deal with the type of economic development that has come to characterize the history of the United States. The task at hand consists of three parts. The first entails an attempt to describe the salient characteristics of the poverty that has emerged. This characterization is presented in the form of a series of propositions. Next, there is the task of selecting an analytical framework sufficiently comprehensive to include conditions under which economic progress can give rise to increasing disparity of income. And, finally, there is the difficult undertaking of determining the conditions that are necessary for increasing disparity in income to occur. It is my belief that the results of this approach are meaningful in the formation of policies to diminish poverty in American agriculture. The policy implications, however, are left for another occasion.

In this paper I take the American scene as it has developed during the comparatively few decades that have elapsed since the settlement of this continent as the empirical setting of the problem. I neglect, for the most part, the effects of sudden changes in the main economic magnitudes of either world war or of the great depression. Accordingly, in order to make my task manageable, I abstract from short-run fluctuations in the basic argument. I take poverty to mean being too poor to afford the level of living[1] that has become generally established and that most people can afford. I am not, however, concerned with the poverty of any particular farm family but, instead, with that of an aggregate consisting of all the families located in a given community or neighborhood.[2] More specifically, whenever I refer to "level of living" or to "income," I mean the average level of living or the per capita income of the community. Accordingly, this study does not focus upon isolated farm families, no matter how poverty-stricken they may be, but upon a group of families comprising a community or neighborhood. Thus in any given community one or more families may be beset by poverty as compared to the average level of living of the community. This *within*-community poverty is not, however, the object of this study. The analysis is restricted to *between*-community comparisons. It follows, therefore, that not all the families in a poor community are necessarily equally poor and that some families in such a community may be better off than are many families located in a comparatively rich community.

In order to simplify the problem, let me treat one of the empirical propositions as an assumption at this point. Let it be assumed that these communities had about the same distribution in wealth and natural endowments at the time of settlement or at the time that the developments associated with the industrial revolution began to make their impact. This means that within a community some families had more than average talents while others fell below that mark; for, even at the outset of settlement, it is only reasonable to suppose that some families were poorer than others both in natural endowments and in material possessions, including the "investment" that had already been made in themselves in ways that enhanced their productive capacity. I take it to be a rough approximation of the facts that the distribution of "talents" and "capital" within most, if not all, communities at the time of settlement or at the time that industrialization began to make itself felt was probably not significantly different from one community to another. Meanwhile, they have moved far apart in income, and therefore, on that score, the distributions of families have come to differ greatly. Whether, however, a similar drift has occurred in the case of the endowments of people within communities is a disputed point. Although the evidence is tenuous, it may be held that, whereas there are now poor and rich communities in agriculture, they are still essentially more alike than they are unlike one another, in the distribution of natural human endowments.[3]

2 Simplifying Empirical Propositions

The propositions that follow are intended to direct attention to certain salient characteristics of our economic development. They are an attempt to describe one of the economic aspects of that development, namely, the differences between communities in the rates of growth or of progress, expressed in terms of per capita income or level of living. To isolate this aspect, it is necessary to simplify greatly and, in the process, to leave aside many other historical facts and issues. Nor is it my belief that no qualifications are required along the way. These propositions may be stated as follows:

1   In general, the differences in per capita income and level of living among communities were not so great at the time when people pioneered new areas or at the time industrialization began as they have become since then.[4] Poverty of whole communities did not generally exist under pioneering conditions because levels of living were in their essentials quite similar, although, if we look back, people were undoubtedly exceedingly poor by present-day standards.

2   The marked differences in level of living that have emerged within agriculture are not mainly the result of a deterioration on the part of those communities in which people are not living under conditions of poverty, but largely the consequences of the increases in per capita incomes that have been realized by people in other communities.[5] This proposition means that families in some localities have been virtually stationary in their level of living. Others have advanced somewhat in their level of living, and still others have shown marked advances. The gap between the first and third types of community has become exceedingly wide, is becoming ever wider, and will continue to increase as long as the first type remains stationary or advanced less rapidly than does the third.

3   These gaps, consisting of differences in level of living, are basically consequences of the way in which the economy of the United States has developed and not primarily the results of any original differences in the cultural values or capabilities of the people themselves.

Each of these propositions is meaningful in the sense that it is possible, by making an appeal to empirical experience, to determine whether each is a valid statement about economic history. Actually, the first two are not essential to the argument proper; for they merely specify a particular set of conditions at the beginning of settlement and outline the changes that have occurred in the relative positions of neighborhoods since that time. It is the third of these that is central and most important to the argument, as may be seen when it is stated as follows: The differences in the per capita income and the level of living that have come to exist *among* neighborhoods in agriculture are basically the consequences of the way in which the economy of the United States has developed. The principal difficulty that arises in putting this statement to the test is largely in specifying the components that go to make up the way in which the economy has developed and in determining their effects upon the local fortunes of people. Before undertaking this task, however, it should be possible to clear away some underbrush by calling attention to several fairly obvious implications of this formulation of the problem of poverty in agriculture.

If poverty, as herein defined, is the result of economic development, it cannot be a consequence of the differences in the physical characteristics of land unless it can be shown that the differences in land per se are a significant factor in that development. It will become evident as I proceed that there are strong reasons for believing that the differences in land suitable for farming, in themselves, have not been an important factor in shaping the course of our economic development. The industrial "Ruhr" of the United States developed across the middle states to the north not because the farm land of the Corn Belt was better than that of the Cotton Belt generally, but for quite other reasons. The main effect has been the other way around, that is, the economy, essentially as an independent variable, has developed in such a way as to give some farm land a comparative advantage over other land in potential adjustments to economic progress. This statement means that people who settled on poor land located in or near the main stream of economic development have benefited from the economic progress growing out of that development as much as have people situated on highly productive land in or near this stream. On the other hand, people who settled on good land that was located away from the centers of active development, and thus at a disadvantage in terms of making the necessary social and economic adjustments, lost ground relative to those people who settled on either poor or good land located in or near the main stream. The term "disadvantage" in this context is not a matter of physical distances and therefore cannot be measured in miles. It must be expressed in terms of adverse effects upon efficiency and capacity of the entry and exodus of resources that can be transferred, especially of the human agent. The milk sheds are a case in point that firmly support these remarks regarding the role of farm land. The milk sheds are the closest of all farm land to the active centers of the main stream of economic development because of the overwhelming importance of the industrial-urban sectors in generating economic progress. The differences in the physical characteristics of land among major milk sheds is exceedingly great, some of it consisting of rough, hilly, poor, land by any standards and some of level, highly fertile land. Yet nowhere within a milk shed, attached to a major industrial-urban area, can it be said that there exist whole communities of poverty-stricken farmers, as is the case in large parts of American agriculture located at a disadvantage relative to such areas.

The main import of these remarks on land is simply that studies concentrating on land may describe the location of poverty but cannot analyze its underlying causes, inasmuch as land is essentially passive in the process that has brought about the poverty under consideration.

Another implication of the argument set forth above pertains to the drift of prices. It may be stated thus: If poverty is the result of economic development and if this development is not incompatible with changes in the level of particular prices, the long-run decline (or rise) of a farm-product price is not necessarily a factor contributing to the poverty that has come to exist among communities in agriculture. Product upon product may be cited in which, over the years, the price has declined relative to other prices and the industry producing the product has prospered, in that it has attracted additional capital and labor into its productive effort. On the other hand, there are many cases in which a decline in price has necessitated less output, and the adjustment has been made without generating poverty. It can, therefore, be demonstrated both in theory and in practice that a decline in price is not incompatible with economic development; in fact, on the contrary, it has usually been an essential part of the process. This is not to argue that prices that fluctuate greatly are as efficient in guiding production as are steadier and more dependable prices.[6] Nor do I wish to imply that contraction is necessarily easy – certainly not in the short run. An appeal may be made to certain obvious empirical observations with regard to agriculture. Take any major farm product, and, regardless of whether the price has declined or risen over the years relative to other farm products, there are farmers – in fact, whole communities of farm families – who are distinctly well-to-do and who are mainly dependent for their income on that product. The view that I am advancing is simply that long-run price flexibility has not brought about the kind of poverty that is under consideration in this paper. It has, of course, enhanced greatly the efficiency and the size of the national product.

3   Increasing Disparity in Income

Progress that increases income may be viewed either in the aggregate or in per capita terms. The argument on which this paper rests presupposes an economy in which both are increasing and in which the per capita income in some communities seems to remain virtually stationary while that of others increases, although the rates of increase may vary. To gain perspective, it may be helpful to look afresh at the classical conception of economic progress. The older economists – Ricardo, Malthus, Mill – conceived of "the dynamics of political economy"[7] as a process in which the aggregate income increases under circumstances where per capita income tends to remain constant. Their analytical apparatus was built around the rates of change of two important magnitudes; they were inclined to call one of these the "power of production" and the other the "power of population."[8] Various rates of increase in production were considered, but, under their assumption, it did not matter whether production moved forward gradually or took a sudden spurt, since extra population soon took up the slack. Their theory in its main outlines is simple and remains powerful. Whenever conditions are such that the growth in population absorbs any increase in production to the point that per capita incomes tend to remain constant, it necessarily follows that the power of production becomes the limitational factor not only of the size of the population but also of economic progress expressed in terms of increases in aggregate income. The conditions on which this classical conception of dynamics rests are no longer generally applicable, but as a special case they continue to apply. Where they do apply, a great deal of insight can be had by the use of this apparatus.

We need, however, a formulation with greater generality; for it is clear that, when the concept of economic progress is restricted to an increase in aggregate income with per capita income remaining constant, it is conceived altogether too narrowly. The following statement is proposed: Economic progress consists of an increase in aggregate income with changes in per capita income unspecified, except that no community becomes worse off. Actually, the most important part of this undertaking is to specify and identify the conditions that are necessary in economic progress, that generate disparity in per capita incomes, and that perpetuate these inequalities functionally considered, once they have become established.

A few observations on the economic developments that have characterized the industrial revolution of western Europe suggest that there is a close parallelism between those developments and the central propositions underlying the main argument of this paper regarding poverty in

American agriculture. There is no firm basis for believing that the level of living that existed in most of the communities (or neighborhoods) comprising the bulk of the population of western Europe prior to the events associated with the industrial revolution were as different one from another as they have become since then.[9] The level of living of the mass of the people was obviously very low everywhere compared to levels that emerged subsequently, if we neglect the courts and a few of the trading towns. The levels of living were, with few exceptions, low in virtually all communities and did not differ nearly so much from one community to another as they do at present. The way in which the economy developed by increasing overall production is noteworthy. The per capita income and level of living began to rise in the countries experiencing the increases in production. One should note also that, instead of a migration of people from other parts of the world toward these countries, attracted by the rising per capita incomes and levels of living, there occurred, in fact, an extraordinary migration out of western Europe not only to the United States but to Asia and to other countries overseas.[10] Was it the poor, the people in the communities that were being by-passed by the industrial revolution, who migrated abroad; and did they do so because they found it easier to go abroad than to participate in the growing fortunes of people generally in communities benefiting from economic progress?

This brief reference to the economic history of western Europe since about 1650 suggests that the advances in technology and in economic organization usually ascribed to the industrial revolution, gave rise (1) to a much larger aggregate production; (2) to an increase in per capita income and in level of living generally in Europe, despite the fact that the European population multiplied five times from 1650 to 1950;[11] (3) to an increasing disparity in per capita incomes and in levels of living between western Europe (certainly up to World War II) and those parts of the world that had not benefited from the process of industrialization;[12] and (4) to conditions which impeded the migration of non-Europeans into Europe, a development that would have equalized returns to human agents of European and non-European communities had it occurred in sufficient numbers. But what actually happened was a migration of millions of Europeans to other parts of the world.

4 Conditions Necessary for Increasing Disparity in Income

There can be no doubt that the economic progress that has characterized the industrial development of the Western world, including our own, has brought about a disparity in incomes. One observes that the disparity in per capita incomes between the advanced and the undeveloped industrial countries has become ever greater; and also, within a country like the United States, communities at or near centers of economic progress have pulled further and further away in terms of productivity and income per head from those communities situated less favorably.[13] I shall endeavor to indicate the conditions responsible for the increasing disparity in incomes.

The accumulation of capital that is put to productive uses will, of course, other things being equal, increase the income of those who are the recipients of such earnings. The concentration of productive assets in the hands of people of advanced industrial countries is a commonplace; the unequal distribution of such assets among families within a country is also well known. This aspect of the growth of capital and its effects on the distribution of income is certainly not new. Nor has it been neglected in economics. In the formation of policy for agriculture, however, sight is often lost of the fact that many farm families possess valuable property that earns for them very considerable income and that such families are not necessarily poor even when farm prices are low.

Abstracting from changes in income contributed by the growth of capital other than that "invested" in the human agent, there are three sets of conditions inherent in economic progress, each of which can bring about a disparity in income. A disparity will occur in favor of people in communities located at or near the centers of economic progress under each of the following conditions: (1) those that alter the proportion of the population engaged in productive work in one community relative to that of another; (2) those that change the abilities of a population to produce, of one community relative to that of another; and (3) those that impede factor-price equalization of comparable human agents between communities.

5   Changes in the Proportion of a Population Contributing to Income

The ratio of contributors to non-contributors becomes larger as communities participate in economic progress. Obviously, this ratio is important; for, if only a few people are active at productive work, there will be less income per head than if many people in a given community are contributors, other things being equal. The conditions that determine this ratio arise out of a number of complex developments; there are (1) the changes in composition of the population associated with economic progress, (2) the changes in the continuity of employment and in the specialization permitted by the division of labor that emerge as a result of economic developments, and (3) differences that arise from the way in which income is measured and in which the income accounting is done. [14]

Probably the most important of these developments is the demographic evolution of the population of a community. Students of population have observed that there are, from a demographic point of view, basically three population types in the world at present. [15] The first of these is the *pre-industrial type*, with very high birth and death rates, with a large proportion of the population in the lower-age brackets of the population pyramid, and with a short life-expectancy. It fulfils the essential conditions of the Malthus-Ricardo-Mill idea of dynamics, inasmuch as the potential increase in population is such that it can readily absorb substantial increases in production should they occur and thus tends to keep the level of living constant. The basic consideration in this context, however, is the fact that a large proportion of the population consists of nonproducers. The second type of population is usually referred to as *transitional*, with its diminishing birth and death rates but with the death rate dropping first [16] and for a time faster than the birth rate, with a marked increase in population taking place as a consequence. The advanced *industrial type* comes into existence when the birth and death rates are again approaching a balance at rates about one-third to one-half as high as those that characterize the pre-industrial populations. Life-expectancy becomes fully twice as high, and the age distribution characterizing the population pyramid is such that a large proportion of the people are in the ages where they can contribute to productive economic effort.

We are inclined to think of the United States as approaching a demographic stage characteristic of an advanced industrial country, but it is true that within agriculture the pre-industrial and the transitional demographic population types predominate. Moreover, one of the major consequences of these demographic differences is to be found in the proportion of the farm population that can contribute to production. For example, in comparing Grundy County, Iowa, with Breathitt County, Kentucky, we find that, in 1940, 62 percent of the farm population of the Iowa County was twenty-one years of age and over, as against 42 percent of the Kentucky country. [17] The farm population seventy years of age and over in both cases was slightly more than 2 percent.

A second development altering the proportion of the population that contributes to income arises out of changes in the continuity of employment and the specialization afforded by the division of labor as economic progress has proceeded. Again, it may be assumed that, until industrialization got under way, most communities were essentially alike in this respect; but they have drifted apart because some communities in agriculture have emerged with more continuous employment and with work more specialized than have the communities that have been by-passed in the course of economic development.[18] The result is fairly obvious; in the communities that have been favored, people who can work may do so more of the time during the year; and the division of labor has been carried further, thus permitting them to specialize to better account. Here, again, to illustrate the consequences one needs only to refer to farming in central Iowa comapred to that in eastern Kentucky.[19]

We conclude this section with the observation that it would appear from even these brief explorations that the conditions which determine the proportion of a population of a community that contributes to income is a consequence of the social evolution of our society set in motion by the character of our economic development.

6   Abilities of a Population to Produce Income

It will be convenient to classify abilities into those with which people are naturally endowed and those which they acquire. As to the first, we have already indicated that it would seem plausible to state that most communities at the time that industrialization began or at the time of settlement were roughly the same in the distribution of native talents. Moreover, communities in agriculture at present may not differ substantially on this score.[20] However, as for the abilities that can be acquired, differences have arisen as a result of the way in which our economy has developed. We can achieve considerable insight into this matter by abstracting from certain social and physical aspects in order to isolate (1) the process by which capital is "invested" in human agents, (2) the amount of capital thus invested, and (3) the effect of this investment upon the productivity of a population. An analysis of the formation of capital in this sphere is beset by many major difficulties. It is exceedingly hard to draw a line of demarcation between inputs for consumption and those that act as capital. Many of these inputs undoubtedly make contributions both ways; and, when it comes to measurement, the existing capital market gives us little or no information because it is not organized to finance "investments" that enhance the abilities of people as producers. Where men are not slaves but free, a mortgage on capital which in the process of formation becomes imbedded in a person requires the kind of instrument that has had no appeal to financial institutions, even though the earnings on such investments in many cases would prove very attractive.[21] Consequently, as one would expect, the supply of capital employed to improve the abilities of a population have come from two major sources – from the family and from the community in which a person lives. Furthermore, with few exceptions, the capital is made available without recourse, that is, the individual is under no obligation to repay his family or community. In substance, then, we have, for all practical purposes, no capital market serving this need. The institutions that exist, namely, the family and the community, bear the brunt of this function, and the results are all too evident. The amount that is invested per human agent is extremely unequal from one community to another. Where the community is poor, families are also poor, and therefore neither of them can afford to make these investments; the converse, of course, is true in a rich community. The implications of this process to our argument are clear; economic development has been uneven; some communities have been left behind; these communities and the families in them have few resources per head and fewer still per child at hand to train and rear their children, while the communities and families situated in the main stream of economic development have many resources available for these purposes.[22]

There is not much that one can say on the amount of capital that is invested in human agents except to express the belief that it has become very large indeed in countries with an advanced industrial economy and especially so in the best-situated communities in the United States. Any attempt to measure this outlay encounters major obstacles, for reasons already touched upon.

There remain, then, the effects of investments of this nature upon the productivity of a population. It will be useful to distinguish between (1) the effects that alter the comparability of human resources in terms of abilities to do a given type of work equally well and (2) the effects that express themselves in awareness of alternative opportunities, in the capacity to communicate, and in willingness to migrate. In the case of the first of these two effects – that pertaining to comparability – it is evident that where the investment consists of preparing an individual for a task that requires years of careful and systematic training, such as is necessary to become a doctor, a lawyer, a scientist, or a skilled technologist, the person who has received this training is no longer comparable to a person who has not had similar preparation. What about the bulk of the work in agriculture, where advanced technology is employed, and in industry generally? It appears that in the short run a significant difference in productivity exists between those who have had the advantages that go with the class of investment as compared to those who have not. To illustrate, a young migrant from eastern Kentucky would probably find himself at some disadvantage on a typical Iowa farm or in doing a given job in industry compared to a young migrant from a rich farming community and from a fairly prosperous family in western Kentucky; but this margin of disadvantage in most cases is likely to disappear rather rapidly. The two men would differ appreciably in the short run, that is, for a month or two or even for as long as a year, but, after that, they would be on about equal footing in terms of the abilities that are required to do such work. The second of these effects, involving awareness of opportunities and a willingness to migrate, is, so it seems to me, by all odds the more important of the two in accounting for the unequal incomes earned per person within agriculture. These effects, however, are basic in getting at the imperfect factor-price equalization that exists and therefore takes us to the third set of conditions underlying the disparity in incomes under consideration.

7   Conditions that Impede Factor-Price Equalization

We have explored briefly the conditions that increase the proportion of the population contributing to income and that improve the abilities of a population to produce, and I have endeavored to show how the forces of economic development, expressing themselves through the existing family and community institutions, alter these conditions. There still remains a third set of conditions which appear to play an important role in contributing to the growing disparity in income among communities within agriculture.

Two questions may be helpful in putting certain aspects of the problem of achieving factor-price equalization into focus. Does economic progress, as we have known it, require a vast and unprecedented transfer of human agents? The answer is, I am sure, without qualification in the affirmative. Does economic progress give rise to major impediments to migration? The answer to this query may seem to be less unequivocal. It will become evident, however, as we proceed that an equally affirmative reply is warranted. What happens in this connection is about as follows: We have seen how economic development sets the stage for the emergence of the advanced industrial demographic type of population alongside what was formerly a common form, that is, the pre-industrial demographic type. As the differences between these two types increase, the cultural impediments to migration become greater. It is these impediments to a transfer of the human factor that bring about a series of short-run equilibria, which, as time goes on, fall increasingly short of achieving an optimum in the allocation of resources.[23]

Two aspects require further elaboration; namely (1) the comparability of a typical human agent located in a poor, pre-industrial demographic-type community and the typical person situated in an advanced community and (2) the nature of the cultural impediments and their role as costs to the economy. Before touching on these, an observation on factor-price equalization among pre-industrial communities may be instructive. Let us take two communities of this demographic type with the same cultural values, including similar standards of living, and let us assume, further, that the fortunes of the one improve. To make this concrete, let the increase in production come from an irrigation project without cost to the community. Is it necessary for people to migrate from the less fortunate community to the one that has the windfall afforded by irrigation in order to attain factor-price equalization? The answer is that, even without a common market for either factors or products – that is, *without either migration or trade* – factor-price equalization will occur as a consequence of the upward surge in population in the community with the new irrigation project under the assumptions as I have formulated them. Factor-price equalization, however, cannot occur when the community benefiting from a windfall is of the advanced industrial demographic type and the other a pre-industrial community, unless a transfer of factors takes place.[24]

The question of comparability of human agents as factors in this context raises a number of issues which are exceedingly difficult to resolve. Entirely too little work has been done on this problem;[25] and, as is obvious, the answer must come, in the last analysis, from an appeal to empirical reality. All that one can do with the fragmentary materials now available is to express one's belief on the matter. It seems to me that most of the people located at present in poor communities within agriculture are essentially comparable to most of the people situated in rich communities in terms of their capacities to produce if allowance is made for the short-run acclimatization required for the improvement in abilities which I have already considered. If this is true, it follows that the cultural impediments are indeed a heavy burden because the income earned by these (human) factors is very unequal between communities. Is it possible that the cultural impediments can be so great and so costly? Here the researches of the sociologists are making important contributions, and their results indicate quite clearly that it is no easy matter for people to pull up their roots and leave the folk society, with its strong local-personal-informal relations, and transplant themselves into an impersonal-formal, less locally oriented, urban-minded community. The economist must leave it to the sociologist to isolate and identify the nature of these cultural impediments; the economist, however, can and should come to grips with the cost aspects. The burden of these impediments is obviously a continuing one. If anything, measured in terms of the unequal factor prices that exist, they have become greater over time. If the "price" of eliminating, or even only substantially diminishing, these impediments is a non-recurring cost for any given migrant, then the probabilities are high that society could achieve a very considerable gain by taking positive actions to diminish the adverse effects of these impediments upon factor-price equalization and, in so doing, diminish significantly the disparity in incomes on which we have concentrated our attention in this paper.

Notes and References

1   The concept of "level of living" refers to the possession of goods, services, and opportunities. It consists in what people have, that is, the opportunities available to them and the goods and services that they use and consume. For the distinction between "level of living" and "standard of living" see Carl C. Taylor et. al., *Rural Life in the United States* (Alfred A. Knopf, New York, 1949), chapter xvii.

Margaret Jarman Hagood, of the Bureau of Agricultural Economics, has made a number of studies concentrating on the level of living of farm people. Her study, *Farm Operator Family Level of Living Indexes for Counties of the United States 1940 and 1945* (May, 1947), is exceedingly instructive. With the United States county average for 1945 equal to 100, one finds that her indexes of the level of living for the ten lowest counties in Kentucky range from 5 to 16, as follows:

1945 Level of Living

Counties	Index (10 Lowest Counties in Kentucky)
Breathitt	5
Leslie	6
Elliott	9
Knott	12
Owsley	13
Magoffin	13
Clay	14
Lawrence	15
Lee	15
Knox	16

Her data for the ten highest counties in Iowa show indexes ranging from 188 to 196, as follows:

1945 Level of Living

Counties	Index (10 Lowest Counties in Kentucky)
Ida	188
Buena Vista	189
Hamilton	189
Cherokee	190
Marshall	190
Wright	191
O'Brien	192
Sac	192
Benton	194
Grundy	196

2 I am inclined to follow fairly closely the idea of a community (or neighborhood) as it is set forth in Taylor et. al., *Rural Life in the United States*, chapter iv. For most of the conditions under consideration, the rural neighborhood can be used instead of the community. Accordingly, I shall use the two terms "neighborhood" and "community" as being quite interchangeable.

3 Dorothy S. Thomas, in reviewing the research that has been done on selective migration, finds that four conflicting hypotheses have emerged as to the direction of this selection and its effects upon rural areas:

"1 City migrants are selected from the superior elements of the parent population;

2 Cityward migrants are selected from the inferior elements;

3 Cityward migrants are selected from the extremes, i.e., both the superior and the inferior elements; and

4 Cityward migration represents a random selection of the parent population."

Professor Thomas concludes that there is some evidence to support each of these hypotheses. Although the evidence is tenuous, it is nonetheless probable that "selection does operate positively, negatively, and randomly, at different times, depending on a variety of factors that, up to the present, have not been adequately investigated". See "Selective Migration", *Milbank Memorial Fund Quarterly*, XVI, No. 4 (Oct. 1948), 403–7.

4 Chester W. Wright, *Economic History of the United States* (McGraw-Hill Book Co., New York, 1941), discusses the agriculture of the late Colonial period in these words: "The outstanding feature that characterized colonial agriculture was the fact that the greater portion of the products raised was for the family's own consumption. This was typically the situation except in the regions such as the souther plantations where . . . [tobacco, rice, indigo]

dominated" (p. 89). For an account of the level of living about 1770, covering housing, food, clothing, and medical care, see pp. 1010–22.

5   A cogent study of this point is that of Mandel Sherman and Thomas R. Henry, *Hollow Folk* (Thomas Y. Crowell Co., New York, 1933).

6   The effects of variations in prices (in terms of the economic uncertainty that these impose upon farmers) on the productions plans of farmers is the central subject of my article, "Spot and Future Prices as Production Guides", *American Economic Review, Papers and Proceedings*, xxxix (May, 1949), 135–49.

7   This John Stuart Mill's phrase in opening Book IV, "Influence of the Progress of Society in Production and Distribution", of his *Principles of Political Economy* (1848).

8   Best expressed in David Ricardo's *The Principles of Political Economy and Taxation* (Everyman's Library edn., 1943), chapter v, p. 58.

9   In *Review of Economic Progress*, vol. I, No. 4 (april 1949), Colin Clark presents data that permit the following comparisons among countries in terms of levels of real national product per man-hour, showing the period when they reached a specified level (in international units).

At 0.03	0.10–0.15		At about 0.30	
France before 1800	Britain before	1800 (0.14)	Britain,	1890 (.31)
Germany before 1800	France,	1850 (.10)	U.S.A.,	1890 (.34)
India by 1860	Sweden,	1860 (.10)	Denmark,	1913 (.30)
Japan by 1890	Greece,	1880 (.13)	Germany,	1913 (.31)
China by 1930	Eire,	1880 (.11)	Nether-	
	Belgium,	1890 (.11)	lands	1913 (.29)
	Italy,	1890 (.10)	Norway,	1920 (.33)
	Norway,	1890 (.14)	Spain,	1920 (.31)
	Switzer-		Sweden,	1920 (.30)
	land,	1890 (.15)	France,	1924 (.30)
	U.S.S.R.,	1900 (.15)	Switzer-	
	Estonia,	1913 (.11)	land,	1925 (.31)
	Hungary,	1913 (.14)	Eire,	1926 (.30)
	Portugal,	1913 (.11)	Belgium,	1930 (.33)
	Japan,	1922 (.10)	Argentina,	1935 (.35)
	Turkey,	1927 (.10)	Finland,	1937 (0.32)
	Ecuador,	1940 (.11)		
	Brazil,	1946 (.11)		

10   Dudley Kirk, in his book *Europe's Population in the Interwar Years* (League of Nations, Geneva, 1946), chapter iii, puts the migrations out of Europe as follows: "The number of Europeans living outside of Europe was negligible in 1650; it has been estimated that since that time some 60 million

Europeans have sought homes overseas . . . Millions more crossed the low barriers of the Urals to settle in Siberia and the Interior of Asia."

11   Ibid., p. 17.

12   The increasing disparity in income per head is documented by a wealth of data brought together by Colin Clark, *The Conditions of Economic Progress* (Macmillan Co., New York, 1940), esp. chapter iv. In my paper, "Food, Agriculture and Trade", *Journal of Farm Economics*, XXIX (1947), 7, I drew upon Clark to show how rapidly this disparity had occurred since about 1870.

13   It may be of interest to note that, taking Colin Clark's figures appearing in *Review of Economic Progress*, vol. I, No. 4, and assuming that his $0.03 per hour (in terms of his international unit) is the lowest level of real national produce per man-hour, we get the following spread between the low and the high countries:

Year	No. of Times Highest Country is above Lowest
Before 1800	5
1800–1825	7
1910	17
1930	25
1940	33
1947	39

The last figure, that for 1947, is obtained by assuming that China has not risen above the $0.03 reported for 1930 and relating it to the $1.19 reported for the United States. That the level-of-living index of farm operators in the United States in 1945 should also show Grundy County, Iowa, thirty-nine times as high as Breathitt County, Kentucky (see Hagood, *Farm Operators Family Level of Living Indexes*) is a similarity that should not be dismissed too lightly.

14   I will not elaborate the third in this paper because it would take me somewhat afield and because it would require an entire paper to do it satisfactorily.

15   An excellent essay on this subject is that of Frank W. Notestein, "Population – the Long View", in *Food for the World*, ed. Theodore W. Schultz (University of Chicago Press, Chicago, 1945); see also Warren Thompson, *Population and Peace in the Pacific* (University of Chicago Press, Chicago, 1946), chapter ii.

16   To quote Notestein, "Population – the Long View", pp. 39–40 on this point: ". . . Fertility was much less responsive to the processes of modernization. So far as we can tell from available evidence, no substantial part of the modern population growth has come from a rise in fertility. On the other hand, neither did fertility decline with mortality. The reasons why fertility failed to decline with mortality are clear enough in general terms. Any society having to face the heavy mortality characteristic of the premodern

era must have high fertility to survive. All such societies are therefore ingeiously arranged to obtain the required births. Their religious doctrines, moral codes, laws, education, community customs, marriage habits, and family organizations are all focused toward maintaining high fertility. These change only gradually and in response to the strongest stimulation. Therefore, mortality declined, but a fertility high enough to permit survival in an earlier period began producing rapid growth."

17 Based on data from the 1940 Census. Note that Grundy County had a level-of-living index of 196, while that of Breathitt was 5 in 1945, according to Hagood, *Farm Operator Family Level of Living Indexes.*

18 "Underemployment", which is unproductive employment in the sense that a person produces a smaller product than he could elsewhere in the economy, is not included here, for it properly belongs under the set of conditions that impede factor-price equalization.

19 There are many clues in the available statistics, although the data are not on a county basis. One comparison may be cited. In the fall of 1945 an attempt was made by the Bureau of Agricultural Economics, by means of an enumerative survey, to ascertain the average hours that farm operators worked during the week September 16–22 (see facing page). These data by type of farming regions show that in the dairy areas farm operators worked nearly twice as many hours (59) as did those in the general and self-sufficing areas (31). For the Corn Belt, the equivalent figure was 57 hours. The following table has been taken from unpublished data made available by Louis J. Ducoff, of the Bureau of Agricultural Economics:

20 Howard W. Beers, in *Mobility of Rural Population* (Bull. 505, Kentucky Agr. Exper. Stat., June 1947, p. 40), advances the hypothesis that rural-urban migration has selected the less able youths, leaving on farms those who are most capable. For a more comprehensive review see Thomas, "Selective Migration".

21 Earl Hamilton has called my attention to the excellent observations of Marshall on certain aspects of this problem (*Principles of Economics*, 8th edn., Macmillan & Co Ltd, London, 1930), esp. pp. 560–63.

22 In 1938, Mississippi allocated about 5.4 percent of its income to the support of secondary and elementary schools, while Iowa used about 3.9 percent of its income for this purpose; and yet the amount that was available per enrolled student was about $22.00 in Mississippi compared to $74.00 in Iowa.

23 When factor-price equalization is based upon given wants, the cultural differences under consideration are taken as attributes of the existing pattern of wants. When the problem is approached in this way, the cultural differences between a community that has been by-passed by economic growth and progress and a community located at or near the centers of industrialization are not impediments to factor-price equalization but a part of the existing wants of the people in the two communities. It follows from this formulation that the two communities may be in equilibrium in terms of

Average Hours Worked by Farm Operators

	WEEK OF SEPTEMBER 16–22, 1945	WEEK OF JULY 14–20, 1946
Regional Areas:		
United States	43	48
General and self-sufficing areas . .	31	37
Cotton Belt	35	35
Western specialty-crop areas . . .	48	50
Range and livestock area	53	58
Corn Belt	57	65
Dairy areas	59	65
Wheat areas	59	69
Type-of-Farming Areas:		
South, general and self-sufficing areas	25	29
South, Cotton Belt	35	34
North-central, general and self-sufficing areas	40	46
West, wheat areas	44	60
Western specialty-crop areas	48	50
Northeast, general and self-sufficing areas	48	59
Northeast, dairy areas	52	59
West, range and livestock areas . .	55	57
North-central, Corn Belt	58	65
North-central, dairy areas	64	67
North-central, wheat areas	65	76

resource allocation, although great differences in the level of living exist. Another approach, the one on which this analysis rests, proceeds on the assumption that wants are not given and constant but that they are the result of cultural developments which are not independent of industrialization. One may view the changes in wants that emerge as industrialization proceeds as a movement away from a pre-industrial pattern of wants toward new, more dominant industrial-urban patterns and that the differences in wants are the result of lags in this adjustment. It is better, however, in order to simplify the analytical problem, to introduce a value judgment explicitly in this connection. This value judgment is simply to the effect that the wants that characterize the communities that have been by-passed by industrial growth and progress are inferior to the wants which are emerging in the main stream of industrialization. Given this valuation, it follows that the cultural factors that isolate the backward community and press upon it the relatively inferior wants operate as cultural impediments and, as such, impede factor-price equalization.

24 P. A. Samuelson, in two articles in the *Economic Journal*, "International Trade and Equalization of Factor Prices" (68, June 1948) and "International Factor-Price Equalization Once Again" (69, June, 1949), has attempted to show that free commodity trade will, under certain conditions, inevitably lead to complete factor-price equalization. The conditions that are specified in his analysis are, however, far removed from the hard realities that underlie the existing geographical inequalities.

25 A major research program made possible by a grant from the Rockefeller Foundation on the malallocation of resources that characterize agricultural production, was carried out at the University of Chicago, largely by Professor D. Gale Johnson. This research program had as one of its objectives the determination of the comparability of resources within agriculture and between agriculture and other sectors of the economy and in the connection focusing primarily on the human agent.

5

Our Welfare State and the Welfare of Farm People[*]

The distinguished economist Jacob Viner acutely and in my judgment correctly characterizes the style of organization of the American economy as that of a "welfare state." The welfare state is neither "liberal" in the nineteenth-century sense nor authoritarian in the form that calls itself "People's Democracy." Thus the welfare state represents a partial rejection of laissez-faire as it prevailed fairly widely in the Western world during the nineteenth century, in which "the emphasis was on freedom for the individual from government, not on service to him by government."[1] It is also a rejection of the modern form of the authoritarian state, in which emphasis is placed on service to the individual, service determined from above and enforced by abandoning political and civil freedom. Between these two systems there has emerged the welfare state which "tries to find a middle path between service without freedom and freedom without service."[2]

Long before the New Deal farmers in the United States had had a large hand politically in developing our welfare state. The earlier agrarian movements protested strongly against the doctrine of laissez-faire, not because farm leaders had been schooled in European socialism or in Marxian thought. Their protests were a direct, indigenous response to the raw industrialism of the decades after the Civil War and to the long decline in the general level of prices. More recently, mainly after World War I, farmers turned to the federal government to intervene on their behalf in adjusting agricultural production and in supporting particular farm prices in what J.D. Black called "Assisted Laissez-Faire."[3] But, despite the strong political influence they have had in the development of the welfare state, farmers have not acquired many of the social services that it renders to others. The puzzle, is why?

[*]First published in *Social Service Review*, xxxviii, No. 2 (June 1964) 123–29. Reproduced by permission of University of Chicago Press (copyright 1964 by the University of Chicago).

My aims here are, first, to recount briefly the objectives of the agrarian movements of the 1880s and 1890s; second, to list several social services that specifically benefit farm people; third, to examine the social aspects of the needs of farm people; and, last, to give reasons for the government's neglect of social services for farm people.

1   Early Political Objectives

The agrarian protest movements that appeared soon after the Civil War repeatedly challenged the nineteenth-century doctrine of laissez-faire. In practice, laissez-faire, so it seemed to many farm people, sheltered all manner of monopolies. The agrarian movements demanded that trusts be "busted," and they eventually won the enactment of far-reaching anti-trust legislation. They were also convinced that private banks, with an eye to profits, had all too free a hand in determining the supply of money and thus to the general level of prices, regardless of what happened to the economy and to farmers as debtors. William Jenning Bryan electrified a political convention by espousing the agrarian cause in his "Cross of Gold" speech. Then, as a response, although after a long lag, the Federal Reserve System was established.[4]

In retrospect, it is noteworthy that these early farm leaders anticipated what has since become a major purpose of modern monetary-fiscal policy.[5] They also protested the then extreme inequalities in the distribution of personal income and wealth. The response came during the first term of the Wilson administration, when a constitutional amendment was finally approved; progressive taxation was enacted to redress the existing inequalities in personal income and wealth. But, for all these important modifications of the doctrine of laissez-faire, farm people have not acquired for themselves many of the major social services of the United States welfare state.

2   Distribution of Social Services

Farmers did acquire, among others, the following: rural free delivery of the mail (RFD); improved farm roads often better, at least until recently, than the roads in our cities; co-operatives to provide electricity and telephone services to farmers; and some credit to improve farm homes. The land grant colleges and universities began mainly as an agricultural venture. They are undoubtedly one of our outstanding institutional innovations. While they have contributed to the dignity of farming and to its modernization and productivity, the economic benefits have become widely diffused among consumers who are predominantly nonfarm people. These are all welfare services for which farm people have taken political action.

But there are other important services now provided by the welfare state that farm people have been reluctant to share in or have been opposed to strongly enough to have been by-passed. Farm people generally are opposed to extending to hired farm labor the unemployment and related benefits available to non-farm laborers. There is virtually no concern on the part of farm people about the social deprivation of migratory farm workers or about the social costs of cheap imported farm labor. For years there appeared to be widespread uneasiness among farm people in having old age and survivors' insurance extended to farmers, although it has become in less than a decade a major source of benefits, more important in terms of welfare than much of the farm legislation enacted on behalf of agriculture.[6] Except for agricultural vocational training and for land-grant teaching, research, and extension work, there is strong opposition to any and all federal aid to education. There is also objection to public measures for medical care and health facilities. The puzzle with which I began is not resolved by this review of the role that farm people have had in the development of our welfare state, although their reluctance in having some of the major services come to them provides a clue.

3   Is There Less Need?

The reluctance of farm people to participate in the social services of the welfare state may simply mean that there is no need. Just what is meant by "need" is hard to say. Is it a matter of already having such services or of not wanting them? Equivalent social services may be supplied presumably by private endeavor, or the demand for them may be very weak.

It is probably true that farm families are still somewhat more closely knit personally than urban families; thus, for any given level of income and wealth, they do more than urban families for the aged and other family members who are in need. This assistance is also cheaper, at least to the extent that there is something for them to do. Moreover, in terms of wealth, the net asset position of farmers who are actually farming has been impressively large, approximately $35,800 per farmer in 1963.[7] While there are $125 billion of net assets back of it, this average figure hides a vast amount of inequality in the personal distribution of wealth among farm families. But our statistics are bad when it comes to determining how many farm families are too poor to acquire even a minimum level of consumption, including housing, health and recreational services, and education for their children compatible with our national income and values.

We have long been complaisant about American poverty, saying to each other that we are the affluent society. Our President is now focusing attention on poverty in the United States. But unfortunately we are ill prepared to act because we have been out of touch. Our ideas of poverty, mostly of New Deal vintage, are obsolete. Both politically and intellectually there has been long neglect of the inequalities in consumption, in levels of living, and in education among American families. All we have is a handful of crude data, mostly on family incomes, and they tell us very little.

Despite the lack of data and relevant studies, we know that there are many poor people. Some are old people, but the numbers are not nearly as large as our crude income data might lead us to believe,[8] because many old people are drawing on assets which they had accumulated for precisely this purpose. Data aside, we know that, in general, the American Indians, Mexican nationals, and Negroes are not in the main consumption stream. There is a large concentration of poor people in the South, white and Negro. Among our Negroes there is much poverty, whether in the metropolitan slums, in the South, or on farms. There are many poor people in agriculture.

Except for the highly controversial New Deal Farm Security Administration, farm policy and programs have been blind to the welfare needs of Negroes in agriculture. There are still many Negroes on farms, and they are mostly very poor. According to the 1960 Census, nearly 8 percent of all farm operators were non-white. In the South, fully 16 percent of the farm operators were Negroes; while the value of farms operated by whites was $25,400 – quite low, compared to the rest of the United States – the value of farms operated by Negroes was only $6,200 per farm. In terms of median income, white farm families were three times as well off as non-white farm families. White farm males, aged twenty-five and over, had completed 8.7 (median) years of schooling, compared to only 4.8 years for the non-white males. In addition, the quality of schooling of non-whites was much inferior to that of whites.[9] School drop-outs tell a similar story: the figures for farm males, fourteen to twenty-four years of age, are 22 percent for whites and 41 percent for non-whites.

The reluctance of farm people to participate in the social services of the United States welfare state cannot be attributed to lack of need for such services. In addition to the low economic and social lot of American Indians, Mexican nationals, and Negroes on farms, there are also many other poor farm families. One sees poverty in what these families can afford to consume and in how they live; one sees it in many rural farm communities in the low quality of schooling and of health facilities.

4 Reasons for Neglect

The United States welfare state contributes relatively few social services benefiting farm people. Why this should be true is the puzzle with which I began. This neglect cannot be attributed to lack of need or to commitment to the nineteenth-century doctrine of laissez-faire. The Grange, Populists, and Non-Partisan League were all protest movements demanding that this doctrine be modified. The roots that fed these earlier protests are still very much alive. One cannot claim that farm people hold that all property rights, including rights to farm property, are inalienable as is clear from the many laws that have been passed, in general with the consent of farm people, on grazing, erosion control, watershed protection, dam sites, forestry, and mineral rights. I doubt also that farm people are substantially more concerned than other people about the presumed corruption of the moral fiber of people to work and hustle and earn their keep once the state becomes a large source of social services.[10]

As I interpret our political and economic history, there are four major reasons for governmental neglect of the social aspects of welfare of farm people.

(a) *Influence of the Southern Tradition*

Lest we forget, the South is a key, critical part of agriculture. It accounted for over 45 percent of all farms when the 1959 agricultural census was taken. Jefferson's agricultural views are often featured. But what is not emphasized is the political influence of the southern tradition long supported by an undemocratic political structure. The weakness of this tradition with respect to social responsibility is evident in an indifference and antagonism to public schools. William H. Nicholls' study leaves no room for doubt on this matter.[11] The social services of the United States welfare state, with few exceptions, are an anathema to the South politically, although these services are used heavily once they become available.

(b) Conflicts of Interest

Who represents whom with respect to the interests of farm people? Or, more narrowly, which classes of farmers are represented? Precisely, which particular interests of particular farmers? The conflicts among farm commodity groups, though well known, have little direct bearing on the welfare issues under consideration. What is relevant here is the conflict in interest between imported farm laborers and the farmers who want cheap labor. Migratory farm laborers of domestic origin are situated somewhat like hired farm workers generally. There is also the long-standing animosity of poor whites toward Negroes. Another conflict exists when one considers national sharing of some of the costs of schooling, with its implied tax burden on the North and West, to assist the South, where taxes on farm land to support local schools are often less relative to the value of farm land than in the rest of the country. Patently, the poorest whose needs are the greatest have the least political influence, which is necessary to gain access to the social services of the welfare state.

(c) Lack of Knowledge

Farm people and their leaders are not in general conversant with the ideas, the philosophical basis, and the historical processes inherent in the urbanization and industrialization of which modern agriculture is an integral part. The scientific and technological knowledge underlying modern agriculture is well understood by farm people, but the changing social and economic framework is still largely in the realm of myth. If blame we must, we must look at our land grant colleges and universities. Where are the county agents who can hold forth competently on these cultural, economic, and historical issues? They are not to blame, for where is the instruction to prepare them for this task? Even today there are few instructors who can match, for example, Allan Kline's understanding of modern monetary-fiscal analysis. In the area of cultural and historical analysis, there is a great void in research and instruction.

(d) Price-Production Programs

This brings us to the principal reason for the neglect by government of the welfare of farm people. These price supports, acreage restrictions, and subsidies hold top priority in United States farm policy. Virtually all of the time and thought of the United States Department of Agriculture, the agricultural committees of Congress, and the farm organizations is spent on them. They exhaust the political influence of farm people. But these programs do not improve the schooling of farm children; they do not reduce the inequalities in personal distribution of wealth and income; they do not remove or alleviate poverty in agriculture. On the contrary, they worsen the distribution of income within agriculture.

But is this summary of their income effects not a flat contradiction of what really happens? Surely, it will be said, high price supports, with or without large government payments, must mean that farm income is larger than it would otherwise be, and hence farm people must be able to afford the consumption underlying welfare. Faith in this false proposition has lasted unbelievably long. Ever since the period of parity prices, parity income, acreage allotments, government payments, and then an expensive round of supply management have held the center of the United States farm-policy stage. Who benefits most? Landowners. who least? The poorest farm families. By any meaningful welfare test, helping least those who need help most is absurd.

There are signs that some farm people have lost faith in these acreage restrictions, marketing quotas, and price support programs. Nevertheless, alternative programs designed to reduce the real poverty in agriculture, to raise the level of consumption of those who are very poor, and to provide first-class primary and secondary schooling for farm children are not welcomed by the agricultural committees of Congress or demanded politically by the strongest farm organization. The belief is still strong that there must be some way of putting a bell on the cat by tying farm welfare to the production-price programs.

A system of forward prices,[12] provided they are set with an eye to clearing the market could enhance the efficiency of agriculture and protect farmers against major fluctuations in the prices of what they sell. But even well-conceived programs of this type will not resolve the need for social services for farm people.

The combination of the political influence of southern tradition, the conflicts of interest among farm families, and the extraordinary commitment to having the government enact and administer production-price programs — all these create a formidable barrier to welfare. It is a high wall against the social services of the welfare state.

Notes and References

1 Jacob Viner, "The United States as a 'Welfare State'," in Sanford W. Higginbotham (ed.), *Man, Science, Learning and Education* (Rice University, Houston, 1963), p. 215.

2   Ibid.

3   John D. Black, *Agricultural Reform in the United States* (McGraw-Hill Book Co, New York, 1929), chapter xiii.

4   The Farm Bureau, led by Ed O'Neal during the New Deal period, continued to support these aims. Christiana McFadyen Campbell, in her excellent study, *The Farm Bureau and the New Deal* (University of Illinois Press, Urbana, Ill., 1962) p. 48, notes that "the old agrarian stand-bys of trust-busting and currency reform . . . were still doggedly in the Farm Bureau's resolutions." Also (p. 187), "Farm Bureau support for the anti-trust campaign of the Department of Justice (under Thurman Arnold) was not confined to good wishes, but was applied where it counted most – that is, to Congressional appropriations." The remainder of her study on this matter is most telling.

5   The economic sophistication with respect to monetary policy of Allan B. Kline, who followed Ed O'Neal as president of the Farm Bureau, was probably not excelled by any lay reader in either business or labor of that period.

6   The extension of old age and survivors' benefits to farm people explains in large part the sharp improvement in their lot since the mid-1950s. In 1954, the median incomes of farm families with heads of family aged sixty-five and over was only 57 percent that of rural non-farm families – $1,091 and $1,929 respectively. By 1960 this gap had virtually disappeared; for farm families, head aged sixty-five and over, it was $2,294, and for non-rural farm families, $2,352.

7   The estimate is based on a value of all farm real estate – $144 billion – of which about 37 percent was owned by landlords who were not farming (although some of them lived on farms). Attributing 63 percent to farmers equals $90.7 billion. Add to this livestock, machinery, motor vehicles, and crops, and the total is $136.3 billion. Financial assets amounted to $18.4 billion; thus altogether $154.7 billion. Claims (debts) were as follows: farm real estate, $15.2 billion, and "other debts" of $14.8 billion; attributing all of this to farmers (none to landlords not farming, even though they surely have some of it), the total debt of farmers would be $30 billion. Subtracting this sum from $154.7 billion leaves $124.7 billion of net assets. If this is divided between 3,481,000 farmers, net assets owned per farmer equal $35,832. (Source: *Economic Report of the President*, 1964, table C-76.)

8   For an example of this type of overestimation, see table 4 of the *Economic Report of the President, 1964.*

9   This picture is not nearly so bleak for younger farm males aged fourteen to twenty-four years, for whom the years of school completed were 10 for whites and 8 for non-whites.

10 I am of course aware that the Farm Bureau currently (1964) issues some statements pertaining to governmental social services that read as if they were pure nineteenth-century laissez-faire. But every special-interest group is to some extent a victim of its own oversimplification of political issues in its attempts to "sell" its policy approach.

11 *Southern Tradition and Regional Progress* (University of North Carolina Press, Chapel Hill, 1960).

12 See D. Gale Johnson, *Forward Prices for Agriculture* (University of Chicago Press, Chicago, Ill., 1947).

6

Economic Puzzles Pertaining to Poverty[*]

How much does theory tell us about poverty? Since Ricardo the winding course of theory and its ever-changing income distribution implications have challenged economists. Harry Johnson dealt cogently with these issues in his, "The Theory of Income Distribution."[1] Jan Pen was concerned about numerous gaps and inconsistencies between observed facts and received theories.[2] I am particularly struck by puzzles in our understanding of the size distribution of income and the secular changes in factor shares and in personal shares. Seeing these puzzles, I have become increasingly uneasy about the state of our knowledge pertaining to poverty.[3]

A major problem with our perspective of poverty is that it is too parochial. It is very difficult for us in the United States, with our astronomically high incomes, to perceive what the economic implications of being poor are throughout most of the world. Our life style and national data thwart our perception of how poor people in low income countries manage to live and how in times past Europeans, when they too were very poor, maintained their households and families.

There are two studies that are useful in acquiring a broad historical perspective on the micro attributes of poverty. Peter Laslett's book[4] is especially rewarding in showing the size and structure of households and the state of family life over the past three centuries in England, France, the Netherlands, Serbia, Japan, and colonial North America. A rare body of agricultural production and household consumption data appears in the *Resurvey of Matar Taluka* by Vimal Shah and C. H. Shah of the University of Bombay.[5] (Along with the study of Shah and Shah the all too brief lectures by M. L. Dantawala[6] should be read.) These data are cogently analyzed to show what took place between 1930 and 1967

* Based on my 1977 paper on the "Economics of Being Poor", in Robert O. Coppedge and Carlton G. Davis (eds), *Rural Poverty and Policy Crisis* (Iowa State University Press, Ames, IA, 1977, pp. 35–42). The opening page of this 1977 paper has been omitted. In 1979 I adopted the 1977 title for my Nobel lecture (Part I, No. 1).

when the population doubled and per capita expenditure in real terms increased by a fourth. In general, however, studies of poverty in low income countries should be approached with caution. Currently available per capita income data for these countries are subject to large errors, and the real value of the income per dollar is unknown for lack of a standard for measuring the consumption value of these income statistics.

The advantages of treating evidence pertaining to poverty in its cultural context are featured by anthropologist Lloyd Fallers. In his *Inequality*[7] Fallers states that his thinking on income distribution has been "tempered and rendered more mature by direct experience in East Africa and Turkey." Fallers sees income inequality as a subset within the cultural domain of inequality. Since it is not a stationary domain, we are well advised to take account of such changes. Fallers is effective in showing that we are culturally bound in our views about inequality.

Within the existing cultural context, my hypothesis is that the actions of the poor are finely attuned to marginal costs and returns. They tend to make the most out of what they have. Accordingly, for me it is an axiom that poor people live close to their economic optimum, poor as their circumstances are; it follows that being poor does not imply being inefficient.[8]

We have to look beyond our own economy, and beyond our own history to get a more complete picture of the economics of being poor. Worldwide economic trends matter.[9] Economists often ignore long-range international trends at their peril.

1   Poverty Related to Land

In economics the relationship between poverty and land is unclear. Although the shadow of Henry George and the Single Tax is now dim, the emphasis is still on land reform as a means of alleviating rural poverty in most of the world. Meanwhile, the current doomsday pronouncements project increasing poverty and famine as world population grows while the land suitable for growing crops remains virtually fixed. In retrospect, however, we see that the households and families in Western Europe, according to Laslett,[10] were in general very poor, despite the fact that the population was much smaller then and the natural endowment of land was what it is now. This observation suggests the first puzzle with which I am concerned.

Within the very low income heart of Asia are two city states with virtually no cropland or minerals, with only human resources, in which personal incomes are far above Asian standards. Although Hong Kong, as of 1975, was crowded with more than 4 million people, the per capita gross domestic product (GDP) was equal to about $1,000, US dollars. Singapore had more than 2 million people and a per capita GDP equal to about $1,200, U.S. dollars. The study by Geiger and Geiger[11] is a major contribution in analyzing and in explaining the remarkable economic success of these two city states.

It is evident that in many countries with a *low* population-land density ratio the rank and file are very poor, and that they are similarly poor in many countries with a *high* population-land density ratio. The puzzle is, why has this difference in the ratio of people to cropland in these countries not produced comparable difference in incomes? Until we have the answer to this question, it behooves us not to treat land as a key variable in explaining income differences among all low income countries.

2   Income Inequality Related to Life Span

It is clear from historical records and from current data that the difference in the life spans of human beings is a critical index of the difference in their well-being. This index has been rising rapidly in low income countries. Since 1950 the life expectancy in many low income countries has risen about 40 percent; from 35–40 years to approximately 52 years.[12] By this important measure of human well-being the gap between the low and the high income countries has been substantially reduced. The puzzle is that there are all kinds of data on the per capita availability of food, and of the state of housing and of employment, that presumably show that the standard of living has not improved. Since I am quite convinced from the available evidence that life expectancy has risen in many low income countries, I have begun a search for the explanatory factors. Early English history provides some clues, but none of the western countries, to the best of my knowledge, ever came close to matching the above gains in life span. In this context I am fascinated by the economic logic and the quantitative importance of Dan Usher's attributing changes in life expectancy to the measure of economic growth.[13] In the case of Ceylon, his analysis shows that the growth rate of GNP more than doubled when the value of the increase in life expectancy between 1946 and 1963 is taken into account. The point to ponder is the inconsistency between this rise in life expectancy and our "data" on food supplies, nutrition, and health in low income countries.

3   Human Capital and Property Income Shares

In the rhetoric on factor shares, capitalists are rich and workers are poor. Analytically, however, we deal with two forms of capital, property assets and human capital. In western countries the stock of human capital has been increasing relative to that of property assets, and it is a well-established fact that the share of national income accruing to labor has become much larger than it was when the early English economists had their say. As this share has increased, the level of family income has risen and the personal distribution of income has become less unequal. Simon Kuznets[14] taking the long view of economic processes in western countries, saw labor's share as having risen from 55 to 75 percent in the last century, while the share accruing to property assets declined from 45 to 25 percent. But the reasons for these secular changes in factor shares have received too little attention in economics. I will comment on two aspects: the decline in the income share accruing to landlords and the rise in the value of human time.

At the time when Ricardo wrote, about half the income of the rank and file of people in England went for food. Wages were very low and the rents accruing to the owners of farmland accounted for 20 to 25 percent of the national income. Thus, according to Kuznets' estimates cited in the previous paragraph, about half the income accruing to property assets at that time consisted of farmland rent. What we observe in many non-western countries today is a similar economic picture. Since Ricardo's day, however, landlords as an economic class in western countries have been fading away. Economic theory has little to offer in explaining why this has occurred; what we know we learn from the data. Suffice it to say that the increases in productivity of cropland are largely man-made and that a vast array of substitutes for cropland are being developed. In terms of theory we fail to see these developments. No one has been as cogent as Jan Pen in analyzing the historical decline in farmland rents as a share of income.[15]

I cannot resist noting the current lack of perspective in what is being said and written about farm products, raw materials, energy, and oil. I foresee that the trends of the decades prior to 1972 will prevail: the owners of natural resource assets will lose income as man-made substitutes for these assets are developed, and as ways of exploiting natural resources are improved. Even the oil lords who are now collecting large rents will see their rents diminishing for the same basic reasons that account for the decline of landlords as an economic class.

One thing is certain: in the western countries, as the income share accruing to farmland has declined, the income share accruing to labor has increased, and the economic lot of poor people has improved. It is this increase in the income share accruing to labor that holds the key to the secular rise in income for most families. If we knew the economic reasons for the marked, persistent rise in the value of human time in high-income countries, we would be able to explain in large part why the income share of labor has been increasing.[16]

What determines the long-term changes in the supply of and the demand for labor? Recent advances in economic thought have supplied a substantial portion of the theory which functionally relates changes in the supply of labor to the *quality attributes* of labor. The useful abilities people acquire should be viewed as forms of human capital. The investment in these abilities or skills occurs in response to favorable investment opportunities. Individuals, families, and public bodies build up the supply of skills through their expenditures (sacrifices) on education, health, on-the-job training, the search for information, and geographical migration to take advantage of better jobs or consumption opportunities. People are willing to make these sacrifices because the return in future earnings and personal satisfaction is high. And it is high because of the increase in the demand for skilled work in western countries.

But the demand side is still largely an unexplored frontier. The puzzle is, why does the demand for a highly trained work force increase so persistently in the advanced economies, notably in the United States? This growth in demand is implicit in the fact that between 1929 and 1957 the educational capital embodied in the labor force of the United States increased at an average annual rate twice as high as that of reproducible tangible wealth. We know the simple answer to the implied question of why the accumulation of human capital occurs at a higher rate than that of nonhuman capital. Theory and empirical analysis both imply that this difference is a response to the difference in rates of return.

But this response to the difference in rates of return sheds no light whatsoever on why the rate of return to human capital has tended to be relatively high. The basic question is this: what is it about these economic processes that increases the demand for skilled labor services and why have those services long maintained a relatively high rate of return to human capital investment?

Thinking about the demand problem considered here, I am convinced that we can explain simultaneously two critical factual puzzles. The first is that diminishing returns to capital have not occurred generally despite the vast accumulation of capital in advanced economies. The second fact is the relatively high rate at which the formation of human capital has occurred. The resolution of the first puzzle also provides a solution for the second.

The key to both puzzles is the continuous growth of knowledge. The acquisition, adoption, and efficient utilization of new knowledge provides new sources of investment opportunities, so it maintains the growth process and keeps the returns to capital from diminishing over time. Furthermore, these additions to the stock of knowledge increase opportunities for human capital more than investment opportunities for material capital.

Studies of the last decade tell us that people in the United States who are poor over their life span possess relatively few skills, or human capital. Lack of training limits not only the job skills they might invest in, but also their skills in coping with a complex modern environment. The consequences are that their lifetime earnings are low. They are especially vulnerable to unemployment. They experience the most disabilities for reasons of poor health, they are relatively inefficient in their financial affairs, in household production, in searching for information, and in dealing with economic disequilibria over their life span. In this context it is important to take into account the acquired entrepreneurial ability of housewives, laborers, students, farmers, and businessmen. The economic value of the ability to deal with disequilibria is substantial, and the effects of education and experience in enhancing this particular ability are strong and clear.[17]

4 Human Capital Related to Personal Income

Conceptually, personal income is beset with ambiguities. Decisions about the use made of personal income are not vested equally among all members of the family. Consumer units are very heterogeneous. Theoretically, the economic interactions between functional and personal income are far from clear. What would be the consequences for personal income shares if the economy were open and competitive, if total national income were rising secularly, and if there were no public income transfers? Not having theory to generate implications, we are short on economic explanations that have been tested. We know very little about the economics of intergenerational transfers of property assets or about the effects of differences in family wealth on the investment that parents make in the human capital of their children. Empirically, we can learn much from Dorothy Projector and Gertrude Weiss.[18] As expected, the ownership of investment assets, which accounted for 33 percent of the total wealth in their 1962 survey, is distributed very unequally, despite progressive inheritance taxes. But, quite unexpectedly to me, 27 percent of our total wealth consisted of owners' equity in their homes, and this form of personal wealth was distributed almost equally among consumer units by income classes.

Most of the story of personal income shares is linked to human capital and its personal distribution. Gary Becker has advanced a theoretical approach to analyze the function of human capital in this context.[19] Empirical tests of its implications are still fragmentary. There are plenty of difficulties in using the theory. Several issues need to be considered further if we are to explain the relationship of human capital to personal income. Personal priorities affect the jobs that people take since among those with the same human capital some more than others prefer pleasanter jobs with fewer earnings. Transitory earnings should be distinguished from permanent earnings; the life-cycle of earnings is important; and the measure of full returns to human capital should not omit the value of time devoted to household production, the value of entrepreneurial skill, the value of human capital after retirement, and the value of skill in making consumer choices. (Bruce Gardner, in his study of rural poverty in the United States[20] has made commendable progress in analyzing several of these issues.)

There are many mansions when theory and data talk to each other about the economics of being poor. There is hope for all.

Notes and References

1 Harry G. Johnson, *The Theory of Income Distribution* (Gray-Mills Publishing, London, 1973).

2 Jan Pen, *Income Distribution: Fact, Theories, Policies*, translated from the Dutch by Trevor S. Preston (Praeger, New York, 1971).

3 See Edgar S. Furniss, *The Position of the Laborer in a System of Nationalism* (Houghton Mifflin, Boston, 1920).

4 Peter Laslett, assisted by Richard Wall, *Household and Family in Past Times* (Cambridge University Press, Cambridge, 1972).

5 Vimal Shah and C. H. Shah, *Resurvey of Matar Taluka* (Vora and Co., Bombay, 1974).

6 M. L. Dantwala, *Poverty in India – Then and Now, 1870–1970* (Macmillan Co of India, Bombay, 1973).

7 Lloyd A. Fallers, *Inequality: Social Stratification Reconsidered* (University of Chicago Press, Chicago, Ill., 1973).

8 Theodore W. Schultz, *Transforming Traditional Agriculture* (Yale University Press, New Haven, Conn., 1964).

9   See Bernard Berelson et. al., "World Population: Status Report 1974," in *Reports on Population and Family Planning* (Population Council, New York, 1974).

10 Laslett, *Household and Family in Past Times.*

11 Theodore Geiger and Frances M. Geiger, *Tales of Two City-States: The Development Progress of Hong Kong and Singapore* (National Planning Association, Washington, 1973).

12 Bernard Berelson et. al., "World Population," p. 7.

13 Dan Usher, "An Imputation to the Measure of Economic Growth for Changes in Life Expectancy" in Milton Moss, ed., *Measurement of Economic and Social Performance* (Columbia University Press, National Bureau of Economic Research, New York, 1973).

14 See Simon Kuznets: "Economic Growth and Income Inequality," *American Economic Review*, 45: 1–28; "Quantitative Aspects of the Economic Growth of Nations: VIII. Distribution of Income by Size," *Economic Development and Cultural Change* 2(2), 1–80; *Modern Economic Growth* (Yale University Press, New Haven, Conn., 1966); *Economic Growth and Nations* (Harvard University Press, Cambridge, Mass., 1971).

15 Jan Pen, *Income Distribution*, esp. pp. 208–14.

16 See below, Part III, No. 2, "The Increasing Economic Value of Human Time."

17 Theodore W. Schultz, "The Value of the Ability to Deal with Disequilibria", *Journal of Economic Literature* 13 (Sept. 1975).

18 Dorothy S. Projector and Gertrude S. Weiss, *Survey of Financial Characteristics of Consumers* (Board of Governors of the Federal Reserve System, Washington, 1966).

19 Gary S. Becker, *Human Capital and the Distribution of Personal Income: An Analytical Approach* (Woytinsky Lecture No. 1, Institute of Public Administration, University of Michigan, Ann Arbor 1967).

20 Bruce L. Gardner, "An Analysis of Recent Changes in Rural Poverty in the U.S.," unpublished paper (State University of North Carolina, Aug. 1974).

Part II

Investing in Skills and Knowledge

Part II

Investing in Skills and Knowledge

1

*Investment in Human Capital**

Although it is obvious that people acquire useful skills and knowledge, it is not obvious that these skills and knowledge are a form of capital, that this capital is in substantial part a product of deliberate investment, that it has grown in Western societies at a much faster rate than conventional (nonhuman) capital, and that its growth may well be the most distinctive feature of the economic system. It has been widely observed that increases in national output have been large compared with the increases of land, man-hours, and physical reproducible capital. Investment in human capital is probably the major explanation for this difference.

Much of what we call consumption constitutes investment in human capital. Direct expenditures on education, health, and internal migration to take advantage of better job opportunities are clear examples. Earnings foregone by mature students attending school and by workers acquiring on-the-job training are equally clear examples. Yet nowhere do these enter into our national accounts. The use of leisure time to improve skills and knowledge is widespread and it too is unrecorded. In these and similar ways the *quality* of human effort can be greatly improved and its productivity enhanced. I shall contend that such investment in human capital accounts for most of the impressive rise in the real earnings per worker.

I shall comment, first, on the reasons why economists have shied away from the explicit analysis of investment in human capital, and then, on the capacity of such investment to explain many a puzzle about economic growth. Mainly, however, I shall concentrate on the scope and substance of human capital and its formation. In closing I shall consider some social and policy implications.

* First published in *American Economic Review* li, No. 1 (March 1961), 1–17, and reproduced by permission of the American Economics Association.

1 Shying Away from Investment in Man

Economists have long known that people are an important part of the wealth of nations. Measured by what labor contributes to output, the productive capacity of human beings is now vastly larger than all other forms of wealth taken together. What economists have not stressed is the simple truth that people invest in themselves and that these investments are very large. Although economists are seldom timid in entering on abstract analysis and are often proud of being impractical, they have not been bold in coming to grips with this form of investment. Whenever they come even close, they proceed gingerly as if they were stepping into deep water. No doubt there are reasons for being wary. Deep-seated moral and philosophical issues are ever present. Free men are first and foremost the end to be served by economic endeavor; they are not property or marketable assets. And not least, it has been all too convenient in marginal productivity analysis to treat labor as if it were a unique bundle of innate abilities that are wholly free of capital.

The mere thought of investment in human beings is offensive to some among us.[1] Our values and beliefs inhibit us from looking upon human beings as capital goods, except in slavery, and this we abhor. We are not unaffected by the long struggle to rid society of indentured service and to evolve political and legal institutions to keep men free from bondage. These are achievements that we prize highly. Hence, to treat human beings as wealth that can be augmented by investment runs counter to deeply held values. It seems to reduce man once again to a mere material component, to something akin to property. And for man to look upon himself as a capital good, even if it did not impair his freedom, may seem to debase him. No less a person than J. S. Mill at one time insisted that the people of a country should not be looked upon as wealth because wealth existed only for the sake of people.[2] But surely Mill was wrong; there is nothing in the concept of human wealth contrary to his idea that it exists only for the advantage of people. By investing in themselves, people can enlarge the range of choices available to them. It is one way free men can enhance their welfare.

Among the few who have looked upon human beings as capital, there are three distinguished names. The philosopher-economist Adam Smith boldly included all of the acquired and useful abilities of all of the inhabitants of a country as a part of capital. So did H. von Thünen, who then went on to argue that the concept of capital applied to man did not degrade him or impair his freedom and dignity, but on the contrary that the failure to apply the concept was especially pernicious in wars; "... for here ... one will sacrifice in a battle a hundred human beings in the prime of their lives without a thought in order to save one gun." The reason is that, ". . . the purchase of a cannon causes an outlay of public funds, whereas human beings are to be had for nothing by means of a mere conscription decree"[3]. Irving Fisher also clearly and cogently presented an all-inclusive concept of capital.[4] Yet the main stream of thought has held that it is neither appropriate nor practical to apply the concept of capital to human beings. Marshall,[5] whose great prestige goes far to explain why this view was accepted, held that while human beings are incontestably capital from an abstract and mathematical point of view, it would be out of touch with the market place to treat them as capital in practical analyses. Investment in human beings has accordingly seldom been incorporated in the formal core of economics, even though many economists, including Marshall, have seen its relevance at one point or another in what they have written.

The failure to treat human resources explicitly as a form of capital, as a produced means of production, as the product of investment, has fostered the retention of the classical notion of a labor as a capacity to do manual work requiring little knowledge and skill, a capacity with which, according to this notion, laborers are endowed about equally. This notion of labor was wrong in the classical period and it is patently wrong now. Counting individuals who can and want to work and treating such a count as a measure of the quantity of an economic factor is no more meaningful than it would be to count the number of all manner of machines to determine their economic importance either as a stock of capital or as a flow of productive services.

Laborers have become capitalists not from a diffusion of the owner-ship of corporation stocks, as folklore would have it, but from the acquisition of knowledge and skill that have economic value.[6] Knowledge and skill are in great part the product of investment and, combined with other human investment, predominantly account for the productive superiority of the technically advanced countries. To omit them in studying economic growth is like trying to explain Soviet ideology without Marx.

2   Economic Growth from Human Capital

Many paradoxes and puzzles about our dynamic, growing economy can be resolved once human investment is taken into account. Let me begin by sketching some that are minor though not trivial.

When farm people take nonfarm jobs they earn substantially less than industrial workers of the same race, age, and sex. Similarly non-white urban males earn much less than white males even after allowance is made for the effects of differences in unemployment, age, city size and region.[7] Because these differentials in earnings correspond closely to corresponding differentials in education, they strongly suggest that the one is a consequence of the other. Negroes who operate farms, whether as tenants or as owners, earn much less than whites on comparable farms.[8] Fortunately, crops and livestock are not vulnerable to the blight of discrimination. The large differences in earnings seem rather to reflect mainly the differences in health and education. Workers in the South on the average earn appreciably less than in the North or West and they also have on the average less education. Most migratory farm workers earn very little indeed by comparison with other workers. Many of them have virtually no schooling, are in poor health, are unskilled, and have little ability to do useful work. To urge that the differences in the amount of human investment may explain these differences in earnings seems elementary. Of more recent vintage are observations showing younger workers at a competitive advantage; for example, young men entering the labor force are said to have an advantage over unemployed older workers in obtaining satisfactory jobs. Most of these young people possess twelve years of school, most of the older workers six years or less. The observed advantage of these younger workers may therefore result not from inflexibilities in social security or in retirement programs, or from sociological preference of employers, but from real differences in productivity connected with one form of human investment, i.e., education. And yet another example, the curve relating income to age tends to be steeper for skilled than for unskilled persons. Investments in on-the-job training seems a likely explanation, as I shall note later.

Economic growth requires much internal migration of workers to adjust to changing job opportunities.[9] Young men and women move more readily than older workers. Surely this makes economic sense when one recognizes that the costs of such migration are a form of human investment. Young people have more years ahead of them than older workers during which they can realize returns on such an investment. Hence it takes less of a wage differential to make it economically advantageous for them to move or, to put it differently, young people can expect a higher return on their investment in migration than older people. This differential may explain selective migration without requiring an appeal to sociological differences between young and old people.

The examples so far given are for investment in human beings that yield a return over a long period. This is true equally of investment in education, training, and migration of young people. Not all investments in human beings are of this kind; some are more nearly akin to current inputs as for example expenditures on food and shelter in some countries where work is mainly the application of brute human force, calling for energy and stamina, and where the intake of food is far from enough to do a full day's work. On the "hungry" steppes and in the teeming valleys of Asia, millions of adult males have so meager a diet that they cannot do more than a few hours of hard work. To call them underemployed does not seem pertinent. Under such circumstances it is certainly meaningful to treat food partly as consumption and partly as a current "producer good," as some Indian economists have done.[10] Let us not forget that Western economists during the early decades of industrialization and even in the time of Marshall and Pigou often connected additional food for workers with increases in labor productivity.

Let me now pass on to three major perplexing questions closely connected with the riddle of economic growth. First, consider the long-period behavior of the capital-income ratio. We were taught that a country which amassed more reproducible capital relative to its land and labor would employ such capital in greater "depth" because of its growing abundance and cheapness. But apparently this is not what happens. On the contrary, the estimates now available show that less of such capital tends to be employed relative to income as economic growth proceeds. Are we to infer that the ratio of capital to income has no relevance in explaining either poverty or opulence? Or that a rise of this ratio is not a prerequisite to economic growth? These questions raise fundamental issues bearing on motives and preferences for holding wealth as well as on the motives for particular investments and the stock of capital thereby accumulated. For my purpose all that needs to be said is that these estimates of capital-income ratios refer to only a part of all capital. They exclude in particular, and most unfortunately, any human capital. Yet human capital has surely been increasing at a rate substantially greater than reproducible (nonhuman) capital. We cannot, therefore, infer from these estimates that the stock of *all* capital has been decreasing relative to income. On the contrary, if we accept the not implausible assumption that the motives and preferences of people, the technical opportunities open to them, and the uncertainty associated with economic growth during particular periods were leading people to maintain roughly a constant ratio between *all* capital and income, the decline in the estimated capital-income ratio[11] is simply a signal that human capital has been increasing relatively not only to conventional capital but also to income.

The bumper crop of estimates that show national income increasing faster than national resources raises a second and not unrelated puzzle. The income of the United States has been increasing at a much higher rate than the combined amount of land, man-hours worked and the stock of reproducible capital used to produce the income. Moreover, the discrepancy between the two rates has become larger from one business cycle to the next.[12] To call this discrepancy a measure of "resource productivity" gives a name to our ignorance but does not dispel it. If we accept these estimates, the connections between national resources and national income have become loose and tenuous over time. Unless this discrepancy can be resolved, received theory of production applied to inputs and outputs as currently measured is a toy and not a tool for studying economic growth.

Two sets of forces probably account for the discrepancy, if we neglect entirely the index number and aggregation problems that bedevil all estimates of such global aggregates as total output and total input. One is returns to scale; the second, the large improvements in the quality of inputs that have occurred but have been omitted from the input estimates. Our economy has undoubtedly been experiencing increasing returns to scale at some points offset by decreasing returns at others. If we can succeed in identifying and measuring the net gains, they may turn out to have been substantial. The improvements in the quality of inputs that have not been adequately allowed for are no doubt partly in material (nonhuman) capital. My own conception, however, is that both this defect and the omission of economies of scale are minor sources of discrepancy between the rates of growth of inputs and outputs compared to the improvements in human capacity that have been omitted.

A small step takes us from these two puzzles raised by existing estimates to a third which brings us to the heart of the matter, namely the essentially unexplained large increase in real earnings of workers. Can this be a windfall? Or a quasirent pending the adjustment in the supply of labor? Or, a pure rent reflecting the fixed amount of labor? It seems far more reasonable that it represents rather a return to the investment that has been made in human beings. The observed growth in productivity per unit of labor is simply a consequence of holding the unit of labor constant over time although in fact this unit of labor has been increasing as a result of a steadily growing among of human capital per worker. As I read our record, the human capital component has become very large as a consequence of human investment.

Another aspect of the same basic question, which admits of the same resolution, is the rapid postwar recovery of countries that had suffered severe destruction of plant and equipment during the war. The toll from bombing was all too visible in the factories laid flat, the railroad yards, bridges, and harbours wrecked, and the cities in ruin. Structures, equipment and inventories were all heaps of rubble. Not so visible, yet large, was the toll from the wartime depletion of the physical plant that escaped destruction by bombs. Economists were called upon to assess the implications of these wartime losses for recovery. In retrospect, it is clear that they overestimated the prospective retarding effects of these losses. Having had a small hand in this effort, I have had a special reason for looking back and wondering why the judgments that we formed soon after the war proved to be so far from the mark. The explanation that now is clear is that we gave altogether too much weight to nonhuman capital in making these assessments. We fell into this error, I am convinced, because we did not have a concept of *all* capital and, therefore, failed to take account of human capital and the important part that it plays in production in a modern economy.

Let me close this section with a comment on poor countries, for which there are virtually no solid estimates. I have been impressed by repeatedly expressed judgments, especially by those who have a responsibility in making capital available to poor countries, about the low rate at which these countries can absorb additional capital. New capital from outside can be put to good use, it is said, only when it is added "slowly and gradually". But this experience is at variance with the widely held impression that countries are poor fundamentally because they are starved for capital and that additional capital is truly the key to their more rapid economic growth. The reconciliation is again, I believe, to be found in emphasis on particular forms of capital. The new capital available to these countries from outside as a rule goes into the formation of structures, equipment and sometimes also into inventories. But it is generally not available for additional investment in man. Consequently, human capabilities do not stay abreast of physical capital, and they do become limiting factors in economic growth. It should come as no surprise, therefore, that the absorption rate of capital to augment only particular nonhuman resources is necessarily low. The Horvat formulation of the optimum rate of investment[13] which treats knowledge and skill as a critical investment variable in determining the rate of economic growth is both relevant and important.

3 Scope and Substance of These Investments

Is it at all feasible to identify and measure them? What do they contribute to income? Granted that they seem amorphous compared to brick and mortar, and hard to get at compared to the investment accounts of corporations, they assuredly are not a fragment; they are rather like the contents of Pandora's box, full of difficulties and hope.

Human resources obviously have both quantitative and qualitative dimensions. The number of people, the proportion who enter upon useful work, and hours worked are essentially quantitative characteristics. To make my task tolerably management, I shall neglect these and consider only such quality components as skill, knowledge, and similar attributes that affect particular human capabilities to do productive work. In so far as expenditures to enhance such capabilities also increase the value productivity of human effort (labor), they will yield a positive rate of return.[14]

How can we estimate the magnitude of human investment? The practice followed in connection with physical capital goods is to estimate the magnitude of capital formation by expenditures made to produce the capital goods. This practice would suffice also for the formation of human capital. However, for human capital there is an additional problem that is less pressing for physical capital goods: how, to distinguish between expenditures for consumption and for production. This distinction bristles with both conceptual and practical difficulties. We can think of three classes of expenditures: expenditures that satisfy consumer preferences and in no way enhance the capabilities under discussion – these represent pure consumption; expenditures that enhance capabilities and do not satisfy any preferences underlying consumption – these represent pure investment; and expenditures that have both effects. Most relevant activities clearly are in the third class, partly consumption and partly investment, which is why the task of identifying each component is so formidable and why the measurement of capital formation by expenditures is less useful for human investment than for investment in physical goods. In principle there is an alternative method for estimating human investment, namely by its yield rather than by its cost. While any capability produced by human investment becomes a part of the human agent and hence cannot be sold, it is nevertheless "in touch with the market place" by affecting the wages and salaries the human agent can earn. The resulting increase in earnings is the yield on the investment.[15]

Despite the difficulty of exact measurement at this stage of our understanding of human investment, many insights can be gained by examining some of the more important activities that improve human capabilities. I shall concentrate on five major categories: (1) health facilities and services, broadly conceived to include all expenditures that affect the life expectancy, strength and stamina, and the vigor and vitality of a people; (2) on-the-job training, including old-style apprenticeship organized by firms; (3) formally organized education at the elementary, secondary, and higher levels; (4) study programs for adults that are not organized by firms, including extension programs notably in agriculture; (5) migration of individuals and families to adjust to changing job opportunities. Except for education, not much is known about these activities that is germane here. I shall refrain from commenting on study programs for adults, although in agriculture the extension services of the several states play an important role in transmitting new knowledge and in developing skills of farmers.[16] Nor shall I elaborate further on internal migration related to economic growth.

Health activities have both quantity and quality implications. Such speculations as economists have engaged in about the effects of improvements in health,[17] have been predominantly in connection with population growth, which is to say with quantity. But surely health measures also enhance the quality of human resources. So also may additional food and better shelter, especially in underdeveloped countries.

The change in the role of food as people become richer sheds light on one of the conceptual problems already referred to. I have pointed out that extra food in some poor countries has the attribute of a "producer good." This attribute of food, however, diminishes as the consumption of food rises, and there comes a point at which any further increase in food becomes pure consumption.[18] Clothing, housing and perhaps medical services may be similar.

My comment about on-the-job training will consist of a conjecture on the amount of such training, a note on the decline of apprenticeship, and then a useful economic theorem on who bears the costs of such training. Surprisingly little is known about on-the-job training in modern industry. About all that can be said is that the expansion of education has not eliminated it. It seems likely, however, that some of the training formerly undertaken by firms has been discontinued and other training programs have been instituted to adjust both to the rise in the education of workers and to changes in the demands for new skills. The amount invested annually in such training can only be a guess, H. F. Clark places it near to equal to the amount spent on formal education.[19] Even if it were only one-half as large, it would represent currently an annual gross investment of about $15 billion. Elsewhere, too, it is thought to be important. For example, some observers have been impressed by the amount of such training under way in plants in the Soviet Union.[20] Meanwhile, apprenticeship has all but disappeared, partly because it is now inefficient and partly because schools now perform many of its functions. Its disappearance has been hastened no doubt by the difficulty of enforcing apprenticeship agreements. Legally they have come to smack of indentured service. The underlying economic factors and behavior are clear enough. The apprentice is prepared to serve during the initial period when his productivity is less than the cost of his keep and of his training. Later, however, unless he is legally restrained, he will seek other employment when his productivity begins to exceed the cost of keep and training, which is the period during which a master would expect to recoup on his earlier outlay.

To study on-the-job training Gary Becker[21] advances the theorem that in competitive markets employees pay all the costs of their training and none of these costs are ultimately borne by the firm. Becker points out several implications. The notion that expenditures on training by a firm generate external economies for other firms is not consistent with this theorem. The theorem also indicates one force favoring the transfer from on-the-job training to attending school. Since on-the-job training reduces the net earnings of workers at the beginning and raises them later on, this theorem also provides an explanation for the "steeper slope of the curve relating income to age," for skilled than for unskilled workers, referred to earlier.[22] What all this adds up to is that the stage is set to undertake meaningful economic studies of on-the-job training.

Happily we reach firmer ground in regard to education. Investment in education has risen at a rapid rate and by itself may well account for a substantial part of the otherwise unexplained rise in earnings. I shall do no more than summarize some preliminary results about the total costs of education including income foregone by students, the apparent relation of these costs to consumer income and to alternative investments, the rise of the stock of education in the labor force, returns to education, and the contribution that the increase in the stock of education may have made to earnings and to national income.

It is not difficult to estimate the conventional costs of education consisting of the services of teachers, librarians, administrators, of maintenance and operating expenses of the educational plant, and interest on the capital embodied in the educational plant. It is far more difficult to estimate another component of total cost, the income foregone by students. Yet this component should be included and it is far from negligible. In the United States, for example, well over half of the costs of higher education consists of income foregone by students. As early as 1900, this income foregone accounted for about one-fourth of the total costs of elementary, secondary and higher education. By 1956, it represented over two-fifths of all costs. The rising significance of foregone income has been a major factor in the marked upward trend in the total real costs of education which, measured to current prices, increased from $400 million in 1900 to $28.7 billion in 1956.[23] The percentage rise in educational costs was about three and a half times as large as in consumer income, which would imply a high income elasticity of the demand for education, if education were regarded as pure consumption.[24] Educational costs also rose about three and a half times as rapidly as did the gross formation of physical capital in dollars. If we were to treat education as pure investment this result would suggest that the returns to education were relatively more attractive than those to nonhuman capital.[25]

Much schooling is acquired by persons who are not treated as income earners in most economic analysis, particularly of women. To analyze the effect of growth in schooling on earnings, it is therefore necessary to distinguish between the stock of education in the population and the amount in the labor force. Years of school completed are far from satisfactory as a measure because of the marked increases that have taken place in the number of days of school attendance of enrolled students and because much more of the education of workers consist of high school and higher education than formerly. My preliminary estimates suggest that the stock of education in the labor force rose about eight and a half times between 1900 and 1956, whereas the stock of reproducible capital rose four and a half times, both in 1956 prices. These estimates are, of course, subject to many qualifications.[26] Nevertheless, both the magnitude and the rate of increase of this form of human capital have been such that they could be an important key to the riddle of economic growth.[27]

The exciting work under way is on the return to education. In spite of the flood of high school and college graduates, the return has not become trivial. Even the lower limits of the estimates show that the return to such education has been in the neighborhood of the return to nonhuman capital. This is what most of these estimates show when they treat as costs all of the public and private expenditures on education and also the income foregone while attending school, and when they treat all of these costs as investment, allocating none to consumption.[28] But surely a part of these costs are consumption in the sense that education creates a form of consumer capital[29] which has the attribute of improving the taste and the quality of consumption of students throughout the rest of their lives. If one were to allocate a substantial fraction of the total costs of this education to consumption, say one-half, this would, of course, double the observed rate of return to what would then become the investment component in education that enhances the productivity of man.

Fortunately, the problem of allocating the costs of education in the labor force between consumption and investment does not arise to plague us when we turn to the contribution that education makes to earnings and to national income because a change in allocation only alters the rate of return, not the total return. I noted at the outset that the unexplained increases in US national income have been especially large in recent decades. On one set of assumptions, the unexplained part amounts to nearly three-fifths of the total increase between 1929 and 1956.[30] How much of this unexplained increase in income represents a return to education in the labor force? A lower limit suggests that about three-tenths of it, and an upper limit does not rule out that more than one-half of it came from this source.[31] These estimates also imply that between 36 and 70 percent of the hitherto unexplained rise in the earnings of labor is explained by returns to the additional education of workers.

4   A Concluding Note on Policy

One proceeds at one's own peril in discussing social implications and policy. The conventional hedge is to camouflage one's values and to wear the mantle of academic innocence. Let me proceed unprotected!

1   Our tax laws everywhere discriminate against human capital. Although the stock of such capital has become large and even though it is obvious that human capital, like other forms of reproducible capital, depreciates, becomes obsolete, and entails maintenance, our tax laws are all but blind on these matters.

2   Human capital deteriorates when it is idle because unemployment impairs the skills that workers have acquired. Losses in earnings can be cushioned by appropriate payments but these do not keep idleness from taking its toll from human capital.

3   There are many hindrances to the free choice of professions. Racial discrimination and religious discrimination are still widespread. Professional associations and governmental bodies also hinder entry; for example, into medicine. Such purposeful interference keeps the investment in this form of human capital substantially below its optimum.[32]

4   It is indeed elementary to stress the greater imperfections of the capital market in providing funds for investment in human beings than for investment in physical goods. Much could be done to reduce these imperfections by reforms in tax and banking laws and by changes in banking practices. Long-term private and public loans to students are warranted.

5   Internal migration, notably the movement of farm people into industry, made necessary by the dynamics of our economic progress, requires substantial investments. In general, families in which the husbands and wives are already in the late thirties cannot afford to make these investments because the remaining payoff period for them is too short. Yet society would gain if more of them would pull stakes and

move because, in addition to the increase in productivity currently, the children of these families would be better located for employment when they were ready to enter the labor market. The case for making some of these investments on public account is by no means weak. Our farm programs have failed miserably these many years in not coming to grips with the costs and returns from off-farm migration.

6   The low earnings of particular people have long been a matter of public concern. Policy all too frequently concentrates only on the effects, ignoring the causes. No small part of the low earnings of many Negroes, Puerto Ricans, Mexican nationals, indigenous migratory farm workers, poor farm people and some of our older workers, reflects the failure to have invested in their health and education. Past mistakes are, of course, bygones, but for the sake of the next generation we can ill afford to continue making the same mistakes over again.

7   Is there a substantial underinvestment in human beings other than in these depressed groups?[33] This is an important question for economists. The evidence at hand is fragmentary. Nor will the answer be easily won. There undoubtedly have been overinvestments in some skills, for example, too many locomotive firemen and engineers, too many people trained to be farmers, and too many agricultural economists! Our schools are not free of loafers and some students lack the necessary talents. Nevertheless, underinvestment in knowledge and skill, relative to the amounts invested in nonhuman capital would appear to be the rule and not the exception for a number of reasons. The strong and increasing demands for this knowledge and skill in laborers are of fairly recent origin and it takes time to respond to them. In responding to these demands, we are heavily dependent upon cultural and political processes, and these are slow and the lags are long compared to the behavior of markets serving the formation of nonhuman capital. Where the capital market does serve human investments, it is subject to more imperfections than in financing physical capital. I have already stressed the fact that our tax laws discriminate in favor of nonhuman capital. Then, too, many individuals face serious uncertainty in assessing their innate talents when it comes to investing in themselves, especially through higher education. Nor is it easy either for public decisions or private behavior to untangle and properly assess the consumption and the investment components. The fact that the return to high school and to higher education has been about as large as the return to conventional forms of capital when all of the costs of such education, including income foregone by students, are allocated to the investment component, creates a strong presumption that there has been underinvestment since, surely, much education is cultural and in that sense it is consumption. It is no wonder, in view of

these circumstances, that there should be substantial underinvestment in human beings, even though we take pride, and properly so, in the support that we have given to education and to other activities that contribute to such investments.

8   Should the returns from public investment in human capital accrue to the individuals in whom they are made?[34] The policy issues implicit in this question run deep and they are full of perplexities pertaining both to resource allocation and to welfare. Physical capital that is formed by public investment is not transferred as a rule to particular individuals as a gift. It would greatly simplify the allocative process if public investment in human capital were placed on the same footing. What then is the logical basis for treating public investment in human capital differently? Presumably it turns on ideas about welfare. A strong welfare goal of our community is to reduce the unequal distribution of personal income among individuals and families. Our community has relied heavily on progressive income and inheritance taxation. Given public revenue from these sources, it may well be true that public investment in human capital, notably that entering into general education, is an effective and efficient set of expenditures for attaining this goal. Let me stress, however, that the state of knowledge about these issues is woefully meager.

9   My last policy comment is on assistance to underdeveloped countries to help them achieve economic growth. Here, even more than in domestic affairs, investment in human beings is likely to be underrated and neglected. It is inherent in the intellectual climate in which leaders and spokesmen of many of these countries find themselves. Our export of growth doctrines has contributed. These typically assign the stellar role to the formation of nonhuman capital, and take as an obvious fact the superabundance of human resources. Steel mills are the real symbol of industrialization. After all, the early industrialization of England did not depend on investments in the labor force. New funds and agencies are being authorized to transfer capital for physical goods to these countries. The World Bank has already had much experience. Then, too, measures have been taken to pave the way for the investment of more private (nonhuman) capital abroad. This one-sided effort is under way in spite of the fact that the knowledge and skills required to take on and use efficiently the superior techniques of production, the most valuable resource that we could make available to them, is in very short supply in these underdeveloped countries. Some growth of course can be had from the increase in more conventional capital even though the labor that is available is lacking both in skill and knowledge. But the rate of growth will be seriously limited. It simply is not possible to have the fruits of a

modern agriculture and the abundance of modern industry without making large investments in human beings.

Truly, the most distinctive feature of our economic system is the growth in human capital. Without it there would be only hard, manual work and poverty except for those who have income from property. There is an early morning scene in Faulkner's *Intruder in the Dust*, of a poor, solitary cultivator at work in a field. Let me paraphrase that line, "The man without skills and knowledge leaning terrifically against nothing."

Notes and References

1   This paragraph draws on the introduction to Theodore W. Schultz, "Investment in Man: An Economist's View," *Social Service Review*, 33 (June 1959), 109–17.

2   J. S. Nicholson, "The Living Capital of the United Kingdom," *Economic Journal*, 1 (Mar. 1891), 95; see J. S. Mill, *Principles of Political Economy*, ed. W. J. Ashley (London, 1909), p. 8.

3   H. von Thunen, *Der isolierte Staat*, trans. B. F. Hoselitz, 3rd ed., vol. 2, Part 2 (1875; reproduced by the Computer Education Centre, University of Chicago), pp. 140–52.

4   Irving Fisher, *The Nature of Capital and Income* (New York, 1906).

5   Alfred Marshall, *Principles of Economics*, 8th edn (London, 1930), Appendix E., pp. 787–8.

6   See H. G. Johnson, "The Political Economy of Opulence," *Canadian Journal of Economics and Political Science*, 216 (Nov. 1960), 552–64.

7   See Morton Zeman, *A Quantitative Analysis of White-Non White Income Differentials in the United States*, unpublished PhD dissertation (University of Chicago, 1955).

8   Based on unpublished preliminary results obtained by Joseph Willett in his PhD research at the University of Chicago.

9   Simon Kuznets, *Income and Wealth in the United States* (Cambridge, 1952), section IV, "Distribution by Industrial Origin."

10 P. R. Brahmanand and C. N. Vakil, *Planning for an Expanding Economy* (Bombay, 1956).

11 I leave aside here the difficulties inherent in identifying and measuring both the nonhuman capital and the income entering into estimates of this ratio. There are index number and aggregation problems aplenty, and not all improvements in the quality of this capital have been accounted for.

12 Solomon Fabricant, *Basic Facts on Productivity Change* (National Bureau of Economic Research, Occasional Paper 63, New York, 1959), table 5.

13 B. Horvat, "The Optimum Rate of Investment," *Economic Journal*, 68 (Dec. 1958), 747–67.

14 Even so, our *observed* return can be either negative, zero or positive because our observations are drawn from a world where there is uncertainty and imperfect knowledge and where there are windfall gains and losses and mistakes aplenty.

15 In principle, the value of the investment can be determined by discounting the additional future earnings it yields just as the value of a physical capital good can be determined by discounting its income stream.

16 Schultz, "Investment in Man."

17 Health economics is in its infancy; there are two medical journals with "economics" in their titles, two bureaux for economic research in private associations (one in the American Medical and the other in the American Dental Association), and not a few studies and papers by outside scholars. Selina J. Mushkin's survey, "Toward a Definition of Health Economics," *Public Health Reports* (US Department of Health, Education, and Welfare, Sept, 1958, 73, 785–93), is very useful with its pertinent economic insights, though she may have underestimated somewhat the influences of the economic behavior of people in striving for health.

18 For instance the income elasticity of the demand for food continues to be positive even after the point is reached where additional food no longer has the attribute of a "producer good."

19 Based on comments made by Harold F. Clark at the Merrill Center for Economics, summer 1959; see also H. F. Clark, "Potentialities of Educational Establishments Outside the Conventional Structure of Higher Education," *Financing Higher Education 1960–70* (New York, 1959).

20 Based on observations made by a team of US economists of which I was a member: see *Saturday Review*, Jan. 21, 1961.

21 Gary S. Becker, preliminary draft of study undertaken for National Bureau of Economic Research (New York, 1960).

22 Becker has also noted still another implication arising out of the fact that the income and capital investment aspects of on-the-job training are tied together, which gives rise to "permanent" and "transitory" income effects that may have substantial explanatory value.

23 See below, Part II, No. 2, "Capital Formation by Education."

24 Had other things stayed constant this suggests an income elasticity of 3.5. Among the things that did change, the prices of educational services rose relative to other consumer prices, perhaps offset in part by improvements in the quality of educational services.

25 This of course assumes among other things that the relationship between gross and net has not changed or has changed in the same proportion. Estimates are from Theodore W. Schultz, "Education and Economic Growth," in *Social Forces Influencing American Education*, ed. H. G. Richey (Chicago, 1961).

26 From Schultz, "Education and Economic Growth," section 4. These estimates of the stock of education are tentative and incomplete. They are incomplete in that they do not take into account fully the increases in the

average life of this form of human capital arising out of the fact that relatively more of this education is held by younger people in the labor force than was true in earlier years; and they are incomplete because no adjustment has been made for the improvements in education over time, increasing the quality of a year of school in ways other than those related to changes in the proportions represented by elementary, high school, and higher education. Even so the stock of this form of human capital rose 8.5 times between 1900 and 1956 whiel the stock of reproducible nonhuman capital increased only 4.5 times, both in constant 1956 prices.

27 In value terms this stock of education was only 22 percent as large as the stock of reproducible physical capital in 1900, whereas in 1956 it already had become 42 percent as large.

28 Several comments are called for here. (1) The return to high school education appears to have declined substantially between the late 1930s and early 1950s and since then has leveled off, perhaps even rising somewhat, indicating a rate of return toward the end of the 1950s about as high as that to higher education. (2) The return to college education seems to have risen somewhat since the late 1930s in spite of the rapid influx of college trained individuals into the labor force. (3) Becker's estimates based on the difference in income between high school and college graduates, based on urban males adjsuted for ability, race, unemployment, and mortality show a return of 9 percent to total college costs including both earnings foregone and conventional college costs, public and private and with none of these costs allocated to consumption (see Gary S. Becker, "Underinvestment in College Education?", Proc., *American Economic Review*, 50 (May 1960), 346–54). (4) The returns to this education in the case of nonwhite urban males, of rural males, and of females in the labor force may have been somewhat lower (ibid.). (5) My own estimates, admittedly less complete than those of Becker and thus subject to additional qualifications, based mainly on lifetime income estimates of Herman P. Miller ("Annual and Lifetime Income in Relation to Education: 1939–1959," *American Economic Review*, 50 (Dec. 1960), 962–86), lead to a return of about 11 percent to both high school and college education as of 1958. See Schultz, "Education and Economic Growth," section 5.

Whether the consumption component in education will ultimately dominate, as in the sense that the investment component in education will diminish as these expenditures increase and a point will be reached where additional expenditures for education will be pure consumption (a zero return on however small a part one might treat as an investment), is an interesting speculation. This may come to pass, as it has in the case of food and shelter, but that eventuality appears very remote presently in view of the prevailing investment value of education and the new demands for knowledge and skill inherent in the nature of our technical and economic progress.

29 The returns on this consumer capital will not appear in the wages and salaries that people earn.

30 Real income doubled, rising from $150 to $302 billion in 1956 prices. Eighty-nine billions of the increase in real income is taken to be unexplained, or about 59 percent of the total increase. The stock of education in the labor force rose by $355 billion, of which $69 billion is here allocated to the growth in the labor force to keep the per-worker stock of education constant, and $286 billion represents the increase in the level of this stock. See Schultz "Education and Economic Growth," section 6 for an elaboration of the method of the relevant estimates.

31 The lower estimate came out to 29 percent and the upper estimate to 56 percent.

32 See Milton Friedman and Simon Kuznets, *Income from Independent Professional Practice*, National Bureau of Economic Research (New York, 1945).

33 See Becker, "Underinvestment in College Education?"

34 I am indebted to Milton Friedman for bringing this issue to the fore in his comments on an early draft of this paper. See the Preface to Friedman and Kuznets, *Income from Independent Professional Practice*, and also Jacob Mincer's pioneering paper, "Investment in Human Capital and Personal Income Distribution," *Journal of Political Economy*, 66 (Aug. 1958), 281–302.

2

Capital Formation by Education[*]

I propose to treat education as an investment in man. Since education becomes a part of the person receiving it, I shall refer to it as *human capital*. Since it becomes an integral part of a person, it cannot be bought or sold or treated as property under our institutions. Nevertheless, it is a form of capital if it renders a service of value. The principal hypothesis underlying this treatment of education is that some important increases in national income are a consequence of additions to the stock of this form of capital. Although it will be far from easy to put this hypothesis to the test, there are many indications that some, and perhaps a substantial part, of the unexplained increases in national income in the United States are attributable to the formation of this kind of capital.[1]

Education can be pure consumption or pure investment in production, or it can serve both these purposes. But, whatever it is in these respects, education in the United States requires a large stream of resources. The principal task of this paper is to present a set of estimates of the value of the resources that have been entering into education. These resources consist chiefly of two components – the earnings that students forego while attending school and the resources to provide schools. Our estimates begin with 1900, cover the next five decennial years, and close with 1956. The annual factor costs are given in current prices. A major section is devoted to the earnings that students forego while they attend school, both because of their importance and because these foregone earnings have heretofore been neglected. More than half the total resources that enter into high school, college, and university education consist of the time and effort of students. The section on costs of the educational services that the schools provide introduces estimates of the

*First published in *Journal of Political Economy*, 68, No. 6 (Dec. 1960), 571–83, and reproduced by permission of the University of Chicago Press (copyright 1960 by the University of Chicago). This study was started during 1956–57 while I was a Fellow at the Center for Advanced Study in the Behavioral Sciences. I was assisted by Marto Ballasteros and Jacob Meerman, who checked my calculations and questioned some of the assumptions underlying my tables as I first prepared them. I benefited from the criticisms made by Gary S. Becker, Zvi Griliches and Albert Rees on an early draft of this paper.

value of school property used for education, along with current expenditures for salaries, wages, and materials.

Capital formation by means of education is neither small nor a neat constant in relation to the formation of non-human capital. It is not small even if a substantial part of the total cost of education were strictly for consumption. What our estimates will show is that the stream of resources entering into elementary education has increased less than that entering into either high school or higher education. But, even so, it has been increasing at a higher rate than has the gross formation of physical capital. In 1900 the total cost of elementary education was equal to about 5 per cent of gross capital formation compared to 9 per cent in 1956. Comparable figures for high school and higher education combined are 4 percent in 1900 and almost 25 percent in 1956.

Two more introductory comments seem necessary, one on the neglect of the study of human capital and the other on the moral issue of treating education as an investment in man. A serious fault in the way capital is treated in economic analysis has been the omission of human capital; this was a major part of the burden of my Teller lecture.[2] Had economists followed the conception of capital laid down by Fisher,[3] instead of that by Marshall,[4] this omission, so it seems to me, would not have occurred.

It is held by many to be degrading to man and morally wrong to look upon his education as a way of creating capital. To those who hold this view the very idea of human capital is repugnant, because for them education is basically cultural and not economic in its purpose, because education serves to develop individuals to become competent and responsible citizens by giving men and women are opportunity to acquire an understanding of the values they hold and an appreciation of what they mean to life. My reply to those who believe thus is that an analysis that treats education as one of the activities that may add to the stock of human capital in no way denies the validity of their position; my approach is not designed to show that these cultural purposes should not be, or are not being, served by education. What is implied is that, in addition to achieving these cultural goals, some kinds of education may improve the capabilities of a people as they work and manage their affairs and that these improvements may increase the national income. These cultural and economic effects may thus be joint consequences of education. My treatment of education will in no way detract from, or disparage, the cultural contributions of education. It takes these contributions for granted and proceeds to the task of determining whether there are also some economic benefits from education that may appropriately be treated as returns on capital that can be identified and estimated.

Ideally, we should like to have estimates of the formation of human capital, both gross and net, and of the size of the stock. We should also like to know how much, if any, of the increase in national income is attributable to increases in the stock of human capital and what the "rate of return" on investment in education has been. There will then be the question, how do parents and students and public authorities respond to these investment opportunities?[5] In this paper, however, I take only one small step toward answering these questions.

Let me now present the sources of the estimates that follow, making explicit the underlying assumptions and commenting on the data so that the reader may have a basis for determining the limitations of these estimates. The more important economic implications that emerge from this study will be left until later.

1 Earnings that Students Forego

It will be convenient to draw an arbitrary line between elementary and secondary schools and to assume that no earnings are foregone on the part of children who attend elementary schools.[6] Beyond the eighth grade, however, these earnings become important. The time and effort of students may usefully be approached as follows:

1 Students study, which is work, and this work, among other things, helps create human capital. Students are not enjoying leisure when they study, nor are they engaged wholly in consumption; they are here viewed as "self-employed" producers of capital.

2 Assume, then, that if they were not in school, they would be employed producing (other) products and services of value to the economy, for which they would be "paid"; there is, then, an opportunity cost in going to school.

3 The average earnings per week of those young men and women of comparable age and sex who are not attending school or of students while they are not in school are a measure of the (alternative) value productivity of the students' time and effort.

4 The cost of living of students and non-students may be put aside because they go on whether young people go to school or enter the labor market and are about the same except for minor items, such as books, extra clothes, and some travel in getting to and from school.

Estimates of the earnings that students have foregone were made in the following manner: High school students were treated separately from college and university students. The year 1949 was taken as a base year

Table 2.2.1 Estimates of Earnings Foregone by High School and College or University Students in 1949

Age	Median income (Dollars) (1)	Weeks worked (2)	Income per week (Dollars) (3)	Annual earnings foregone in attending school (Dollars) (4)	In weeks equivalent to average earnings of workers in manufacturing (5)
14–17:					
Male	311	24	13.00	520	....
Female	301	20	15.00	600	....
18–19:					
Male	721	32	22.50	900	....
Female	618	29	21.30	852	....
20–24:					
Male	1,669	40	41.70	1,669	....
Female	1,276	36	35.40	1,416	....
25–29:					
Male	2,538	44	57.70	2,308	....
Female	1,334	33	40.40	1,616	....
Per Student:					
High School				583[a]	11 weeks
College or University				1,369[b]	25 weeks

[a] Students enrolled in high school were approximately half males and half females: 92.7 per cent were allocated to the age group 14–17, and 7.3 per cent to ages 18–19. In making this allocation, it was assumed that those below the age of 14 offset those above the age of 19 (*Statistical Abstract of the United States*, 1956, table 126).
[b] College or university students were distributed as follows:

Ages	Males (Per Cent)	Females (Per Cent)
14–17	3.5	5.0
18–19	18.2	16.0
20–24	30.6	11.5
25–29	14.7	0.5
	67.0	33.0

These percentages were used as weights in calculating the estimate of $1,369 (based on *Statistical Abstract of the United States, 1956*, table 126).

* *Sources and notes:*
Column 1: *United States Census of Population, 1950, Special Report on Education*, 1953, table 13, except for figures for age group 20–24, which are from Herman P. Miller, *Income of the American People* (John Wiley & Sons, New York, 1955) table 29. Virtually all the income in these age groups would appear to be from "earnings" according to Miller's table 34.

Column 2: *United States Census of Population, 1950, Special Report on Employment and Personal Characteristics*, 1953, table 14. Of the persons who did work in 1949, the Census shows the percent who worked 1–13, 14–26, 27–39, 40–49, and 50–52 weeks and, on the assumption that these classes averaged out to 7, 20, 33, 45, and 51 weeks, respectively, these were used as weights.

Column 3: col. 1 divided by col. 2.

Column 4: Assumes that students forego, on the average, 40 weeks of earnings: col. 3 multiplied by 40.

Column 5: *Economic Report of the President, January 1957*, table E-25. The average gross weekly earnings for all manufacturing was $54.92: Col. 4 divided by 54.92.

in determining the "earnings" per week of young people, both males and females, for each of four age groups. Students' foregone earnings were calculated on the assumption that, on the average, students forego 40 weeks of such earnings, and then expressed in earning-equivalent weeks of workers in manufacturing in the United States. The results appear in table 2.2.1; they indicate that high school students forego the equivalent of about 11 weeks and college or university students about 25 weeks of such warnings. These 1949 earnings ratios were applied to particular years between 1900 and 1956; an adjustment was then made for unemployment, as set forth in table 2.2.2.

Two sorts of limitations need to be borne in mind in interpreting and in using these estimates. The first pertains to the *11-week* and *25-week* estimates for the base year 1949; the other is inherent in applying the 1940 relationships to other years.

Many of the young people who did work in 1949 were employed for only a few weeks during the year. It seems plausible that their earnings per week would be below those of workers of equivalent abilities who worked most or all of the year. To this extent, our estimates are too low.[7] Also, it could be that students rate somewhat higher per person in the particular abilities for which earnings are received than do those not in school who are earning income. To the extent that there are such differences, other things being equal, our estimates of earnings foregone are again too low. On the other hand, some students have held jobs while they were attending school; the earnings they have received from such jobs should have been subtracted from our estimates. Then, too, young people are probably burdened with more unemployment relative to the number employed than is the labor force as a whole.[8] Thus, of the four factors just mentioned, two pull in one direction and two in the other. They may be compensating factors.

There is also the question: What would the earnings of school age workers have been if all of them had entered the labor market? But the question is not relevant because our problem is not one that entails a large shift in the number of human agents. The elasticity of the demand, either in the short or the long run, for such workers over so wide a range is not at issue. Instead, we want to know what earnings a typical student has been foregoing. Even so, our estimates of earnings foregone are substantially reduced by the effects of the large shift of students into summer employment;[9] the earning figures that we are using, drawing on the 1950 Census, are heavily weighted by this summer employment. As pointed out above, many who did work for pay worked only a couple of months or so.[10]

Table 2.2.2 Annual earnings foregone by students, adjusted and not adjusted for unemployment, 1900–1956, in current prices

| | | Annual earnings foregone per student while attending | | | |
| | | High School | | College or University | |
Year	Average weekly earnings, all manufacturing (Dollars) (1)	Unadjusted (Dollars) (2)	Adjusted for un-employment (Dollars) (3)	Unadjusted (Dollars) (4)	Adjusted for un-employment (Dollars) (5)
1900	8.37	92	84	209	192
1910	10.74	118	113	269	259
1910	26.12	287	275	653	626
1930	23.25	256	224	581	509
1940	25.20	277	236	630	537
1950	59.33	653	626	1,483	1,422
1956	80.13	881	855	2,003	1,943

Sources:
Column 1: *Economic Report of the President, January, 1957,* Table E-25 and U.S. Department of Labor: and *Historical Statistics of the United States, 1789–1945,* a supplement to *Statistical Abstract of the United States, 1949,* Ser. D, pp. 134–44.
Column 2 : For high-school students, col. 1 multiplied by 11; based on table 2.2.1
Column 4: For college and university students, col. 1 multiplied by 25; based on Table 2.2.1.
Columns 3 and 5: The percent unemployed is based on Clarence D. Long, *The Labor Force under Changing Income and Employment* (N.B.E.R. study Princeton: Princeton University Press, 1958), Appendix C, table C-1 and, for 1956, table C-2. Unemployed adult male equivalents in percent of the labor force were as follows: 1900, 8.2; 1910, 3.9; 1920, 4.2; 1930, 12.4; 1940, 14.7; 1950, 4.1; and 1956, 3.0.

The other difficulties stem from applying the 1949 "structural" relationships to other periods, especially to earlier years. The only adjustment that has been introduced is that for movements in unemployment. It is not easy to isolate the changes resulting from legislation. Stigler[11] suggests that "on the whole compulsory school attendance laws have followed more than led the increase in enrollments of children over 14." Child labor laws may have done likewise. In any case, these laws may be viewed as a comprehensive private and public effort to invest in education, the child labor laws having the effect of eliminating some job opportunities.[12]

There is a presumption in favor of the view that high school students in 1949 were attending school more weeks per year than did high school students in earlier years. Such evidence as I have been able to uncover, however, suggests that for 1900, 1910, and 1920 most high school students, including those who were attending secondary preparatory schools, were being instructed so that they could win entrance into a college or university and that these students were attending school about as many weeks per year as high school students in more recent years. Between the early 1920s and the mid 1940s, there may have been a small dip in this variable as a consequence of the large increases in high school enrolment and the fact that high school instruction was no longer devoted primarily to the preparation of students for college.[13]

The weekly earnings of workers who possess the capabilities of students and who are of that age group may have changed substantially since 1900 relative to the earnings of those employed in manufacturing. But it is not possible even to guess whether their earnings have become more or less favorable relative to the earnings of workers in manufacturing. The age groups that appear in table 2.2.1 represent young people who had had more years of schooling than did the same age groups in 1900. But this would also be true of workers in manufacturing. The fact that the wage ratio between skilled and unskilled workers has narrowed may imply that our estimates of earnings foregone by high school students during the earlier years are somewhat too high, or more plausible, that the estimates for college and university students are on the low side for those years.[14] It would be exceedingly difficult, however, to isolate the effects of these changes.

2   Costs of Services Provided by Schools

Ideally, we want a measure of the annual flow of the inputs employed for education. This flow consists of the services of teachers, librarians, and school administrators, of the annual factor costs of maintaining and operating the school plant, and of depreciation and interest. It should not include expenditures to operate particular auxiliary enterprises, such as providing room and board for students, operating "organized" athletics or other non-educational activities. School expenditures for scholarships, fellowships, and other financial aids to students should also be excluded, because they are in the nature of transfer payments; the real costs involved in student time are already fully covered by the opportunity-cost estimates.

Tables 2.2.3 and 2.2.4 give these costs of schools for elementary, secondary, and higher education. Each table is essentially self-contained, with sources and notes.

3   Total Costs of Education

The estimates of the costs of elementary education were complete as set forth in column 11 of table 2.2.3, inasmuch as no earnings were forego in accordance with our assumption.

Table 2.2.5 summarizes the principal components entering into the costs of high school education. A comparison of columns 3 and 6 shows at once the importance of the earnings that students forego relative to total costs of this education. That such foregone earnings should have been a larger proportion of total costs of high school education during the earlier years (and a larger proportion of total costs of high school than of college and university education in all years) comes as a surprise. Earnings foregone while attending high school were well over half the total costs in each of the years; they were 73 percent in 1900 and 60 percent in 1956; the two low years were 1930 and 1940, when they fell to 57 and 58 percent of total costs. During 1950 and 1956 they were 62 and 60 percent, respectively. Other and more general economic implications of these changes in resource costs of high school education will be considered later.

Table 2.2.6 provides similar estimates for college and university education. Here, too, earnings foregone by students are exceedingly important (see cols. 3 and 6). In 1900 and 1910 these earnings were about half of all costs, rising to 63 percent in 1920 and then falling to 49 percent in 1930 and 1940. With inflation and full employment, they then rose to 60 and 59 percent in 1950 and 1956.

Table 2.2.3 Annual resource costs of educational services rendered by elementary and secondary schools in the United States, 1900–1956, in current prices
(millions of dollars except column 4 in billions)

| | Public Schools | | | | | | Private Schools | | Public and Private Schools | | |
Year	Gross expenditures (1)	Capital outlay (2)	Net expenditures (3)	Value of property (4)	Implicit interest and depreciation (5)	Total public (6)	Gross expenditures (7)	Total private (8)	Total (9)	Secondary (10)	Elementary (11)
1900	215	35	180	.55	44	224	27	28	252	19	233
1910	426	70	356	1.1	88	444	54	56	500	50	450
1920	1,036	154	882	2.4	192	1,074	104	108	1,182	215	967
1930	2,317	371	1,946	6.2	496	2,442	233	246	2,688	741	1,947
1940	2,344	258	2,086	7.6	608	2,694	227	261	2,955	1,145	1,810
1950	5,838	1,014	4,824	11.4	912	5,736	783	769	6,505	2,286	4,219
1956	10,955	2,387	8,568	23.9	1,912	10,480	1,468	1,404	11,884	4,031	7,853

Sources and Notes:

Column 1: Lines 1–6, from *Statistical Abstract of the United States, 1955*, table 145; line 7 from *Biennial Survey of Education in the United States, 1954–56*.

Column 2: Lines 1–6, from *Biennial Survey of Education in the United States, 1948–50*, chap. 2, table 1; line 7 from the 1954–56 survey.

Column 3: Obtained by subtracting col. 2 from col. 1.

Column 4: From same source as col. 2.

Column 5: Obtained by taking 8 per cent of col. 4. The distribution of physical assets is placed at 20 percent land, 72 percent buildings, and 8 percent equipment, following Robert Rude's study, "Assets of Private Nonprofit Institutions in the United States, 1890–1948" (N.B.E.R., April 1954, not published), table 11.2a. With no depreciation or obsolence on land, 3 per cent on buildings (more obsolescence than for colleges and universities because of changing local and community populations to which high schools must adjust) and 10 per cent on equipment, and with an implicit interest rate of 5.1 per cent, we have an 8 per cent rate per $100 of assets per year.

Column 6: Obtained by adding cols. 3 and 5.

Column 7: From same sources as col. 1, except that line 1 is based on the same ratio as line 2 between cols. 1 and 7; line 3 is based on the same ratio as line 4; and line 7 is based on the same ratio as line 6.

Column 8: Obtained by taking the percentage that col. 7 is of col. 1 and multiplying by col. 6. The gross expenditures of private schools ranged from 9.7 to 13.4 percent of that of public schools. This procedure assumes that capital outlays, value of physical property, and imputed interest and depreciation bear the same relationship to gross expenditures for private as for public schools.

Column 9: Obtained by adding cols. 6 and 8.

Column 10: Obtained by allocating the total of col. 9 between elementary and secondary schools on the basis that it costs 88 percent more per student in secondary than in elementary schools. Expenditures for high schools determined by using George J. Stigler's estimates appearing in *Employment and Compensation in Education* (Occasional Papers, No. 33, New York: National Bureau of Economic Research, 1950, tables 7 and 12. Enrolment in elementary schools is given as 3.3, and in secondary schools as 21 per teacher (using average for last five years in Stigler's table); and average salary of elementary school teachers in 1938 was $1,876 and of secondary school teachers it was $2,249. This is as 100 to 120. Accordingly, per student, we have:

$$\frac{120 \div 21}{100 \div 33} \times 100 = \text{an index of 188 for teacher salary per student in secondary schools compared to 100 for that in elementary schools. A slightly}$$

lower ratio appears in *Biennial Survey of Education in the United States, 1939–40*, chapter 10.1, table 42, n. 1, in which secondary school costs per student are placed 74 percent higher than that in elementary schools. There are, however, no estimates in the 1939–40 survey which permit one to determine expenditures per student for elementary and secondary schools.

Table 2.2.4 Annual resource costs of educational services rendered by Colleges and Universities in the United States, 1900–1956, in current prices (Millions of dollars)

Year	Gross expenditures (1)	Auxiliary enterprises (2)	Capital outlay (3)	Net expenditures (4)	Value of physical property (5)	Implicit interest and depreciation (6)	Total (7)
1900	46	9	17	20	254	20	40
1910	92	18	30	44	461	37	81
1920	216	43	48	125	741	59	184
1930	632	126	125	381	1,925	154	535
1940	758	152	84	522	2,754	220	742
1950	2,662	539	417	1,706	5,273	422	2,128
1956	4,210	736	686	2,788	8,902	712	3,500

Sources and notes:

Column 1: Lines 1–6, from *Statistical Abstract of the United States, 1955*, table 145; and line 17 from *Biennial Survey of Education in the United States, 1954–56*. These expenditures by public and private institutions were as follows:

	Public	Private
	(in Million Dollars)	
1920	116	100
1930	289	343
1940	391	367
1950	1,429	1,233
1956	2,375	1,835

Column 2: Lines 5–7, same source as col. 1. For the two sets of institutions these were as follows:

	Public	Private
	(in Million Dollars)	
1940	59	93
1950	255	284
1956	364	372

Lines 1–4 were obtained by letting these auxiliary enterprises equal one-fifth of gross expenditures.

Column 3: Lines 4–7 from *Biennial Survey of Education in the United States, 1954–56,* chapter iv, sec. II; lines 1–3 obtained by taking 6.5 percent of col. 5, lines 1–3.

Column 4: Obtained by subtracting the sums of cols. 2 and 3 from col. 1.

Column 5: From *Biennial Survey of Education in the United States, 1948–50,* chapter iv, sec. II, Table I, and *1954–56.* These estimates check closely with those of Robert Rude, "Assets of Private Nonprofit Institutions in the United States, 1890–1948," (National Bureau of Economic Research, April 1954, not published).

Column 6: Obtained by taking 8 percent of col. 5; they assume no depreciation and obsolescence on land, 2 percent on buildings and improvements, and 10 percent on equipment. Following Robert Rude's study cited above, table II–2a, these physical assets were distributed 15 percent to land, 70 percent to buildings and improvements, and 15 percent to equipment. Assuming an interest rate of 5.1 percent, we have per $100 of assets:

Interest on all assets	£5.10
Depreciation and obsolescence	
On buildings and improvements	1.40
On equipment..	1.50
Total	$8.00

Column 7: Is the sum of cols. 4 and 6.

Table 2.2.5 Earnings foregone and other resource costs represented by High School education, in the United States, 1900–1956, in current prices

Year	Number of students (Millions) (1)	Earnings foregone per student (Dollars) (2)	Total earnings foregone (3)	School costs (4)	Additional expenditures (5)	Total (6)
				(Millions of Dollars)		
1900	.7	84	59	19	3	81
1910	1.1	113	124	50	6	180
1920	2.5	275	688	215	34	937
1930	4.8	224	1,075	741	54	1,870
1940	7.1	236	1,676	1,145	84	2,905
1950	6.4	626	4,006	2,286	200	6,492
1956	7.7	855	6,584	4,031	329	10,944

Sources:
Column 1: *Statistical Abstract of the United States, 1955* table 145; and *Biennial Survey of Education in the United States, 1954–56* chap. 2, table 44.
Column 2: From table 2.2.2, col. 3.
Column 3: Col. 1 multiplied by col. 2.
Column 4: From table 2.2.3, col. 10.
Column 5: Expenditure for books supplies, extra clothes, and travel to and from school estimated at 5 percent of total earnings foregone; hence, 5 percent of col. 3.
Column 6: Cols. 3 + 4 + 5.

Table 2.2.6 Earnings foregone and other resource costs represented by College and University education in the United States, 1900–1956, in current prices

Year	Number of students (Thousands) (1)	Earnings foregone per student (Dollars) (2)	Total earnings foregone (3)	School costs (4)	Additional expenditures (5)	Total (6)
			(Millions of Dollars)			
1900	238	192	46	40	4	90
1910	355	259	92	81	9	182
1920	598	626	374	184	37	595
1930	1,101	509	560	535	56	1,151
1940	1,494	537	802	742	80	1,624
1950	2,659	1,422	3,781	2,128	378	6,287
1956	2,996	1,943	5,821	3,500	582	9,903

Sources:

Column 1: *Statistical Abstract of the United States, 1955* table 145; and *Biennial Survey of Education in the United States, 1954–56* chapter. 2, table 44.

Column 2: From table 2.2.2, col. 5.

Column 3: Col. 1 multiplied by col. 2.

Column 4: From table 2.2.4, col. 7.

Column 5: Expenditure for book supplies, extra clothes, and travel to and from school estimated at 10 percent of earnings foregone; thus, 10 percent of col. 3.

Column 6: Cols. 3 + 4 + 5.

4   Concluding Observations

When costs of all levels of education are aggregated, the proportion of total costs attributable to earnings foregone has clearly risen over time. This is due to the much greater importance of secondary and higher education in more recent years, a change that outweighs the decline in the foregone earnings proportion of high school education alone. For all levels of education together, earnings foregone were 26 percent of total costs in 1900 and 43 percent in 1956. Probably the actual 1900 figure should be somewhat higher than this because of foregone earnings of children in the higher grades of elementary school (ignored here), but such an adjustment would not substantially alter the picture.

Between 1900 and 1956, the total resources committed to education in the United States rose about *three and one-half times* (1) relative to consumer income in dollars and (2) relative to the gross formation of physical capital in dollars. Accordingly, if we look upon all the resources going into education as "consumption" based on consumer behavior, our estimates would not be inconsistent with the hypothesis that the demand for education has had a high income elasticity.[15]

If, however, we treat the resources entering into education as "investments" based on the behavior of people seeking investment opportunities, our estimates then are not inconsistent with the hypothesis that the rates of return to education were relatively attractive; that is, they were enough larger than the rate of return to investments in physical capital to have "induced" the implied larger rate of growth of this form of human capital.[16]

Again, it should be stressed that the underlying private and public motives that induced the people of the United States to increase so much the share of their resources going into education may have been cultural in ways that can hardly be thought of as "consumption," or they may have been policy determined for purposes that seem remote from "investment." Even if this were true, it would not preclude the possibility that the rates of return on the resources allocated to education were large simply as a favorable by-product of whatever purposes motivated the large increases in resources entering into education. If so, the task becomes merely one of ascertaining these rates of return. If, however, consumer and investment behavior did play a substantial role in these private and public decisions, then, to this extent, economic theory will also be useful in explaining these two sets of behavior.

Not only have the streams of resources entering into elementary, high school, and higher education increased markedly, but they have changed relative to one another (see table 2.2.7).

Table 2.2.7 Total costs of Elementary, High School, and College and University education in the United States, 1900–1956, in current prices

Year	Elementary (1)	High School (2)	College and University (3)	Total (4)
		(Millions of Dollars)		
1900	230	80	90	400
1910	450	180	180	810
1920	970	904	600	2,510
1930	1,950	1,870	1,150	4,970
1940	1,810	2,900	1,620	6,330
1950	4,220	6,490	6,290	17,000
1956	7,850	10,950	9,900	28,700

*Sources (figures have been rounded):
Column 1: From table 2.2.3, col. 11.
Column 2: From table 2.2.5, col. 6.
Column 3: From table 2.2.6, col. 6.
Column 4: Cols. 1 + 2 + 3.

1   Though elementary education by this measure has increased at a slower rate than has either of the other two, it has come close to doubling its position relative to gross physical capital formation; it rose from about 5 to 9 percent of the latter between 1900 and 1956.[17]

The total costs of elementary education have been strongly affected by changes in enrolment and attendance. Increases in the average number of days that enrolled students have attended school played almost as large a part as did the increase in enrollment; the first of these rose 60 and the second 73 percent between 1900 and 1956. However, it should be noted that this factor of attendance has nearly spent itself: average daily attendance is now without about 10 percent of its apparent maximum. Enrolment, on the other hand, will turn upward in response to the growth in population. Meanwhile, the salaries of elementary school teachers have been declining relative to wages generally.[18] Altogether, however, it seems plausible that investment in elementary education will not continue to rise at the rate that it did during the period covered by our estimates.

As previously noted, some earnings were undoubtedly foregone by elementary pupils, especially by children attending the upper grades. We have come upon bits of data that suggest that these earnings may have been appreciable during the early part of this period. Farm families at that time still placed a considerable value on the work that their children could do for them; moreover, fully a third of the population had farm residences in 1900 and 1910. Surely, a poor country endeavoring to establish a comprehensive program of elementary education must reckon the cost entailed in the earnings that older children will have to forego.

2   The annual national cost of high school education has risen markedly, so much so that in 1956 it was equal in amount to nearly 13 percent of gross physical capital formation compared to somewhat less than 2 percent in 1900.[19]

Enrolment in high school increased from 0.7 to 7.7 million between 1900 and 1956. It had already reached 7.1 million in 1940. The effect of the upsurge in population that began in the early 1940s had started to make itself felt by 1956, the proportion of young people embarking upon a high school education being very large – indeed, it was approaching its maximum. The increases in this ratio were striking; for example, in 1900 only about 11 percent of the fourteen to seventeen age group was enrolled in secondary schools; by 1956 the percentage was about 75.[20]

Let me emphasize once more the fact that earnings foregone have made up well over half the total costs of high school education. In 1956 they were three-fifths of total costs, which is somewhat less than at the beginning of this period. From this experience one may infer that poor countries, even when they are no less poor than were the people of the United States in 1900, will find that most of the real costs of secondary education are a consequence of the earnings that students forego while attending school.

3 The trend of total cost of higher education has been similar to that of high school costs. It rose at a slightly smaller rate than did total high school cost in the early part of the period, and at a larger rate later. Relative to gross physical capital formation, it was about 2 percent in 1900 and slightly less than 12 percent in 1956.

Enrolment in higher education increased from 328,000 in 1900 to 2,996,000 in 1956. Of the eighteen to twenty-one age group, 4 percent were in residence and enrolled as undergraduates in higher education in 1900; by 1956, 32 percent of this age group were thus enrolled. The numbers in the college age group will increase substantially soon, as the children born when the upsurge in birth rates of the early 1940s reach these ages. The proportion of this age group that will begin higher education is not readily discernible. The upper limit is not near at hand, as it is for elementary and high school education; there are many indications that it will continue to increase for some time to come.

Earnings foregone by students attending colleges and universities were also about three-fifths of total costs in 1956. Here, however, we appear to observe an upward trend between 1900 and 1956.

4 Altogether, total costs of education have increased much more rapidly than have the total costs of the resources entering into physical capital. Between 1900 and 1956, the total costs of the three levels of education covered by this study rose from 9 to 34 percent of the total entering into the formation of physical capital.

Several more steps must be taken, however, before we can gauge the increases in the stock of capital developed by education and its contribution to economic growth. These steps will entail allocating the costs of education between consumption and investment, determining the size of the stock of human capital formed by education, and ascertaining the rate of return to this education.

Notes and References

1 By "unexplained", I mean here the increases in measured national income that exceed the increases in measured resources, treated as inputs. For approximately the same period covered by this study, Solomon Fabricant, in *Basic Facts on Productivity Changes*, National Bureau of Economic Research, Occasional Paper 63 (New York, 1959), table 5, presents estimates

that show the output of U.S. private domestic economy as having increased at an average annual rate of 3.5 percent between 1889 and 1957, whereas total inputs increased at an annual rate of only 1.7 percent. For the latter part of this period, that is, between 1919 and 1957, these annual rates of increase were 3.1 and 1.0 percent respectively.

2 See Theodore W. Schultz, "Investment in Man: An Economist's View", *Social Service Review*, 33 (June 1959), 109–17.

3 Irving Fisher, *The Nature of Capital and Income* (Macmillan & Co., New York, 1906).

4 Alfred Marshall, *Principles of Economics* (8th edn., London: Macmillan & Co., 1930). In discussing definitions of capital, Marshall commented on Fisher's precept as follows: "The writings of Professor Fisher contain a masterly argument, rich in fertile suggestion, in favour of a comprehensive use of the term. Regarded from the abstract and mathematical point of view, his position is incontestable. But he seems to take too little account of the necessity for keeping realistic discussions in touch with the language of the market-place . . ." (Appendix E).

5 Surely some individuals and families make decisions to invest in some kinds of education, either in themselves or their children, with an eye to the earnings that they expect to see forthcoming from such expenditures on education. It should be possible to analyze these decisions and their consequences as one does other private decisions that give rise to physical capital formation throughout the economy.

6 This assumption is plausible enough in the case of our society at the present time. But back no further than 1900, many of these children were of considerable economic value as workers, and some parents were keeping them from school for that reason.

7 Of males aged fourteen to seventeen who worked in 1959, 44 percent worked only about 7 weeks and 19 percent worked about 20 weeks (averages). Similarly, in the case of females aged fourteen to seventeen who worked, 53 percent worked only about 7 weeks and 21 percent about 20 weeks (averages). For ages eighteen to nineteen, these figures are smaller, i.e., for males, 24 percent worked only 7 weeks and 19 percent about 20 weeks; and for females aged eighteen to nineteen, the two figures are 29 and 31 percent respectively. For ages twenty to twenty-four, they are 10 and 12 percent for males and 17 and 15 percent for females.

8 *The Economic Report of the President, January, 1960*, table D-18, gives some figures that appear relevant. They show total unemployed equal to 5.2 percent of the total employed, whereas for the fourteen to nineteen age group it was 11.8 percent.

9 In 1955, for example, 1.2 million individuals aged fourteen to nineteen entered the labor force between May and July, in contrast to about 0.4 million in the ages twenty to twenty-four.

10 One can know something about the relation of the number of individuals in these age groups who are gainfully employed to the number enrolled in school. As one might expect, in the youngest of the three age groups, the

number gainfully employed (April, 1950) was a little more than one-third the number enrolled in school (October, 1950), whereas for the age group twenty to twenty-four there were fully seven times as many in the gainfully employed group as there were enrolled in school. The figures for 1950 are as follows:

Ages	Enrolled in school (October) (millions)	Gainfully employed or in labor force (April) (millions)
16–17	3.06	1.12
18–19	1.19	2.39
20–24	0.96	7.09
Total	5.21	10.60

11 George S. Stigler, "Employment and Compensation in Education," National Bureau of Economic Research, Occasional Papers 33 (New York, 1950), p. 8 and Appendix B.

12 In commenting on child labor laws, Albert Rees has called my attention to the *Census of Manufactures* of 1890, which shows that 121,000 children (males under sixteen and females under fifteen) were employed and that their annual earnings were 31 percent of those of all manufacturing wage earners. This is a substantially higher ratio than that implied for this age group in tables 2.2.1 and 2.2.2. Thus using 11 weeks' earnings foregone for 1900 may understate the investment in high school education at the beginning of this period.

13 Unfortunately for our purposes, data for the United States do not separate elementary and high school attendance. The data are mainly for the five to seventeen age group with two sets of figures: (1) the average number of days that schools were in session and (2) the average number of days attended by each enrolled pupil five to seventeen years of age. These are: 1900, 144 and 99 days, respectively; 1910, 156 and 113 days, 1920, 163 and 121 days; 1930, 173 and 143 days; 1940, 175 and 152 days; 1950, 178 and 158 days; and 1956, 178 and 159 days. Thus there has been a 60 per cent increase in the average number of days that each enrolled student attended schools. This rise, however, has been dominated by changes that have occurred in the attendance of elementary students. In the early years, high school students were heavily concentrated in states that had already established long school sessions and good attendance records. For example, the average number of days attended by high school students in a sample of such states was 170 days in 1920; a 1925–26 set of 31 states shows 151 days, and another set of states for 1937–38 shows 168 days, rising to 178 days in 1945–6 and 176 days in 1959–60.

14 Paul G. Keat, "Changes in Occupational Wage Structure, 1900–1956", unpublished PhD dissertation, (University of Chicago, Mar. 1959), p. 77,

estimates the wage ratio of skilled to unskilled workers to have been 205 in 1900 and 149 in 1949.

15 A 1 percent increase in real income was associated with a 3.5 percent increase in resources spent on education, implying an income elasticity of 3.5 had other things stayed constant. Among other changes, the price of educational services rose relative to other consumer prices, offset perhaps in considerable part by improvements in the "quality" of educational services.

16 Of course, other relevant factors may not have remained constant. For example, it seems plausible to believe that the grip of capital rationing is much less severe presently than it was during earlier years covered by this study.

17 Whenever I refer to estimates of gross nonhuman or gross physical capital formation, I shall base them on Simon Kuznets' *Annual Estimates 1869–1953* (National Bureau of Economic Research, New York, 1958), table T-8, technical tables in supplement to summary volume on *Capital Formation and Financing*, mimeographed, used with his permission. Estimates for 1956, roughly comparable with that of Kuznets' series, is the 67.4 billion appearing in *Economic Report of the President, January, 1960*. Table D-1 raised by 26.4 (the percentage by which Kuznets' estimate for 1950 exceeds commerce estimate of that year). Thus we have the total costs of elementary education increasing from $7,850m and gross physical capital costs increasing from $4,300 to $85,200m.

18 Keat, "Changes in Occupational Wage Structure", table 7, p. 25, presents estimates showing that these teachers in 1903 received 58 percent more earnings than did the average full-time employee in manufacturing during the year, compared to only 19 percent more in 1956. Comparable figures for high school teachers are 188 and 36 percent; and for professors, 261 and 73 percent.

19 Beginning with 1940, the total costs of high school education exceeded that of elementary education; by 1956 they were almost 40 percent larger. In 1900 it was the other way around, with elementary education nearly three times as large as that of high school, measured in resources used (see cols. 1 and 3 of table 2.2.7).

20 However, of this fourteen to seventeen age group, 88 percent was enrolled either in elementary school, high school, or college.

3

*Rates of Return on Education**

The advance that has been made in determining the economic value of education, since I last considered this problem,[1] is impressive. This symposium affords an opportunity to take stock, with a view of re-examining this problem and of seeing where we have arrived. I shall comment, first, on the advantages of thinking in terms of the rate of return, provided allowance is made for the lack of efficiency prices in the capital market serving private investment in education and for omissions of particular forms of capital when planning for economic development. I shall then evaluate the new crop of estimates of earnings from education and of the costs of education. Mainly, however, I shall concentrate on the limits of the rate of return as a guide in allocating investment resources to education.

The formation of capital by education is obviously relevant in planning for economic development when the objective is that of achieving an efficient allocation of investment resources in accordance with the priorities set by the relative rates of return on alternative investment opportunities. But economists are still far from clear on the connections between the rate of return, capital theory, growth theory, and technical change. It is now fairly evident that these connections are unclear because of the partial (incomplete) specification of capital and because of the confusion about the distinction between capital and technical change. Conventional concepts and measures of capital include only a part of all capital. There are, of course, no compelling reasons why the stock of any particular class of capital should not fall (rise) relative to national income over time. Producer goods – structures, equipment, and inventories – are such a class.

*First published as "The Rate of Return in Allocating Investment Resources to Education," in *Journal of Human Resources*, II, No. 3 (Summer 1967), 293–309. Reproduced by permission of University of Wisconsin. I benefited much from dialogues with Yoram Ben-Porath and Zvi Griliches, from Harry G. Johnson's critical and clarifying pen, from incisive comments by Robert M. Solow, Dale W. Jorgenson, Edward F. Denison, Mary Jean Bowman, and Jacob Mincer, and from a correction and suggestions by Samuel Bowles, Martin Carnoy, W. Lee Hansen, and Finis Welch.

The clarification of the concept of human capital and its identification have set the stage for a more complete specification and measurement of the accumulation of modern capital. It has also made us aware of changes in the quality of material capital. Thus treating education as human capital is but a step toward a more complete accounting of all capital. Once we embark on this road, it may soon be possible to transform most, if not all, of *technical change* into forms of capital heretofore omitted in capital accounting.

But how to do it is another matter. *Technical change* is ever so elusive. What is it? How can it be identified? Acceptable answers are as yet not at hand. Is it a matter of *definition* or of *evidence*? The distinction between solutions of this problem that depend on definitions and those that rely on evidence is, so it seems to me, a relevant distinction. Jorgenson has advanced and clarified this distinction in his argument that "one can never distinguish a model of embodied technical change from a model of disembodied technical change on the basis of factual evidence."[2] An alternative approach is to specify the services of different forms of capital (labor too) and of the stock of each form in terms of refutable hypotheses by confronting the data.[3]

Although there are still many unresolved questions, what really matters is that we are moving toward an all-inclusive concept of capital, and, in doing so, we are greatly strengthening the connections between capital and income and between capital accumulation by investment and economic growth.

The advantages of thinking in terms of the rate of return are presented cogently by Solow in his de Vries Lectures at Rotterdam.[4] In searching for "the relation between capital accumulation and economic growth in industrial countries,"[5] he finds capital theory unsettled and beset with many analytical difficulties. Solow is convinced, however, that from a planning point of view in dealing with saving and investment, "the central concept in capital theory should be *the rate of return on investment*."[6] I too am convinced that the rate-of-return approach has many advantages; yet it does not tell enough of the story of capital accumulation and economic growth. My plan is to show that the investigations of the economic value of education reveal important supplementary parts of the process of capital accumulation and growth.

Although thinking in terms of the rate of return is fundamental, it will remain an inefficient approach in planning economic development until at least the more important forms of capital, which are the sources of income and economic growth, have been identified. But on this score the omissions of particular forms of capital continue to plague economic growth theory. Human capital is one of the major omissions. Improvement in the quality of nonhuman capital is another. I do not want to imply that such omissions are endemic to all growth thinking. Yet it comes close to that when "techniques" are treated as exogenous and not as new forms of capital, for this capital must also be identified in allocating investment resources in accordance with priorities set by relative rates of return on alternative investment opportunities.

It may be helpful to comment once again on the attempts to explain the large, unexplained part of modern growth. The challenge, of course, has been the *residual*. I am sure economists will long be indebted to Denison[7] for his pioneering endeavor at identifying and measuring the sources of growth despite all the criticism that has been heaped upon it. Although Denison underestimates, in my view, by a large margin the increases in the contributions of nonhuman capital because so much of the improvement in the quality of such capital is concealed in his "increases in output per unit of input,"[8] a large part of which he attributes to "advance in knowledge," his *labor input* nevertheless represents a marked advance, because it takes account of changes in the quality of labor, including education.[9]

Although the challenge of the residual made "technical change" fashionable, it also gave us Denison's contributions. Furthermore, it led to a realization that there is an accumulation of human capital; and, to cope with it and with conventional capital forms, an all-inclusive concept of capital began to emerge as set forth by Harry G. Johnson in his comment in *The Residual Factor and Economic Growth*,[10] "Towards a Generalized Capital Accumulation Approach to Economic Development." It is now becoming clear that the question pertaining to technical change has been badly posed. The question facing policy-makers, planners, and entrepreneurs is as follows: How can they allocate investment resources efficiently to the production (formation) of particular new forms of capital?

The advantage of the rate-of-return approach is also limited, especially in the private sector when it comes to investing in education, by the lack of efficiency or shadow prices. This limitation is inherent in the way the capital market functions in financing students.

Let me turn, however, to the stages through which the investigations of human capital are proceeding for some clarifying clues with respect to unsolved problems inherent in capital accumulation and economic growth. Consider education: Is it a source of earnings? Is it a significant variable in a production function? Can its resource cost be determined? Is it an important form of capital? Do students and schools respond to changes in rates of return? Is the production function applicable to educational activities? Answers to these questions cannot be had without theory and data; and, as might be expected, the analytical task is beset with difficulties on both scores. But some answers are in; others are still in doubt; and, for some of the questions, the search for answers has hardly begun.

1   Earnings from and Costs of Education

The first stage was simply a matter of determining whether there is any growth mileage whatsoever in education. That there is some mileage of this sort from some education in some countries is now firmly established. Rough as the estimating procedures were at the outset, they showed that it would undoubtedly be worthwhile to undertake more refined and complete analyses of the attributes of earnings from education. Denison found that education seemed to account for about a fifth of the growth of the US economy from 1929 to 1957.[11] Is education therefore a good investment? His study obviously was not intended to answer that question. My admittedly very rough estimates, which preceded those of Denison, derived from my factor cost of education and some very preliminary notions of the relevant rates of return, were in general consistent with Denison's results – namely, that education appeared to account for at least a fifth of the increase in U.S. national income during that period.[12] Complementary evidence of a different sort had come from the work of Miller[13] and Houthakker,[14] from Becker's first paper[15] in this area, and from a discovery of the relevance of the 1945 study by Friedman and Kuznets.[16] Mincer's study,[17] which dealt with human capital and the distribution of personal income, provides still another type of supporting evidence. But the availability of data on earnings and schooling differs widely from country to country. There are some usable data covering recent decades for the United States, Israel, and Canada. They are better for India than might have been expected, as is clear from the study by Nalla Gounden.[18] But they are not available from census sources for European countries.[19] One of the favorable surprises, however, is how much can be learned by taking a small sample as Carnoy[20] did in Mexico, Bowles[21] in Nigeria, and as Blaug did using a British sample of data on earnings and schooling.

Once it had been established, however, that earnings were related positively to some extent to schooling, a number of important advances were soon made in developing theoretical models and in using them in estimating earnings from schooling. Becker's *Human Capital*[22] is a landmark. Hanoch's[23] estimation technique and data for estimating the earnings function which relates expected earnings to age and education, after standardizing for other relevant factors, gives us, in my judgment, the best estimates presently available for the United States. Where self-employment predominates, as in agriculture, one turns to Welch's estimates of the relevant earnings function.[24] Meanwhile, in a theoretical paper, Ben-Porath relates the shape of the life cycle of earnings of individuals to properties of the production function of human capital and examines the implications of these relations.[25] From his model he derives a number of promising hypotheses which await testing. In another direction, Bowles has developed a linear programing model for the efficient allocation of resources in education.[26]

Educated labor can be introduced as an input in a production function. The presumption here is that, if the estimates of the earning function of education are valid, education should be one of the relevant variables in estimating the production function of firms. If this variable were significant and its coefficient were positive and well behaved, there would be additional assurance that education is a real source of part of the observed production. Although there is the supposition that education would be less relevant in agriculture than in most sectors of industry, the lack of suitable data except for agriculture has restricted the use of this method of analysis predominantly to agriculture. But the indications are that even in agriculture the education of labor is an important input. Griliches, in his search for the sources of measured productivity growth of U.S. agriculture, uses an aggregate production function for that sector. His studies indicate that *education* "is a statistically significant variable with a coefficient that is not very different from the coefficient of the man-years worked variable."[27] Gisser, Welch, and Evenson, analyzing other economic attributes of U.S. agriculture in their Ph.D. research, also have used an implicit production function with education as a variable.

Another method for determining the value of education in production is a planning approach, a linear programing model, of the type developed by Bowles. In applying his model to Northern Nigeria, using a discount rate of 5 percent, he obtained the present value of the net benefits associated with the four educational activities listed below to be as follows:[28]

Present Value of Net Benefits in £s

Primary school	990
Secondary school	1,210
Technical training school	840
University studies	10,080

But all these studies omit the consumption value of education, as Solow correctly reminds me. It is a serious omission. In my papers and in

The Economic Value of Education, I have stressed the importance of this consumption value. The available estimates of earnings from education in this respect all underestimate the real value of education. Except for Becker's study, ability differences are not reckoned.

To calculate the rate of return, we must have estimates not only of the earnings from education but also of its cost. But the estimates of cost are presently not as good as Hanoch's estimates of earnings. The work to measure these costs has fallen behind, and there are deficiencies that affect the reliability of cost estimates, and these in turn affect the calculated rates of return.

The deficiencies I refer to are not those asserted by Vaizey, who among other criticisms of past work seems to make a main point of the assertion that earnings foregone by students should not be included in the cost of education.[29] The economic logic which makes earnings foregone a part of the opportunity cost of education has been presented with care by Bowman and need not be repeated here.[30] Carnoy, Nalla Gounden, and Bowles, for Mexico, India, and Northern Nigeria, respectively, have done as well as they could with their data; but workers on U.S. data have ignored many factors that influence the cost of education by region, community and type.[31] I am not so much troubled by our national (aggregate) cost estimates as I am about the way these national estimates are then allocated to various subgroups by region and race without taking account either of the large differences in cost arising from the differences in the regional mix of low-cost community colleges and high-cost private colleges, or of the differences in earnings of students attending school between both regions and types of communities in the same region. I am also sure that there are vast differences in the quality of education at all levels among regions – between the farm and nonfarm sectors and between whites and Negroes which are not unrelated to differences in the cost of education.[32]

2   As Allocative Guides

I turn now to a consideration of how real and relevant are rates of return in efficiently allocating investment resources to education.[33] The following questions appear pertinent.

1   Should we be worried whether the allocation of resources to education is efficient or not? Yes, because education absorbs a large share of resources, as I shall show, so that misallocations *within* that sector and *between* education and alternative expenditures could be wasteful.

2 Is there evidence that private educational choices are privately efficient, that is, do private rates of return on education tend (a) to be equal as among educational options and (b) to be comparable to private rates of return on other private investments? The evidence implies inefficiencies.

3 Are social rates of return and private rates of return proportional in all activities? Evidence is insufficient.

4 If private choices are privately inefficient, are they nevertheless socially efficient as a consequence of the allocation of public subsidies to education? No evidence on it.

If the amount of resources spent on education were trivial, there would be no point in being worried about rates of return as allocative guides in the area of education. But surely in the United States the amount of resources allocated each year to education is far from negligible. In 1956 the total outlay on formal education was $28.7 billion,[34] of which $12.4 billion was earnings foregone, compared with a total gross material capital formation for that year of $79.5 billion.[35] We learn from Kuznets[36] how much investment in man increases the share of GNP that is allocated to the formation of capital. Starting with the conventional concept of material capital, 30 percent of GNP, net of intermediate products, is accounted for in gross capital formation. The direct costs of formal education along with some other investments in man increase the gross capital formation to 42 percent of GNP. Kuznets then adds earnings foregone to GNP, which increases the conventional estimate of GNP by 10 percent; and since earnings foregone are all part of human capital formation the share of GNP allocated to gross capital formation rises to 47 percent.[37] In actual amounts, by 1959–60, the total outlay on formal education in the United States reached $39.5 billion.[38]

On the second question, the evidence shows very high private rates of return to elementary schooling (e.g. see Carnoy for Mexico, Hansen and Hanoch for the United States). They are also high for high school and have risen secularly (see Becker's *Human Capital*). These high private rates of return imply that private educational choices are privately inefficient with respect to elementary and secondary schooling. As I see this evidence, it implies that there is an underinvestment partly in quantity but *predominantly in the quality of such schooling*. The private rates of return to college education are, in general, comparable to private rates of return on other private investment, when no allowance is made for the consumption value of such education. On the third and fourth questions, as already noted, there is too little evidence to support firm answers.

Another unsettled question is the response of students (or of their parents) and of the decision-making bodies that organize and operate schools – i.e., the suppliers of educational services – to changes in the rates of return. If these responses were nil, it would be pointless to attribute any behavioral importance to these rates of return as allocative guides in the area of education. Such a lack of response on the part of students and schools would imply that the concept of investment in education is meaningless in terms of such economic behavior or that our measures of the rate of return to education are wrong. But what we observe is not a lack of response. Although the story of these responses of students to attend schools and of those who decide to supply schooling to changes in rates of return has not yet been told in the language of a Nerlovian dynamic-response model, there is an abundance of historical evidence which leaves little room for doubt that such responses are occurring and that, in general, they are in the right directions.[39] The search is for behavior models that would be appropriate in analyzing these investment responses.[40]

What is the relevant educational investment horizon in education? It is useful to distinguish between the *apparent behavioral horizons* of students and the *ex post horizons* underlying the estimates of rates of return. In thinking about the first of these – i.e., the investment horizon which will explain the behavior of students and schools – there are strong reasons for believing that it is, in general, fairly short. It is impossible to predict lifetime earnings; for the student to do so he would have to predict the changes in the demand for his type of education and the supply consequences of the decisions of others like himself to enter his particular field on his earnings up to 40 and more years ahead. The relevant information available to the student would seem to be mainly of two parts: (1) starting salaries and (2) the relative earnings position of people in their forties at the time the student's decision is made. (His parents will be comparing themselves with contemporaries in other occupations and with respect to those who have made good.[41]).

Thus I would proceed on the assumption that the investment horizon of students is relatively short, except for such traditional occupations as law and medicine. In the case of engineers, Freeman finds that starting salaries of engineers provide a strong clue to the behavior of students entering or leaving this field.[42] But we do not know the relationship between starting salaries and the earnings profiles which we use in calculating the rates of return to education which take account of earnings that accrue from education through the fourth decade after the education is completed. Nor do we know how sensitive these starting salaries are to changes in the real rates of return.

An approach to get at these relatively short investment horizons is to think (1) in terms of the subjective discount rates of students and (2) in terms of the uncertainty which they face. The two could be closely linked. But I would presume that the linkage between them is quite loose. The fog of uncertainty is everywhere concealing the more distant value of education. The subjective discount rates will differ depending upon differences in preferences and in the supply price of capital for this purpose; and, despite such differences, these subjective discount rates may be, in general, not high but close to the going interest rate. Thus, it is possible that the relatively short investment horizon, which I have postulated, is a consequence of the general fog of uncertainty.

I do not want to imply that we should dismiss out of hand the possibility that we might find that some of the relevant subjective rates of discount are high. We should therefore search for ways of ascertaining what these rates appear to be, hard as it is to secure any data which might reveal them to us. Students from families with low incomes and with little wealth in general cannot, even if they wanted to, borrow funds in the capital market to finance education. Even if they could, many of them may impose on themselves forms of internal capital rationing which would keep them from turning to the market for such funds.

But the fog of uncertainty is there. How low and how dense it is really matters. Yet we are ever so vague when it comes to identifying and measuring the level and density of this fog. It is in the nature of things, as a part of the human predicament that we must face. Reason and probabilities and the search for solutions will not dispel all this fog, as Shackle reminds us in his presidential address "Policy, Poetry and Success."[43] The future economic value of education is no exception. Estimates of the profiles of lifetime earnings from education are pictures of the past. They reveal *ex post* supply and demand intercepts of the capabilities acquired from education. But when it comes to projecting these estimates into the future reason, economic logic and theory, and appeals to probabilities are quite imperfect in making projections that will prove to be right. This limitation of our knowledge about the future is, of course, not unique to investment in education; for this uncertainty is also ever present in the realm of investment in material capital. What we do know is that the dynamics of our type of economy is continuously changing not only the demands for final products and the intermediate components entering into them, but even more important, is improving the quality of old forms of capital and also developing new and better forms of capital. The obsolescence of capital, including the capital that is formed by education, is *real*, in large part *unpredictable*, and *important*.

In planning for economic development, when investment decisions are made by a governmental agency, the investment horizon with regard to education is likewise, so it seems to me, relatively short. Those who make these public decisions are up against the same fog of uncertainty with respect to the more distant economic value of education. They have one advantage, however, namely, that such an agency can pool some types of risks that confront a student and treat them in terms of ascertainable probabilities; for example, the probability that a particular student is capable of completing some additional education.

If this view of the relevant investment horizons should prove to be valid, it strongly implies that appropriate steps should be taken to maximize the returns from built-in flexibilities for taking advantage of any lifting of the fog as it occurs over time. Such flexibility can be had by postponing specialization in education and thus not only starting with but staying with general education longer than would be warranted if there were no uncertainty with respect to future earnings from the investment in education. The characteristics of this fog also imply that more (not all) of the specialized skills should be acquired from on-the-job training than would thus be acquired if there were less or no uncertainty.

My purpose here is not to present a catalogue of particulars but to clarify somewhat the problem at hand. We know that the rapid change in the demand for skills is a function of our type of economic growth. The secular shift, which shows that an increasing part of on-the-job training is being acquired by those with a college education, is consistent with the sort of flexibility that my approach implies. In 1939, only one-third of all on-the-job training of males in the United States (which at that time was as large as all formal education) was acquired by college level males. In 1958, two-thirds of it was acquired by males who already had attained a college education.[44]

It should also be said that our task as educators is to provide instruction which will best serve students in adjusting their skills to the rapidly changing economy in which they will live. Thus, we ought to give a low rating to instruction that is specific. We ought to give a high rating to learning principles and theories. We should give the highest priority to instruction which is devoted to problem solving analytical methods. If you ask how this can best be done, don't expect answers. What is odd, however, is that we do not search for answers so relevant to the efficiency of our own work. As economists we search for ways that will make producers more efficient. We tell everybody else how they can do their work better. But we fail to bring hard, analytical thinking to bear on our task as teachers. Surely the rate of obsolescence of what we teach and what students learn is higher than it need be.[45]

In using the distinction between the investment horizon of students and the horizon underlying our estimates of rates of return, I have concentrated on the first of these. If the estimated lifetime earnings profiles, costs, and rates of returns could be projected with certainty, could students then privately invest efficiently in their education if they were informed with respect to only the first half, or some larger part, of such lifetime earnings profiles? Evidence pertaining to this possibility using Hanoch's estimates shows, as one would expect, that it would lead to an inefficient investment in education.

This evidence comes from Hanoch's estimates for males in the United States, for whites in the North in 1959.[46] It is restricted to a comparison of the investment in 16 years of schooling over that of 12 years of schooling. Since the net present value at age 20 and the internal rate of return give the same results, I shall refer only to the internal rates of return. They show, using 4 years for college, large differences.

Time span after age 20 of	Internal rate of return
10 years	2.5
15 years	7.5
20 years	9.6
Full life	11.5

The inference from this evidence, given the conditions set by the problem under consideration, is that there would be an underinvestment in college education if the information on earnings covering, e.g., only the first 15 years, were to guide such private investment decisions. The results shown imply that an expected rate of return of 7.5 percent would then be the guide, whereas the lifetime rate that would be realized is 11.5 percent, which is half again as high, thus calling for additional investment.

Lastly, there is the distinction between the internal rate and the net present value. Much has been written attributing important theoretical advantages to the present value over the internal rate approach, citing as a rule Hirshleifer's paper[47] but unaware of Bailey's classic paper,[48] which shows that Hirschleifer's analysis is not sufficient to solve the multi-period case in full generality. Bailey demonstrates formally that "the general solution of investment decision problems cannot rely solely on either the present value or rate of return reasoning."[49] Thus, as with techniques of analysis in empirical work, neither technique is wholly satisfactory formally. Aside from these formal limitations, each has its advantage. Given the data in this area, the results in terms of the relative internal rates and the relative net present values tend to be about the same; and, since the internal rate of return is a much easier (less costly) statistic to calculate, it has by this token an advantage. But where the data permit, the net present value has an advantage in identifying the large net return from a large additional investment (the extra years in becoming a surgeon), with a relatively small rate of return above the market rate, compared with the small net return from an extra year of elementary schooling (going from the seventh and completing the eighth), although it produces a relatively high rate of return.

3   Conclusions

In conclusion, the advantages of thinking in terms of the rate of return are cogent in searching for solutions to investment, capital accumulation, and growth problems, including the problem of an efficient allocation of investment resources to education. I prefer to think of the reciprocal of the rate of return as the *price of an income stream* and then treat this price of an additional income stream as the price of growth. But (staying with the rate of return), my endeavor here at clarifying particular issues would seem to support the following conclusions:

1   The best of the estimates showing the profiles of earnings from education are in good repair (Hanoch). But they omit the consumption value of education and ability differences.

2   Factor costs of education, however, are still far from satisfactory.[50]

3   Estimates of the private rates of return to the different levels of education, despite the limitations with respect to costs, are becoming useful indicators of particular *ex post* disequilibria in the supplies of educated labor viewed privately.

4   The social rates of return are not in good repair, either theoretically or empirically. There is all too little evidence on the relationship between the social and private rates of return.

5   The alleged advantages of present value estimates over internal rate estimates are questionable in theory and in practice; each has its particular advantage.

6   We know very little about the tendency to equilibrium or about the responses of students and schools to the relative rates of return.

7   When it comes to private investment in education, the private investment horizon of students is not known. Despite the substantial additional earnings from education that accrue to the person during the later part of his life span, my feeling is that the private investment horizon is, in fact, relatively short.

8 The economic linkage between recent *ex post* rates of return and future rates of return from investments, in general – including investment indifferent levels of education – are tenuous. Growth theory does not as yet provide us with any strong links.

9 An approach that treats investment in education as a means of improving the quality of the human agent is an important step leading to the specification and measurement of the quality of both human and nonhuman capital, and thus accounting for the increases in macro production without any appeal to technical change as Griliches and Jorgenson have shown.[51]

10 In terms of capital accounting, we are moving toward an all-inclusive concept of capital, and in terms of growth, we have the beginnings of a "generated capital accumulation approach to economic development,"[52] in which the reciprocal of the rate of return is in theory and in fact the price of growth.

Notes and References

1 Theodore W. Schultz, *The Economic Value of Education* (Columbia University Press, New York, 1963).

2 Dale W. Jorgenson, "The Embodiment Hypothesis", *Journal of Political Economy*, 74 (Feb. 1966), 1–17. I am indebted to Jorgenson for this distinction. This distinction is somewhat too strong if one were to say the embodiment approach solves the problem wholly by definition. It too leads to an appeal to data but in a manner and under what seem to be implausible assumptions – e.g., that there is a constant relationship between the rate of technical progress and the rate of investment. On the other hand, although the capital approach is a way of identifying and measuring new forms of capital, it is not possible empirically to account for all of it, and the notion of a once-and-for-all refutable hypothesis settling the measurement problem is too strong. As Zvi Griliches has taught me, his approach to input and capital accounting succeeds in reducing the unaccounted part. His search in appealing to new information has been highly rewarding. (See his "Research Expenditures, Education, and the Aggregate Agricultural Production Function", *American Economic Review*, 54 (Dec. 1964), 961–74. In terms of capital accounting, see Zvi Griliches and Dale W. Jorgenson, "Sources of Measured Productivity Change: Capital Input", *American Economic Review*, 61 (May 1966), 50–61.

3 Despite my strong inclination to rely on "refutable hypotheses", I realize that Solow (see note 4) can point out that not all of the observable total factor productivity may be of this sort. A part of it may still prove to be a "residual", whether it is labeled a "return to scale" or something else. Thus, it is possible that a part of it may not be imputable to any resource cost, or

that whoever makes such a residual technical change is unable to collect the return.

4 Robert M. Solow, *Capital Theory and the Rate of Return* (North-Holland Publishing Company, Amsterdam, 1963).

5 Ibid., p. 8.

6 Ibid., p. 16. The italics are Solow's.

7 Edward F. Denison, *The Sources of Growth in the United States and Alternatives Before Us* (Committee for Economic Development, New York, 1962). In his presentation at the American Economic Association meetings at San Francisco, December 17, 1966, "Sources of Postwar Growth in Nine Advanced Countries", Denison indicated that he had somewhat modified some of the estimating techniques that he had used in his early US study. My comment here does not take account of these modifications. I have not had an opportunity as yet to study them.

8 Ibid., p. 266, table 32.

9 Denison sees this issue differently. In his view, his "incorporation of education into the measurement of labor input has the effect of putting labor input on a par with conventional measures of capital input . . . When labor input is measured by applying weights to education groups, this is comparable to weighting different types of capital by their value in a base year . . . I don't think you really object to my estimates as such but to my classification." (Quoted from a letter, with Denison's permission.)

10 Harry G. Johnson, *The Residual Factor and Economic Growth* (Paris: OECD, 1964).

11 Denison, *Sources of Growth*, p. 266, table 32, see second to last column.

12 Theodore W. Schultz, "Education and Economic Growth," in Nelson B. Henry (ed.), *Social Forces Influencing American Education* (University of Chicago Press, Chicago, Ill., 1961), pp. 78–82. See table 18 covering the period between 1929 and 1956.

13 Herman P. Miller, "Annual and Lifetime Income Relation to Education," *American Economic Review*, 50 (Dec. 1960), 962–86. Also an earlier paper by Paul C. Glick and Herman P. Miller, "Educational Level and Potential Income," *American Sociological Review*, 21 (June 1956), 307–12.

14 H. S. Houthakker, "Education and Income," *Review of Economics and Statistics*, 41 (Feb. 1959), 24–28.

15 Gary S. Becker, "Underinvestment in Education?", *American Economic Review*, 50 (May 1960), 346–54.

16 Milton Friedman and Simon Kuznets, *Income from Independent Professional Practice*, National Bureau of Economic Research (New York, 1945).

17 Jacob Mincer, "Investment in Human Capital and Personal Distribution of Income," *Journal of Political Economy*, 66 (Aug. 1958), 281–302.

18 A. M. Nalla Gounden, "Education and Economic Development," PhD dissertation (Kurukshetra University, India, 1965).

19 Mark Blaug has noted that Sweden is a possible exception. Edward Denison found the earnings data collected by INSEE in a special survey in France useful.

20 Martin Carnoy, "The Cost and Return to Schooling in Mexico," PhD dissertation (Department of Economics, University of Chicago, 1964).

21 Samuel S. Bowles, "The Efficient Allocation of Resources in Education: A Planning Model with Applications to Northern Nigeria," PhD dissertation (Department of Economics, Harvard University, Cambridge, Mass., 1965).

22 Gary S. Becker, *Human Capital* (Columbia University Press, New York, 1964). A major part of Becker's theoretical analysis first appeared in the Universities-National Bureau of Economic Research, *Investment in Human Beings*, published as a supplement to the *Journal of Political Economy*, 70 (Oct, 1962), 9–49.

23 Giora Hanoch, "Personal Earnings and Investment in Schooling," PhD dissertation (Department of Economics, University of Chicago, 1965).

24 F. Welch, "The Determinants of the Return to Schooling in Rural Farm Areas, 1959," PhD dissertation (Department of Economics, University of Chicago, 1966).

25 Yoram Ben-Porath, "The Production of Human Capital and the Life Cycle of Earnings," unpublished, *Investment in Human Capital* series, paper No. 66.06 (University of Chicago, Nov. 1966).

26 Bowles, "The Efficient Allocation of Resources in Education."

27 Zvi Griliches, "Estimates of Aggregate Agricultural Production Function from Cross-Sectional Data," *Journal of Farm Economics*, 45 (May 1963), 419–28; and "The Sources of Measured Productivity Growth: United States Agriculture, 1949–60," *Journal of Political Economy*, 71 (Aug. 1963), 331–46; and his "Research Expenditure, Education and the Aggregate Agricultural Production Function," *American Economic Review*, 54 (Dec. 1964), 961–74. The coefficient of "man-years" of labor is .524 and that of "education" is .431 for 1949, with US agriculture classified into 68 regions.

28 Bowles, *The Efficient Allocation of Resources in Education*, table 6.4.1. Bowles informs me that the figure for secondary schools should be 1,206 instead of 906, before rounding.

29 Commenting on Vaizey's view, Harry G. Johnson notes that they "seem to be partly motivated by concern about the political implications," and thus are scarcely relevant to a scientific search for the underlying real cost of education. If the political motive were that of persuading the body politic to increase the governmental appropriations for education, it could of course be convenient to omit earnings foregone. Omitting them in the case of the United States would fully double the calculated rate of return to high school and college education. But this is not the road that leads to economic knowledge. See The *Residual Factor and Economic Growth*, pp. 225–27.

30 Mary Jean Bowman, "The Costing of Human Resource Development," in E. A. G. Robinson and J. E. Vaizey (eds.), *Economics of Education* (St. Martin's Press, New York, 1966), pp. 421–50. Also set forth above, Part II, No. 2, in my "Capital Formation by Education;" and elaborated in Theodore W. Schultz, *The Economic Value of Education* (Columbia University Press, New York, 1963), chapter II.

31 There is much merit in attaining some historical perspective of the changing

composition of the cost of education and thereby improving our understanding of changes affecting these costs, as revealed by Albert Fishlow, "Levels of Nineteenth Century American Investment in Education," *Journal of Economic History*, 26, No. 4 (Dec. 1966), 418–36; and from the PhD research of Lewis Solomon at the University of Chicago, concentrating on about the same period.

32   The economic importance of differences in the quality of schooling is revealed in the work of F. Welch, building on his PhD research, in "Labor Market Discrimination: An Interpretation of Income Differences in the Rural South," *Investment in Human Capital* series, paper No. 66.02 (University of Chicago, May 25, 1966); and in Theodore W. Schultz, "Underinvestment in the Quality of Schooling in Rural Farm Areas," in *Increasing Understanding of Public Problems and Policies* (Farm Foundation, Chicago Ill., 1964), pp. 12–34.

33   In clarifying these issues I owe much to Harry G. Johnson.

34   Schultz, "Capital Formation by Education," (Part II, No. 2 above), tables 2.2.5, 2.2.6, and 2.2.7.

35   Simon Kuznets, *Modern Economic Growth* (Yale University Press, New Haven, Conn., 1966), p. 228.

36   Ibid., pp. 228–30.

37   Ibid., table 5.2, p. 231, lines 4, 5, and 7.

38   Lewis C. Solomon's estimate, using the same method as that used in Schultz, "Capital Formation by Education;" the earnings foregone component was $17.7 billion.

39   But it would be a mistake to conclude from such evidence that these responses are *efficient* and that there is no *malinvestment* in education, there is still a tendency toward one or the other of two opposite biases – i.e., as extremes, that these responses are close to perfect in equating marginal returns or that the acquisition of education is determined wholly by social and cultural factors which are beyond the economic calculus.

40   The first study of this type known to me was by W. Lee Hansen, "Shortages and Investment in Professional Training" (Labor Economics Workshop Paper No. 62.1, University of Chicago, Oct. 16, 1961). See also his paper, "The Shortage of Engineers," *Review of Economics and Statistics*, 43 (Aug. 1961), 251–56. Bruce W. Wilkinson, "Present Values of Lifetime Earnings for Different Occupations," *Journal of Political Economy*, 74 (Dec. 1966), 556–72, compares the behavior of teachers and engineers between 1957–58 and 1961–62 in Canada, table 4, p. 570. Richard B. Freeman, "Labor Market for B.S. Engineers, 1948–1965," PhD research, Harvard University, as presented before the Labor Economics Workshop, University of Chicago, January 23, 1967, used a cobweb model. Harry G. Johnson in "The Social Sciences in an Era of Opulence," *Canadian Journal of Economics and Political Science*, 32, No. 4 (Nov. 1966), sees the relevance of a cobweb model in explaining changes in the demand-supply of teachers.

41   Johnson, "The Social Sciences in an Era of Opulence;" also from his comments on my preliminary draft of this paper.

42 Freeman, "Labor Market for B.S. Engineers." These responses of engineers to starting salaries do not necessarily imply short investment horizons; such starting salaries could be good proxies for lifetime earnings.

43 G. L. S. Shackle, "Policy, Poetry and Success," *Economic Journal*, 76 (Dec. 1966), 755–67.

44 See Jacob Mincer, "On-the-Job Training: Costs, Returns and Some Implications," *Journal of Political Economy*, Supplement, 70 (Oct. 1962), 50–79.

45 In this paragraph I draw upon my "Reflections on Teaching and Learning in Colleges of Agriculture," *Journal of Farm Economics*, 47 (Feb. 1965), 17–22. Johnson also considers these issues in "The Social Sciences in an Era of Opulence."

46 Hanoch, "Personal Earnings," table 4.

47 J. Hirshleifer, "On the Theory of Optimal Investment Decision," *Journal of Political Economy*, 66 (Aug. 1958), 329–52.

48 Martin J. Bailey, "Formal Criteria for Investment Decisions," *Journal of Political Economy*, 67 (Oct. 1959), 476–88.

49 Ibid., p. 477.

50 Wilkinson, "Present Values of Lifetime Earnings," p. 561, for example, proceeds as follows: "Information is not available on incidental high school costs or summer and part-time earnings of high school students, so it will be assumed that they are equal." Hanoch, "Personal Earnings," p. 74, is quite aware of the weakness of his cost data in noting that "direct costs of schooling constitute a main component of these initial sections of the profiles. But due to the shortage of satisfactory data, we actually used here a crude assumption, that direct costs equal the earnings of students."

51 Griliches and Jorgenson, "Sources of Measures Productivity Change."

52 See Johnson's comment on this approach in *The Residual Factor and Economic Growth*, pp. 219–25.

4

Resources for Higher Education[*]

It would be convenient, in good grace, and not too difficult to make a strong case for more funds for higher education. Such a case could be made convincing by simply projecting the recent high rate of increase in higher education, as student enrolment and cost per student continues to rise, by proclaiming that soon virtually every high school graduate will require some higher education. This would set the stage for universal higher education with the implication that it should become more nearly free to students and would stress the necessity of supporting more quantity and more quality everywhere. Thus, it would seem that there are reasons aplenty for more funds, preferably without public control, and for a public package that would finance everybody.

But I would serve you badly by making such a case. The problems here that await solution cannot be treated in so convenient a manner. Even the preliminary task of identifying the problems that matter is a major undertaking. I am attracted to Professor Shackle's distinction between poetry as a search for beauty and policy as a search for solutions to problems.[1] Our search is for solutions to the problem of financing higher education. Raising money falls on the University President, whereas the task of finding beauty is left to students. While bards with beards protest, poets command a low price. University administrators who are successful financiers are scarce and dear.

Why is it better to maintain an old college than to move it to a superior location, better to add new university functions than to eliminate those that have become obsolete, better to accommodate classes that have become virtually empty than to reallocate faculty to gain efficiency, better simply to project past upward trends than to explain them with the view of altering their course for the better; and better to obtain additional outside funds than to raise tuitions?

[*] First published in *Journal of Political Economy*, 76, No. 3 (May/June 1968), 327–47. Reproduced by permission of University of Chicago Press (copyright 1968 by the University of Chicago). C. E. Bishop, Mary Jean Bowman, Milton Friedman, Zvi Griliches, A. C. Harberger, Lewis C. Solomon, and Finis Welch commented critically on my first draft, and I am indebted to them.

Turning to economic analysis, my plan is to begin with a comment on some of its limitations; then to present a set of propositions and their implications for higher education; and last, to sketch the search for solutions to financing higher education.

1 From Preferences to an Agenda of Problems

Consider first the cultural values that determine the preferences of parents, students, and society for higher education. How they may be changed for the better is beyond the economic calculus; such a reform must rest on cultural and political considerations rather than on economic choices among economic opportunities. Economists start with preferences and build on them, treating them as given. Economists have developed useful techniques, and they are skillful in using them in identifying the "revealed preferences" of people. With regard to the technical properties of resources, there are some that are "fixed entities." They consist of particular "original" resources and their attributes – for example, the physical dimensions and space of the United States and the inherited abilities of students and teachers. Other technical properties are not altogether fixed but nevertheless cannot be altered much in any short period of time – for example, the magnitude of the endowment of human and material capital, including the state of knowledge. At best, this endowment can be enlarged somewhat but it would be small, and to this extent economics would have something to say on the worthwhileness of such small changes.

When you ask economists for their agenda of problems pertaining to education you are asking for additional trouble. Propositions about education that have long been treated as self-evident and settled are placed in doubt. The grand monolithic social value of higher education is seen as many little values, each of which is up against a schedule of marginal costs. There is no free instruction. Thus, one must ask: Is the additional cost worth the additional satisfactions and earnings? Is it worth as much as the value from an equal expenditure in some other private or public activity? If the federal government were prepared to appropriate an additional billion dollars, would society gain as much from allocating it to higher education as it would from using it for the conservation of natural resources, reducing water and air pollution, providing more medical care, slum clearance, or for the reduction of poverty? Would an additional billion dollars reduce the job discrimination? Would Negroes face the rate of economic obsolescence of acquired education, or the inefficiency with which resources are allocated within higher education? Would it improve the career choices of students?

Would it reduce the social and economic inequities which presently characterize the personal distribution of resources going into higher education? These are some of the troublesome problems on the economists' agenda.

2   From Propositions to Implications

While altruism is not at the heart of the relationship between education and economics, both gain from an exchange of products. To broaden the exchange, economists are offering some new propositions which should prove useful in planning and in financing education. Of these, there are seven which I shall offer for your consideration. Let me indicate what they are about. Organized education produces an array of different forms of human capital of varying durability. Higher education is engaged in three major types of production activities which entail discovering talent, instruction, and research. But it is not renowned for its gains in the productivity of teachers and students. Educational planning overlooks most of the real costs of higher education because of its omission of earnings foregone by students. Long-term projections of the demand for higher education are conjectures that undervalue flexibility and over-value formulas. The advantages of thinking in terms of the rates of return to investment in education and the requirement of efficiency prices in allocating investment resources in accordance with the standard set by the relative rates of return on alternative investment opportunities are strong and clear. There is, however, much confusion with regard to the welfare consequences of higher education, including the consequences of the way in which it is financed and the resulting personal distribution of costs and benefits. I now turn to the meaning of these propositions.

3   Education as Human Capital

It is *human* because it becomes a part of man, and it is *capital* because it is a source of future satisfactions, or of future earnings, or both of these. Thus far, however, the concept of human capital has contributed more to economic thinking than it has to the solution of problems in education. In economics it has become a seminar concept entering into many parts of economic analysis. In international trade it points to the solution of the Leontief paradox, showing why capital rich countries nevertheless export goods which are labor intensive; for we discover that labor entering into these goods requires much human capital. The differences among countries in their capital endowments, when both physical and human capital are taken into account and under the assumption of factor price equalization, go a long way toward explaining the differences in income per worker among them.[2] When considering the international movement of human capital and the growing international markets for particular high skills, the so-called brain drain is straightaway a form of maximizing economic behavior. In internal migration also, human capital is a critical explanatory factor. In solving the long-standing puzzle of the *residual*, where the rate of increase in output exceeds the rate of increase in inputs, it has contributed much. As a part of an all-inclusive concept of capital, advances in specification and measurement of the services of capital explain most of the observable economic growth.[3] Furthermore, it sets the stage for a generalized theory of capital accumulation in which investment resources are allocated in accordance with the priorities set by the relative rates of return on all material and human investment opportunities.[4]

There are the following particular implications of this proposition for planning and financing higher education:

1 The human capital that is formed by higher education is far from homogeneous. Parts of it are for consumption and parts are for production. Moreoever, both the consumer and producer components are of many different types. To lump them in allocating resources to higher education is bad economics.

2 The value of each type of human capital depends on the value of the services it renders and not on its original costs; mistakes in the composition and size of the stock of each type, once made, are sunk investments.

3 The formation of most of these types of capital requires a long horizon because the capabilities that the student acquires are part of him during the rest of his life.

4 The value of the benefits of higher education accruing to students privately consists of future earnings and of future non-pecuniary satisfactions. Although it is difficult to measure the latter, they are nevertheless real and important.

5 Although human capital as such cannot be bought and sold, it is possible to estimate the value of the producer services of this capital when they are priced in terms of wages and salaries in the labor market.

6 Human capital, like reproducible material capital, is subject to obsolescence. The traditional tax treatment of depreciation is outmoded inasmuch as it excludes human capital. Although earnings

foregone do not enter into taxable income, none of the direct private costs is treated as capital formation. The upper limit of the life of this capital is the remaining life span of individuals after they have completed their formal education. An increase in longevity may decrease the rate of depreciation; earlier retirements may work in the opposite direction. More important is the obsolescence from changes in demand for high skills, changes which are a consequence of the characteristics of our type of economic growth. It should be possible to provide instruction that would be less subject to this type of obsolescence than it is presently. Educational research should search for ways and means of improving higher education in this respect, by substituting long-life for short-life instructional components so that it can ride better the changing demands for high skills. Continuing education after graduation is a form of maintenance.

7   Capital formation by education sets the stage for thinking of education as an investment.

4   Major Functions of Higher Education

Each of these activities requires analysis to determine how efficiently it is organized and whether too few or too many resources are allocated to it. But it must be admitted that hard facts and valid inferences pertaining to these issues are scarce. What is an efficient organization of each of these three activities in higher education, thinking in terms of scale of organization, specialization, location of colleges and universities, and importantly, the *complementarity between the discovery of talent, instruction, and research?*

Taking the system of higher education as it is, with regard to instruction, economists have made substantial progress in specifying and identifying the economic value of higher education as it increases the value productivity of human agents as workers. Less, although some progress, has been made in getting at the economic value of university research. The much neglected activity is that of discovering talent. It, too, can be approached by treating it as a process which provides students with opportunities to discover whether they have the particular capabilities that are required for the type and level of education at which they are working.

The value of the research function has received a lot of puffing but little analysis. It has prestige, but what about performance? With regard to organized agricultural research, where it is a part of land grant universities, there are some studies with some hard facts. The payoff on this type of research has been high.[5] But there are no economic studies to my knowledge of other types of organized university research. Is it organized efficiently in terms of combinations of scientific talent, scale of organization, complementarity with Ph.D. research and with other research centers, and division of labor between basic and applied research? Is it for profit or on public account? Despite the importance of these questions and the wide array of experience from which we can learn, scientists are woefully unscientific in the impressionistic answers they give to this question.[6]

The economic value of instruction is appropriately considered under the section on the rate of return.

There are many signs that indicate that one of the strongest features of U.S. higher education is in discovering talent. The payoff to additional resources used for this purpose is still in all probability very high. If so, three implications are worthy of note: (1) relatively more resources should be committed to this activity; (2) resources should be allocated specifically to support it; and (3) the organization and budgets of higher education should be planned to perform this activity efficiently.

5 Measured Productivity from Higher Education

It follows that if the price of this labor rises and if its productivity remains constant (other things unchanged), the price of the services it renders must rise; that is, the cost of higher education per student must rise. The crude facts, as we observe them, are consistent with this proposition. But these facts do not measure changes in the quality of the educational product which has been rising in many fields. Advances in knowledge are probably the main reason; and here we have a strong clue to the complementarity between instruction and research.

Nor do we know the possibilities of economizing on the labor entering into education by substituting other educational inputs for this labor or by reorganizing the educational process and thereby obtaining gains in the productivity of teachers and students in terms of the time they spend teaching and learning. These possibilities are undoubtedly of substantial importance, but it is doubtful that they will be found predominantly in new learning machines, television instruction, or in the computerization of educational activities; instead, they are mainly to be had by many small innovative reorganizations of the instructional interplay between teachers and students that will reduce the time spent by each in achieving a given educational product.

The reasons why it is so difficult to make these gains are fairly obvious. The product of teaching and learning is highly labor intensive, like that of barbers. At best, it would appear that there is little room for non-labor inputs. Nor are cheaper labor inputs the solution, that is, substituting low quality, less costly teachers and students for high quality persons. Although the difficulties here may seem insurmountable, it should be remembered that in classical economics, manufacturing carried the promise of decreasing cost whereas the outlook for agriculture was increasing cost per unit of product. But economic development in Western countries has more than offset the drag of diminishing returns to land in farming, and the gains in labor productivity in agriculture have been exceeding those in manufacturing. Not so long ago, the conventional view was that the retail sector could not gain appreciably from labor-saving developments, but it has in fact made much progress on this score. The present conventional view that the educational sector is destined to continue as it is in the amount of time required of students and teachers may also prove wrong.

The major real problems awaiting solution in higher education in economizing on the time of students and teachers are in large part a consequence of the traditional decision-making process in colleges and universities, the ambiguity which conceals the value of the product that is added, and the lack of strong incentives to innovate. On theoretical grounds there is room for more progress. Decision-making theory is not empty as a guide in improving the traditional process. A theory of the allocation of time is now at hand for determining how efficiently the time of students is allocated.[7] Requiring college students to spend twenty hours a week in class, as is required of many students, may be anything but efficient. The implication is that we might find fifteen, or ten, or even fewer hours more efficient. But we really will not know what could be achieved by such innovations until we have undertaken carefully planned experiments to discover what the results would be. The specifications of the value added to the capabilities of students by the educational process are being clarified, for example, in the search for a better mix of instructional components which would have a longer life than the present mix.

6　Do Not Omit Earnings Foregone by Students

In 1959–60, US "direct" expenditures for higher education minus auxiliary enterprises and capital outlay plus implicit interest and depreciation of physical property came to about $4,350 million, but the earnings foregone by college and university students exceeded this figure. Yet we omit these earnings foregone in our planning and financing approach to higher education. We keep them concealed by not entering them in our college and university plans or in our national income and capital formation accounts. The omission of these earnings foregone by students seriously distorts our view of the economics of higher education. Let me turn to the major implications of this omission of earnings foregone: (1) higher education (leaving university research aside) is more than twice as costly as is revealed in our budgets; (2) it is simply impossible to plan efficiently when over half of the real costs are treated as "free" resources; (3) there is no incentive to economize on the time of students in educational planning under existing circumstances; (4) educational planners receive no signals that the value of the time of students is rising relative to material inputs; (5) the rate of return to investment in higher education is grossly overestimated when earnings foregone are omitted; (6) so-called free education is far from free to students and their parents, which in turn implies that many families with low incomes cannot afford to forego the earnings of their children; and (7) savings, investment, and capital formation are all substantially understated in terms of national accounting.[8]

7 Projections of Demand for Higher Education Beset by Uncertainty

These projections are conjectures that can be very misleading. As a consequence, flexibility is undervalued and formulas are overvalued in educational planning. Economic logic tells us that in coping with uncertainty it is worthwhile to remain sufficiently flexible so that one can act efficiently when new and better information becomes available. But such flexibility is not costless; thus, the prospective additional gains from flexibility must be reckoned against the additional costs. Furthermore, to the extend that these projections can be made more reliable, the need for and cost of acquiring flexibility can be reduced.

The now available projections of the demands for higher education can be substantially improved. What we have are numbers which are not a reliable source of information. The concept of demand for education requires clarification; as it is presently used, it is beset with ambiguity. So-called need is not demand, because the concept of demand implies prices and quantities. But the relevant prices, whether they are shadow prices or actual prices, are not specified in the numbers which are being projected. The demand behavior of students for places in colleges and universities is a useful approach. Another approach is to determine the demands for the particular capabilities that come from the teaching and learning in higher education – demands that are derived from the production activity of the economy. But it is unfortunately true that there is as yet no satisfactory theory which connects ex post rates of increase in the demands for the satisfactions and earnings that accrue to college and university students with future rates of increase in these demands. Projections, of course, abound, but they are in principle as naïve as exponential population projections. You can take your choice, and if you happen to be correct, it will not be because of reason but because of luck. Manpower studies do not provide the answer, nor are the sophisticated programming models as yet providing an answer.

The rise in income per family undoubtedly increases the demand for the consumer satisfactions from higher education; the income elasticity of the demand for this consumer component is probably such that it is a superior good with a fairly high elasticity. But the demand for the producer component is very hard to determine because it is derived from the production activity of the economy and because the sources of change in these derived demands over time are still far from clear. Furthermore, the observable responses of students to the array of different prices that students pay for higher education are confounded by all manner of pricing policies and changes in these policies over time.

The lessons to be drawn from all of this are as follows:

1 The game of numbers as it is now played produces unreliable projections of the demand for higher education.
2 Some improvements can be achieved by clarifying and analyzing the economic demands in terms of the factors that determine changes in these demands.
3 But this approach is also severely limited because as yet there is no economic theory for determining the changes in the demands for higher education that are derived from our type of economic growth.
4 At best, any long-term projections of the demands for higher education are subject to many unknowns and to much uncertainty.
5 To be prepared to cope with these, it is better to pay the price of developing flexibility in the institutional structure of higher education, and also within colleges and universities, so that they will be capable of adapting their activities to new information, with regard to demands, as it becomes available.
6 Fixed formulas, like the parity formula in agriculture, lead to inflexibility and, over time, to serious distortions. They should be avoided in planning and financing higher education.

8 Financing Higher Education[9]

The advantages of this concept are that it has a firm foundation in economic theory, that it is applicable to both private and public allocative decisions, that in practical economic affairs it is widely used and understood, and that it leads to efficient allocations when all investments are made in accordance with the priorities set by the relative rates of return on alternative investment opportunities. Although it is difficult to use this concept as an allocative guide in view of the way in which education is organized, it is the economist's key in solving the problem of allocating resources; the solution is in equalizing the rates by always allocating investment resources in favor of the highest rate of return.

The practical difficulties in using this concept in education are predominantly consequences of a type of organization which is not designed to provide most of the necessary information and which lacks strong incentives to use the available information. Consider the cost of college and university instruction: earnings foregone by students, which are well over half of the real cost, are concealed; the depreciation and the rate of interest on the investment in buildings used for classrooms, laboratories, offices, and libraries are also as a rule concealed; the cost of university research and of discovering talent is rarely identified and separated from the cost of instruction. It is also true that the price that the student pays for educational services is only remotely related to the real cost of producing them, and therefore private choices by students, however efficient they are privately, are not necessarily efficient socially. Nor can the allocation of public funds to higher education be made socially efficient under circumstances where information on cost is so inadequate. The organization of higher education provides little or no economic information on returns, pecuniary and non-pecuniary, to guide students in making their career choices – not even the starting salaries of college graduates. Foundation and public subsidies are accepted and awarded to students to get them to enter particular fields without regard to the depressing effects of the increase in supply that is thereby induced upon the lifetime earnings of those who are and will be in these fields. There is inadequate information on the effects upon returns of differences in innate ability of students, in their motivations, and of the differences in the effectiveness of college teaching. Although these returns are subject to uncertainty, it is not a unique, distinguishing mark, because other investments are also subject to uncertainty. In general, colleges and universities and public bodies that provide funds are poorly organized to provide the necessary information on cost and returns or to use whatever information is available.

Meanwhile, economists, who have taken a hand in estimating the returns to education, have made substantial progress.[10] These estimates and those pertaining to cost have reached the stage where they are becoming useful allocative guides. But so far, the returns from the non-pecuniary satisfactions that accrue to students have not been reckoned. Nor are the estimates of social returns in good repair.

Turning back to the rate of return as the central concept, the alternative investment opportunities are of course numerous, not only between human and material capital but within each of these two sets. Is there evidence that private educational choices are privately efficient; that is, do private rates of return on education tend (1) to be equal among educational options and (2), to be comparable to private rates of return on other private investments? The evidence implies inefficiencies (see table 2.4.1). To illustrate, consider the available estimates on alternatives within education: In terms of equalizing the rates of return, elementary and secondary schooling appear to have priority. All of the estimates with which I am familiar show the highest rates of return to elementary schooling. We need to remind ourselves that there are still some children who are not completing the elementary grades. Even more important, perhaps, is the underinvestment in the quality of elementary schooling in many rural areas.[11] While the private rate of return on the investment resources entering into high school education is not as high as that on elementary schooling, it nevertheless appears to be about twice as high as that indicated for private investment in completing college. In table 2.4.1, the private rates of return to white males after personal taxes, in 1958, are 28 percent for high school graduates and 14.8 percent for college graduates. Thus, in allocating resources within education with a view to equalizing the rates of return, the implication is that elementary and secondary schooling appears to be subject to underinvestment relative to higher education. Nevertheless, comparing columns (2) and (4) in table 2.4.1, the private rates of return to white male college graduates after personal taxes, without any allowance for the private satisfactions that accrue to students, are on a par with the private implicit rates of return to material capital *before personal taxes* on the income from this capital.

9   Education Changes Distribution of Personal Income

The general extension of education and the additional earnings from these forms of human capital have probably been a major factor during

Table 2.4.1 Estimates of Private Rates of Return, United States

Year	High School Graduates: White Males after Personal Taxes (%)[a] (1)	College Graduates: White Males after Personal Taxes (%)[a] (2)	Corporate Manufacturing Firms after Profit Taxes but before Personal Taxes (%)[b] (3)	U.S. Private Domestic Economy: Implicit Rate of Return after Profit Taxes but before Personal Taxes (%)[c] (4)
1939	16	14.5		...
1949	20	13.+		12.6
1956	25	12.4	7.0	14.4 (1955–56)
1958	28	14.8	(for	12.3 (1957–58)
1959	Slightly higher than in 1958	Slightly higher than in 1958	period	9.7
1961	Slightly higher than in 1958	Slightly higher than in 1958	1947–57)	11.2 (1960–61)
1963–65	...	...		13.3

Sources:
[a] From Becker, *Human Capital*, p. 128.
[b] Also from ibid., in which Becker draws on a study by G. J. Stigler (see p. 115 and n. 2).
[c] From Jorgenson and Griliches "The Explanation of Productivity Change," p. 268.

recent decades in changing the distribution of personal income. Not only has the supply of educational opportunities increased markedly over time, but the inequality in the differences in the supply of these opportunities has been reduced, without doubt, in elementary and secondary schooling.

The differences in the innate capacity of individuals to benefit from investment in education probably remains unchanged for the population as a whole, but the distribution of this capacity of those attending college changes over time as the proportion of individuals of particular ages attending college classes increases. Becker treats human capital as the key to a theory of the distribution of personal income.

Higher education is certainly *not neutral* in its personal income distribution effects; some individuals and families undoubtedly gain future income streams partly at the expense of others. Whether it is, in general, regressive or progressive depends on the distribution of the personal costs and personal benefits of higher education. There are many opinions but few hard facts on this issue.[12]

In clarifying public policy choices it is necessary to distinguish between the objective of economic efficiency and that of reducing the inequality in the distribution of personal income. There are circumstances when a particular policy will advance the economy toward both objectives; for example, when there is excessive unemployment, a fiscal-monetary policy that reduces such unemployment would normally contribute to both objectives. Similarly, when there is an underinvestment in elementary schooling (that is, a high rate of return to additional investment in such schooling) a policy to invest more in universal elementary schooling of high quality contributes both to economic efficiency and to reducing the inequality in personal income. But under other circumstances the attainment of one of these objectives is in part at the expense of the other. At this point, the rating of social values underlying such policy choices enters.

I assume that it is not necessary to belabor the fact that economic efficiency rates high among the social values of our society.[13] This assumption is implicit in my formulation of the six propositions already considered; the principal implications derived from them all pertain to economic efficiency. But how high a social value does our society place on reducing the inequality in personal income? The rating of this social value is not so clear as that which is socially assigned to economic efficiency. Nevertheless, there are strong indications that it also is an important social value. I shall proceed on the assumption that there is a social preference for less inequality in the distribution of personal income than that which prevails presently. Moreover, I shall assume that this social preference is such that society is prepared, should it be necessary, to forego some economic efficiency to bring about somewhat less inequality in the distribution of personal income. Proceeding on this assumption, it becomes relevant and important to determine what the income distribution effects of higher education are, and how they can be altered for the better at the least cost in terms of allocative efficiency.

Although higher education is in all probability far from neutral in its effects on the distribution of personal income, it is surprising how little is actually known about these effects. It could be that the financing of higher education is in general regressive. It is plausible that it is regressive because it adds to the value of the human capital of those who attend college relative to those who do not go to college, and because it increases the lifetime earnings of college graduates in part at the expense of others. Higher education provides educational services predominately for students from middle and upper income families; a part of the cost of these educational services is paid for by taxes on poor families. It appears to be true that a much smaller proportion of the undergraduate students in publicly financed institutions receive financial aid, for reasons of their having inadequate income, than do undergraduate students in private colleges and universities. In either case, the financing is such that substantial amounts of valuable assets are being transferred by society to a particular intellectually elite set of individuals.

In retrospect, given the type of growth that has characterized our economy and the remarkable increase in the stock of education per worker in the labor force, the gains in elementary and secondary schooling and in higher education taken as a whole have been instrumental, it seems to me, in reducing the inequality in the distribution of personal income. The hypothesis which I proposed some time back with regard to this issue continues to be consistent with the evidence thus far available. [14] In terms of the income effects of additional education per worker, this hypothesis is: The rise in the investment in education relative to that invested in non-human capital increases total earnings relative to total property income, and property income is distributed much less equally than the earnings of persons from labor. Therefore, investment in schooling reduces the inequailty in the distribution of personal income. The hypothesis proposed here is that these patterns of investment are an important part of the explanation of the observed reductions in the inequality of distribution of personal income.

Becker and Chiswick have been analyzing the effects of schooling on the distribution of personal income. For adult white males and for the states within the United States, they report that "about one-third of the differences in inequality between states is directly explained by schooling, one-third directly by the residual, and the remaining one-third by both together through the positive correlation between them.[15]

In a more recent report, Chiswick gives the following results from his analysis of North–South differences: "The education component . . . can 'explain' half of the North–South differences in income inequality. The proportion is slightly lower for white males and slightly higher for all males."[16]

But neither the hypothesis which I have advanced nor the evidence on the income effects of schooling from Becker and Chiswick implies that the income effects of higher education per se are progressive rather than regressive. It is indeed regrettable that studies to determine what these income effects are have not been undertaken.

In developing an analytical approach bringing economic theory to bear on the effects of human capital on the distribution of personal income, the recent pioneering work of Becker is full of promise.[17] His distinction between the "egalitarian" and "elite" views is helpful in clarifying the problem. He identifies the egalitarian view with supply conditions; the objective is to reduce the inequality in the differences in the supply of educational opportunities. The elite view, on the other hand, turns on the demand conditions; the actual investment and earning differences are primarily a consequence of differences in the capacity of individuals to benefit from investment in education and from other forms of human capital. What Becker's analytical approach will show when it is applied to higher education is still in the realm of unfinished business.

10   Searching for Solutions

My list of problems that await solution is indicated by the implications that have been derived from the preceding propositions. Although it is a long list, it consists of two major parts in terms of economic logic. The first part pertains to resources for higher education allocated in accordance with the test of economic efficiency; the second part pertains to allocations that reduce the inequality in the distribution of personal income. Rest assured, I shall not present a national budget for higher education all properly allocated. I shall try, however, to clarify some of the organizational changes that would strengthen the tendency toward a more efficient allocation of resources in the area of higher education.

The purpose of the organizational changes on which I shall concentrate is to improve the possibilities of making optimum allocative decisions pertaining to higher education. The substantive changes relate to economic incentives and information. The decisions that are dependent on these incentives and the state of information consist of economic decisions by students, college and university administrators, and public (social) bodies. The ideal, from an economist's point of view, is a form of organization that would assure the necessary incentives coupled with optimum information in allocating investment resources to higher education in accordance with the relative rates of return on alternative investment opportunities, an organization in which the rate of return is functionally the price at the intercept of the supply of education services and the demand for them.

But, in making these organizational changes, it will be important not to lose sight of the advantages of the existing organization of higher education that are consistent with this ideal. Among them are:

1   in terms of career choices, higher education in the United States offers students many options;
2   in discovering talent, it has in all probability no equal;
3   the process of admitting many students who do not graduate is not necessarily wasteful, especially when they can readily enter the labor force;
4   there is substantial economic complementarity between discovering talent and instruction and between research and instruction, despite the common view to the contrary;
5   although it is obvious that colleges and universities tend to serve an elite, measured in terms of intellectual capacity to benefit, they provide places for a much larger proportion of college age youth than is traditionally served, for example, in western Europe;
6   no college or university has a monopoly of the supply of these educational services, and, on the contrary, there are many more institutions than would be necessary to assure competition if it were strictly a business sector;
7   as suppliers of these services, colleges and universities show some tendency to adjust to changes in demand, although this tendency could be substantially strengthened;
8   last, and very important, there is much more economic competition within higher education, and between it and other sectors of the economy, than meets the eye.

Colleges and universities purchase virtually all of their instructional inputs in competitive markets. Most of the budget is for faculty, and the job market for their services in this country is actively competitive among colleges and universities and between them and government. Business, too, bids for many of these skills. The range in salaries is subject to some constraints, partly corrected by adjustments in work arrangements. The earnings foregone by students are also determined in a competitive job market. Surely it would be short sighted to overlook or impair these advantages in our quest to improve the possibilities of making optimum allocative decisions.

How, then, can we strengthen the tendency toward a more efficient allocation of resources? The required changes in organization to achieve this objective are fundamentally of two parts, namely, better economic incentives and better information for those who make the allocative decisions.

But who should make these allocative decisions? Who is best qualified? There are those who contend that students and their families are best qualified. To support this contention, they appeal to consumer sovereignty and to private self-interest for privately efficient investment in education. Others contend that there are external economies or social benefits that accrue not to the student but to others in society and that these decisions can best be made by public or other social bodies. Those who know and administer the affairs of our colleges and universities see the importance of academic entrepreneurship in managing this complex set of activities, and it can be argued that they are best qualified.

How much truth is there in each of these contentions?

11   On Student Sovereignty

The key to student sovereignty is the private self-interest of students, which provides the necessary economic rationale. Student self-interest is also sufficient to bring about an efficient allocation of investment resources to education under the following conditions: (1) competition in producing educational services along with efficient prices of these services, (2) students acquiring optimal information, (3) an efficient capital market serving students, and (4) no social benefits (losses) from higher education.

A clear view of the gains to be had from hitching higher education to the private self-interest of students is blurred by arguments about the underlying conditions. But surely competitive pricing of educational services is in the realm of possibilities. Student loans from public and private sources can be devised to supply the necessary capital. How to reckon the social benefits (losses) of higher education is much more difficult.

In enlarging the scope and improving the performance of student sovereignty in allocating resources in higher education, the gaps in information and the distortions in incentives really matter.[18] On earnings foregone, students are well informed, but on their capabilities as students they are in doubt. With regard to the benefits that will accrue to them, the state of information is far from optimum. But much worse still is the lack of information on the differences in the quality of the educational services of different colleges and universities. Nowhere are students confronted by prices for these services that are equal to the real cost of producing them, and therefore the prices to which they respond are not efficient prices. As a consequence, no matter how efficient students are privately in their decisions, from the point of view of the economy as a whole, the allocation of resources to higher education will not be efficient.

12   On Reckoning Social Benefits and Losses

When this box is opened, we are in trouble. There is so little agreement on what this box contains. It is hard to distinguish between fact and fiction because the task of specifying and measuring these benefits has been grossly neglected. No wonder that claims and counterclaims are the order of the day. Most of us have a vested interest in higher education which is hard on objectivity. We are prone to lay claim to most of the advances in knowledge from which social benefits are undoubtedly large. University research and instruction are as a rule joint products; at the PhD level, graduate instruction and research are highly complementary. Are there identifiable social benefits from instruction that do not accrue to the college student from his private investment in education? It is plausible that having neighbors who are educated gives a family with such neighbors some positive satisfactions. It is also plausible that having co-workers who are educated is a source of additional satisfactions. It has been argued that parts of our public administration, namely, individuals coping with our "income tax forms," give rise to an administrative social benefit. But it is also plausible that the private benefits of education accruing to college students leave some other persons worse off. It is argued that some elementary school teachers *favor* the children from homes with (college) educated parents and that this favoritism leaves other children worse off. It is also alleged that in buying and selling homes some educated families act to exclude uneducated families from acquiring property (homes) in their particular neighborhoods.

But it is all too convenient to engage in double counting. Education, no doubt, increases the mobility of a labor force, but the benefits in moving to take advantage of better job opportunities are predominantly, if not wholly, private benefits. Educated labor has access to more of the relevant economic information than uneducated labor; but here, too, the benefits from this advantage presumably accrue to the persons who have the education. The cultural component embodied in higher education is the source of another benefit which invites double counting. There is also a tendency to claim that higher education makes for better citizens and for a better political democracy. It could be, but our belief with respect to these benefits is a matter of faith. It is not obvious that the political self-interest of college graduates results either in more responsible citizenship or in a more perfect government than the self-interest, say, of high school graduates.

To the extent that there are benefits that accrue to persons other than to the student acquiring the education, there could be underinvestment in higher education, regardless of how efficient students are privately in their investment in education. But there is an important set here that does not qualify, namely, those benefits accruing to the student, that make the private investment at least as good an investment, in terms of the rate of return, as that on alternative investment opportunities. Under these circumstances, presumably, privately efficient investment by students would suffice to bring forth the required education and assure whatever benefits might accrue to others, as was true in the case of Henry Ford and his very profitable Model T.

Suppose, however, that there are some potential college students who would not benefit enough privately to warrant the investment privately and that there were some social benefits which were sufficient, when added to the benefits accruing to the student privately, to raise the (social) rate of return sufficiently to make it a good investment by the standard set by the priorities of the relative rates of return on alternative investment opportunities. Under these circumstances, some underinvestment in higher education at the margin would be implied.

It follows, of course, that if there were no such social benefits, this bit of economic logic would be wholly empty. Thus, we are back to a question of fact – namely, are there in fact any such benefits that can be identified and that are subject to measurement?

13   On Academic Entrepreneurship

In terms of managerial decisions, the complexity of the modern university places an extraordinary burden on its administrators. But by what economic test are their decisions to be judged? The market test is severely circumscribed by the constraints placed on student sovereignty. Endowment income, private gifts, and public funds confound any economic test of an efficient allocation of resources. Innovation should be rewarded, but where are the incentives to innovate? Surely under the dynamic conditions that now characterize higher education, academic entrepreneurship should be given a vastly better opportunity than is presently possible to allocate resources efficiently.

These observations with respect to student sovereignty, social benefits, and academic entrepreneurship would appear to lend support to the following organizational changes in higher education.

The Private Decision Domain of Students

In providing economic incentives that would be allocatively efficient, the ideal price to students for the educational services they acquire should be neither more nor less than the real cost of producing these services. But much of the argument on the differences between private and public tuitions is beside the point. Equalization of tuitions would merely replace one type of price distortion by another type because of the marked differences in the quality and real cost of the educational services that colleges and universities supply.

This important organizational change implies, however, several complements: (1) that there be developed a capital market that would provide funds to students so they could invest in themselves, which would call for large increases in funds for public loans to students in view of the limitations of the private capital market, (2) that a program of private and public subsidies would be required to finance those, and only those, qualified students who for welfare or social efficiency reasons should attend college but who privately would not enroll, even if there were student loans, and (3) that although the improvement in information that is implicit in the change in pricing set forth above would be very substantial, much more would have to be spent in moving to an optimum in producing and distributing the other types of information already referred to.

The Social Benefits of Higher Education

In producing these education services, the required organizational changes pertaining to incentives and information are not easy to determine. Consider the problem that arises in planning and financing these components so that public and social bodies would become efficient in allocating investment resources for these purposes: what are the pertinent educational activities that render social benefits? University research is in substantial part one of them. So is a part of the activity pertaining to the discovery of talent. Let me elaborate briefly on why this may be true.

My conception of the cost and returns pertaining to the *discovery of talent* could qualify here. There are many colleges that admit at least two freshmen for everyone who will survive to graduation. If these colleges charged full costs, I would assume that this ratio of entering freshmen to graduating seniors would decline sharply – and suppose then that for every ten freshmen, nine could graduate. Presently, the half of entering freshmen who discover that they lack the capabilities and motivation to complete college drop out and enter the labor market, benefiting sufficiently from the year or more they spent in college to have made their private investment in that amount of college work a good investment privately, although when the subsidy entering into their instruction is taken into account, it was in itself a poor investment. But suppose now that out of the entering freshmen who would not have sought admission at full costs there were a substantial number of students (say, a tenth of the seniors who complete college) who did not know they had the necessary capabilities. These discovered students could (should) pay full cost; but they would not have become college educated had it not been for the extra cost of the discovery process. It would be a matter for public policy to decide whether this extra cost was worthwhile. A part of instruction may also belong here; but the instruction that accrues wholly to the benefit of students is excluded. It must be admitted that it is exceedingly difficult to specify the particular types of information and the nature of the incentives that would prove strong and clear in attaining these purposes. Here we have one of the major unsolved problems in planning and financing higher education.

Academic entrepreneurship can be made much less frustrating and at the same time much more efficient, once the private decision making domain of students is made subject to the constraints of a pricing policy, complemented by adequate student loans and by subsidies to attain the particular welfare and social efficiency purposes set forth above. But more than this would be required in terms of information and incentives. The value of the time of students would have to enter; it is, however, easy to measure, using earnings foregone. The value of faculty time is also readily available information, in view of the open market competition for their services; but the internal organization of colleges and universities is anything but efficient in allocating their services within the institution. The most important informational component that is lacking is the *value added* by the instruction, research, and the activity which I have called "discovering talent." But if we put our minds to it, I am sure we could do a good deal in determining the amount of value added by each of these different activities and proceed from there to internal organizational changes that would provide incentives to take advantage of such information in our academic entrepreneurial and management endeavors.

Notes and References

1 G. L. S. Shackle, "Policy, Poetry and Success," *Economic Journal*, 76 (Dec. 1966).

2 Here I am indebted to Professor Anne Krueger for her paper, "Factor Endowments and *Per Capita* Income Differences among Countries" (unpublished MS, Department of Economics, University of Minnesota, 1967).

3 See Dale W. Jorgenson and Zvi Griliches, "The Explanation of Productivity Change," *Review of Economic Studies*, 34 (July 1967), 249–83.

4 See above, Part II, No. 3, "The Rate of Return in Allocating Investment Resources to Education."

5 Theodore W. Schultz, "World Agriculture in Relation to Population Science, Economic Disequilibrium and Income Inequality: Reflections and Unsettled Questions," Part II (unpublished paper presented at International Association of Agricultural Economists, Sydney, Australia, Aug. 1967).

6 For a thoughtful exception see Harvey Brooks, "Can Science be Planned?", in *Problems of Science: Seminar at Jouy-en-Josas on Science* (OECD, Paris, 1967).

7 Gary S. Becker, "A Theory of the Allocation of Time," *Economic Journal*, 75 (Sept. 1965), 493–517.

8 See the excellent treatment of these issues by Simon Kuznets in *Modern Economic Growth* (Yale University Press, New Haven, Conn., 1965), pp. 228–34.

9 For a more extended treatment of this approach see above, Part II, No. 3.

10 See especially Gary S. Becker, *Human Capital* (Columbia University Press, New York, 1967); and Giora Hanoch, "Personal Earnings and Investment in Schooling" (PhD dissertation, Department of Economics, University of Chicago, 1965).

11 See Theodore W. Schultz, "Underinvestment in the Quality of Schooling: The Rural Farm Areas," in *Increasing Understanding of Public Problems and Policies* (Farm Foundation, Chicago, Ill., 1964); and Finis Welch, "The Determinants of the Return to Schooling in Rural Farm Areas, 1959" (PhD dissertation, University of Chicago, 1966).

12 For a general approach to the many factors entering here, see Mary Jean Bowman and C. Arnold Anderson, "Distributional Effects of Educational Problems," in *Income Distribution Analysis* (N.C. State University, Raleigh, 1966), pp. 177–214.

13   A. L.Macfie, *Economic Efficiency and Social Welfare* (Oxford University Press, London, 1943).

14   Theodore W. Schultz, "Reflections on Investment in Man," *Journal of Political Economy*, 70, Part II, Suppl. (Oct. 1962), 2.

15   Gary S. Becker and Barry R. Chiswick, "Education and the Distribution of Personal Income," *American Economic Review*, 56 (May 1966), 368.

16   Barry R. Chiswick, "Human Capital and the Distribution of Personal Income by Regions" (PhD dissertation, Columbia University, New York, 1967), p. 35.

17   Gary S. Becker, "Human Capital and the Personal Distribution of Income: An Analytical Approach" (W. S. Woytinsky Lecture No. 1, University of Michigan, Ann Arbor, 1967).

18   See E. G. West, "Private versus Public Education," *Journal of Political Economy*, 72 (Oct. 1964), 465–75.

5

*Reckoning Education as Human Capital**

The mainstream of the analytical work on human capital pertains to the economic properties of education. My reflections on this and related work are threefold. I shall begin with a comment on the advances in economic knowledge from this work coupled with some observations on its apparent shortcomings; I shall, then, consider briefly aspects of the aggregation problem in the treatment of human capital, whatever its source, in analyzing costs and returns, economic growth, migration, educated labor in a production function, and of human capital in explaining the personal distribution of income. Thirdly, I shall direct attention to some major omissions.

1   As Economic Knowledge

There is the rediscovery of Margaret Reid's *Economics of Household Production*.[1] The advances are mainly joint products of theoretical and empirical analysis. Those that stem from theoretical analysis are predominantly the work of Gary S. Becker. Beginning in the area of investment in human capital, Becker distinguished between specific and general human capital forms. Next he recognized the importance of earnings foregone in an array of economic activities and developed a theory for the allocation of time.[2]

Clearly, in economic thinking and measuring, the concept of human capital is a source of many new analytical insights with respect to particular classes of economic behavior. Seminal economic properties are being attributed to human capital. Mark Blaug, in his *Economics of Education*,[3] reviews the progress in this area[4]. His annotated bibliography lists literally several hundred contributions.[5] In determining the role of human capital in the comparative advantage of nations, we turn to

* First published in *Education Income, and Human Capital* (National Bureau of Economic Research, New York, 1970), pp. 297–306.

Kenen. Human capital has received even more attention in analyzing international migration, as is clear from the survey by Scott. The findings of Krueger, in her pioneering paper on factor endowments and per capita income, attribute an important new dimension to human capital. Her conclusion is "that the difference in human resources between the United States and the less-developed countries accounts for more of the difference in *per capita* income than all of the other factors combined."[6] While we await confirmation of her findings, it behooves us to begin thinking through the radical economic implications of her conclusions for economic development. In explaining the personal distribution of income, first Mincer,[7] and more recently, Becker[8] and Chiswick[9] have turned to human capital. Advances in economic knowledge pertaining to internal migration keyed to education and to costs of migrating as a form of human capital are also impressive (Sjaastad,[10] Bowman and Myers,[11] Schwartz,[12] and others). Needless to say, there are also other classes of economic behavior and approaches that stem from human capital.

But when we turn to the other side of the coin of these discoveries, there are growing pains, omissions, and a generation gap between those who espouse human capital and those who guard the establishment. Although the guardians of capital theory and economic growth theory may be defending a weak fort, the walls have not come tumbling down.

The beauty of accounting and discounting is that we can take the cost of education or we can transform the earnings from education and call it human capital. But this acquired beauty only conceals the difference between them where there is economic growth. Then, too, the fine art of capital aggregation hides the key to the economic information that makes for economic growth. The aggregation of human capital from education is no exception. As an input, it is well behaved in a production function and it contributes to the output, thus adding to our confidence that educated labor matters in production. But it does not tell us whether all or only a part of this education is worthwhile. Studies of international migration have not been designed to determine whether a well behaved international market for particular high skills is emerging. The going prices for high skills are not made explicit. Nor has the introduction of human capital in analyzing international trade revealed the effects that trade has upon the prices of high skills. Then, too, we consider only a part of education and find it convenient to neglect only parts, notably the large investment in the education of women. By concentrating on education, we are in danger of losing sight of other sources of human capital and, not seeing their contributions, credit some of them to education.

2 Aggregation Ambiguities

It will not do to continue to by-pass the ambiguities of capital theory or of capital in economic growth models because human capital, as a part of it, is subject to the same ambiguities. The different faces of capital, both theoretically and empirically, lack analytical integrity. What they tell us about economic growth, which is a dynamic process, are inconsistent stories. As the alternative investment opportunities change over time, it alters the difference between the factor cost of a particular form of capital and the discounted value of the stream of services that it renders. But worse still is the capital homogeneity assumption underlying capital theory and the aggregation of capital homogeneity assumption underlying capital theory and the aggregation of capital in economic growth models. As Hicks[13] would have it, capital homogeneity is the disaster of capital theory. This assumption is demonstrably inappropriate in analyzing economic growth in a dynamic world that is afloat on capital inequalities, whether the capital aggregation is in terms of factor costs or in terms of the discounted value of the lifetime services of its many parts. Nor would a catalogue of all existing models prove that these inequalities are equals. But why try to square the circle? If we were unable to observe these inequalities, we would have to invent them because they are the mainspring of economic growth. They are the mainspring because they are the compelling economic force of growth. Thus, what is interesting and what matters in economic growth is concealed by capital aggregation.

One of the major advances of recent years in economic knowledge is the approximate solution of the problem of the residual. Jorgenson and Griliches have shown us a way of explaining productivity change.[14] The improvement in the quality of labor is an important part of the explanation and this part is a consequence of investment in human agents, restricted in their empirical work to education. A decade ago the then growing awareness of investment in human capital followed the observed rise in the quality of labor, and now we have fortified the quality approach in explaining productivity change. The improvements in the quality of nonhuman capital have, also, been large, perhaps a good deal larger than the best available estimates indicate. But the investment activities that account for this part of the additional quality have not been adequately clarified. In large measure, these activities pertain to advances in scientific and technological knowledge, advances which are truly, in some ultimate sense, a consequence of investment in the scientific skills of man.

Now that we have disposed of the residual, where do we go from here? Clearly, so it seems to me, the real unfinished business is to reckon the costs of and returns to each of these quality components along with the traditional components. But it cannot be done with the family of growth models that presently dominate the literature in economics. These models, including capital theory, begin with the wrong questions for the purpose at hand. What we want to know are the relative rates of return to investment opportunities and what determines the change in the pattern of these rates over time. To get on with this analytical task we must build models that will reveal the very inequalities that we now conceal, and proceed to an explanation of why they occur and why they persist under particular dynamic conditions. The solution obviously is not in the art of producing ever larger capital aggregates.

The growth problem, thinking in terms of economic decisions, requires an investment approach to determine the allocation of investment resources in accordance with the priorities set by the relative rates of return on alternative investment opportunities. It is applicable not only to private decisions, but also to public decisions guided by economic planning. The production and distribution of public goods (services) are a necessary part of the process, for example, the investment in research where the fruits of it do not accrue to the researcher or his financial sponsor but are captured by many producers and consumers. Thus, we move toward Harry Johnson's "generalized capital accumulation approach."[15]

While this approach may be paved with good economic logic, it is in fact a rough road with many detours. For particular investments, and there are many such in the domain of human capital, the value of the investment is exceedingly hard to come by. It is all too convenient to leave the hard ones out, yet each and every omission falsifies the true picture of the full range of alternative investment opportunities. In analyzing education, we cling to differential earnings and leave aside differential satisfactions with no more than a pious acknowledgment that they exist. Another rough part of this road is the determination of investment sources and the price of each. The facile assumption of a well behaved capital market serving the formation of human capital is far from true. When it comes to private investment in human capital, poor people are subject to a great deal of capital rationing. Bruce Gardner's analysis of farm family income inequalities in the United States suggests that neither schooling nor migration has been a solution because of the inability of those poor people to respond to shifts in the structure of demand for skills by migrating or acquiring additional skills.[16] The explanation is to be found in capital rationing.

3   Some Omissions

Let me turn to some major omissions in the work on education, thinking in terms of the formation of human capital. If one were to judge from the work that is being done, the conclusion would be that human capital is the unique property of the male population, that the only services rendered by it are earnings, that the instructional activities of the educational enterprise are the only source of the educational capital produced by formal education, that the response to changes in educational investment opportunities is restricted to the private decisions of students of their parents, and that advances in knowledge are not altering the quality and value of instruction. There is enough substance to this image of what is being done for us to be troubled.

If it is true that investment in human beings is only for males, we would do well to drop the term "human capital" and replace it with "male capital." It would serve notice that human capital is sex specific! Despite all of the schooling of females and other expenditures on them, they appear to be of no account in the accounting of human capital. If females are capital free, in view of all that is spent on them, we are in real trouble analytically, unless we can show that it is purely for current consumption. There is no way of hiding the fact that females attend elementary and high school to the same extent as males and probably perform a bit better than males.

In college attendance they fall behind somewhat; of the 4.9 million college students enrolled in October 1966, about two-fifths were women. Even so, in terms of median years of school completed, of all persons twenty-five years and older in the United States, females are ahead of males slightly and the difference in favor of females has been increasing over time.[17] Surely, it cannot be denied that the factor costs of all this schooling of females is real and large. Nor is it plausible that all of these direct and indirect costs are only for current consumption. The investment component must be large. But if there is little to show for it, how do we patch-up the economic behavioral assumption underlying the investment in education?

Mincer[18] and Becker[19] have each devoted some research to women. Mincer found that on-the-job training is not for women. Becker observes that the rate of return to female college graduates may not be lower than for males "because direct costs are somewhat lower and opportunity costs are much lower for women."[20] But differential earnings are a small part of the story. The two main reasons for the failure to get at the returns to schooling of women are, it seems to me, (1) concealment by aggregation and (2) the lack of any accounting of the differential satisfactions that correspond with the differentials in schooling.

There are many puzzles about the economic behavior of women that can be resolved once their human capital is taken into account. Young females leave the better parts of agriculture more readily than young males; these females have a schooling advantage and they are not held back by any specific on-the-farm training as are males. The explanation of the preponderance of women in most Negro colleges before school integration is to be found in the differences between the job opportunities open to Negro women and Negro men graduates. At a more general level, there is the slow, yet real, economic emancipation of women. It may be viewed as a consequence of growth and affluence. But it is also true that a part of this growth and increase in family income is some function of the rise in the education of women, much more than is revealed by the increasing participation of women in the labor force. At the micro level of the household there is the shift from household work to work for pay; while a part of the explanation is undoubtedly the relative decline in the price of the services rendered by consumer durables, an important part is a consequence of the rise in the value of the time of women which in turn is in large measure the result of the education of women.

Turning now to another major component that is omitted in our work, there is the human capital represented by human agents without any education and by children before they enter upon schooling. The distinction between people with some schooling and those with none, educated labor versus raw labor is useful for some analytical purposes as Welch has shown.[21] Pre-school children are also a form of human capital. I find it hard to believe that there is no economic rationality in the acquisition of this form of human capital. Surely parents derive some satisfactions from their pre-school children. But the acquisition of children has its price. An approach that treats the production of children, viewed as human capital, in all probability will tell us a great deal about the economics of family planning.[22] In determining the costs of children, it is already clear that the level of schooling of women and changes in job opportunities for women – or more generally, the economic emancipation of women – and the required school attendance of children, whether cultural or legal, are among the important cost factors.

My conclusions are in two parts. First, there is a class of research, which I have not discussed, in which the very idea of reckoning priorities violates the essence of the process of discovery. It is not possible to reckon priorities for this class because the problem to be solved is one of the unknowns awaiting to be discovered. Consider the original theoretical analysis of investment in human capital by Becker.[23] I think it is fair to say that he started with the aim of estimating the returns to college and high school education in the United States. In pursuing this aim, he discovered that the investment activities associated with education were akin to other investments in people and that all these activities had basic attributes in common for which received theory, tailored to investment in structures and equipment, required reformulation.[24] Then, later in pursuing the many implications of earnings foregone, he discovered the problem that could be solved by a theory of the allocation of time.[25] I find it intuitively plausible that advances pertaining to this part will come largely from microanalysis, mainly, in response to puzzles and paradoxes revealed by economic data, for example, Telser's[26] modification of specific human capital and its formation by firms in his search for the determinants of the differences in the rates of return in manufacturing. Thinking in terms of the activities of the household, it may prove especially rewarding in coping with human capital formation by the family to approach it as a part of the production activities of the household and, also, in getting at the satisfactions that it renders to the family in consumption.[27] The differences in the motivation of students in their school work associated with the differences in job market discrimination, following the approach of Welch, is another case in point.[28]

Turning to the second part of my conclusions; a good deal can be said for a reckoning of priorities. Specifically, from this limited endeavor at reckoning priorities, my conclusions are as follows:

(1) As a device for preliminary exploration, it is not wrong to use national aggregates whether it be to determine the costs and returns to higher education or to secondary schooling, or to ascertain the amount of human capital in commodities entering into international trade or that which highly skilled people who migrate possess or as a quality input in a national production function, *provided that such use is viewed as exploratory*. In fact, it has been a necessary first step in discovering whether or not there is any economic value in education or in other forms of human capital.

(2) Now that it is established that human capital is both real and important, the question becomes: where does it stand within the full range of alternative investment opportunities? In entering upon this analytical task, we are beset by the ambiguities of capital theory and of capital, including human capital aggregates, in economic growth models and in national accounting of change in the quality of labor. It is, also, true that the art of capital aggregation conceals a critical part of the information that we must have to understand and explain the dynamics of economic growth.

(3) An investment approach, not only to the many different forms of human capital but also to research activities and to traditional nonhuman forms, is in principle the next analytical step.

(4) In the work that has been done, the omission of human capital in females and in children before they enter upon schooling should give us pause. But this troublesome omission, so it seems to me, can be taken on, and the rewards in terms of additional knowledge are likely to be large.

Notes and References

1 Margaret G. Reid, *Economics of Household Production* (New York, 1934).
2 Gary S. Becker, "A Theory of the Allocation of Time," *Economic Journal*, 75 (Sept. 1965), 493–517.
3 M. Blaug, *Economics of Education* (Baltimore, Maryland, 1968).
4 Ibid., "Introduction," pp. 7–9.
5 M. Blaug, *Economics of Education: A Selected annotated Bibliography* (Oxford & New York, 1966). See also more recent mimeographed supplements by Blaug, bringing this bibliography up to date.
6 A. O. Krueger, "Factor Endowments and *Per Capita* Income Differences Among Countries," *Economic Journal*, 78 (Sept. 1968), 641–59; see p. 658.
7 Jacob Mincer, "Investment in Human Capital and Personal Income distribution," *Journal of Political Economy*, 66 (Aug. 1958), 281–302.
8 Gary S. Becker, "Human Capital and the Personal Distribution of Income: An Analytical Approach" (W. S. Woytinsky Lecture No. 1, University of Michigan, Ann Arbor, 1967).
9 Barry R. Chiswick, "Human Capital and the Distribution of Personal Income," unpublished doctoral dissertation (Department of Economics, Columbia University, 1967).
10 Larry A. Sjaastad, "Income and Migration in the United States," unpublished doctoral dissertation (Department of Economics, University of Chicago, 1961). Also "The Costs and Returns of Human Migration," *Journal of Political Economy*, 70, Supplement, No. 5, part 2 (Oct. 1962), 875–98.
11 Mary J. Bowman and Robert Myers, "Schooling Experience and Gain and Losses in Human Capital Through Migration," *Journal of the American Statistical Association*, 62 (Sept. 1967), 875–98.
12 Aba Schwartz, "Migration and Life Time Earnings in the US," unpublished doctoral dissertation (Department of Economics, University of Chicago, 1968).
13 John Hicks, *Capital and Growth* (Oxford, 1965), chapter III, see p. 35.
14 Dale W. Jorgenson and Zvi Griliches, "The Explanation of Productivity Change," *Review of Economic Studies*, 34 (3), No. 99 (July 1967). The references listed in this paper cover the relevant contemporary literature.

15 H. G. Johnson, "Towards a Generalized Capital Accumulation Approach to Economic Development," *The Residual Factor and Economic Growth* (OECD, Paris, 1964), pp. 219–25.

16 Bruce L. Gardner, "An Analysis of US Farm Family Income Inequality, 1950–1960," unpublished doctoral dissertation (Department of Economics, University of Chicago, 1968).

17 US Bureau of the Census, *Statistical Abstract of the United States, 1965*, table 147, p. 112.

18 Jacob Mincer, "On-the-Job Training: Costs, Returns and Some Implications," *Journal of Political Economy*, Supplement, 70 (Oct. 1962), see pp. 66–68.

19 Gary S. Becker, *Human Capital* (New York, 1964), pp. 100–102.

20 Ibid.

21 Finis Welch, "the Determinants of the Return to Schooling in Rural Farm Areas, 1959," unpublished doctoral dissertation (Department of Economics, University of Chicago, 1966).

22 T. Paul Schultz, *An Economic Model of Family Planning and Fertility* (The Rand Corporation, P-3862-1, Santa Monica, California, July 1968); also *A Family Planning Hypothesis and Some Empirical Evidence from Puerto Rico* (The Rand Corporation, M-5404, Santa Monica, California, Nov. 1967).

23 Gary S. Becker, "Investment in Human Capital: A Theoretical Analysis," *Journal of Political Economy*, 70, Supplement (Oct. 1962), pp. 9–49.

24 Here I have drawn upon Theodore W. Schultz, "Reflections on Investment in Man," *Journal of Political Economy*, 70 Supplement (Oct. 1962), p. 2.

25 Becker, "A Theory of the Allocation of Time."

26 L. G. Telser, "Some Determinants of the Rates of Return in Manufacturing," unpublished paper (Department of Economics, University of Chicago, Sept. 1968).

27 My reading of an unpublished paper by Gary S. Becker modifying consumption theory is an approach along these lines.

28 Finish Welch, "Labor-Market Discrimination: An Interpretation of Income Differences in Rural South," *Journal of Political Economy*, 75 (June 1967), 225–40.

6

Equity and Efficiency in
College Instruction[*]

It could be argued that higher education as it had developed in the United States is a "model" of competition and welfare inasmuch as college students have many subsidized options and no college or university has a monopoly of the supply of these educational services. There are more than 2,500 institutions competing for faculty and students[1], and they compete not only with each other but also with other sectors of the economy for talent and materials. They acquire virtually all their instructional inputs in competitive markets. Moreover, to the extent that growth enhances competition, higher education has been a growth sector par excellence with enrollment rising since 1940 from 1.5 million to more than 7 million students in 1968 (see table 2.6.1).

It is also true that in terms of career choices higher education in the United States not only offers students many options, but also subsidizes them, in part directly and nearly all of them indirectly, in large amounts. There is a strong presumption that the economic organization of higher education has a built-in tendency to be inefficient. It is certainly true that the social rates of return and private rates of return are not proportional in all higher educational activities. Furthermore, there is a tendency to transfer wealth in the form of human capital to select classes of the population.

In general, the private rates of return to investment in higher education tend to be comparable to the private rates of return to other private investments. Whether there are long-standing disparities among private rates of return to the various higher educational opportunities awaits disaggregation and analysis. The changing economy implies that certain disparities are inevitable. Richard Freeman's study (1971) shows, however, that as these disparities occur, the lags in adjustment are relatively short.[2] The efficiency with which public resources are allocated

*First published in *Journal of Political Economy*, 80, No. 3, Part 2 (May–June 1972), S2-S30. Reproduced by permission of University of Chicago Press. I benefited and gained assurance from the cogent criticism of Gary S. Becker, Richard B. Freeman, W. Lee Hansen, Robert W. Hartman, and T. Paul Schultz.

Table 2.6.1 US Higher Education, selected data for 1940 and 1968

	Public			Private			Total			Public/Private		
	1940 (1)	1968 (2)	1968/ 1940 (3)	1940 (4)	1968 (5)	1968/ 1940 (6)	1940 (7)	1968 (8)	1968/ 1940 (9)	1940 (10)	1968 (11)	1968/ 1940 (12)
a) Number of institutions	600	940	1.6	1,150	1,440	1.3	1,750	2,380	1.4	0.5	0.6	1.2
b) Enrollment (thousands)	800	4,850	6.1	700	2,110	3.0	1,490	6,960	4.7	1.1	2.3	2.0
c) Direct total instruction costs ($ million)	300	7,900	26.5	340	4,800	14.3	630	12,700	20.0	0.9	1.6	1.9
d) Net instruction expenditures ($ million)	230	6,710	30.0	250	4,070	16.6	470	10,780	22.8	0.9	1.6	1.8
e) Implicit interest, depreciation ($ million)	71	1,190	16.7	90	730	8.1	160	1,920	11.9	0.8	1.6	2.1
f) Tuition and fees ($ million)	55	1,210	22.0	150	2,180	15.0	200	3,390	16.9	0.4	0.6	1.5
g) Student aid expenditures ($ million)	7	330	47.4	22	390	17.6	29	720	24.8	0.3	0.9	2.7
h) Enrollment per institution	1,320	5,170	3.9	610	1,460	2.4	1,170	2,920	2.5	2.2	3.5	1.6
i) Per student direct total instruction costs ($)	370	1,630	4.4	480	2,270	4.7	420	1,820	4.3	0.8	0.7	0.9
j) Per student net instruction expenditures ($)	280	1,380	4.9	350	1,930	5.5	320	1,550	4.9	0.8	0.7	0.9
k) Per student interest and depreciation ($)	89	240	2.8	130	350	2.7	110	270	2.5	0.7	0.7	1.0
l) Per student tuition and fees ($)	69	250	3.6	210	1,030	4.9	140	490	3.6	0.3	0.2	0.7
m) Per student financial aid ($)	9	69	7.6	32	180	5.7	19	100	5.4	0.3	0.4	1.3

Note – Table prepared by Anne Williams. Data sources and bases of calculations are in Appendix. Col. 3 = col. 2 ÷ col. 1; col. 6 = col. 5 ÷ col. 4; col 9 = col. 8 ÷ col. 7; col. 10 = col. 1 ÷ col. 4; col. 11 = col. 2 ÷ col. 5; col. 12 = col. 11 ÷ col. 10.

to the many parts of higher education is another story. When it comes to equity consequences, the evidence is fragmentary; it is inconceivable, however, that they are neutral in their effects on the distribution of personal income.

The classical economists divided on the question of efficiency with respect to alternative ways of providing education.[3] This controversy is still with us.[4] Nor have the proponents of "equal educational opportunities" settled the problem of equity in distributing the benefits of education. The continuing disagreements suggest that we have not been asking the right questions. With respect to the United States, I have become convinced that the problems of efficiency and equity in higher education, especially as they have come to the forefront during recent decades, are in large part the consequences of modern increases in income. This view implies the following question: Under the changing conditions that characterize our economy, how efficient are we in allocating private and public resources to higher education and in using these resources to produce educational services? I believe the equity question should be formulated along similar lines.

With respect to the problems of disparities in the distribution of private and social costs and benefits, these disparities are strongly related to developments that characterize modern growth. When an economy arrives at an equilibrium that prevails over an extended period, it is in general true that the efficiency disparities tend to become small. But under conditions of modern growth, disequilibria are the order of the day and, although adjustments are made, new disparities continue to emerge. In approaching growth via the process of investment, what is required, ideally, is a generalized optimal investment model that encompasses both human and nonhuman capital and that accounts for all of the nonmarket benefits, including the personal satisfactions that accrue to students from their investment in higher education. But we will have to settle for less because of the limitations of the state of economic knowledge. I shall examine four interrelated issues: (1) three economic growth-education puzzles, (2) the rise in the student's opportunity cost and in his allocative benefits associated with growth, (3) the growth-related enlargement of the student's capacity to finance and to benefit from education, and (4) the equity-efficiency quandary in a growing economy.

1   Three Economic Growth-Education Puzzles

Growth is not an equilibrium state. For the purpose at hand, growth implies responses to investment opportunities in acquiring additional income streams at a price lower than the equilibrium price. In terms of investment decisions, growth is a consequence of the allocation of investment resources in accordance with the priorities set by the relative rates of return to alternative investment opportunities. The reciprocal of the highest rate of return option is, in theory and in fact, the lowest price of additional growth. On the one hand, investment in human capital by means of higher education occurs as a response to the demand derived from growth, and, on the other, it contributes to the growth of an economy. The particular acquired ability associated with higher education is, in all probability, complementary to the new, superior material inputs that have their origin in scientific advances and the associated developments in technology. Then, too, modern research and development activities are dependent upon particular subsets of these abilities.

Thus, a satisfactory theory of economic growth should explain the mechanism that determines the formation of human and nonhuman capital, including the accumulation of knowledge.[5] Razin extended growth theory along these lines.[6] Growth theory, however, also should explain the *sources of the investment opportunities that maintain the growth process* and keep it from settling into a stationary long-run equilibrium. This more difficult part of growth theory is lacking.

In thinking about the economics of education, I find it instructive to distinguish between the investment mechanism that determines the formation of capital and the sources of the new investment opportunities that account for growth. The mechanism appears to be sufficient to explain various puzzling interactions between growth and education. In retrospect, taking the long view, there are three such puzzles: (1) Why has the accumulation of human capital represented by education occurred at a higher rate than that of nonhuman capital? (2) Why has the difference in relative earnings between workers with little education and those with much decreased? (3) Why, as growth proceeds, does the inequality in the distribution of personal income show signs of decreasing?

There is some evidence. Human capital consisting mainly of education accounts for a smaller part of the production (income) in the less-developed countries than in those classified as developed. This implies that, as growth proceeds, the complementarity and substitution among factors are such that the role of human capital becomes increasingly important. Krueger's study is most telling on this point.[7] In explaining the large absolute differences in per capita income between poor and rich countries in terms of factor endowments, she concludes "that the difference in human resources between the United States and the less developed countries accounts for more of the difference in *per capita* income than all the other factors combined" (p. 658). The attribute of human resources that matters most in her study is education. My estimates of the average annual rates of increase of different stocks of capital in the United States between 1929 and 1957 provide some additional evidence[8]: reproducible tangible wealth, 2.0 percent; educational capital in the labor force, 4.1 percent.

From 1900 to 1957 the educational capital in the labor force rose sharply relative to the stock of reproducible nonhuman capital; it was 22 percent as large as the nonhuman capital in 1900, and by 1957 it had risen to 42 percent.[9] Here the implication is that the rate of return to education was sufficiently higher than the rate of return to reproducible nonhuman capital to have induced this pattern of investment. Although there are no clues in this evidence of the sources of this favorable rate of return to investment in education, it supports the presumption that investments were responding to opportunities that imply disequilibrium, and the further presumption that there have been continuing sources of new opportunities that have kept the rates of return from settling into a long-run equilibrium state.

The next puzzle for consideration is: What is it about growth that reduces the difference in relative earnings between workers who have little and those who have much education?[10] Kothari investigated the extent and the sources of the disparities in earnings in the city of Bombay, India, and the United States.[11] His data, by occupations and education, appear in table 2.6.2. His summary of the income ratios with the earnings of unskilled workers as the base (equal to 1.0) follows:

> The relative income ratios for skilled manual occupations in Bombay as well as the United States were 1.4. The Bombay ratio for clerical personnel was 2.1, as against 1.5 for the United States, i.e., nearly 50% higher. For lower professions the Bombay ratio was 25% higher than the United States ratio. For Higher Professions the ratio in Bombay was 7.8 as against the United States ratio of 3, i.e., nearly 2½ times as high. The differences in ratios in case of business and government executives in higher posts were even sharper. The Bombay ratio was 11.2, as against the United States ratio of 2.4. This contrast is all the more striking in the light of the educational content of different occupations. In Bombay City an unskilled worker had only 2 years of schooling while the clerical workers had 10.3 years of schooling. The corresponding figures for the United States were 8.2 years and 11.6 years. For the skilled manual occupations the years of schooling were 3.7 in Bombay and 9.5 in the United States. . . .
>
> The real puzzle, however, is the very much higher relative income ratio in Bombay for the higher professions and the higher posts in business and government . . . [than in] the United States.
>
> (Kothari, pp. 607–8)

Table 2.6.2 Mean income, relative income ratio, and education in City of Bombay (1955, 1956) and in the United States (1959) by broad groups of occupations (males)

Occupation	Mean income		Relative Income Ratio		Years of Schooling	
	City of Bombay (Rupees per Month)	U.S. (Dollars per Year)	City of Bombay	U.S.	City of Bombay	U.S.
Higher professionals	622	9,890	7.78	3.00	15.1	15.7
Business and government executives in higher posts	897	7,831	11.21	2.37	13.0	12.7
Lower professionals	207	6,628	2.59	2.01	10.0	13.0
Subordinate officers in business and government	261	6,935	3.26	2.10	10.6	11.6
Clerical personnel	168	4,902	2.10	1.49	10.3	11.6
Skilled manual laborers	110	4,627	1.38	1.40	3.7	9.5
Unskilled manual laborers	80	3,301	1.00	1.00	2.0	8.2

Source: Kothari, "Disparities in Relative Earnings," (table 2, p. 609).

I see four interferences with respect to growth and education that are supported by Kothari's study:

1   As growth increases the general level of earnings, the absolute differences in earnings by level of education increase; and it is well known that the returns to education depend on the absolute, not the relative, differences in earnings. In Bombay, although college graduates were earning twice as much as matriculants, this difference was only 323 rupees per month, whereas in the United States college graduates were earning $4,158 per year more than high school graduates;[12] Kothari's estimates of the private rates of return for these college graduates are about the same for both locations – 12 percent for the United States and 14 percent for Bombay.

2   Restrictions on entry into the "higher professions" are more telling in a less developed country such as India than in the United States. Among the college graduates in Bombay, those who had managed to

enter those professions were enjoying a 33 percent private rate of return, presumably because of such restrictions to entry as barriers associated with the caste system and the lack of facilities for engineering and medical education.

3   Higher education in the less-developed countries tends to be more elite oriented and less subject to competition than in the United States, where higher education has become mass oriented.

4   In adjusting education to growth, competition in providing educational services is an important institutional requirement.

Kuznets devoted his American Economic Association presidential address in 1955 to growth and income inequality;[13] he pointed out that there are long-term trends toward less inequality and noted that the reduction in this "inequality in the secular income structure is a puzzle" (p. 7). He later quantitatively analyzed these trends,[14] and then in his *Modern Economic Growth* offered explanations emphasizing the relative decline in income from property, accompanied by a compensatory relative rise in income from the "greater investment in training and education".[15] Thus, presumably, growth alters the functional distribution in a manner that reduces the inequality in the distribution of personal income. Mincer and Chiswick provide both theory and evidence to explain the distribution of labor incomes.[16]

My interpretation of the role of growth in the above three puzzles can be summarized as follows: (1) As growth proceeds investment in education occurs at a higher rate than investment in nonhuman capital, in response to the investment mechanism when the rates of return are favorable to investment in education. (2) The rise in the general level of earnings is accompanied by sufficiently large absolute differences in earnings to make the investment opportunities in education relatively attractive, even though the difference in relative earnings between unskilled and skilled workers declines; one of the long-term effects of this growth, as rates of return tend toward equality, is to reduce the income inequality within countries. (3) As growth proceeds education becomes less elite and more mass oriented.

Although each part of this interpretation is derived from the investment mechanism of growth, the mechanism by itself tells us nothing about the *sources* of the investment opportunities that have maintained the growth process. Despite the vast accumulation of capital from the long continuing, ever increasing investments, diminishing returns to investment have not prevailed in bringing about a long-run general equilibrium as traditional theory would imply. The critical unanswered question about growth is, what are the sources of the new investment opportunities that have counteracted the theoretically expected tendency toward diminishing returns to investment? Let me advance the following hypothesis: The acquisition of additional knowledge that becomes useful in reducing the cost of production and in enlarging consumer choice accounts in large part for the continuation of growth. Since the "production" of knowledge also requires scarce resources, it has the attributes of an investment.[17] Research-oriented universities are among the major contributors to the advances in knowledge.[18]

2   Rise in Opportunity Costs and Allocative Benefits Associated with Growth

One of the attributes of economic growth is that it increases the value of time; thus the *earnings foregone* by students tend to rise. Another attribute of growth is that it affords new production and consumption opportunities and, as a result, there are *allocative benefits* to be had by responding promptly to these opportunities. Education is not organized to take account of earnings foregone, and most studies of the returns to education tend to omit these allocative benefits. Moreover, both components have efficiency and equity implications.

Although most economists include earnings foregone as a cost in analyzing the rates of return to investment in education, such costs are not taken into account in educational planning. Nor do earnings foregone appear in official educational statistics. It is fair to say that, in determining education policy, in authorizing programs, and in allocating resources to finance education we go on ignoring earnings foregone although they are well over half of the real cost of higher education. Despite the marked upward trend in the value of the time of students, educational administrators and faculties appear to be virtually unaware of this development. There is no search for ways of economizing on the time of students. The standard of 4 years for a bachelor's degree is enforced, with rare exception, regardless of differences in the capacity of students to learn and regardless of the increases in value of their time. Such a standard is inefficient. Students stand in long lines to get what is subsidized; it is rationing by queuing instead of by pricing the instructional services at cost.

Among the benefits of education there is an *allocative benefit* that is determined by the ability to respond to the opportunities afforded by growth. This particular benefit increases as the level of education rises, with the least educated persons slowest in responding to the new opportunities. In production, the allocative benefit accrues initially to those persons who are among the first to respond; then, under competition, it is transferred and accrues to consumers sooner than it would have if the production response had occurred more slowly. Economists in their studies of education, with a few exceptions, have put this class of benefits aside although they are of major economic importance. The approach has been, in estimating the lifetime earnings function from cross-sectional earnings data associated with education, to adjust this function downward for growth over time on the assumption that the rate of growth is wholly independent of the allocative behavior of educated people.

While I have argued that growth favors investment in education, it is also plausible that if the economy were to experience no growth for an extended period the benefits from education would decline. Less education would suffice as economic life became more placid. The disequilibria that are the result of growth would diminish, and fewer economic adjustments would be required because the domain of economic activity would become more routine in character. It follows that the economic value of one of the abilities developed by education is not only dependent upon growth but also contributes to growth. This is the ability *to discern the new opportunities, to evaluate them, and to act promptly and effectively* in taking advantage of them. These are opportunities that are inherent in the disequilibria associated with growth. I contend that the contribution of this particular ability to growth is omitted in reckoning the benefits of education.

The discovery of the allocative benefit here under consideration owes much to Welch's perceptive treatment of the "allocative effects" of education.[19] His conceptual distinction between the worker effect and the allocative effect of education in production is clear and cogent. To the extent that increases in "education enhance a worker's ability to acquire and decode information about costs and productive characteristics of other inputs" (p. 42), there is an allocative effect. He argues that, in a technically changing economy, educated persons are more adept than less educated individuals at critically evaluating new opportunities because they can distinguish more quickly between the systematic and random elements in such an economy; thus they are more productive than uneducated persons. In addition to Welch's evidence (drawn from U.S. agriculture) in support of the allocative-effects hypothesis, there is the evidence provided by Chaudhri's studies of education and the productivity of agriculture in India.[20]

The allocative benefits from this particular ability developed by education are not restricted to farmers in the modernization of agriculture. There are reasons for believing, and there is some evidence, that they are pervasive under the dynamic conditions of growth. Schwartz[21] found that differentials in lifetime earnings provide a better explanation of migration than do the differentials in current earnings and also that the response to the differences in lifetime earnings is lowest for the least educated persons and increases monotonically with education. His findings are consistent with the hypothesis that one of the effects of education is to reduce the cost of obtaining information about job opportunities. O'Neill confirms Schwartz's results with respect to responses to job opportunities.[22] She also found that the effects of consumption opportunities upon migration show a comparable pattern of response by level of education.

I interpret Freeman's finding[23] of relatively short lags by college students in adjusting to changes in job opportunities among the fields in which they specialize as also supporting the argument that there are allocative benefits associated with education.

In studying the effects of education upon the management of the household, Michael showed that efficiency is lowest for the heads of households with the least education and increases with education.[24] Here, too, one of the effects of education would appear to be a reduction in the cost of acquiring information to respond to new consumer opportunities which come with growth. At every turn in the application of the new micro (household) approach to fertility (population), the level of the woman's education appears to be a strong explanatory factor in connection with the wage effect, the efficiency effect in the household, and the contraception effect.

What then are the efficiency and equity (income-distribution) implications of these allocative benefits? In production, as better production possibilities become available, the allocative benefits are the sum of two parts: (1) the benefits that accrue to the educated person as a reward for his expeditious response to the opportunity, and (2) the benefit that accrues to the consumer sooner than it would have if the production response had occurred with a longer lag. The logic of economics implies that, under the assumption of competition, the opportunities arising as a result of growth disequilibria will be fully realized when equilibrium is attained. The educated person who is capable of exploiting such opportunities first (fastest) stands to gain relative to those who respond less expeditiously. Then, as these opportunities are realized under competition, the gains from a set of better production possibilities for example, are transferred to the intermediate, and through them to the final product, where they become consumer surpluses. The consumer acquires these surpluses soonest where the responses in production occur with the shortest lag. Herein is the consumer's part of the gain from the allocative benefit attributed to the education of producers.

Welch's study[25] provides a useful framework by way of summary. In production, the distribution of the allocative benefits among producers depends on the differences in their ability to respond. Welch found that more educated farmers have an advantage compared with less educated farmers in responding to the dynamics of growth. The sooner the better production possibilities are attained, the sooner the additional efficiency from them is added to the real income of the economy. Resulting reductions in real factor cost are thus transferred to consumers in terms of lower food prices, and, as a special case, when this occurs in agriculture it tends to improve the income position of low-income families relatively more than that of higher-income families. Thus, to some extent for agriculture, this process under competition reduces the inequality in the distribution of personal income in general, *although it tends to widen the inequality among farm families.*[26]

3 Enlarging the Student's Capacity for Educational Finance and Benefits

Turning to the investment by college students in their own human capital, I will examine a set of attributes of economic growth with the view of determining their effects upon the capacity of students to finance and to benefit from higher education. I will treat *the student (family) as a firm, his capacity to finance as the supply, and his capacity to benefit as the demand.* Although institutions and policy also are altered by growth, I will abstract from these alterations. I will concentrate on the investment decisions of college students (families) in acquiring human capital by means of some form of higher education for which they incur costs and from which they obtain benefits. The primary growth attributes to be examined are (1) the rise in the personal income of families, (2) the enlargement of the student's capacity to learn, (3) the increase in the value of time, and (4) the improvements in the entrepreneurial ability of students, including the allocative benefits they obtain in managing their investment decisions.

The connection between the value of the student's time and his *earnings foregone* has been examined briefly above. Likewise, the importance of the *allocative benefits* that increase with education under conditions of growth is formally clear and consistent with a growing body of evidence. Earlier, in accounting for a higher rate of investment in education than in nonhuman capital, we found that economic growth favors the investment in education. In solving the puzzle of the narrowing difference in relative earnings between those with little and those with much education, we were led to reaffirm that the difference in absolute earnings, not the relative difference, accounts for the investment opportunities in successive levels of education.

My approach to the changing pattern of the supply curve and demand curve here under consideration is basically the optimal investment in human capital model developed by Becker.[27] The demand curve represents the marginal benefit measured by the ratio of return to the student on each additional dollar of investment, the supply curve and the marginal financing cost measured by the rate of interest on each additional dollar invested. I will extend the Becker model somewhat in treating the attributes of economic growth.

The rise in the personal income of families is the key that alters these supply and demand curves over time. The number of students and their respective marginal financing cost account for the aggregate supply curve; their respective marginal benefits account for the aggregate demand curve. The general direction of the changes in supply and demand as income rises can be inferred. If social and legal institutions and policy remain constant and if the distribution of personal income remains unchanged, or becomes less unequal, it follows that, as incomes rise, the marginal financing cost declines, and the per students supply curve shifts down and becomes more elastic.[28] More important, however, in determining the increases in investment in higher education associated with growth, is that the rise in income under these conditions increases the marginal benefits from higher education and the per student demand curve shifts up.[29] The inference with respect to the supply as personal incomes rise is fairly evident, but that pertaining to the demand is far from obvious and is generally neglected in examining the economics of higher education.

4   Changes in Supply

The supply curves do not reveal the cost of producing college education. They represent the marginal cost borne by students (families) in financing additional units of education. To simplify the analysis, I treat the distribution of personal income as a dichotomy consisting of families who are rich and those who are not rich. Thinking in terms of US 1969 incomes, I shall arbitrarily classify all families who have had over a period of years an annual permanent income of $15,000 or more as rich, and all of the families with less income as not rich.[30] I shall assume that the families who are here classified as rich have sufficient resources to finance their students and that their own capital is the cheapest source for the purpose. Moreover, the financial resources of these families would be sufficient even if college students from these families were to pay the full cost of providing the education with no scholarships, fellowships, or subsidized student loans. The characteristics of the per student supply of this set of families are as follows: (1) it is below that of families who are not rich, (2) it is relatively elastic, and (3) it is not segmented.

It is evident that many families who are not rich, in contrast, lack sufficient income and wealth to finance from their own resources the full cost of higher education for their children. Accordingly, they must depend, for a part of the capital required, on borrowed funds that entail relatively high transaction costs because of legal restrictions on lending funds to invest in human capital. It is for these reasons that the per student supply curve of students from families who are not rich is segmented, less elastic, and above that of students of rich families.[31]

Although the value of the time of students rises with growth, actual earnings foregone are held in check by more part-time work by students. This has occurred during recent years in the United States; such work may, however, impair a student's education.[32] Thus, the dominant factors shifting the per student supply curve down and making it more elastic are: (1) the increase in the proportion of all families who become rich with growth, and (2) the rise in the personal incomes of the rest of the families that reduces their marginal cost of financing education.

5   Changes in Demand

The interactions between economic growth and the marginal benefits measured by the rate of return to students on each additional dollar of investment in higher education are complex, and they have received all too little analytical attention. The key to the analysis is in the enlargment of the capacities of potential and actual students made possible by the rise in personal incomes. In examining this process with respect to changes in demand, I again appeal to the simplified dichotomy of rich and not rich families.

Both the students' *capacity to learn* in benefiting from college work and their *entrepreneurial capacity* in combining their own time with the services of teachers and with other resources come into play. I contend that the rise in personal incomes associated with growth results in parents making additional expenditures to enlarge these capacities in their children; as this occurs, the per student demand curve shifts up.

Presumably it is the task of geneticists, psychologists, and students of education to explain the changes and the differences among students in their capacity to learn. While it is exceedingly hard for economists to interpret their findings, it would be naïve to treat the capacity to learn as if it were identical with innate ability. To do so can only lead to a serious misspecification of the factors that account for the observed differences in the capacity of the youth of college age to learn. A convenient framework, albeit a much oversimplified one, is to treat this capacity as a product of both innate ability and acquired ability. The amount of acquired ability is obviously dependent not only upon the years of schooling, but, importantly, upon the quality of the elementary and secondary schooling. Equally, if not more, important is the preschool home environment and experience of the child; this is in no small part determined by the education of the mother. It is nevertheless true that the rate at which these acquired abilities are accumulated depends in part on the innate ability that each child inherits.

The proposition is here advanced that the *proportion* of the youth of college age who have this capacity to learn *increases* as relatively more of the members of this age group benefit from precollege investments that add to their acquired ability. At some point, however, as this process continues, the innate abilities that are required to benefit from college work will become exhausted. My interpretation of the available evidence is that the supply of the relatively high level of innate ability distributed among the college age population is as yet less scarce than the supply of acquired studies that is necessary to a sufficient capacity to learn enough to warrant the investment in college work.

In supporting the above proposition, it is not necessary to assume that the distribution of innate ability of students from rich families is the same as that of students from families who are not rich. This interpretation by no means implies that all youth of college age or all who now enter college have enough innate ability to benefit from college work, measured in terms of the going rate of return, to undertake such an investment compared with alternative investment opportunities. On this score, my view of the facts is that the lack of sufficient innate ability is somewhat greater in the United States among college students from rich families than among students from families who are not rich. This difference between them is concealed, however, because students from rich families are long on acquired ability whereas those from the other set tend to be short on the necessary acquired abilities. As of October 1969, 66 percent of US rich families with dependent members of 18–24 years old had dependants in college full time contrasted with only 16 percent from the very poor families. Surely no one would argue that this difference of four to one implies that the genetic difference between them is equally wide. The complete classification of families by income[33] is shown in table 2.6.3.

Table 2.6.3 Classification of Families by income

Family Income	No. of Families with 18- to 24-Year-Old Dependants (in Thousands)	Families with Dependants in College Full Time (%)
Under $3,000	690	16
$3,000–$4,999	940	24
$5,000–$7,499	1,440	33
$7,500–$9,999	1,470	42
$10,000–$14,999	2,100	49
$15,000 and over	1,410	66
Not reporting	720	39
Total	8,770	42

Becker, in his perceptive and cogent argument on why the demand curves for human capital are negatively inclined and not horizontal,[34] digresses to suggest that persons investing in human capital are "firms." Since entrepreneurial time is required by students in combining their learning time with the services of teachers and with other resources, the differences among students in their entrepreneurial capacities alter their respective demand curves. A part of the "profit" attributed to this capacity is an allocative benefit of the type already presented. This particular benefit increases for the same reasons advanced earlier, namely, from both improvements in the quality and quantity of the schooling and in pre-school investments that enlarge this part of the student's entrepreneurial capacity. But the primary attribute of entrepreneurship is the capacity to cope with risk and uncertainty, and the source of it is far from settled. It is probably true, in general, that students from poor families who have managed despite all manner of difficulties to acquire a college capacity to learn possess more entrepreneurial capacity than students from rich families who have had at their disposal without stint or effort the best facilities and instruction in acquiring such a capacity to learn.

In summary, the first conclusion is that the per student supply curve that represents the financing cost of students who come from rich families is not altered by additional increases in their personal income resulting from economic growth. Their supply curve remains low, unsegmented, and relatively elastic. Since relatively more families, however, become rich, the general per student supply curve is altered to that extent. The important change in the supply curve occurs as a consequence of the rise in the personal income of families who are not rich. For this class of families the supply curve shifts down and becomes less segmented and more elastic as growth proceeds toward the arbitrary $15,000 dividing line that I have imposed. It should be noted, once again, that this analysis rests on the assumptions that social and legal institutions and policies remain constant and that the distribution of personal income does not become more unequal with growth.

The second conclusion is that the demand curve representing the marginal benefits measured by the rate of return to students on each additional dollar of investment depends on their capacity to learn and on their entrepreneurial capacity. The sources of the capacity to learn are innate abilities coupled with acquired abilities; the supply of the first component presently in our college age population is less restrictive than the supply of the second. Here, too, the per student demand curve of dependents from rich families is not altered appreciably by additional increases in personal incomes that come to them from growth. Their demand curve remains high and relatively inelastic. Since relatively more families become rich as growth proceeds, to this extent the general per student demand curve shifts up. The larger change in the demand curve takes place, however, as a consequence of the rise in the personal incomes of families who are not rich. The per student demand curve of this class rises and probably becomes less elastic. The allocative benefits arising from the entrepreneurial capacities of students in managing their college affairs suggest a similar pattern of effects on the demand. But the sources and the consequences of the entrepreneurial capacity required to cope with risk and uncertainty are not clear.

6 The Equity-Efficiency Quandary

Are we, because of our commitment to economics, not seeing the beauty of the higher education rainbow? Our concern about allocative efficiency and the welfare implications of the distribution of personal income serves us in choosing those issues that are amenable to our analytical skills. But this convenience does not make economics the right forum if the issues are matters of taste in appreciating beauty. It is undoubtedly true that the perplexities of higher education reach far beyond economic calculus; higher education is an involved state of affairs that has become embodied in a large number of public and private institutions strongly rooted both socially and politically.

Although higher education has long been institutionalized in our society, there is much disagreement on the essentials of an ideal model of higher education. This lack of consensus arises primarily out of basic inconsistencies associated with attributes that are deemed to be essential for higher education. The view that higher education should be free of any manner of government control and that public bodies should appropriate most of the funds for it is inconsistent because government cannot abdicate its responsibility in accounting for uses of public funds. The view that, ideally, the services of higher education should be free to all qualified students is inconsistent with the will and capacity of private donors and public bodies to pay the bill. The incompatibility between "free" and "scarce" is paramount in understanding this lack of agreement. It is little wonder that a major controversy is underway with regard to those goals of higher education appropriate to our democracy with its equalitarian values. The two goals at the center of the controversy may best be identified as "predominantly free higher education" and "optimal investment in higher education." The proponents of the first of these goals still dominate public discussions, mainly because the investment approach has emerged out of economics only fairly recently. The proponents of predominantly free higher education appeal to the political process as the means for attaining their goal – primarily to the legislatures for appropriations and secondarily to the courts for legal standards and their enforcement. They overlook the *limits* of the enforcement powers of the courts and of the taxing and spending powers of the legislatures. As these limits become increasingly evident, the optimal investment goal gains ascendancy in this controversy. While it is clear (to economists) that this shift with respect to goals sets the stage for more allocative efficiency, it still is a matter of doubt that it also could serve to reduce the inequality in the distribution of personal incomes.

The argument for predominantly free higher education is postulated basically as a "social principle" – an established preference of society revealed by widely held and consistent social values of our people.[35] The political process is the means by which it is to be attained. Thus it is an appeal to the legislative bodies and to the courts to maintain and extend predominantly free higher education.

I shall not belabor the weakness of the foundation of the "social principle." Suffice it to say that it is built on shifting sand because our social values, as they are in fact revealed by the political process, are not only far from consistent but fluctuate and change over time. This argument also fails to take account of the *limits* of the judicial process in enforcing, and of the legislatures in financing, such a goal – and that is the critical reason it leads to false conclusions.

In *Brown* v. *Board of Education*, the Supreme Court in a rare unanimous decision declared that education today is perhaps the most important function of state and local governments and that success in life depends on the opportunity of an education. It said: "Such an opportunity, where the state has undertaken to provide it, is *a right which must be made available to all on equal terms*.'[36]

The lucid and cogent analysis of Kurland when applied to higher education in the United States leaves little room for doubt that "the Supreme Court is the wrong forum for providing a solution" to the problem of inequality in higher educational opportunities. A part of the legal argument presented by Kurland is that there are three necessary conditions for the success of any fundamental decision of the Court: The constitutional standard must be a simple one, as it is in the reapportionment cases: one man—one vote. Second, the public must acquiesce. Clearly, in reapportionment, there has been an "unwillingness of any large segment of the population to do battle with it". The third condition is that "the judiciary have adequate control over the means of effectuating enforcement".[37] In satisfying this condition, the problem of enforcement of the "one man—one vote" principle has thus far not arisen; should a case arise that applied this principle to the US Senate, however, the Court would be in difficulty. Turning to equal opportunity in higher education, there is no simple standard. Universities are made to resist governmental authority, and it is inconceivable that the judiciary could enforce such a fundamental decision in the area of higher education.

I take it to be obvious that the judiciary does not have the means of effectuating the enforcement of the principle, for example, that all public colleges and universities provide the *same quality* of educational services. If the courts could enforce all public colleges and universities throughout the United States to be the same in this respect, the results would be absurd. Moreover, if this principle could be enforced, students (families) who wanted higher quality could escape by retreating to private colleges and universities, and the courts would be incapable of preventing it. The powers of the courts are essentially negative, not affirmative. Kurland's quotation from Hamilton is indeed pertinent in considering the possibilities of attaining equal opportunity in higher education via the decisions of the judiciary: "The judiciary . . . has no influence over either the sword or the purse; no direction either of the strength or the wealth of society."[38] *Herein lie the limits of the judiciary.*

The legislatures hold the power of the public purse that consists of two parts: taxing power and spending power. The reports of the Carnegie Commission on Higher Education have not examined the limits of these two powers. According to the commission, it is all very simple: the state and local authorities should increase their appropriation for higher education to $7 billion by 1976–77 and the federal government should jump its contribution from $3.5 billion (1967–68) to $13 billion by 1976–77 – as if there were no limits to the taxing powers of the respective legislatures. Nor is there any analysis of the effects of this financing proposal upon the control by the federal authority over the affairs of higher education. The current confusion over the sharing of federal revenue brings to the fore the problem of developing politically acceptable standards of control, along with the problem of the federal government administering, over the whole of the United States, the spending of vast federal funds in accordance with such standards. Clearly, the spending power of the government also has its limits. Since these limits arise out of the scarcity of resources, their allocation, and the uses to which they are put, economics is to this extent not the wrong forum for providing solutions for the problems here under consideration.

Returning to the quandary, surely the instructional services of higher education embodied in the student are not a public good inasmuch as a "pure public good is one for which enjoyment by one individual does not in any degree exclude the enjoyment" by others.[39] With somewhat less assurance, I would contend that a college graduate generates only a few externalities that accrue as benefits to other persons, with one major exception, namely, the important benefit the eductaion of a woman gives her children in terms of preschool training and experience. It is internalized in the family, however. I take it to be self-evident that the differences in the quality of educational services among colleges and universities are inconsistent with the "principle" of equality of opportunity, and on practical grounds it can be argued that preferential treatment of qualified students who are in need has a priority over the equal treatment of all students. If these conditions and propositions are granted, a good deal of progress can be made in clarifying the underlying perplexities of higher education that account for existing inequities and inefficiencies.

Higher education is not organized to bring about an optimal investment in its instructional services. The source of the difficulty is in the *financing, pricing,* and *supplying* of these services. The financing tends to subsidize the wrong educational activities. The pricing bears no meaningful relation to the differences in the costs of producing the services, and the suppliers of these services are, therefore, substantially sheltered from the discipline of competition, notwithstanding the large number of colleges and universities in the United States. Current endeavors to cope with the financial adversities arising out of the pause in the educational boom of the sixties are efforts to "save" the existing organization. They are not seeking solutions for the basic underlying difficulty that has become increasingly acute, especially since World War II, as a consequence of the doubling since 1940 of personal per capita disposal income (in 1958 prices).

The reasons for the failure to comprehend the sources of organizational difficulties confronting higher education can be put quite simply. It is obvious that most families in the United States, who have members (students) enrolled in higher education, now have the income and wealth to pay the full cost of the education. What have not been perceived clearly are the following points:

1   the allocation of public revenue (even if all of it were collected by means of progressive income taxes) to subsidize *all* publicly supported college and university instruction is bound to be socially inefficient;

2   the optimal investment in this form of human capital is basically dependent upon the micro decisions of students functioning as firms, and these are as efficient as any other large set of private firms;

3   the underpricing of instructional services to all students in supplying them with these services thwarts the possibility of the privately efficient investment decisions of students bringing this sector of the economy into a socially efficient state;

4   the function of private gifts and public funds is in financing and subsidizing, in accordance with some socially agreed upon standards, the qualified students from low-income families (and of on-campus research).

In support of the proposition that private educational choices of college students are privately efficient, there is a growing body of evidence that shows that private rates of return tend to be equal among educational options and comparable with the private rates of return to other private investment that range in general between 10 and 15 percent.[40] The widely held belief of the critics of this interpretation who maintain that college oriented students are too immature to be informed with respect to the economic value of the fields in which they might best specialize is far from valid. The short lags in their responses to changes in job opportunities for the various specialized skills leave little room for doubt that college students become informed about these opportunities and respond to them fairly promptly, as Freeman's study clearly shows.[41] The large shifts, during the sixties, by Negro college students from specializing in teaching to preparing for business, law, and engineering careers where this option was available, as Freeman's ongoing work reveals, strongly support the responsiveness of these students to changes in job opportunities.

In citing this evidence, I am *not* implying that all the youth of college age who have the necessary innate ability have had the opportunity in their precollege schooling to accumulate the necessary acquired ability to qualify for college, or that all who have the necessary capacity to learn at that age can finance the cost of a college education, or that those who enter college can obtain adequate information to determine fully the differences in the quality of the educational services among fields and among the institutions that provide these services.

To see more clearly the extent to which our system of higher education is socially inefficient in terms of optimal investment, it may be helpful to compare it with a hypothetical system designed to be "perfectly" inefficient socially.[42] The requirement would be free tuition, free board and room, free transportation, and a monthly payment to each student to compensate him fully for his earnings foregone, adjusted for the difference between the free board and room and the cost of living were he to take a job. On-campus living would become a way of life for students, and it would have lifetime possibilities once terminal dates were abolished and free child care centers for the children of students were assured! Unless some social purpose were served by maintaining college students in this privileged manner, the rate of return to the cost borne by society would be zero.

Compared with Turkey, higher education in the United States must be grossly antisocial! In the United States tuitions and fees charged by private institutions rose from $210 in 1940 to $1,030 in 1968, per student.[43] Even the cherished free tuition banner of public institutions has become slightly tattered, for their tuitions and fees have risen from $69 to $250 per student during this period. (Four state universities, however, still charge no tuition.) Tuition and fees minus financial aid per student in 1968 averaged $850 in private and $182 in public institutions. Board and room are generally subsidized, more so at public than at private institutions, but the amount of the subsidization is a well-kept secret. But, all told, what students pay the colleges and universities is the smaller part of the direct educational costs per student (see table 2.6.1).

Although it may not be obvious, the logic of economics clearly implies that *the solution of the inefficiencies and inequities here under consideration is not in simply allocating more state and federal funds in support of higher education, even if all such funds were collected by highly progressive taxation.*[44] The problem to be solved is in the choice of educational activities that are to be subsidized by such funds. For example, since university research that is primarily "basic" in character is indeed a public good, it must be subsidized if it is to be undertaken. In supporting needy students, subsidies are required.[45] But, to be allocatively efficient, such subsidization must go directly to the students and not into the funds of colleges and universities, leaving it to them to distribute the financial aid to students by all manner of standards. Until those educational activities that require subsidization are identified and the amounts required determined, to simply proceed in allocating even more funds to subsidize *all* students is not only socially inefficient but grossly inequitable.

One of the necessary conditions in developing a socially efficient system of higher education is full cost pricing of each of the different classes of instructional services, modified (reduced) in the amount of known social benefits if, and only if, the social benefits are ascertainable and worthwhile in terms of the going rate of return to alternative investment opportunities.[46]

Yet, for all manner of reasons, it is widely held that the economic logic of full cost pricing, as modified above, is impractical, unrealistic, and contrary to all historical experience. It is deemed to be wrong by the proponents of predominantly free higher education. It is viewed with suspicion by the rank and file of faculty, by college and university administrators, and probably by many legislators. The students' self-serving interests (however rich the students may be) in demanding that everything they want be free is understandable, if they do not see that this would be at the expense of other persons in society.

It may be true that virtually all colleges and universities have always been subsidized and there may have been good and sufficient reasons for institutionalization of this traditional practice. But it is also true that institutions that perform economic functions, as I have attempted to show in "Institutions and the Rising Economic Value of Man," become obsolete.[47] Higher education clearly is not an exception. Another strongly held view is that it is impossible to determine the real costs of each of the many classes of the services (educational) that students receive from the university. It is true that the economic accounting within a university is not designed for this purpose. But it is no more impossible than it is for firms that are producing a complex set of different products, many of which are joint products of many different production activities within such firms. *Necessity imposed by competition makes it possible.*

There is then the argument that full cost pricing of the instructional services would reduce the supply of college graduates far below the demand for persons with these particular high skills. Recent graduates who specialized in the sciences may now be entertaining the thought that the supply is all too large, but these ex post thoughts in view of the present depressed market for these particular skills have no bearing on the argument. The full cost implications of the direct educational expenditures per student in 1968 (assume that students from rich families paid it) are that average tuition and fees per student would be increased from $490 to $1,820 (see table 2.6.1). When earnings foregone are taken into account, it would increase the cost to these students about two-fifths. Meanwhile, the approach taken here is that more students from low-income families would be subsidized. Even so, the supply of particular skills may be reduced sufficiently to bring the intercept up along the demand curve where the returns to the investment would again assure the going rate of return to alternative investment opportunities. The adjustments would take place with a relatively short lag in view of the known responsiveness of students to changes in the economic value of these forms of human capital.

As a last resort, there is always the argument that the social benefits of higher education are not only ever present, but that they are large and all-pervasive, both in bringing about gains in productivity from which the noncollege population benefits and in improving the quality of life. Although these claims have been with us for ever so long, they continue, with the exception of benefits to children from a mother's education, to remain unsubstantiated. They have the ring of special pleading for more funds to maintain the existing system of higher education. The exception noted is not among those social benefits commonly cited. It has been advanced only recently as a result of the extension of economic theory to analyze the microeconomics of the household. Even this important "social" benefit accrues in large part to the parents in terms of satisfactions. Moreover, and to repeat, most families have sufficient income and wealth to pay for this particular value added to the female members of their families. But the existence of this class of "social" benefits argues for the subsidization of needy students, whether they are males or females.

7   Conclusion

My analysis implies that the rise in personal incomes associated with economic growth, which has doubled real personal incomes in the United States between 1940 and 1968, makes the traditional financing, pricing, and supplying of the instructional services of higher education ever more obsolete. The general conclusion is that the instructional part, especially undergraduate instruction, has become increasingly less efficient socially, and that an inordinate part of the subsidies to higher education is used to provide these educational services below cost to students from families who have the income and wealth to pay the full cost. Thus, in providing instruction higher education is in general both socially inefficient and inequitable.

I am aware that my analysis at a number of points rests on evidence that is still fragmentary. A critical point throughout the analysis is the interpretation of the evidence at hand that college students are privately fairly efficient in investing in themselves. Then, too, if the personal distribution of income, as per capita income has risen, has become in fact more unequal, it would undermine a part of my argument. If colleges and universities were allocating a substantial, and an increasing, part of the funds they receive from public and private sources to provide college instruction in subsidizing needy students, it would impair my conclusions with respect to social inequities. If the supply curves – the capacity of students to finance the cost of their education – were becoming more segmented, less elastic, and were moving upward over time, despite the rise in personal incomes, it would weaken my argument appreciably. Similarly, if the demand curves – the capacity of students to benefit sufficiently from their education to warrant the investment – were not moving upward as personal incomes rose, the argument would lose some of its strength. Although the allocative benefits associated with education imply that there are gains from them that are transferred to consumers, I have not treated these particular gains as social benefits because, in the process of adjusting to the dynamics of a growing economy, less educated persons may become less well-off in competing with more educated persons. If this were not true, there would be a part of these allocative benefits that should be treated as one of the social benefits of education. My argument rests squarely on the concept that students behave as economic firms. The validity of the underlying assumption of this concept implies a hypothesis that awaits more complete testing.

Appendix

Data Sources and Bases of Calculations for table 2.6.1

Data for 1940 are for the continental United States only; those for 1968 are for the "aggregate U.S." (fifty states, District of Columbia, Canal Zone, Guam, Puerto Rico, and the Virgin Islands).They are for the school years ending in 1940 and 1968. Totals may not add due to rounding.

a) *Number of institutions.* **1940** (cols. 1, 4, and 7): US Office of Education, *Biennial Survey of Education in the United States 1938–40* (Government Printing Office, Washington, 1947), vol. 2, chapter 1, table 2, p. 3. **1968** (cols. 2, 5, and 8): US Office of Education, *Digest of Educational Statistics 1970*, table 9, p. 7.

b) *Enrollment (opening fall).* **1940** (cols. 1, 4, and 7): resident degree-credit enrollment; Bureau of the Census, *Statistical Abstract 1970*, table 146, p. 104. **1968** (cols. 2, 5, and 8): degree-credit enrollment includes both resident and extension students; it is available for the United States (fifty states and District of Columbia) in US Office of Education, *Projections of Educational Statistics to 1978–79* (Government Printing Office, Washington, 1947), table 6, p. 23. For total enrollment (United States and outlying areas), see US Office of Education, *Digest of Educational Statistics*, table 84, p. 65. Degree-credit enrollment for aggregate United States is estimated by applying the U.S. degree credit/total enrollment ratio to total enrollment in outlying areas (see table A1).

Table A1

		Enrollment (in thousands)		
		Total	Public	Private
1	U.S. degree credit	6,390	4,350	2,040
2	U.S. total	6,910	4,820	2,100
3	Degree credit/total ratio (= col. 1 ÷ col. 2)	0.9	0.9	0.9
4	Outlying areas, total	52	34	18
5	Outlying areas, degree credit (= col. 4 × col. 3)	48	31	18
6	Aggregate U.S. degree credit (= col. 1 + col. 5)	6,960	4,850	2,110

c) *Direct total instruction costs.* Calculated as (*d*) + (*e*).

d) *Net instruction expenditures.* These are educational and general costs, excluding extensions and public service, other sponsored activities, and 50 percent of organized research. **1940** (cols. 1, 4, and 7): source is US Office of Education, *Biennial Survey of Education*, vol. 2, chapter 4, table 16, p. 90. **1968** (cols. 2, 5, and 8): from US Office of Education, *Digest of Educational Statistics*, table 129, p. 96.

e) *Implicit interest and depreciation.* Calculated as 8 percent of value of physical property, multiplied by ratio of net instruction expenditures to sum of educational and general expenditures and expenditures on auxiliary enterprises (see table A2).

f) *Tuition and fees.* **1940** (cols. 1, 4, and 7): US Office of Education, *Biennial Survey of Education*, vol. 2, chapter 4, table 13, p. 68. **1968** (cols. 2, 5, and 8): US Office of Education, *Digest of Educational Statistics* table 126, p. 5.

g) *Student aid expenditures.* **1940** (cols. 1, 4, and 7): data are for "other noneducational activities" (US Office of Education, *Biennial Survey of Education*, vol. 2, chapter 4, table 16, p. 90. The same figures are given as "Scholarships, Fellowships and Prizes" in Bureau of the Census *Statistical Abstract 1970*, table 191, p. 127. **1968** (cols. 2, 5, and 8): US Office of Education *Digest of Educational Statistics*, table 129, p. 96).

Table A2

	Total		Public		Private	
	1940	*1968*	*1940*	*1968*	*1940*	*1968*
1. Value ($ million)	2,750	34,590	1,260	21,180	1,490	13,410
2. 8 percent of col. 1	220	2,770	100	1,690	120	1,070
3. Ratio of net instruction expenditures to those for educational and general and auxiliary enterprises	0.7	0.7	0.8	0.7	0.7	0.7
4. Implicit interest and depreciation chargeable to instruction (= col. 2 × col. 3)	160	1,920	71	1,190	90	730

Source: **1940**: US Office of Education, *Biennial Survey of Education*, vol. 2, chapter 4, table 17, p. 92. **1968**: US Office of Education *Digest of Educational Statistics*, table 133, p. 99.

h)   *Enrollment per institution.* Calculated as (b) ÷ (a).
i)   *Per student direct total instruction costs.* Calculated as (c) ÷ (b).
j)   *Per student net instruction expenditures.* Calculated as (d) ÷ (b).
k)   *Per student interest and depreciation.* Calculated as (e) ÷ (b).
(l)   *Per student tuition and fees.* Calculated as (f) ÷ (b).
(m)   *Per student financial aid.* Calculated as (g) ÷ (b).

Notes and References

1   The number of institutions in late 1969 was 2,525; see U.S. Office of Education, *Digest of Educational Statistics, 1970* (Government Printing Office, Washington, 1970), table 113, p. 85.

2   Richard B. Freeman, *The Market for College-Trained Manpower: A Study in the Economics of Career Choice* (Harvard University Press, Cambridge, Mass., 1971).

3   E. G. West, "Private versus Public Education," *Journal of Political Economy*, 72 (Oct. 1964), 465–75.

4   A. C. F. Beales, Mark Blaug, Sir Douglas Veale, and E. G. West, *Education: A Framework for Choice*, (Institute of Economic Affairs, London, 1967).

5   Useful knowledge that is appropriated can be treated as capital, but knowledge that enters the public domain and is available to everyone is another matter: see Theodore W. Schultz, *Investment in Human Capital: The Role of Education and of Research* (Free Press, New York, 1971), chapter 12.

6 Assaf Razin, "Investment in Human Capital and Economic Growth: A Theoretical Study," PhD Dissertation (University of Chicago, 1969).

7 A. O. Krueger, "Factor Endowments and *Per Capita* Income Differences among Countries," *Economic Journal*, 78 (Sept. 1968), 641–59.

8 Schultz, *Human Capital*, table 5.1.

9 Ibid., table 5.1.

10 I know of no studies of the changes in relative earnings associated with differences in education during recent decades in the United States. The following data on estimated lifetime mean incomes (Bureau of the Census, *Statistical Abstract of the United States* (Government Printing Office, Washington, 1969), table 155, p. 108) suggest that the relative differences declined somewhat between 1949 and 1967.

Lifetime Mean Incomes
(Males, aged 25 Years and older)

Years of Schooling	1949		1967	
	Thousands of Dollars	Relative Difference	Thousands of Dollars	Relative Difference
8	123	100	246	100
12	175	142	338	137
16 or more	287	233	558	227

11 V. N. Kothari, "Disparities in Relative Earnings among Different Countries," *Economic Journal*, 80 (Sept. 1970), 605–16.

12 Ibid., p. 611

13 Simon Kuznets, "Economic Growth and Income Inequality," *American Economic Review*, 45 (Mar. 1955), 1–28.

14 Simon Kuznets, "Quantitative Aspects of the Economic Growth of Nations, VIII: Distribution of Income by Size," *Economic Development and Cultural Change*, vol. II, part 2 (Jan. 1963).

15 Simon Kuznets, *Modern Economic Growth* (Yale University Press, New Haven, Conn., 1966), p. 218.

16 Jacob Mincer, "Investment in Human Capital and Personal Income Distribution," *Journal of Political Economy*, 66 (Aug. 1958), 281–302; also "The Distribution of Labor Incomes: A Survey with Special Reference to the Human Capital Approach," *Journal of Economic Literature*, 8 (Mar. 1970), 1–26. See also Barry R. Chiswick, "Human Capital and the Personal Income Distribution by Regions," PhD dissertation (Columbia University, 1967); and "Earnings Inequality and Economic Development," *Quarterly Journal of Economics*, 85 (Feb. 1971), 21–39.

17 My critics urged me to extend my comments on this issue, but I shall forego this opportunity because a major paper would be required to develop the analysis and because earlier I examined some aspects of the issue (Schultz,

Human Capital, chapters 1, 2, 12). Suffice it here to say that the argument in *Science* among scientists, beginning with Bentley Glass on "Science Education – Process or Contents?" (Mar. 5 1971, p. 851), is not helpful. While it is obviously true that the acquisition of additional knowledge is, in some ultimate sense, subject to diminishing returns, merely to argue that the "exponential growth (of science) is self-limiting" is rather pointless in clarifying the funding of science in a world of scarce resources.

18 Schultz, *Human Capital*.

19 Finis Welch, "Education in Production," *Journal of Political Economy*, 78 (Jan/Feb. 1970), 35–59.

20 D. P. Chaudhri, "Education and Agricultural Productivity in India," PhD dissertation (University of Delhi, 1968); also "Farmers' Education and Productivity: Some Empirical Results from Indian Agriculture," *Investment in Human Capital* paper No. 69:4 (University of Chicago, 1969).

21 Aba Schwartz, "Migration and Lifetime Earnings in the US," PhD dissertation (University of Chicago, 1968).

22 June O'Neill, "The Effects of Income and Education on Interregional Migration," PhD dissertation (Columbia University, 1969).

23 Freeman, *The Market for College-Trained Manpower*.

24 Robert T. Michael, "Effects of Education on Efficiency in Consumption," PhD dissertation (Columbia University, 1969).

25 Welch, "Education in Production."

26 It may be true, in general, that less educated persons experience losses in terms of the earnings they would have received had not those with more education been present to exploit new opportunities more quickly than they could. Since this may be what happens, I have not treated the particular consumer surplus on which the above paragraph concentrates as one of the social benefits of higher education.

27 Gary S. Becker, "Human Capital and the Personal Distribution of Income: An Analytical Approach," (W. S. Woytinsky Lecture No. 1, University of Michigan, Ann Arbor, 1967).

28 I focus on the supply or demand curve of the per student, a composite of all students, and leave aside the increases in the number of students that occur over time.

29 The logic and evidence on this shift will be presented shortly.

30 Of full-time college students as of October 1969, one-fourth were dependants of families with $15,000 and over of family income during the preceding 12 months, while over one-half were accounted for by families with $10,000 and over of family income. For a detailed specification of concepts and characteristics of the sample, see Bureau of the Census, *Current Population Reports*, Special Studies, Series P-23, No. 34 (Government Printing Office, Washington, Feb. 1 1971). In considering policy choices, families with incomes between $10,000 and $15,000 may be viewed as "comfortably" rich in terms of their ability to finance the education of their dependants.

31 The increase in the value of the time of students, as earnings rise with

growth, obviously increases the student's cost of acquiring a college education. Thus, even if the cost of producing a unit of education by universities and colleges were to remain constant, the total cost that the student would have to finance would rise. For many students from families who are not rich, the supply implications of the rise in earnings foregone are real and harsh.

32 Schultz, *Human Capital*, chapter 7.
33 Bureau of the Census, *Current Population Reports*, table 17, p. 21.
34 Becker, *Human Capital and the Personal Distribution of Income*, pp. 5–9.
35 The prestigious reports of the Carnegie Commission on Higher Education are most explicit in propounding this principle; see, for instance, *A Chance to Learn: an Action Agenda for Equal Opportunity in Higher Education* (McGraw-Hill, New York, 1970).
36 As cited by and with emphasis added by Philip B. Kurland, "Equal Educational Opportunity: The Limits of Constitutional Jurisprudence Undefined," *University of Chicago Law Review*, 35 (Summer 1968), 583–600.
37 Ibid., pp. 592–3.
38 From *The Federalist*, 78, as cited ibid., p. 595.
39 See Harry G. Johnson, *The Two-Sector Model of General Equilibrium* (Allen & Unwin, London, 1971), appendix 3: "A Geometrical Note on General Equilibrium with Public Goods."
40 Gary S. Becker, *Human Capital: A Theoretical and Empirical Analysis with Special Reference to Education* (National Bureau of Economic Research, New York, 1964); see also Schultz, *Human Capital*.
41 Freeman, *The Market for College-Trained Manpower*.
42 I am prompted in suggesting this hypothetical system by the example of higher education in Turkey. A. O. Krueger, in "Rates of Return to Turkish Higher Education" (University of Minnesota, Minneapolis, 1971), informs us that in Turkey "the costs of a university education borne by the student are probably negative". Tuition charges in public universities are nominal, and there "are a host of special concessions available to students; special low fares on intracity bus transportation; subsidized lunches, and sometimes even highly subsidized housing; half-price cinema tickets, etc. Scholarships average about 50 percent of foregone income." Thus it comes as no surprise that "the disparity between the private return and the social return is remarkable . . . While it does not pay, socially, . . . it is privately very profitable to attend college."
43 Not all private institutions charge anywhere near this much. At Berea College, for example, there are upper income limits on the admission of students and there are no tuition charges. Income limits start at $4,000 for a family with one child and go up to $8,500 for a family with seven children, with two exceptions: children of the Berea faculty and from families in the town of Berea (population, 6,000) may also attend tuition-free. The income levels of parents of Berea students are: less than $4,000 for 36 percent of the students; between $4,000 and $6,000, 31 percent; $6,000–$8,000, 19

percent; and between $8,000 and $10,000, 10 percent. This accounts for 96 percent of enrollment. Thus Berea's enrollment is concentrated at the lower tail of the income distribution, whereas higher education is, in general, heavily weighted toward the middle and upper range of family incomes.

44 Surely economists would agree that the economic inefficiencies and gross inequities associated with the several billion dollars of federal funds allocated annually to US farmers cannot be remedied by increasing the progressivity of federal taxation. The same logic applies here to higher education.

45 The point was made repeatedly in the discussions of these papers that the subsidization of needy qualified college students would in principle discriminate on equity grounds against those who could not qualify as college students. Thus, to treat all such youth equally, what is called for would be a subsidy to every youth from a low-income family, comparable in amount with that provided to the needy college student.

46 See W. Lee Hansen and Burton A. Weisbrod, "A New Approach to Higher Education Finance," in *Financing Higher Education: Alternatives to the Federal Government*, ed. M. D. Orwig (American College Testing Program, Iowa City, 1971), pp. 117–42.

47 Schultz, *Human Capital*, chapter 13.

7

Are University Scholars and Scientists Free Agents?*

I begin with the utility of language and I shall treat it as a specialized form of human capital. I then consider why the value of the time of scholars and scientists is so high in our society and some of its implications. Lastly, I ask what we who have high salaries choose to do with our time.

1 Language has an Economic Value

It is obvious that to talk we must have a language, and that for want of a language there can be no conversation. What is not obvious is that a language has the attributes of an economic entity. It is a scarce, acquired human ability and to acquire it entails costs. Its acquisition is an investment in a specialized form of human capital. The utility of this ability matters indeed in getting at the economics of languages. The implication is that a price is attached to language. Scholarship in the humanities specializing in languages is, so it seems, successful in concealing this price; it believes that putting a price on a language would debase its intrinsic or true value. On the contrary, however, a strong case can be made that the underinvestment in language throughout the world is large, and that this underinvestment is in considerable part a consequence of our failure to see the value of the specialized human capital embodied in language.

To be fair it must be said that economists have also erred by their neglect of the economics of language. Would that we had a definitive treatise on the "economics of language". There are abundant examples of issues that have been overlooked. Consider the value of foreign languages in a professional career in economics. In the United States, up to the mid 1960s, two foreign languages – German and French – were

* First published in *Minerva*, xxv, No. 3 (Autumn 1987), 349–57. This paper is an abridged version of Professor Schultz's Franklin Lecture, delivered at Auburn University, Alabama on April 30, 1986.

required for a doctorate in economics. Now English suffices. Unfriendly critics contend that mathematics will soon suffice! Since the Second World War, English has become the international language of economics. This did not occur as a consequence of British and American political influence. Why then did it occur? One important implication for American economists is that their professional language cost has declined markedly. In Canada, meanwhile, the costs in terms of time required to learn the second language must be substantial.

Throughout much of central Africa and also in some other areas of low income, there are spoken languages or dialects that serve small local communities. The value of acquiring such languages or dialects must be very low. There are exceptions. One occurs where such a language is spoken on the radio to provide information where most of the population is illiterate.

Long before human beings can test what they think they know by engaging in a conversation, comes a long list of prerequisites. At the top of that list is the acquisition of the abilities to read efficiently and to write with competence. Not only do these acquired abilities play an important economic role in economic growth, they are in general necessary before individuals proceed to invest in additional human capital through secondary and higher education, in order to become highly competent specialized scholars or scientists.[1] These valuable abilities are in large measure acquired during the early years of schooling. The real cost of learning to read and write is at its lowest during the early years of primary schooling; the cost increases as the value of the time of the maturing student rises. The abilities to read and write are critical components of the quality of the human capital of any population.

It is well known that not only are the rates of return on investment in primary schooling generally higher than in secondary and higher education, but that they also tend to exceed the normal rates of return on investments in physical capital. The implications of these differences in rates of return in investments are clear.

In thinking about the economics of being poor, the English language is richer and more comprehensive than any economic theory. When we turn to the welfare of human beings, our language tells us much that is not captured in our theories of economic welfare. Alms, charity, and gifts have meanings that reach beyond economics. The age old concept of being poor is decidedly richer and broader than the now politicized concept of poverty.

Up to this point the utility of languages has been featured. The specialized languages of the sciences and the humanities do not support the belief in "the two cultures". Scientists and scholars in the humanities are held together by the strong web of language they have in common. The utility of our common language is much undervalued; the poorer the language the lower its value for conversation.

2 Value of the Time of Scholars and Scientists

Lifespans become longer, academic careers become more specialized, permanent tenure remains elusive and mandatory retirement gets set in stone. The time span of the academic career is brief. The economic value of this period of permanent tenure of academic scholars and scientists is at the heart of my story.

The increasing value of the time of human beings may well be the most distinctive attribute of our type of economy. The hourly wage of workers in the United States, measured in constant dollars, has risen well over fivefold since 1900. The value of the time of professors has also marched up and up, as has that of women, including housewives, and not least the value of the time of students; namely the earnings foregone while they attend college or university which now accounts for the largest part of the real cost of their education. We know why our own time has become more valuable, and we also know a good deal about the nature and significance of the resulting effects on income on what university scholars and scientists do in allocating their own time. It would be neat and convenient to assume here that teachers on permanent tenure at our universities are free agents. It is, of course, true they are not indentured servants; they are not legally bound to serve the university until they retire; they can leave when they choose, but the university is not free to dismiss them. But they are subject to governmental regulations, increasingly so, the more they depend on government funds.

There are other important dimensions of time. A perspective on how very brief our period of permanent tenure is – consider the long sense of time as suggested by Professor Karl Weintraub when he cited a story for Hendrik van Loon's *History of Mankind*: "In a fabled land lies a bald granite mountain. Every hundred years a little bird comes to sharpen its beak by grating it against the mountain. When the bird will have worn down the whole mountain, not even one second of eternity will have passed."[2] It is not surprising that historians and scientists view the economist's concept of time as simply the "here and now". What a pity that there is rarely an economist with a long sense of time.

The assumption of the free agent will continue to haunt us. We need to look more closely at universities. We think of our universities as institutions that specialize in activities concerned with the acquisition and transmission of knowledge. We call these activities higher education and research which require libraries, buildings, laboratories, etc. Neither the teachers nor the auxiliary personnel are cloistered, austere monks who "do their thing" for a pittance. Students, governments, foundations, and other patrons pay the bill. Money matters and inflation takes a toll. As institutions, universities have special legal privileges and social responsibilities. Freedom of inquiry is both an essential privilege and a serious responsibility for what we do in our research and teaching.[3]

Higher education is, in some important aspects, fragile in its activities concerned with knowledge. It is vulnerable to interventions by government and to restrictions by foundations and by private patrons who make grants to academics. Caesar is not renowned for providing funds that best serve the "knowledge activities" of universities. Caesar wants support for his policies. Some foundations want policy oriented research linked to the advocacy of particular policies – whereas, not so long ago, members of the teaching staff of unviersities were ever on their guard to keep trustees from encroaching on their freedom of inquiry. Currently they are all too complacent in accepting funds for research that impair their freedom of inquiry.

When we deal with the production and distribution of knowledge, we must consider the contributions of scholars and scientists. Not so long ago a teacher of philosophy, Adam Smith, invented the economic theory of self-interest. His followers have not been inclined to disqualify themselves from placing an economic value on the various components of knowledge.

The late Fritz Machlup, who was every inch an economist, in his *Production and Distribution of Knowledge in the United States*, made a major contribution to his subject.[4] His treatment of the analytical issues implicit in the earnings foregone by students, and in the other opportunity costs of education and the vexing issue underlying the benefits from education – as to whether they are "consumption" or "investment", and whether they accrue to students or to others – is not only formally correct but refreshingly clear and remarkably comprehensive. His concise treatment of inventive effort and patent protection is a classic, and so is his analysis of the complementarity between basic research and higher education.[5]

What then is there to be said about the issues at hand that go beyond Machlup's studies? He did not deal with the acute tensions between governments and universities, and with the increasing vulnerability of the freedom of inquiry brought about mainly by the intervention of the state.

To say that knowledge is man-made, and that it is a measure of the attainment of any civilization, does not require proof. The point which is clear to economists is that the creation, maintenance and distribution of knowledge requires scarce resources. Moreover, these activities have become large and expensive. Scholars and scientists are uneasy about this point. They prefer not to have the economic calculus applied to their activities because they believe doing so will inevitably debase its true value.

Let us proceed cautiously. Some aspects of the distribution of knowledge are not in doubt. Clearly the distribution of knowledge among countries is very unequal. This inequality between countries with low and high incomes *per capita* has been increasing for a long time. Since the 1940s, however, knowledge pertaining to the improvement of health and the growth of agricultural productivity has become somewhat more equal. Even so, differences in the composition and the general level of knowledge between most poor and rich countries are very large.

It is also evident that the production of knowledge is subject to man-made vicissitudes. When the Cultural Revolution was destroying the universities of China, higher education and research in the United States were flourishing. While China was destroying, India was expanding its universities and now has substantial corps of scientists, engineers and other classes of highly skilled persons. During the early 1980s, the knowledge-producing institutions throughout much of Africa were falling apart, as political instability and government intervention took their toll.

We are in an era in which the tensions between the university and the state have become increasingly acute.[6] These tensions are worldwide, although they differ greatly among the more than 150 nation states. In most of them, the intellectual independence of scholarly inquiry is seriously constrained. What most government agencies want is support for their policies and programs, regardless of how harmful these may be.

The pursuit of knowledge is a venture into the unknown. It always entails risk and uncertainty. It was thus for neolithic man and it continues to be so today. Necessity, luck and ideas tell most of the story. Facing a dwindling supply of food provided by men from hunting, neolithic women invented agriculture and they developed many of the food crop species we have today. Our highly skilled plant breeders have produced only one new food crop species, i.e. triticale.[7]

China attained a fairly high state of knowledge and the art of using it many centuries before Europe reached a corresponding level. Chinese farmers used the iron plough, practised crop rotation including multiple cropping, and maintained the productivity of the soil a millennium before European farmers. Anthony Tang, in assessing this legacy of China, shows how striking China's lead was for a long time. "The emergence of the new institutions and agents took place in China when Europe was just setting into the 'Dark Age'. . . ."[8] Yet despite that large early lead, something went wrong in maintaining and increasing the stock of knowledge, long before the Cultural Revolution in China.

Before considering what scholars and scientists do in response to the high value of their time, a summary of some main points is called for. It is our good fortune that salaries are high in the United States. Also, there are enough universities to provide a competitive market, acting as the invisible hand in protecting scholars and scientists. The market for scientists is extended by the demand of profit-oriented enterprises for their services. Nevertheless, the production and distribution of knowledge in universities are fragile, wherever freedom of inquiry is constrained by government or by patrons. The incentive to acquire the ability to obtain grants for research is strong. Prove that you have that ability and your appointment to permanent tenure is assured! Caesar has funds, but woe unto your freedom of inquiry when you sell your intellectual soul to Caesar![9]

3   Having High Salaries, What Do We Choose?

Theory implies that the demand for additional time to pursue leisure activities is enhanced by the income effect of high salaries. What are these leisure activities? If spending more time with one's family is deemed to be a form of leisure, and if the increases in divorce are in some way a consequence, deans and research directors should be extolling the virtues of the traditional work ethic. If scholars in the humanities were to spend a good bit of their additional leisure time reading and enjoying the papers and books created by scientists, and if scientists in turn were to find joy in the papers and books of scholars who are not scientists, and both groups revealed their new happiness, it would please even the most critical students. While there is a lack of evidence to assess the implications of a theory of leisure time, what matters is being free to choose how we allocate the time.

One of the more important new ideas in economics in the hypothesis of permanent income,[10] based on the assumption that both income and consumption are subject to a component of variance. We know that families who derive their income from salaries are favoured by a relatively small variance in income. Since university teachers on permanent tenure are thus favoured, what is their response? Does it create an incentive to reduce exertion, knowing that the variance in their income will be small? Or is it an incentive to be more adventurous in the research they pursue? If the salaries of those on permanent tenure were fixed with no increases based on merit, the economic incentive to break new ground would be blunted. On the second issue, evidence from other occupations indicates that having a substantial source of income that is subject to only a small variance is a condition that favours undertaking enterprises with higher risk. The corresponding response of scholars and scientists is that they also choose to take on the more risky research enterprises, being assured of a steady income.

The teaching staffs and administrators of our universities are dealing with the ever changing research frontier of the natural sciences and of humanistic scholarship. In addition, they are coping with economic conditions that are also changing. Clearly, within our universities academic entrepreneurship is much more important than we realize. Examine a university within which the available resources are allocated in a purely routine manner over any extended period and you will find that it is on a declining path. Senior administrative officers and, to a smaller degree, the overworked heads of departments are also entrepreneurs. Routine teachers are a liability and routine research workers contradict the meaning of research. If, nevertheless, there are such routine teachers and research workers, they are failures.

We need a searching discussion on the persistent dilemma of ever increasing academic specialization. How high is the price of specialization? Most academic economists pay a price for divorcing themselves from history and from the humanities. Professor Hayek has said with good grace that "Nobody can be a great economist who is only an economist"; he added, "an economist who is only an economist is likely to become a nuisance if not a positive danger".[11] As a result of Machlup's ingenious scholarship, we have a rich vein of information about the knowledge-producing professions in the United States. He accounts for the many branches of learning and departments of erudition.[12] The extent and complexity of the knowledge-producing professions touches on the most fundamental issues of the theory of human capital specialization which accounts in large measure for their productivity. But, as is the case with economists, specialized scholars and specialized scientists, notwithstanding their professional achievements, are likely to become a nuisance if not a positive danger when they make grand pronouncements pertaining to public choices.

High salaries, and living in a country with high income *per capita*, reduce our ability to comprehend the lot of scholars and scientists in countries with low income. It may well be easier for a camel to pass through the eye of a needle than it is for us who are so rich to enter into conversations with people who have long been poor. Even when the same words are used, what they mean to them and to us will be different. It stands repeating: there can be no conversation without a language. Moreover, even with a language, we who are rich appear to be incapable of discerning the adverse effects of being poor on the opportunities to do scholarly and scientific work and on the quality of discussion. Where the government is the controlling Leviathan, we fail to understand how precarious academic activities are, regardless of whether or not there is permanent tenure.

4 A Cheerful Conclusion

No one during Adam Smith's day could have anticipated that human capital, consisting of our acquired abilities, would come to predominate, as is the case in the United States where close to four-fifths of our national income is derived from wages, salaries and entrepreneurial rewards.

Henry Adams seeing the United States as it was in 1800[13] could not have anticipated the extraordinary commitment that the people of the United States would make to the promotion of knowledge. Fritz Machlup has documented the vast array and magnitude of such activities. Why is it that we are not satisfied with our success in creating, promoting and distributing knowledge? Instead, there is much criticism. Anti-science movements harass scientists and tend to politicise the sciences.[14] Philip Handler, when he was president of the United States National Academy of Sciences, boldly charged that scientists must expose "the anti-scientific and anti-rationalistic" movements, the "faddist approaches to nutrition", and "unfounded allegations of the environmental hazards". He held that scientists must "unfrock the 'charlatan'" in order to protect the credibility of science, and they must also "contain the feckless debates concerning the magnitude of the risk of innovations and challenge the foolish arguments for a 'risk free society'".[15]

Washington is beset with lobbyists who seek to influence public officials regarding legislation and the appropriation and allocation of funds which will favour the special research interests of their clients. Some foundations are doing the research that they want as an "in-house activity". In this way they establish new policy oriented areas which then serve to determine the type of proposals for support of research that will be considered for the award of grants.

Our government has a large measure of monopoly control over basic research. It is wishful thinking to believe that it will fade away. Professor John T. Wilson found the relationships between the federal government and higher education just short of disastrous. These relationships have been greatly impaired in comparison with what they were during the 1950s and 1960s.[16] Professor Wilson's views are grounded in his experiences as a high official of the National Science Foundation and as president of the University of Chicago.

Gerard Piel has said:

> If the autonomy of American universities is to be secured on public support, the necessary protections cannot be decreed by the Executive Branch of the federal government. Nor can Congress legislate the guarantee. The autonomy of our universities must be negotiated with the electorate. People must be asked to render their support of the university with the full understanding of its mission . . . Some significant percentage of the regular voters must be ready to entertain such a proposal, for thirty million college graduates are at large in the population.[17]

The electorate is understandably confused about the value of what academic scholars and scientists do. Scientists, except for those in agricultural research, have done all too little to inform the electorate and to seek its support.

At best our activities in the production of knowledge are fragile. Of course, we who are employed to do it are not indentured servants and our salaries are high. There is, however, an ever present danger. The harsh truth is that academic scholars and scientists are not free agents.

Notes and References

1 For a stimulating historical perspective on literacy in this context, see Jeffrey Brooks, *When Russia Learned to Read: Literacy and Popular Literature 1861–1917* (Princeton University Press, Princeton, NJ, 1985), especially chapters I and II, "Uses of Literacy" and "Primary Schooling."

2 Karl J. Weintraub, "With a Long Sense of Time . . ." (University of Chicago Press, Chicago, Ill., 1984), pp. 1–20.

3 Here and also later on I draw in part on my "Knowledge Activities of Universities: A Critical View" (unpublished).

4 Fritz Machlup, *Production and Distribution of Knowledge in the United States* (Princeton University Press, Princeton, NJ, 1962).

5 Fritz Machlup, *Knowledge: Its Creation, Distribution, and Economic Significance*, vol. 1, "Knowledge and Knowledge Production" (Princeton University Press, Princeton, NJ, 1980); also *The Economics of Information and Human Capital* (Princeton University Press, Princeton, NJ, 1984).

6 Theodore W. Schultz, "Governments, Foundations and the Bias in Research," *Minerva*, xvii (Autumn 1979), 459–68.

7   Norman E. Borlaug, "The Green Revolution: Can We Make it Meet Expectations," *Proceedings of the American Phytopathological Society*, III (1976).

8   Anthony M. Tang, "The Agricultural Legacy," *Conference on Modern Chinese Economic History* (Academia Sinica, Taipei, 1977), pp. 231–50.

9   Edward Shils, "'Render unto Caesar . . .': Government, Society and the Universities in Their Reciprocal Rights and Duties," *Minerva*, xvii (Spring 1979), 129–77.

10 Milton Friedman, *A Theory of the Consumption Function* (Princeton University Press, Princeton, NJ, 1957).

11 F. A. Hayek, "The Dilemma of Specialization," in *The State of the Social Sciences* (University of Chicago Press, Chicago, Ill., 1956), pp. 462–73.

12 Machlup, *Knowledge and Knowledge Production*, and *The Economics of Information*, also *The Branches of Learning* (Princeton University Press, Princeton, NJ, 1982).

13 Henry Adams, *The United States in 1800* (Great Seal Books, Cornell University Press, Ithaca, NY), p. 52.

14 Edward Shils, "Science, Faith, and the Legitimacy of Science," *Daedalus*, 103 (Summer 1974), 1–15.

15 Philip Handler, "The Future of American Science," an address delivered at Illinois Institute of Technology, Chicago, January 29, 1980.

16 John T. Wilson, *Higher Education and the Washington Scene: 1982* (University of Chicago Press, Chicago, Ill., 1979).

17 Gerard Piel, "On Promoting Useful Knowledge," *Proceedings of the American Philosophical Society* (Dec. 28, 1979), 337–40.

8

*Adam Smith and Human Capital**

I begin with Adam Smith's concept of the useful abilities acquired through education, study, or apprenticeship, always at a real expense, which consists of capital fixed in people. Investment in this form of capital is motivated by the expected rate of return.

I then consider the implications of the lack of a theory of the extension of markets. A compelling theory is still an unfinished part of economics.

Lastly I turn to human capital in the modernizing economy with its proliferation of human capital, vast specialization and its increases in the value of human time and advances in useful knowledge.

The significance of human capital is receiving increasing analytical attention, especially so since World War II. However, an awareness of the existence of this form of capital has a long history. It is clearly evident in many parts of *The Wealth of Nations*. Adam Smith boldly included all of the acquired useful abilities of the inhabitants and members of the society as capital. Smith reckoned that the acquisition of this class of capital by a person through his "education, study, or apprenticeship, always costs a real expense, which is a capital fixed and realized, as it were, in his person .... The improved dexterity of a workman may be considered in the same light as a machine or instrument of trade which facilitates and abridges labour, and which, though it costs a certain expense, repays that expense with a profit."[1] Smith treats the incentives to invest in this class of human capital in much detail along with many historical accounts of such investment processes. Ponder, however, Smith's jaundiced views of the value of public education for women and of the diligence of public teachers being corrupted by the endowments of schools and colleges.[2]

* Presented at the Adam Smith Bicentenary, Edinburgh, Scotland, July 16, 1990, and published in Michael Fry (ed.), *Adam Smith's Legacy: His Place in the Development of Modern Economics* (Routledge, London). Reproduced by permission of Routledge. I am indebted to John Letiche for useful suggestions and to Margaret Schultz for her library search.

A great deal of economics is condensed by Smith in the following paragraph.

> When any expensive machine is erected, the extraordinary work to be performed by it before it is worn out, it must be expected, will replace the capital laid out upon it, with at least the ordinary profits. A man educated at the expense of much labor and time to any of those employments which require extraordinary dexterity and skill, may be compared to one of those expensive machines. The work which he learns to perform, it must be expected, over and above the usual wages of common labour, will replace to him the whole expense of his education, with at least the ordinary profits of an equally valuable capital. It must do this too in a reasonable time, regard being had to the very uncertain duration of human life, in the same manner as to the more certain duration of the machine.[3]

What has been ignored in much of economics is the simple truth that people invest in themselves and that these investments are very large in modern high income countries. Although economists are seldom timid in entering upon abstract analysis, some are even proud of being impractical, they have not been bold in coming to grips with investment in human beings. It is as if when they come even close, they proceed gingerly, afraid that they were stepping into deep water. No doubt there are reasons for being wary.

In my American Economic Association presidential address, "Investment in Human Capital,"[4] I noted some deep-seated moral and philosophical issues. Free men are first and foremost the end to be served by the economy; they are not property, nor are they marketable assets. The mere thought of treating human beings as investment objects is offensive. Our values and beliefs inhibit us from thinking of human beings as capital goods, except in slavery, and this we abhor. We are ever mindful of the long struggle to rid society of indentured servitude and slavery and to evolve political and legal institutions to keep men free of bondage. Hence, to treat a human being as capital could appear to reduce man, once again, to a mere material component, as if he were a bit of physical property.

No less a person than J. S. Mill at one time insisted that the people of a country should not be looked upon as wealth because wealth existed only for the sake of people. But surely, Mill was wrong; there is nothing in the concept of human wealth and for that matter in human capital contrary to his idea that it exists only for the advantage of people. By investing in themselves, people can enlarge their economic opportunities. It is one way free human beings can enhance their welfare.

1 Extensions of Market Critical

Smith's famous theorem is that the division of labor depends on the extent of the market. In today's economic language, this says that the real gains in the productivity of labor, including "the greater part of the skill, dexterity, and judgment with which it is anywhere directed, or applied,"[5] are the consequences of the division of labor. Various components of human capital are specified by Smith. But the conditions and the analytics to explain the extensions of the market, their origins, and the increases in income derived from such extensions were not resolved by Smith.

Smith does appeal to various historical extensions of markets that had their origins in developments that reduced the costs of transportation. The long standing effects of great rivers and that of inland navigation are featured. "It is remarkable that neither the ancient Egyptians, nor the Indians, nor the Chinese, encouraged foreign commerce, but seem all to have derived their opulence from this inland navigation."[6] Explaining extensions of the market is at best a weak part of the division of labor analysis.

Smith could not have anticipated the vast increases in specialized human capital and the large increases in personal income derived from human capital. Ever more specialization is clearly evident in countries that are successful in the modernization of their economy.

Not knowing the economics of extensions of markets, how useful is it to hold fast to Smith's theorem that the division of labor is limited by the extent of the market? Vast increases in specialized human capital imply that the extent of the division of labor and the extent of the market must have increased greatly. I doubt that our knowledge about economic changes over time is sufficient to explain the sources of these vast extensions of the market. When it comes to explaining this source of the increases in income, it continues to receive a low priority in what economists do.

Allyn Young[7] is a notable exception. He perceived that there are latent implications in Smith's theorem that provide clues to explanations.

Young began his classic paper, "Increasing Returns and Economic Progress," with these words, "My subject may appear alarmingly formidable, but I did not intend it to be so." The formidable analytical task was to explain the origins of the changes in the economy that account for the large observed increases in income. There were and there still are many unsolved issues: (1) measured output exceeding measured inputs; (2) unexplained long term increases in per capita income; (3) declines in the economic importance of farm land; (4) increases in the value of time, and (5) the proliferation of human capital in the modernizing economy.

Young turned to latent implications in Smith's theorem. Young reasoned that there exists an economic process in which the interactions between particular extensions of the market and of specific types of extensions in the division of labor that explains increasing returns and economic progress.

The pursuit of investing in specialized human capital to attain increasing returns is not a venture guided by wishful thinking.[8] There are classes of private and public investments that have been and continue to be made guided by expectations of attaining increasing returns. Highly skilled geneticists and biologists, who specialize in their research on food producing plants and animals, have made advances in knowledge that made the recent extraordinary increases in food production possible. Ponder the explanation of the golden age of agricultural research that occurred beginning in the fifties and on into the eighties. All-in-all, the world population doubled. World food production more than doubled. Real expenditures worldwide on agricultural research increased more than seven-fold since 1950. These large increases in investment in research were made and continue to be made in response to the perceived high returns from this class of investments. So too are the sizable investments in research in the case of the remarkable event of the origins, productivity and profitability of the computer. There is one element that all such events have in common; they are all cost saving and income increasing.

Increases in the quality of both physical and human capital originate primarily out of the advances in knowledge. The value of the acquired abilities of human beings is in large measure revealed in wages, salaries, self-employed earnings and entrepreneurial rewards. Engineers who graduate currently will have learned many new elements in their specialization that were not known and therefore not taught to engineers who graduated several decades ago. This is also the case for scientists, medical personnel, technicians of various sorts, and economists. Moreover, the stock of human capital, which consists of a large array of components, has been increasing at a higher rate than that of physical capital.[9]

Smith was not overly occupied with diminishing or with increasing returns. That his division of labor entails specialization was not belabored. That the cost of an education is a form of fixed capital was not treated as an indivisibility to ascertain its effects on returns. That market expansion, division of labor, advances in technology, specialization, and increasing returns go hand in hand in achieving economic progress is implied, but was not featured by Smith.

The private and public investments in the development of highly skilled geneticists and biologists, who in my example become highly specialized in their research on food producing crops and animals, give rise to patterns of returns that are consequences of the indivisibilities that are specific to the human capital of geneticists and biologists.

Sherwin Rosen[10] is both cogent and concise on specialization:

> Incentives for specialization, trade, and the production of comparative advantage through investment are shown to arise from increasing returns to utilization. Hence, the rate of return is increasing in utilization and is maximized by utilizing specialized skills as intensively as possible. Identically endowed individuals have incentives to specialize their investments in skills and trade with each other for this reason, even if production technology exhibits constant returns to scale. The enormous productivity and complexity of modern economies are in good measure attributable to specialization.

Hindsight has some advantages. We now know that advances in technology are endogenous events. These advances are man-made. They originate from within the economy. They are made by people who possess in their person special skills consisting of components of human capital. It is increasingly so in this age of high technology.

We may be well advised to concentrate our analytical work on the following interacting income increasing sources: advances in technology, proliferation of human capital, and the increases in specialization.

We need a theory to analyze the interactions of physical and human capital accumulations that induce investment in specialized human capital. We need to identify the specific external effects of human capital postulated by Robert Lucas.[11] These effects are viewed as a spillover from one person to another. The implication is that people at each skill level are more productive in high than in low human capital environments. Human capital enhances the productivity of both labor and physical capital. Lucas sees "human capital accumulation as a social activity, involving groups of people, in a way that has no counterpart in the accumulation of physical capital."

Given our academic vested interest, dare we ask, does the economics of specialization apply to the professions? Machlup's[12] studies show that a great deal of specialization prevails and that the extent and complexity of our knowledge producing professions bespeak human capital specialization and that it accounts for much of the realized productivity.

When early English economists observed the high rates of increases in production by various manufacturing industries, they attributed a part of the additional income to increases in returns. Favorable changes in economic conditions in manufacturing, transportation, and trade in their day came to be known as the Industrial Revolution. As an economic process it had much in common with what is now referred to as the Green Revolution in agriculture.

Specializations driven by the proliferation of capital and by advances in technology, innovations, and discoveries are income increasing economic events.[13] Most of them are small, micro events, as in the case of a farmer's increase in corn yields made possible by hybrid seed. Such events can, as a rule, be identified and measured. Their economic effects are in general ascertainable. But when increases in income are attributed to large "macro events" – the Industrial Revolution, for example – the specific sources of the increases in incomes are difficult to isolate and measure.

Nature, as Marshall had perceived it, is a minor source of these income increasing events. For most analytical purposes they are consequences of the activities of human beings. They may have their origin either from within or outside of the economic system. Those that originate from within would be included in Schumpeter's theory of economic development.

These income increasing events have become important sources of additional income streams. They spawn related income increasing events. The economy of many countries has a built-in capacity to create income increasing entities, notably by means of organized research, including R and D, university-based science research, and investment in education as well as in the distribution of knowledge.

2   Analytic Leverage of Human Capital

To gauge the relative strength of the leverage of human capital, requires an all-inclusive concept of capital. From Fisher[14] we have the required concept, but it has seldom been used to gauge the economic importance of human capital. The economic effects of various institutions on human capital are rarely on the research agenda of economists. We do have Commons's[15] *Legal Foundations of Capitalism*. Would that economics could have been blessed by a marriage of Fisher's all-inclusive concept of capital and Commons's legal foundations of Fisher's capital. Presently, however, economists who specialize on growth models seldom mention institutions. There is no hiding the fact that our new analytical cupboards are bare on thinking by economists about institutions.

Marshall's[16] economic perceptions pertaining to knowledge, property rights, and organization remain cogent:

> Capital consists in a great part of knowledge and organization: and of this
> some part is private property and the other part is not. Knowledge is our
> most powerful engine of production ... Organization aids
> knowledge ... The distinction between public and private property in
> knowledge and organization is of great and growing importance; in some
> respects of more importance than that between public and private property
> in material things.

Marshall's perceptions are being strongly supported by the large body of
human capital research of the last three decades.

There are significant difference in the nature of property rights
between human and nonhuman capital. Rosen[17] is succinct in his
account of the main ideas in human capital. On the issue of the difference
in property rights he states, "Ownership of human capital in a free
society is restricted to the person in whom it is embodied ... A person
cannot, even voluntarily, sell a legally binding claim on future earning
power." It follows that a person cannot sell asset claims on himself:

> The legal system places many fewer restrictions on the sale and voluntary
> transfer of title of nonhuman capital ... The institution of slavery was the
> primary example of a transferable property right in human capital. To be
> sure, the involuntary elements of slavery are essential, but even voluntary
> systems have not been unknown. Similarly, indentured servitude was an
> example of a legally enforceable long-term contractual claim on the human
> capital services of others.

But keep in mind that there are countries that impose severe political and
legal restrictions on transfers of title to nonhuman capital: the chief
example is collective and state ownership of nonhuman capital in
planned economies.

Thus, at the extreme, people who are bound by the institution of
slavery, have no property rights in their human capital. Poor people who
are free in general have property rights in the small amount of human
capital that is a part of their person. In my *Restoring Economic
Equilibrium: Human Capital in the Modernizing Economy*, I argued the
case for extending property rights in human capital. I concentrated on
high income societies where investments in human capital have been
large, and where the rise in the value of human time has been pro-
nounced, and where the property rights of people in their human capital
have been enlarged and protected.

In societies where wages, self-employment earnings, salaries, and
earnings of entrepreneurs account for three-fourths, or a greater share of
personal income, important institutional changes in favor of human
capital property rights have occurred during recent decades. The political
and legal origins of these changes appear to be fairly easy to document.

There is much to be said for undertaking research using the logic of Yoram Barzel in his *Economic Analysis of Property Rights*,[18] to analyze the various origins of changes in property rights. Self-interest should motivate scholars, scientists including economists to determine the effects on incentives of extending property rights in human capital that go beyond existing patents and copyrights, that increase safety in the work place, safety in travel, and safety where one lives. The effects of tenure rights on incentives are unresolved. To what extent are honors weak substitutes for additional financial rewards for various unprotected intellectual and other human capital components?

The notable advances in human capital theory and in the wide array of supporting empirical studies are evaluated with authority by Rosen[19] in his essay on *Human Capital*. The increasing economic importance of human capital in the modernizing economy is not in doubt. The economic leverage of human capital exceeds that of nonhuman capital in high income countries where it accounts for most of the personal income of people.

The basic element in my approach to human capital is in the linkage of the rate of return to the investment in human capital. This linkage is evident in Smith's explanation of the relative earnings of physicians and other professional workers. The compensatory nature of earnings on prior investments points to opportunities foregone, which is a fundamental cost of undertaking the investment.

Rosen correctly credits Gary Becker for having developed:

> The fundamental conceptual framework of analysis for virtually all subsequent work in this area. Following Schultz's lead, Becker organized his theoretical development around the rate of return on investment, as calculated by comparing the earnings streams in discounted present value to alternative courses of actions. Rational agents pursue investments up to the point where the marginal rate of return equals the opportunity cost of funds[20] . . .

We have a theory of supply of human capital that gives us empirically refutable restrictions on intertemporal and interpersonal differences in the patterns of earnings and other aspects of productivity. In focusing on the development of a person's skills and earning capacity over the life cycle, human capital theory has evolved as a theory of "permanent income" and wealth.

The best studies to date pertain to education as a form of human capital. Moreover, education is the most important component of human capital. In this area Jacob Mincer and Zvi Griliches have made outstanding contributions. An issue of special interest to me is entrepreneurial ability. The advances in the modernization of agriculture has lead to many studies of the entrepreneurship of farmers. The results are that there are few economic regularities that are as valid empirically as is the proposition that the entrepreneurial abilities of farmers are enhanced by their education.

Dale Jorgensen has devoted a great deal of his research over several years to establish the economic value of education. I draw on an up-dating of that research by Jorgenson jointly with Barbara Fraumeni.[21] Their results are based on education in the United States. They reckon ". . . the lengthy gestation period between the application of educational inputs . . . and the emergence of human capital embodied in the graduates of educational institutions. Furthermore, some of the benefits of investing in education, such as greater earning power, are recorded in transactions in the labor market, while others – better parenting or more rewarding employment of leisure – remain unrecorded."

The value of the time spent working has expanded very rapidly in postwar United States. The increases in this value have been greater for women than for men at all levels of educational attainment, which reflects the more rapid increases in labor force participation of women. The proportional increase in the value of market labor time has been greatest for college educated men and women.

The total value of market activities for all educational attainments in the United States, adjusted for the increase in the price level between 1948 and 1984, rose by a factor of 3.3; for males who attained a college education it increased by a factor of 6.6; and for females by a factor of 12.9. The Jorgenson-Fraumeni estimates of the value of nonmarket activities, which rest on a critical assumption, exceeded the value of market activities.

Investments in formal education in 1982–84 dollars increased from 184 to 772 billion dollars, by a factor of 4.2. Investments in college education of males and females combined increased from 36.3 to 523 billion, an increase by a factor of 14.5.

3   Closing Comment

At the outset I cited Adam Smith to show that Smith clearly perceived that the critical economic connection is the rate of return to investment in "education, study, or apprenticeship . . . which is a capital fixed and realized, as it were, in his person." On the basic properties of human capital, Adam Smith stands high, as he does on the division of labor, limited by the extent of the market. But we still do not have a compelling theory of market extensions. Smith presented many particular cases. So do economists presently. Smith could not have anticipated the extraordinary rise in the economic importance of human capital.

In retrospect it has been the increasing economic importance of human capital, consisting of the acquired abilities of people – their education, work experience, skills, and health, that explains most of modern economic progress. It is "human capital" – not space, cropland, energy, or other physical properties of the earth – that is decisive in improving the income and welfare of people in the modernizing economy. A critical view would stress that in making investments land is overrated, whereas effort made to increase the quality of human agents is underrated.[22]

Notes and References

1 This quotation and others that follow are from Adam Smith, *The Wealth of Nations*, ed. Edwin Cannan (Random House, The Modern Library, 1937, New York); see pp. 265–6.
2 Ibid., pp. 733–34.
3 Ibid., p. 101.
4 See above, Part II, No. 1.
5 Smith, *Wealth of Nations*, p. 3.
6 Ibid., p. 20.
7 Allyn A. Young, "Increasing Returns and Economic Progress," *Economic Journal* (Dec. 1928), 527–42.
8 Theodore W. Schultz. "On Investing in Specialized Human Capital to Attain Increasing Returns," in Gustav Ranis and T. Paul Schultz (eds), *The State of Development Economics*, (Basil Blackwell, New York, 1988).
9 I draw here on a part of chapter 14 in my *Restoring Economic Equilibrium: Human Capital in the Modernizing Economy* (Basil Blackwell, New York, 1990).
10 Sherwin Rosen, "Substitution and Division of Labor," *Econometrica*, 45, No. 1 (1976), 861–68. Also, "Specialization and Human Capital," *Journal of Labor Economics*, 1 (1983), 43–49.
11 Robert E. Lucas, Jr., "On the Mechanics of Economic Development" (Marshall Lecture, May 1985), published in *Journal of Monetary Economics*, 22 (1988), 3–42.
12 Fritz Machlup, *The Production and Distribution of Knowledge in the United States* (Princeton University Press, Princeton, NJ, 1962); and his "Knowledge: Its Creation, Distribution, and Economic Significance," in *Knowledge and Knowledge Productivity* (Princeton University Press, Princeton, NJ, 1980): *The Branches of Learning* (Princeton University Press, 1982); and his last, *The Economics of Information and Human Capital*, same press, 1984.
13 Based on a part of chapter 17 of Schultz, *Restoring Economic Equilibrium*.

14 Irving Fisher, *The Nature of Capital and Income* (Macmillan and Co., New York, 1906).

15 John R. Commons, *Legal Foundations of Capitalism* (Macmillan and Co., New York, 1924).

16 Alfred Marshall, *Principles of Economics* (8th edn Macmillan and Co., London, 1930), book IV, chapter 1, 138–9.

17 Sherwin Rosen, "Human Capital," in *The New Palgrave: A Dictionary of Economics* eds John Eatwell, Murray Milgrate, and Peter Newman (The Macmillan Press, London, 1987).

18 Yoram Barzel, *Economic Analysis of Property Rights* (Cambridge University Press, Cambridge, England, 1989).

19 Rosen, "Specialization and Human Capital."

20 Ibid.

21 Dale W. Jorgenson and Barbara M. Fraumeni, "Investment in Education and US Economic Growth," presented at a NBER Conference, May 4–5, 1990.

22 The basis for this assessment is set forth in my *Investing in People: The Economics of Population Quality* (University of California Press, Berkeley, CA, 1981).

Part III
Effects of Human Capital

Part III

Effects of Human Capital

1

Institutions and the Value of Human Capital*

I take it to be true that there is a strong connection between the investment in human capital and the secular rise in the economic value of man. The institutional implications of this development are, however, far from clear. My purpose is to show that this rise in the economic value of human agents makes new demands on institutions, that some political and legal institutions are especially subject to these demands, that there are lags in adjusting to the new demands and these lags are the key to important public problems, and that economic theory is a necessary analytical tool in clarifying and solving these problems.

It might be said that human capital is protesting the status quo of institutions as it seeks participation rights for itself. Be that as it may, there is enough historical perspective to see that the ownership of land is declining as a source of economic leverage, and so is the ownership of physical capital relative to that of human capital. We have long known that Ricardian rent is not the fulcrum of economic values; nor is physical capital the critical historical factor, as Marx believed. The institutions governing private rights in land and in other forms of physical capital, when Ricardo and Marx made their contributions, would be far from adequate in contemporary society with its large investment in human capital. Would that economics could have been blessed by the marriage of Irving Fisher's all-inclusive concept of capital and John R. Commons' legal foundations of that capital.[1]

It is currently a mark of sophistication in presenting economic models not to mention institutions. But for all that, it is a significant trait of contemporary economics that, despite this omission, it manages somehow to find support for institutional changes. It is a neat trick, but it cannot hide the fact that, in thinking about institutions, the analytical cupboard is bare. There are a few old boxes on the back shelf labeled

* First published as "Institutions and the Rising Economic Value of Man," *American Journal of Agricultural Economics*, 50, No. 5 (Dec. 1968), 1113–22. Reproduced by permission of the American Agricultural Economics Association. I am indebted to Earl J. Hamilton, Harry Johnson, and Albert Rees for their incisive comments. I have also benefited from a discussion with Dale Hathaway.

"institutional economics" which have been pushed aside and which have long been thought to be empty. When we look more closely we find that there are virtually no terms of reference, no concepts with specifications that can be identified, and no economic theory to guide the analysis. Yet it is obvious that particular institutions really matter, that they are subject to change and are, in fact, changing, and that people are trying to clarify social choices with regard to alternative institutional change to improve the economic efficiency and the welfare performance of the economy.[2]

My plan is, first, to define and comment on the attributes of the institutions that render services to the economy, then to present and evaluate three approaches for the analytical task at hand, and lastly to use the third of these approaches to explain particular institutional lags in adjusting to the rise in the value of human agents.

1   Institutions that Render Services to the Economy

I shall define an institution as a behavioral rule. These rules pertain to social, political, and economic behavior. They consist, for example, of rules that govern marriage and divorce, rules embodied in constitutions that govern the allocation and use of political power, and rules that establish market capitalism or governmental allocation of resources and of income. Since I shall deal only with those institutions that perform economic functions, I shall leave aside all institutions that perform purely social functions. It is my aim to consider particular political, including legal, institutions that in one way or another influence, or are in turn influenced by the dynamics of economic growth. It is a concept of institutions which takes me into the domain of political economy. A partial list includes the following institutions:

1   those that reduce transaction costs (for example, money, futures' markets)
2   those that influence the allocation of risk among the owners of the factors of production (contracts, share tenancy, cooperatives, corporations, insurance, public social security programs)
3   those that provide the linkage between functional and personal income streams (property, including inheritance laws, seniority and other rights of labor)
4   those that establish the framework for the production and distribution of public goods or services (highways, airports, schools, agricultural experiment stations).

Some elaboration of the economic role of these institutions may be in order. There are those that belong to an older vintage. Money, clearly, is one of them. As the quantity of international transactions increases, the supply of international money may be subject to serious stresses. Consider the process under way to internationalize "paper gold," thus presumably freeing the supply of high-powered money from the constraints that determine the production of gold. Clearly related are credit instruments, including debts. I recall, with pleasure, the first assignment by John R. Commons asking those of us in his class to search for the historical circumstances that gave rise to the negotiability of a debt. The legal assignment of private rights in property is still, obviously, an important institution, the economic implications of which remain high on the agenda at Wisconsin, especially so in agricultural economics. Contracts, of course, are a viable institution, and they also are undergoing change, for example, in obtaining access to the capital market to invest in oneself, the formation of human capital.

A recent vintage includes the legal rights of labor; they now loom large. They, too, are in a state of flux with many unsettled issues. The rights to organize and to use all of the bargaining power that organized labor can muster can impair economic efficiency sufficiently to induce the political process to alter some of these rights. Meanwhile, the rising economic value of man is compelling society to establish additional rights favoring the human agent. Lastly, I shall mention the institutionalization of public transfers of income. But here, too, the guiding principles and the appropriate arrangements are still far from settled.

It is hard to believe that institutions such as these are protected by Nature in ways which make them immune to economic analysis. The analytical job is to specify their functions, measure their influence, and determine when they are efficient. To get on with this task requires a theoretical approach from which testable hypotheses can be derived; and these hypotheses, we may hope, will lead to empirically supported propositions pertaining to the economic performance of these institutions.

2 Approaches to the Economics of Institutions

First, there is the approach that omits or impounds institutions by abstracting from them. As noted at the outset, this is the approach of modern economics. We have a large family of growth models that treat institutions as a part of the "state of nature"; thus, institutions are impounded and they are not subject to change, either exogenously or as a variable adjusting to growth. There are some short-run growth problems that can be treated in this way, but most growth problems cannot be solved in this manner. Modern economics with all of its analytical tools is not up to the job of analyzing the connections between institutional changes and growth dynamics.

Second, there is the approach that treats institutions as subject to change exogenously. In this approach, institutional changes may matter but the critical simplifying assumption is that these changes are independent of economic growth. Accordingly, institutions are treated as an exogenous variable in the sense that they are altered by political acts, including legal decisions, independent of the process of economic growth. There are, undoubtedly, some institutional changes that are of this type and, in considering their economic effects, it is an appropriate approach. But most institutions that perform economic functions undergo change in response to the requirements of economic growth, and the nature and strength of these responses are not within the province of this scheme of analysis.

I would be remiss if I did not give credit to those few hardy economists who remain committed to "institutional economics." They are concerned predominantly with the allocation of property rights in natural resources and they are best known for their analyses of, and arguments for, land reform. The essence of their work is to begin with an ad hoc institutional change. It is, therefore, not an approach that treats an institution as an endogenous variable in an economic growth model. It is primarily concerned with the effects of a particular reform upon the distribution of personal income and welfare. It is not guided by economic theory, no doubt in part because theory has so far not integrated the functional distribution of income and the distribution of personal income. Likewise, institutions that produce human capital (for example, education and on-the-job training), institutions that are the source of technical change (for example, research and development), and laissez-faire competition are also usually treated in this fashion.

Third, I propose an approach that treats these institutions as variables within the economic domain, variables that respond to the dynamics of economic growth. Although not all institutional changes can be treated thus, there is a large and important set that can be taken on analytically in this manner.

Instead of omitting or impounding these institutions in the "state of nature," or introducing them on an ad hoc basis, the analytical task is to bring them into the theoretical core of economics. To get on with this task two key concepts are required, that is, the economic value of the function performed by an institution, and the concept of an economic equilibrium. First, how are we to get at their economic value and the factors that determine their value? We begin with the assumption that these institutions are suppliers of particular services. They may supply a convenience, which is one of the attributes of money; they may supply a contract which reduces transaction costs, as in the case of leases, mortgages, commodity futures; they may supply information, as do markets and economic planning; they may pool particular risks, which is an attribute of insurance, corporations, cooperatives, and public social security arrangements; and they may supply public goods (services), as in the case of schools, highways, health facilities, and experiment stations. For each of these services there is a demand. It is, therefore, within the province of economic theory to approach the determination of the economic value of each of these services by subjecting them to a supply and demand analysis.

The next analytical step is to place this supply and demand approach into an equilibrium framework. The key assumption in taking this step is that an economy arrives at an equilibrium with respect to the value of each of these economic services of institutions when the rates of return represented by these services reach equality.

Consider now several variants of the process of economic growth. Suppose that it were conceivable that an economy could produce additional income streams over a period of time in such a manner that everything would increase in exactly the same proportion. If this were to occur, presumably there would be no disequilibria, and thus the economy would not be confronted by the problem of returning to an equilibrium. But in explaining actual economic growth as we observe it, growth models built on this assumption are, so it seems to me, toys rather than analytical tools.

The process of modern economic growth is beset by all manner of disequilibria which are consequences of the growth process. Institutions that perform economic functions are not spared. Some of these disequilibria persist and even become chronic, as anyone who is informed about economic problems confronting U.S. agriculture knows. It is obvious that we are involved in a long-standing disequilibrium, which has burdened human agents in agriculture greatly and which still persists despite the extraordinary migration out of agriculture. Bishop clearly identified the lags in adjusting community institutions.[3] With respect to this and other disequilibria, the questions to ask are these: How strong is the tendency towards equilibrium? Can it be strengthened? Can the lags in the adjustment be facilitated at a cost where the benefits will exceed the costs?

By way of summary, then, our theory is designed to explain those changes in institutions that occur in response to the dynamics of economic growth. The institution is treated as a supplier of a service which has an economic value. It is assumed that the process of growth alters the demand for the service and that this alteration in the demand brings about a disequilibrium between the demand and the supply measured in terms of long-run costs and returns. Although it is possible for the supply of the service of an institution to be altered independently of economic growth considerations, our theory cannot explain such a change in an institution; it can be used, however, to determine the resulting effects of such a change.

I shall digress at this point and consider briefly several testable propositions pertaining to institutions and agricultural production in countries that have long been in equilibrium of the type that characterizes traditional agriculture.[4] Suppose that the policy objective is to attain a sustained rate of increase in agricultural production and the rate of increase is both efficient in economic terms and higher than the rate associated with population growth (farm labor) in the case of traditional agriculture. In negative terms, I would offer the following propositions: (1) a planned increase in the supply of money at a rate that would be higher than formerly will not suffice to bring about the desired increases in agricultural production, (2) nor will an institutional reform that would increase the supply of credit available to farmers achieve the objective, (3) nor will a change in tenancy laws that would reduce the share rents of tenants bring about the desired sustained rate of increase in agricultural production.

Let me now reformulate these and closely related propositions in positive and more readily testable terms. When agriculture acquires a growth momentum, as it recently has in many parts of Asia (China aside for lack of information and Japan aside for reasons of her prior successful modernization of agriculture) – a growth momentum that is a consequence of favorable farm product prices, the available new varieties of foodgrains that are responsive to fertilizer, and a cheaper and larger supply of fertiizer – the dynamics of that growth will induce farmers in these parts of Asia to demand institutional adjustment. They will demand a larger supply of credit, with stress on its timeliness and terms, and they will organize cooperatives should these be necessary for this purpose. They will demand more flexibility in tenancy contracts. They will join with neighbors to acquire tube wells and undertake minor investments to improve the supply of water. Both tenants and landowners will also use whatever political influences they have to induce the government to provide more and better large scale irrigation and drainage facilities.

These are all testable propositions. There is, so it seems to me, a growing body of evidence in support of each of these propositions.[5] So much by way of digression. I now return to the mainstream of the analysis.

Thinking in terms of the economic incentives for institutional responses, incentives which are a consequence of economic growth, there are several more general propositions:

　1　In a market economy which is achieving growth, the demand for the convenience of money shifts to the right. (This proposition is supported by competent empirical studies.)

　2　In an economy in which the income per family is rising, the demand for contracts and property arrangements serving the economic activities of the nonfarm sectors increases relative to that associated with the farm sector.

　3　As economic growth becomes increasingly dependent upon the advance in useful knowledge, the demand for institutions that produce and distribute such knowledge shifts to the right. Here we have a modern development with respect to which the less developed countries are in generally substantially more in disequilibrium than are the technically advanced countries.[6].

　4　When economic development reaches the stage at which the economy requires increasingly higher skills, the demand for high skills that require schooling, including higher education, increases relative to the demand for low skills and for reproducible forms of nonhuman capital. (There is a strong evidence that the US economy has been in this stage since World War II.)

　5　The proposition on which I shall concentrate during the remainder of this paper is as follows: In an economy where growth increases the economic value of human agents, the demands or services of a number of different institutions are altered by this type of growth. As the value of the time of people rises the demand per worker for additional safeguards protecting workers from accidents shifts to the right; so, does the demand per person for health services and for life insurance. The demand for additional legal protection of personal rights (for example, protection from invasion by police that impairs the privacy of persons) also shifts to the right, as does the demand more generally for civil rights. As a factor in production, human agents demand greater equality in obtaining jobs, especially so with respect to jobs that require high skills. Closely related is the increase in the demand for less discrimination in schooling and higher education to acquire the higher skills. As consumers, human agents demand greater equality in having access to consumer goods and services, notably so in the case of housing and family planning information. Then, too, as the value of a person's time rises, there is allocation toward good-intensive rather than time intensive consumption activities.[7]

3 Institutional Lags in Adjusting to More Human Capital

It is my thesis that the remarkable secular rise in the economic value of human agents that has been, and is occurring in the United States is the source of major disequilibria in the economic functions performed by institutions. Let me be explicit in noting that it is not my contention that all of this rise in the economic value of human agents is wholly a consequence of the type of economic growth that characterizes our economy. A part of it, but surely a small part, is a result of the curtailment of the immigration of persons who are allowed to enter from abroad to become members of the US labor force. The extension of civil rights, the additional public provisions for legal services for the poor, the programs to alleviate poverty,[8] and the Supreme Court's decisions with regard to schooling are developments that have enlarged the choices open to individuals. Although it might be argued that these developments, including urbanization as an intermediate influence, were not dependent upon the growth of the economy enhancing the economic value of human agents, it is a superficial view if it is true, as I contend, since these developments are predominantly a consequence of the type of economic growth which has been and is occurring in the United States. These legislative acts and legal decisions, in large part, were made possible and necessary because of the process of economic growth. In brief, these legislative and legal developments are lagged accommodations to the profound institutional stresses and strains brought about by the marked secular rise in the economic value of human agents.[9]

It is hard to imagine any secular economic movement that would have more profound influence in altering institutions than would the movement of wages relative to that of rents (that is, the price of the services of property). I am sure that economic historians would find the secular movement of wages relative to rents a rich vein. Showing the symmetry of the institutional changes that follow in the wake of such movements, regardless of the type of government, is one of the major contributions of Slicher Van Bath.[10] We are presently in a long secular movement which is running in favor of the economic value of the human agent.

Clearly, then, the institutional changes that occur in response to the rising economic value of the human agent call for a family of new economic models. I shall consider briefly three that belong to this family: namely (1) institutional responses to increases in the market price of work, (2) institutional responses to increases in the rate of return to investment in human capital, and (3) institutional responses to increases in consumer disposable income.

First, assume that economic growth increases the value productivity of workers per unit of time (and thus the wage per hour) relative to the rate of return to investment in property, and also that the value productivity of workers with high skills increases in absolute terms compared to that of workers with low skills. What are the institutional implications? What is implied in terms of substitution possibilities? At the level of allocative decisions made by firms operating for profit we are not burdened with serious institutional rigidities in our type of competitive market economy. Contracts, including leases entered into by tenants in agriculture, are a case in point; there is, of course, a lag, but it is not a long lag in adjusting such contracts to changes to the better earning opportunities of human agents. What is true, however, in a national context is that workers with low skills have access to less job information than workers with high skills, and, in the case of the higher skills, there is job market discrimination against nonwhite workers.

The institutional lags pertaining to wages that arise out of the dynamics of economic growth are predominantly in the realm of internal migration, occupational shifts, and discrimination against nonwhites. These lags are revealed in terms of less than optimum job information, less on-the-job training than is consistent with an equalization of the social benefits and costs of such training, and living accommodations in job expanding areas which are in part rationed by discrimination. In the report, *The People Left Behind*,[11] we have a landmark in analysis and recommendations for lines of public action to reduce the institutional lags in this general area.

Second, in approaching the problem of investing in man, the key assumption was that economic growth is of a type in which the production activities require relatively higher skills than formerly and that the derived demand from these activities increases the rate of return to investment in human agents. Again we ask: What are the institutional implications?[12] Looking back, it would appear that our system of education has been flexible in expanding the supply of education services sufficiently to accommodate the private demands of middle and upper income families. The rub is, however, that it has lagged seriously in supplying additional educational services, both quantitatively and qualitatively, for many children of farm families, for poor whites generally, and, most patently, for black people. In terms of social rates of return to investment in poor people, there is a growing body of evidence that supports the inference of a continuing disequilibrium, especially so with respect to elementary and secondary schooling. Higher education is an institution that raises complex and difficult organizational issues. The tendency toward an efficient allocation of resources is weak; economic incentives and information are in poor repair. The self-interest of students is not mobilized adequately, the accounting of social benefits (losses) is haphazard, and academic entrepreneurship is in a box which provides all too little opportunity for allocating resources efficiently. Since I have considered elsewhere the problems associated with resources for higher education,[12] I shall not elaborate further here.

Third, in thinking about institutional lags that impair consumer sovereignty, the central problem is that of accessibility where rationing occurs as a consequence of discrimination. Here, too, let us assume that disposable consumer incomes rise as a result of economic growth. Although it is true that in general market forces have a strong tendency to adjust to the changing demands of consumers, it is not true in the case where particular consumer goods and services are subject to market discrimination between people by color. There is little room for doubt that many black families with rising incomes are subject to such markets in traveling, at least until very recently, in acquiring health services and family planning information and techniques, and, above all, in renting or purchasing housing.

Finally, it must be said, when the economic value of human agents is rising, we are in the realm of new and better opportunities. The range of private and social choice is enlarged. It is, indeed, an optimistic set of circumstances that all too few people of the world enjoy. But even so, this favorable type of economic growth is not without its institutional stresses and strains. Since we can specify and identify these institutional lags, we can also analyze the benefits in terms of the efficiency and welfare that could be had by reducing these lags. Meanwhile, it is not simply a matter of catching up, because there are strong reasons for believing that the economic value of man will continue to rise.

Notes and References

1   Irving Fisher, *The Nature of Capital and Income* (The Macmillan Co., New York, 1906); John R. Commons, *Legal Foundations of Capitalism* (The Macmillan Co., New York, 1924).

2   A part of the literature pertaining to welfare economics is relevant here. The *Journal of Law and Economics* is a rich source of papers on the economic implications of property rights; the contributions in it by Coase are especially noteworthy. Still another relevant source is the work by Anthony Downs in bringing economic theory to bear on political decisions.

3   C. E. Bishop, "The Urbanization of Rural America: Implications for Agricultural Economics," *Journal of Farm Economics*, 49 (Dec. 1967), 999–1008.

4   Theodore W. Schultz, *Transforming Traditional Agriculture* (Yale University Press, New Haven, Conn., 1964), chapter 2.

5   I am indebted here to W. David Hopper for his formulation in "Regional Economic Report on Agriculture", *Asian Agricultural Survey*, section 3, vol. 1, Asian Development Bank, Manila (Mar. 1968).

6   See Theodore W. Schultz, "Efficient Allocation of Brains in Modernizing World Agriculture," *Journal of Farm Economics*, 49 (Dec. 1967), 1071–82.

7   See Gary S. Becker, "A Theory of the Allocation of Time," *Economic Journal*, 75 (Sept 1965), 493–517.

8   Walter Gellborn, "Poverty and Legality: The Law's Slow Awakening," *Proceedings of the American Philosophical Society*, 112(2) (April 1968), 107–16.

9   Albert Rees has called my attention to the fact that courts are more and more explicitly considering earning power in determining the size of the judgements in cases of accidental injury or death.

10 B. H. Slicher van Bath, *The Agrarian History of Western Europe, A.D. 500–1850* (St. Martin's Press, New York, 1963).

11 President's National Advisory Commission on Rural Poverty, *The People Left Behind* (Government Printing Office, Washington, Sept. 1967).

12 Professor Earl J. Hamilton reminded me of the insights of Alfred Marshall on some aspects of this issue (*Principles of Economics*, 8th edn, Macmillan & Co. Ltd., London, 1930), Book 6, chapters 12, 13.

13 See above, Part II, No. 4.

2

*The Increasing Economic Value of Human Time**

When data and theory talk to each other there is hope for economics. We are very much in need of such talk with a view to explaining the long-term changes in relative prices of the productive services of the factors of production. When we leave the equilibrium static state and endeavor to bring theory to bear on the economic processes that change these prices relative one to another, our factor price economics is wanting. Modern economic growth theory puts this issue aside on the convenient assumption that these prices do not change relative to each other. The classical economists, however, had more courage and a broader perspective of economic processes, and their theories continue to influence our thinking about long-term changes in rents relative to wages and relative to the price of the services of reproducible capital. By their theory, rents would necessarily rise relative to wages. But history has been hard on this theory.

What we observe in countries where per capita incomes are high is that rent per acre declines over time relative to the price of human time. In the United States, for example, the total real compensation per hour at work of all manufacturing production workers increased between 1929 and 1970 more than four times as much as did the rent of farm real estate per acre similarly adjusted.[1]

In explaining long-term changes in the size of the labor force and in wages, if we follow the first edition of Malthus' *Essay on Population*, the price of children remains constant over time and the supply of laborers is highly elastic. The wage implications are obvious. But we now know that the economics of human fertility is not as simplistic as Malthus envisioned it. The Malthusian assumption about bearing and rearing children in response to economic growth led, of course, to the long-standing dismal economic perspective with respect to the population consequences of the accumulation of capital and of any advances in the techniques of production. Economists no longer accept the subsistence standard of

* First published in *American Journal of Agricultural Economics* (Dec. 1972), 843–50. Reproduced by permission of the American Agricultural Economics Association.

living as invariant over time in view of the widely observed rise in standards of living that has occurred.

Contrary to the dismal economic perspective of classical thinking with rents rising and wages constant, the approach to the price of human time to be presented here implies a fairly optimistic perspective of economic processes. It is a long-term view of changes in relative factor prices.

With respect to the price of capital, despite the continuing controversy about underlying fundamentals, the core of economic theory implies a tendency toward a constant long-term real interest rate, and this implication is broadly consistent with the data. There are, however, two major unsettled issues that plague capital theory, namely: (1) how do we treat the heterogeneity of capital and (2) in view of the vast increases in the stock of capital in the advanced economies, why are diminishing returns to capital not evident as would be expected on theoretical grounds? On the latter point, the data are saying there is something missing in the theory.

The central problem to which I now turn can be stated briefly. Although the price of human time is the most important cost component in modern production and although this price has been rising secularly relative to land rent and to real interest rates and markedly so, we have no satisfactory economic theory to explain this persistent and potent rise in the price of human time to guide us in analyzing its economic implications. I shall first present an economic approach to this problem and then consider some of the more important implications.

1 An Economic Approach

What determines the long-term changes in the supply of and the demand for the services of human agents? Recent advances in economics provide parts of the theory for determining the changes in the supply of the *quality attributes* of human agents. The useful abilities that people acquire are viewed as forms of human capital. Investment in these abilities is taken to be the response to favorable investment opportunities. Thus the increases in the supply of these skills depend on current expenditures (sacrifices) made by individuals, families, and public bodies, on education, health, on-the-job training, their search for information, and on geographical migration to take advantage of better jobs or of better consumption opportunities. These expenditures (sacrifices) are presumably made deliberately with an eye to future personal satisfactions and earnings. During the last several years economic analysis has been further extended to cope with fertility behavior to determine the number and quality of children that parents bear and rear.[2] Accordingly, in determining the long-term changes in the supply of the services of human agents, the fundamentals of a theory are at hand along with substantial empirical support.

It may be helpful to be more explicit on the advances in economic analysis that have made the supply part of this approach possible. The idea and the theory of investment in human capital need not be elaborated further. (See Mincer, early work and that of Becker in this area.)[3] The economic significance of the producer attributes of human capital have been summarized succinctly by Harry Johnson.[4] A second important advance is the treatment by Becker of human time in the allocative decisions with respect to both market and non-market activities.[5] The linkage between human capital and this concept of the allocation of time is strong and clear. The usefulness of the new concept of human time is not restricted to work in the labor market, for it is also applicable to work in the household. In the household, predominantly, the housewife's time is allocated in part to shopping for and choosing consumer goods and in part to using them in household production leading to consumption. Then, too, consumption per se also requires time. The central principle underlying this analysis is that in reality each consumer service has two prices attached to it; namely, a money price as in traditional theory of consumer choice, and a time cost of acquiring the consumer good and processing it in the household (including the time cost that is involved in consuming the services obtained from this household activity).[6]

The third advance is the household production function. It was a direct outgrowth of the concepts of investment in human capital and allocation of human time. The household production function provides a comprehensive approach to non-market activities of the household, activities that were foreshadowed by the much earlier work of Margaret Reid.[7] The distinctive merit of Becker's theory of the allocation of human time is in accounting for the use of the individual's time in household production activities. The household production function is for this purpose a new, useful analytical tool.[8]

The fourth advance is a view of the family as a decision making unit maximizing both its utility in consumption and in the allocation of human time in purchasing goods in the production activities of the household. According to this view of the family, the welfare of each member of the family is normally integrated into a unified family welfare function, and shadow (non-market) prices play an important role in the family's producer and consumer activities, including the bearing and rearing of children.

To sum up, we now have in large measure a theory of the changes in the supply of the services of human agents. It is useful in determining changes in the supply of the quality attributes of human agents, attributes that have economic value becuase they render either producer or consumer services. With respect to quantity, it would be premature to claim that we have, as yet, a satisfactory theory of population growth.

But the demand side is still in large part an unexplored frontier. The puzzle is, why does the demand for the quality attributes of human agents increase so persistently in the advanced economies? What are the factors that are functioning in these economic processes that account for the remarkable increases in this demand, notably in the United States? This growth in demand is implicit in the fact that between 1929 and 1957 the educational capital embodied in the labor force of the United States increased at an average annual rate twice as high as that of reproducible tangible wealth.[9] We know the simple answer to the implied question of why the accumulation of human capital occurs at a higher rate than that of nonhuman capital. Theory implies that this difference is a response to the difference in rates of return. Empirical analysis strongly supports this implication of theory.[10]

But this response to the difference in rates of return sheds no light whatsoever on why the rate of return to human capital tends to be relatively high. The basic question is: What is it about these economic processes that increases the demand for the services of human agents that in turn have long maintained the relatively high rate of return to human capital?

Thinking about the demand problem here under consideration, I am convinced that we must explain simultaneously two critical factual puzzles. The first fact, to which I have already alluded, is that diminishing returns to capital have not occurred generally despite the vast accumulation of capital in the advanced economies. The second fact is the relatively high rate at which the formation of human capital has occurred. Of the two, the first factual puzzle is the more fundamental. I shall contend, moreover, that the resolution of the first puzzle also provides a solution for the second.

The key to both puzzles is in the additions to the stock of useful knowledge. The acquisition, adoption, and efficient utilization of this knowledge provides new sources of investment opportunities, maintains the growth process, and keeps the returns to capital from diminishing over time. Furthermore, these additions to the stock of knowledge are relatively more favorable in increasing the investment opportunities in the quality attributes of human agents than in the quality components of material agents of production.

I find support for this approach of the economic role of knowledge in some of the insights of both Marshall and Knight. Marshall, in his 1890 treatment of the agents of production[11] – land, labor, capital, and organization – observed that "capital consists in large part of knowledge and organization," and that "knowledge is the most powerful engine of production." Knight in 1944 in what I now consider to be one of his classic papers, "Diminishing Returns from Investment,"[12] perceived the role of improvements in the quality of the labor force and advances in the sciences as they affect, over time, the rate of return to investment.[13]

I remain convinced that an investment approach is required in coping with the problem at hand; it must be an all-inclusive treatment of investments to determine *all of the sources* of additional income streams. The mainspring that keeps these processes going is the rate of return to investment, and the inequalities in the rates of return then determine the allocation of investment resources among the various investment options. The basic assumption is that the allocation of investment resources is made in accordance with the standard set by the relative rates of return to alternative investment opportunities.[14]

Thus, in a nutshell the persistent increases in demand for the high quality services of human agents are a function of the additions to the stock of useful knowledge. The complexities of the additions to this knowledge have been much greater in recent, modern economic growth than during the early, relatively simple industrialization. The rate at which the stock of useful knowledge has increased has also been higher than the rate at which it took place during the early stages of industrialization. I concur with the historical interpretation of Mark Blaug[15] that the schooling of the labor force played a relatively small role in the early industrialization of England. But it is not presently so in the modernization of either agriculture or industry, an issue to which I shall turn in the next section.

2   On Implications

This approach to long-term economic processes has broad integrative power in that it provides a unifying principle for a consistent explanation of the allocation of investment resources encompassing both human and nonhuman capital as modernization proceeds. It has many implications that can be tested against data. It implies that the value of human time increases relative to the cost of investment resources. It implies that the relative share of national income accruing to labor increases and that the personal distribution of income then becomes less unequal. It implies that there is a special premium for the allocative ability of both males and females in managing firms and households and in allocating their own time, including their investments in themselves and in geographical migration. It also implies that, as the value of the time of mothers increases, fertility declines. Then, too, this approach implies that the social rate of return to expenditures on research is (has been) higher than that on most alternative investment opportunities. I shall consider briefly each of these implications in turn.

Long-term economic processes, under conditions that are characterized by a tendency toward constant cost of investment resources and by a relatively high rate of return to investment in the quality attributes of human agents, imply that the capital component embodied in people, per person, will increase and that the price of human time will increase relative to the time cost of capital resources. As a theoretical proposition, this summarizes an important part of the economic history of advanced economies. The supporting evidence is compelling; both males and females in these economies have become, to an increasing extent over time, capitalists in terms of human capital as a consequence of the investment they have made and are making in education, on-the-job training health, and in migrating geographically. The returns that accrue to them from accumulation of this human capital are in large measure the source of the increases in the economic value of human time.

A theory that is capable of explaining the long-term increases in the value of human time also implies that the relative share of national income accruing to labor will rise. I refer here to the changes in the functional distribution of income between labor and property assets. It is widely observed that the share of national income accruing to labor has been increasing. Kuznets,[16] taking a long view of the economic processes of Western countries, sees labor's share as having risen from 55 to 75 percent, while the share accruing to property assets was declining from 45 to 25 percent. Thus, in fact the share earned by labor increases, relatively as the modernization of the economy proceeds. A simplified way of putting the argument is that as growth occurs, the complementarity and substitution among factors and the rates at which the factors are augmented, are such that the role of human capital increases relative to that of the other forms of capital. Krueger's study[17] is most telling on this issue. In explaining the large absolute differences in per capita income between poor and rich countries in terms of factor endowments, she concludes "that the difference in human resources between the United States and the less developed countries accounts for more of the difference in *per capita* income than all of the other factors combined".[18] The human resource that matters most in her study is education.

Estimates by Lianos[19] of labor's income share in US agriculture are too low because the value of the time of farmers is assumed to be no higher than the wages paid to hired farm workers. The difference in human capital per person between these two groups is much in favor of farmers and members of their family. The omission of this difference, given the model, attributes a good deal more of the current agricultural income to land than is warranted in terms of theory and evidence.

Returning to the main theme, the accumulation of human capital has profound implications pertaining to the broad question of social and economic inequality. Although the theoretical linkage between functional and personal income is still weak in coping with changes in the economy over long periods, important advances in economic analysis are at hand. The data already noted with respect to Western countries make it evident that the share of personal income derived from property has declined, and that personal distribution of the property assets is more unequal than the personal distribution of earnings. It follows that the personal distribution of the total personal income become less unequal.[20]

The long-term increase in the demand for the quality attributes of human agents, as we have envisioned it thus far, is a demand for skills and other abilities to do the many, new (complex) tasks associated with the advances in useful knowledge. There is, however, another important attribute in the roles that males and females perform under such dynamic conditions. It is their *allocative ability*, i.e., the ability to take advantage of the opportunities that such conditions afford. This allocative ability is revealed in the *rates* at which males and females are capable of adjusting their activities, given the disequilibria implied in this approach.

One way of clarifying the source of the economic value of this allocative ability is as follows: Suppose that the investment processes throughout the economy were to arrive at a long-run equilibrium. The relevant implication of such an equilibrium may appear paradoxical in the sense that the economic value of this allocative ability would decline relative to its value prior to the state of equilibrium. Education, for example, gives better educated people greater allocative ability to take advantage of the opportunities associated with advances in useful knowledge, as Welch has shown[21] in analyzing the rates at which US farmers decode, act on, and use efficiently new technical information produced by the research sector.

It is fitting that I turn at this point to agriculture because farmers are both workers and entrepreneurs. I shall feature schooling because it is the major investment in human capital. Starting with traditional agriculture[22] and assuming that the farm and the household activities are in long-run equilibrium and that no events occur to disturb the equilibrium, economic activities under these assumptions become routine. Since there are no new techniques, farm people know from long experience the quality of the factors they employ, the productivity of the crops they grow, and the utility of what they consume. They are not involved in decoding new information with respect to either farm production or household production. What then is the economic value of schooling under these conditions? The implication is that farm people informally acquire the skills and information that are useful to them and that the economic value of formal schooling is small. Thus, there is little or no incentive to make current sacrifices to acquire schooling because the future returns from it do not warrant the sacrifice.

As the modernization of agriculture gets under way, some aspects of farm work call for new skills, but most of them – in my view – may be learned from experience as efficiently as from schooling. But the particular allocation ability of farmers, envisioned by Welch, is dependent on schooling because the ability to read and write now becomes important. Given the expectation that the process of modernization will continue, the demand for elementary schooling emerges.[23]

We are on firmer ground in economic analysis as we turn to the continuing modernization of agriculture in the advanced economies. In these economies, all manner of technical and economic developments are crowding in on farm people. The pace is such that a new input becomes "obsolete before its productivity can be fully explored." Equilibrium is neither at hand nor in sight. Both the farm firm and the farm household are in this dynamic state. In managing their farms and households, farm people are continually reaching for new things, trying them, learning about them, and deciding whether they are worthwhile. They are adjusting their household activities no less than their farming activities to changing technical and economic conditions. Farm people in some of these countries have made extraordinary adjustments during recent decades in trying to stay abreast of changing circumstances. The farm population has declined dramatically and the number of farms has dropped sharply. More of the same is in prospect.

The educational implications of this type of economic development, as already noted, have been investigated by Welch.[24] His findings are that in a technical, dynamic agriculture of this type the explanation of education's productivity is mainly in the difference in the *allocative abilities* associated with the difference in the level of education. The hypothesis is that better educated farm people "are more adept at critically evaluating new and reportedly improved inputs." They "can distinguish more quickly between the systematic and random elements" as they seek to take advantage of the new inputs, whether these be in farm production or in household production. Welch's empirical analysis supports this hypothesis in the domain of farm production to which he limited his test. His results show that this "allocative ability" plays a key role in determining education's productivity in agriculture and is relevant in a dynamic setting.[25]

Clearly, in the United States, as modernization continues at this rapid pace and where farm people in general have high levels of income, the economic value of education is such that the optimum level is not attained by elementary schooling. More education than this is required to satisfy the demand for education of farm people. Farm people with 12 years of schooling are winning out in competition with those who have 8 and less years of schooling. Furthermore, those with 16 years of education have been gaining relative to other levels over time.[26]

I alluded to the apparent paradox that if modernization were not to continue and farm production and household activities were to arrive at a long-run equilibrium, the value of education would decline. Although such an economic state is a theoretical possibility, it is assuredly not in sight. It is, nevertheless, a useful model in thinking about the economic value of education. Under such circumstances, the economic activities of farm people would be repetitive; year after year they would do essentially the same things except as each family made accommodations to meet its life cycle requirements. There would be no new inputs to upset this routine. The information required pertaining to farm and household production would be known. The economic value of the allocative ability associated with education would decline. The optimum level of education would become less than it is when farm people have attained a high level of productivity and modernization is continuing at a rapid pace. Relatively high-level work skills would still be needed but not the allocative ability. Farm people with 12 years of schooling would no doubt do about as well as those with more education.[27] Even less than 12 years could possibly suffice that is, allocative skills might become the optimum under some circumstances.

Let me digress once again. It is well known that a considerable part of the personal income of US farm families is derived from non-farm sources. This part, moreover, has been increasing markedly relative to that from farming. It is presently nearly as large as that from all farming activities. Most of this personal income of farm families from non-farm sources consists of earnings for off-farm work. The size of these earnings is, I am convinced, determined in large part by the human capital of farmers and members of their families who engage in this off-farm work. Yet nowhere, to the best of my knowledge, has anyone seriously analyzed this important development.

Returning to the role of this allocative ability, it is strong and clear at many points in economic behavior. With more education, the rate of adjustment is higher in geographical migration whether the repsonse be to better job or consumption opportunities. It is also evident in consumption and household activities and in the adoption of superior and cheaper contraceptive techniques.

The increases in the value of the time of women parallels that of men. Recent studies of the economics of fertility indicate that increases in the value of the mother's time reduce the number of children that parents bear and rear. When the value of time is measured by education, the relationship between additional schooling of mothers and the number of children is strongly negative for the early years of schooling of mothers. Why this relationship should not continue for additional education at the higher levels remains a puzzle.

It is worthy of note that these studies of fertility reveal various functions that the education of parents perform in household family behavior. The education of parents, notably that of the mother, appears to be an omnibus. It affects the choice of mates in marriage. It may affect the parents' preferences for children. It assuredly affects the earnings of women who enter the labor force. It evidently affects the productivity of mothers in household work including the rearing of their children. It probably affects the incidence of child mortality, and it undoubtedly affects the ability of parents to control the number of births. The task of specifying and identifying each of these attributes of the parents' education in the family context is beset with analytical difficulties on a par with the difficulties that continue to plague the economic analysis of growth in coping with the advances in technology.

Our approach attributes a basic role to the knowledge-producing sector. With respect to this sector, the assumption is that it produces useful knowledge and that one of the major characteristics of this knowledge is that it is the source of new, rewarding investment opportunities in the quality attributes of both human and nonhuman capital. The derived demand for this new, useful knowledge under these circumstances should show a relatively high rate of return to the investment in producing such knowledge. All of the studies known to me support this implication.

Mindful of our vested interest in research, I am, of course, in good grace in featuring the role it plays in the long-term rise in the price of human time. Our knowledge-producing activities are no longer a trivial sector. This sector has become more organized and there is much specialization. Organized agricultural research, as is well known, has a longer history than most of the other organized research activities. It is also the first to have received major attention by economists; we now have several competent econometric studies that provide estimates of the cost and returns to agricultural research. Included are those by Griliches, Tang, Peterson, Evenson, and Ardito-Barletta.[28] The social rate of return to expenditures on non-profit agricultural research is in general high relative to that of most alternative investment opportunities. I have summarized the evidence elsewhere.[29] Robert Evenson and Yoav Kislev have important new studies underway. Meanwhile, I consider it a major advance in economic analysis to treat agricultural research as an endogenous sector as Hayami and Ruttan have succeeded in doing.[30]

In a nutshell, then, the increasing economic value of human time is a consequence of the specific forms of new useful knowledge that characterize modernization. Investment in the *quality attributes* of men and women is the supply response. The income share of labor rises, and the personal distribution of income becomes less unequal. The economic dynamics of the adjustment processes is the source of a special premium for the *allocative abilities* of both males and females. As the value of time of women rises, fertility declines and parents opt for more quality per child in place of numbers of children. This, assuredly, is not a dismal economic perspective.

Notes and References

1   The compensation per hour of work includes fringe benefits which have been increasing relative to wages. These estimates are from the studies of Albert Rees as reported in Bureau of the Census, *Long Term Economic Growth 1860–1965* (Government Printing Office, Washington, 1966), pp. 188–89. I have extended this series to 1970. The farm real estate prices are from *Farm Real Estate Developments*, US Department of Agriculture, Economic Research Service (Washington, Aug. 1971), table 1. I assume that rents have tended to parallel the changes in prices per acre. I should also note that investments in farm real estate improvements were substantial during this period; accordingly, the rise in price of farm real estate reflects the value of these improvements, in addition to any rise in Ricardian Rent.

2   Theodore W. Schultz (ed.), "New Economic Approaches to Fertility", *Journal of Political Economy*, 81, Suppl. (Mar.–April 1973).

3   Jacob Mincer, "A Study of Personal Income Distribution," unpublished PhD dissertation (Columbia University, 1957); also "Investment in Human Capital and Personal Income Distribution," *Journal of Political Economy*, 66 (Aug. 1958), 281–302; "Market Prices, Opportunity Costs, and Income Effects," in Carl F. Christ et al, *Measurement in Economics: Studies in Mathematical Economics and Econometrics in Memory of Yehuda Grun-*

field (Stanford University Press, Stanford, Ca, 1963). See also Theodore W. Schultz, "Investments in Man: An Economist's View," *Social Service Review*, 33 (June 1959), 110–17; see also Part II, No. 1 above, "Investment in Human Capital." Also Gary S. Becker, *Human Caital: A Theoretical and Empirical Analysis, with Special Reference to Education* (National Bureau of Economic Research, New York, 1964).

4   Harry G. Johnson, "The Economic Approach to Social Questions," *Economica*, 36 (Feb. 1968), 1–21; see also Theodore W. Schultz, *Human Resources*, Fifteenth Anniversary Colloquium VI (National Bureau of Economic Research, New York, 1972).

5   Gary S. Becker, "A Theory of the Allocation of Time," *Economic Journal*, 75 (Sept. 1965), 493–517. See also Kelvin J. Lancaster, "A New Approach to Consumer Theory," *Journal of Political Economy*, 74 (April 1966), 132–57.

6   This paragraph and the next two are drawn in part from chapter 5 below, "Children: An Economic Perspective."

7   Margaret G. Reid, *Economics of Household Production* (John Wiley & Sons Inc., New York, 1934).

8   The usefulness of this tool is suggested by its applications in analyzing the derived demand for health, leisure, durable goods, and transportation and in ascertaining the derived demand for children.

9   See Theodore W. Schultz, *Investment in Human Capital: The Role of Education and Research* (Free Press, New York, 1971), table 5.1.

10   Ibid., chapter 10; also Becker, *Human Capital*.

11   Alfred Marshall, *Principles of Economics* (8th edn, Macmillan & Co. Ltd., London, 1930).

12   Frank H. Knight, "Diminishing Returns from Investment," *Journal of Political Economy*, 52 (Mar. 1944), 26–47.

13   See the Preface to Schultz, *Investment in Human Capital: The Role of Education*.

14   I elaborated on this ibid., chapters 2 and 3.

15   Mark Blaug, "The Economics of Education in English Classical Political Economy: A Re-examination," in *Essays of Adam Smith*, bicentenary edition of *The Works of Adam Smith* (University of Glasgow, Glasgow, Scotland, 1972).

16   Simon Kuznets, *Economic Growth and Nations* (Harvard University Press, Cambridge, Mass., 1971).

17   A. O. Krueger, "Factor Endowments and *Per Capita* Income Differences among Countries," *Economic Journal*, 78 (Sept. 1968), 641–59.

18   Ibid., p. 658.

19   Theodore P. Lianos, "The Relative Share of Labor in United States Agriculture 1949–1968," *American Journal of Agricultural Economics*, 53 (Aug, 1971), 411–22.

20   Long-term studies by Simon Kuznets show the personal distribution of income becoming more equal over time in major Western countries: "Economic Growth and Income Inequality," *American Economic Review*,

45 (Mar. 1955), 1–28; "Quantitative Aspects of the Economic Growth of Nations: VIII, Distribution of Income by Size," *Economic Development & Cultural Change*, 11(II) (Jan. 1963), 1–80; *Modern Economic Growth* (Yale University Press, New Haven, Conn., 1966). The vast inequality in wealth (property assets) is set forth by Robert Lampman, *The share of Top Wealth Holders of National Wealth, 1922–1956* (Princeton University Press for the National Bureau of Economic Research, Princeton, NJ, 1962).

T. Paul Schultz has studied the separation of the secular trends from the cyclical behavior in this distribution of income: "Secular Equalization and Cyclical Behavior of Income Distribution," *Review of Economics and Statistics*, 50 (May 1968), 259–67; and "Secular Trends and Cyclical Behavior of Income Distribution in the United States: 1944–1965," in *Six Papers on the Size Distribution of Wealth and Income*, Studies in Income and Wealth, vol. 33, ed. Lee Soltow (National Bureau of Economic Research, New York, 1969), pp. 75–100. He has also examined the puzzle inherent in the fact that the personal distribution of income in the United States has not continued its secular tendency towards less inequality since the late 1940s: see his "Long Term Change in Personal Income Distribution: Mythology, Fact and Explanation," summarized in *American Economic Review*, 62 (May 1972), Proceedings Issue (complete paper available from the Rand Corporation).

21   Finis Welch, "Education in Production," *Journal of Political Economy*, 78 (Jan. 1970), 35–39.

22   See Theodore W. Schultz, *Transforming Traditional Agriculture* (Yale University Press, New Haven, Conn., 1964).

23   There will be a lag on the supply side in adjusting to this demand, for reasons set forth in Theodore W. Schultz, "Investment in Human Capital in Poor Countries," in Paul D. Zook (ed.), *Foreign Trade and Human Capital* (Southern Methodist University Press, Dallas, Texas, 1962). For a general approach to this issue see Theodore W. Schultz, "The Education of Farm People: An Economic Perspective," in *Education and Rural Development, 1972–73, Yearbook of Education* (School of Education, London School of Economics, London, England).

24   Welch, "Education in Production."

25   Ibid., p. 47.

26   In March 1970, 10.8 percent of the employed males in agriculture had one or more years of college (7.6 percent, 1 to 3 years; 3.2 percent, 4 or more years). Of the employed females in agriculture, 12.5 percent had one or more years of college (9.8 percent, 1 to 3 years; 2.7 percent, 4 or more years). The proportion of all farmers and farm managers with one or more years of college appears to have doubled between 1952 and 1970 in US agriculture. Data are from Bureau of Labor Statistics, *Educational Attainment of Workers*, Special Labor Force Reports Nos. 65 (Mar. 1966) and 125 (Oct. 1970).

George S. Tolley, in his study "Management Entry into US agriculture," *American Journal of Agricultural Economics*, 52 (Nov. 1970), 485–93, shows that agriculture is undergoing replacement of one kind of human capital by another because high level management farms experience favorable cost curve shifts; this explains the replacement of many low-level management by fewer high-level management farms.

27   Welch, "Education in Production," notes that agricultural research expenditures in the US per farm were $4.30 in 1940 and $28.40 in 1959 (in constant 1959 dollars). His estimates indicate that "if research were to fall from $28.40 to $4.30 . . . the relative wage of college to high school graduates would fall from 1.62 to 1.43, indicating that one-third of the wage differential would disappear" (p. 55).

28   See: Zvi Griliches, "Research Costs and Social Returns: Hybrid Corn and Related Innovations," *Journal of Political Economy*, 66 (Oct. 1958), 419–31; Anthony M. Tang, "Research and Education in Japanese Agricultural Development, 1880–1938," *Economic Studies Quarterly*, 13 (Feb.–May 1963), 27–42, 91–100; William L. Peterson, "Returns to Poultry Research in the United States," unpublished PhD dissertation (University of Chicago, 1966); Robert E. Evenson, "The Contribution of Agricultural Research and Extension to Agricultural Production," unpublished PhD dissertation (University of Chicago, 1968); and Nicholas Ardito-Barletta, "Costs and Social Returns of Agricultural Research in Mexico," unpublished PhD dissertation (University of Chicago, 1971).

29   Schultz, *Investment in Human Capital: The Role of Education*, pp. 241–44, table 12.1.

30   Y. Hayami and V. W. Ruttan, *Agricultural Development* (Johns Hopkins Press, Baltimore, 1971). I share the assessment of Hayami and Ruttan on the weaknesses of our knowledge about the organization and management of agricultural research (ibid., p. 289). There are several useful leads in some of the papers appearing in Walter L. Fishel (ed.), *Resource Allocation in Agricultural Research* (University of Minnesota Press, Minneapolis, Minnesota, 1971), and in Albert H. Moseman (ed.), *Agricultural Science for the Developing Nations*, Publ. No. 76 (American Association for the Advancement of Science, Washington, 1964). See also Albert H. Moseman, *Building Agricultural Research Systems in the Developing Nations* (Agricultural Development Council, New York, 1970).

3

Woman's New Economic Demands*

The voices of many women are being raised today in demands for a better deal. While much of the rhetoric is shrill, it would be shortsighted not to see that there are basic developments calling for adjustments. These developments are in large measure economic in the sense that the rate of increase in their employment has been four times as high as that of men since 1947, that real earnings of employed women have risen markedly, that women now have as much property as men and that the income of most families supports a standard of living stratospherically above mere subsistence. Increasingly, human capital is being embodied in women, adding to their skills and enhancing their productivity and efficiency in the home and in the labor market. Hard, physical work is no longer available to women, so they join their husbands in camping to satisfy their taste for ruggedness.

Above all, the value of the time of women has been rising rapidly. But there are lags in adjusting the household, the family, and the labor market to these developments; and, as a consequence, the opportunities open to women are not in equilibrium with economic possibilities. Accordingly, there is room for improving these opportunities. Moreover, the bargaining position of women for a better deal should not be underrated; it is strong and it is growing. Home economics in general, however, has not stayed abreast of these fundamental developments. To be specific to the United States:

1   In terms of median years of school completed, females are somewhat ahead of males in our national statistics, but these statistics hide the fact that in higher education women are behind. The school record of females is better, however, than that of males. Women's health has also become better than men's, judging from the rise in life expectancy of women relative to that of men.

2   Although the value of women's time has been rising rapidly, no-where, to the best of my knowledge, is this significant development

* First published as "Woman's New Economic Commandments," in *Families of the Future*, Iowa State University Press (Ames Iowa, 1972), 79–88. Reproduced by permission of the publisher.

explained and its implications analyzed. Traditional marriage arrangements, family organization, and traditional household decision making are all to some extent obsolete in view of the rising value of the time of women.

3 The microeconomics of the household in the allocation of women's time, in acquiring and processing commodities that enhance the family consumption, and in the formation of human capital in children is still neglected in economics generally and in home economics in particular.

4 The economics of the labor markets for women as workers, and the still poor accommodation of this market to the special requirements of women, are receiving too little attention.

No wonder that women are protesting. Economic developments are providing new possibilities, but the better opportunities that should be available to women are delayed because of all manner of lags in social, legal, and economic adjustments. With respect to the required adjustments there is much confusion, as is evident from the rhetoric, which reveals mainly frustrations and which puts forward the panacea that women should be transformed into men. God forbid! The real adjustments, however, do not pertain to sex; they relate to a wide array of mundane yet complex, economic issues. There are no panaceas. Although women and children come first when a ship is being abandoned, it is not so when it comes to climbing the stairs of economic development.

My approach to this climbing is that of an economist. I shall first briefly summarize four recent extensions in economic theory that guide my thinking in this area. I shall then identify seven issues that call for solutions which consist of new directions and rules that would enlarge the choices of women. I shall refer to these as the New Economic Demand of Women.

1 Four Extensions in Economic Theory

Home economics draws on an array of disciplines as do agriculture, engineering, and medicine. During my tenure at Iowa State I became aware of the strong underpinning that home economics derived from the scientific advances in nutrition and from the heritage in the fine arts. From a social point of view, the extension activities in home economics were superior to the agricultural extension programs. But, the economic component in home economics fared less well, partly because economics in general, with the notable exceptions of the work of Elizabeth Hoyt and

Margaret Reid, tended to neglect the value framework of the home and the economics of the household. Recent extensions in theory are helping to rectify this long neglect by economists. The four extensions to which I now turn do not include the permanent income hypothesis (as formulated by Milton Friedman[1]) which owes a good deal to the creative empirical insights of Michael Reid[2] and which has become an integral part of the core of economic theory.

1(a)   The Concept of Human Capital

The pervasive analytical power of this concept emerged in the late fifties. My part in its early development is set forth in three papers.[3] To date the empirical analysis deals predominantly with the schooling and education of men as investments in human capital. On-the-job training and migration have also been analyzed using this concept, but here, too, these studies are still restricted to males because of the availability of data on their earnings. But it should be obvious that human capital is not sex specific.

Harry G. Johnson provides us with an excellent summary of the economic implications of this concept:

> [It pertains] . . . to the economics of the role of human beings in the productive process – based on the concept of "human capital." According to this concept, the skilled [or even the so-called unskilled] worker, and the academically or professionally trained executive, are envisaged as particular types of capital equipment employed in the production process, in the sense that their capacity to make a contribution to the productive process is developed by a process of investment [which means simply the sacrifice of current resources for future returns] incurred in the formal education system and through on-the-job training, and that this investment yields its returns over the life-time of the individual concerned[4] . . .

1(b)   The Allocation of Time

Gary S. Becker in his classic paper published in 1965,[5] seeing the pervasiveness of earnings foregone, developed the theory of the allocation of time. It is especially germane to the value of the time of women for it provides a basic approach to allocative decisions with respect to cost of time in consumption.

1(c)   The New Economics of the Household

The economic analysis of the value of time as a unit of cost in the production activities of the household has rapidly led to the development of the new economics of the household. It provides a comprehensive economic approach to the nonmarket household activities by introducing the "shadow price" of time that women devote to these activities.

Home economists have long known that the classical theory of consumer choice pertained to only a part of the allocative decisions in the household. They had identified many production activities that took place in the households which also required allocative decisions. Margaret Reid already in 1934 dealt exhaustively with these household production activities.[6] As noted, the new extension in theory reveals that each consumer good has two prices attached to it – a money price, as in traditional consumer choice, and a time cost of *acquiring, processing,* and *consuming* the commodity.

1(d)   The Economics of Information

Complete and perfect information in making allocative decisions has long been a convenient assumption in economics. Economic analysis, however, has paid a high price for this assumption. The extension in theory to cope with economics of information is set forth by George J. Stigler.[7] This extension is applicable to the search for information by women as well as by men about job opportunities, whether to move (migrate) to a new location, and about consumer goods and services to be acquired in the market. In making each of these decisions, the information required is not a free good. Thus, costs and returns must be equated.

In sum, the four new analytical tools consist of human capital, the allocation of time, the new economics of the household, and the economics of information.

2   The Search for Solutions

Turning to applications of the extensions in theory, we obtain a new economic perspective of marriage, the household, and children by treating marriage as a particular type of partnership, by treating the household as a complex economic enterprise requiring both management and entrepreneurship, and by treating children as a source of satisfaction and security that entail both pecuniary and nonpecuniary costs. I shall deal exclusively with the allocative decisions that relate to the domain of women. For example, their search for information is guided by the cost of acquiring it in relation to the returns it fetches. This behavioral logic is applicable in analyzing dating and mating for marriage; it applies to the search for information about goods and services purchased for the household, as well as in investing in her children. With respect to each of these activities, a woman must evaluate and allocate her own time.

The applications to be presented deal with secular, dynamic changes; the setting is one of substantial, continuing economic growth – much as it is being maligned these days. The resulting rise in personal income is the primary source of the developments. The resources that we have accumulated have become, in per family terms, very large. They have come in considerable part from the advances in knowledge, especially from the sciences. These additions to our knowledge are embodied both in materials and in our acquired abilities in structures, equipment, improvements in land, and in consumer durables; and, importantly, in human capital – investment in schooling and higher education, adult training, health, migration, and information. As a people we have become affluent at a rapid pace, so rapidly that we have not had time enough to learn how to live with our increase in personal income and how to adjust our institutions. My plan is to comment briefly on seven issues and on the new directions and the changes in rules that would enlarge the opportunities of women.

2(a)   *The Older Single Woman*

She typically has had more education than her counterpart in any other country, she is as a rule a skilled person, usually has a job, and lives in an urban environment. She is a member of an important growing class of women. But the rules of the games discriminate against her. If her earnings are substantial and she acquires some income from property, she is required to pay an unduly high rate of federal income taxes. The 1969 tax reform reduces this tax discrimination, but it is still large compared to those who qualify for joint return rates. This tax discrimination is an unwarranted incentive to become married, in a day when population growth concerns should lead to the provision of public incentives to remain single! More serious, no doubt, are the barriers she faces in having a normal social life which is still strongly oriented by tradition to serve married people to the exclusion of the single woman.

2(b)   The Married Woman in the Labor Force

Her options in acquiring a job with pay are subject to several serious restrictions. Regardless of her skills, even if she has won a major graduate degree, her choice of a job is restricted by virtue of her marriage to the location where her husband happens to work. Being thus tied, the adverse effects upon the incentives she has to specialize in acquiring a high level of skills are strong and clear. Suppose the roles of the husband and wife were reversed by the rules of marriage; if the woman's job opportunities would determine where they would locate, it would follow that the incentives to acquire specialized skills would also be reversed. Another difficulty arises because the labor market is as yet organized quite imperfectly in accommodating the changes in the woman's availability for a job during her married life cycle.

A common pattern is to seek a full-time job for a period before having children, then leave the labor force for a decade and longer to care for the children (especially so if the woman is highly educated), and following this, reenter the job market for an extended period. Then too, if she employs someone to care for the children while she works, the cost is not deductible from the family home in federal income taxation, except for families that earn relatively little income. Meanwhile, child-care centers are viewed as welfare agencies and not as enterprises that are held accountable for the services they render in terms of costs and returns.

2(c)   In Charge of the Household

There are over 60 million household units in the United States. As the number of farms declines the household is, all the more, the predominant small, personal, face-to-face, private enterprise. It requires organization, management, and a good deal of entrepreneurship. The decision making pertaining to the household, borne mainly by the woman, has become increasingly complex when it comes to acquiring information about the goods she purchases, to allocating her own time, and to giving her children a preschool start that paves the way for future investments in their schooling. Although the household processing of purchased goods has been vastly altered and in some respects simplified by ready-made goods and by consumer durables, it is still a complicated task requiring organization and entrepreneurial abilities.

2(d)   Wanted Children

We have become mesmerized by macropopulation projections featuring countries where the population appears to be increasing ever so rapidly. The profitable *Population Bomb* sold by Paul Ehrlich, a modern doomsday book, is filled with fruitflies, benefitting the authority of a laboratory biologist. These macroprojections are at best statistical artifacts. How meaningful they may be, including how stable they are over time, depends on the theory that guides the interpretation. Unfortunately, however, there is as yet no received macrotheory of population that is grounded on microfamily behavior.

Presumably the required microtheory could be forthcoming from any one of the social sciences. In sociology, the treatment of the family by Professor William Goode is a major step in this direction. So is the thinking and work of Professor Sol Tax and his colleagues as anthropologists, exemplified in their studies pertaining to an Indian community in Guatemala. Meanwhile in economics a microeconomic theory is emerging, along with empirical analysis of the behavior of parents in having and rearing children, in the research work underway at the National Bureau of Eocnomic Research, some of it jointly with Columbia University and the City University of New York, at Rand, and in economics at the University of Chicago.

Parents the world over are far from irrational in the number of children they want. Parents value their children. They acquire satisfactions, but as they become more affluent they acquire from their children fewer productive services, and less in terms of old age security. These satisfactions entail two sorts of costs: the opportunity cost of the time of parents in having and rearing a child and the costs of the goods and services for food, clothes, shelter, medical care, and educating a child. In equalizing these satisfactions and sacrifices, parents are in general rational in their behavior. This proposition implies that parents do not behave like robots in having children. Nor do they breed like fruitflies up to the limits of their food supply.

Going beyond the United States, most of the people of the world are very poor and children are in a very real sense the poor man's capital on which parents are dependent for shelter and food when they can no longer provide for themselves. But whether families are poor or rich, the social and economic characteristics of the community of which they are members systematically affect the costs and benefits of having children. The subjective and pecuniary costs encompass (1) the opportunity cost of the woman's time, (2) the value of child labor, (3) family income, (4) education, (5) social, legal, and economic institutions, and (6) contraception information and techniques. The demand of parents for children, both with respect to numbers and quality (for example, investment in the child's health and schooling), is clear and cogent from the recent studies of the microeconomics of the household. Children obviously are not free to the parents. The opportunity cost that determines the value of the time of the woman predominates. These costs and benefits differ widely between poor and rich countries.

It is not amiss to ponder to the reasons for the apparent success of the USSR and the socialist countries of Eastern Europe in reducing the fertility rates, especially of the urban population. Could it be that this has been accomplished unwittingly by bringing most women into the labor force, along with the shortage of housing and free access to legal abortion?

The study sponsored by the National Academy of Sciences, *Rapid Population Growth* is, so it seems to me, the best balanced treatment of the population question that is presently available. But I may be biased because of my involvement in it.

2(e)   Unwanted Children

The burden of having unwanted children is borne primarily by the women. Shifting more of this burden onto the male is long overdue. Meanwhile, the thrust of research on human reproduction with a view of discovering better contraceptive methods is still almost wholly female oriented. This discrimination in biological and related chemical research pertaining to human fertility is clearly unwarranted. Since contraceptive methods are still far from perfect, an ancillary procedure to reduce the number of unwanted births is necessary. Yet, except for a few scattered states, abortion has not been legalized. Here, too, the choices open to women are restricted by man-made laws.

2(f)   Investment in Human Capital: Women

As already noted, the application of the concept of human capital to the investment in schooling and higher education of females has received less attention than that of males. But recent studies of the economics of the household and of the interplay between the earnings of husbands and wives who are in the labor force reveal significant returns to the education of women. There is considerable evidence that suggests that the level of education of the wife has a favorable influence on the earnings of the husband; it appears to be true that, as the level of education of wives rises, other things equal, the earnings of their husbands also rise. Why?

The explanation of this puzzle is not at hand. It may require a woman's intuition to provide the key to this puzzle. It also appears that the organizational efficiency of the household in its contribution to family consumption depends in substantial part on the level of the education of the woman. Those who have twelve years or more of education obtain measurably more consumption from a given level of family income than is obtained by women with eight years and less of schooling.

It is well known that young, unmarried, farm reared females are more successful than are young males in leaving agriculture, a declining industry in terms of labor requirement, and that the degree of success in this out-migration depends in large part on the level of schooling. It comes as a surprise to find that, even when family incomes are the same, most married women with sixteen years of schooling who have entered the labor force prior to having children, leave the labor force for a decade or more during the early years of their children, whereas relatively few of those with less schooling leave the labor force in order to be in their homes while the children are young. The implication appears to be that the productivity and efficiency of the more educated woman in the home during this period makes her time more valuable there than the earnings she foregoes by leaving the labor force, whereas this trade-off in favor of the home for the less educated woman is not such that she is induced to make this shift.

The social benefits of the education of women are undoubtedly both real and important. This fact has a bearing on the controversy about the social benefits derived from higher education. It is becoming increasingly clear that most of the social benefits that the advocates of more subsidies for higher education attribute to higher education are not supported by any convincing evidence. The notable exception, which these advocates have not featured, is the social benefit of the education of women.[9] The main source of this social benefit arises out of the marked advantage that children derive from being reared in homes where the mothers have had this education. This line of thinking argues for more subsidization of the education of females than of males!

2(g)   *The Rising Value of Women's Time*

The most pervasive factor that accounts for the required adjustments in social, legal, and economic institutions pertaining to marriage, the household, contraception knowledge, and the rearing of children is the persistent marked rise in the value of the time of women. It calls for more flexible marriage arrangements. Consensual marriage prior to entering upon legal marriage is one form of flexibility. The husband and wife developing arrangements so that they can work in different locations is another resolution. Traditional dowries are passé. Equality in the division of the investment portfolio of the family is another step, an arrangement which fortunately is consistent with the incentives provided in federal income and inheritance taxation.

Economizing on the time of women in performing household work and in managing this enterprise requires all manner of adjustments. The role of consumer durables plays an important part in these adjustments; the achievements in this connection are impressively good. But the state of information about goods and services that households purchase is far from satisfactory. Meanwhile, it is still true that many women are poorly equipped in terms of the level of the education required to manage skillfully the household of which they are in charge. In my thinking, the most serious lag is in learning how to live satisfactorily in our age of affluence. The standard of values to be placed on additional things, on one's time, and the standard that is to be applied in rating the additional opportunities that are associated with becoming rich are hard to learn. But learn we must. Not least is the value to be placed on children, the costs of which depend primarily on the opportunity cost of the woman's time.

Would that more women might become top-flight economists and bring the analytical techniques of economics to bear in solving these and related issues.

Notes and References

1 Milton Friedman, *A Theory of the Consumption Function* (Princeton University Press for the National Bureau of Economic Research, Princeton, NJ, 1957).

2 Margaret Reid, *Economics of Household Production* (John Wiley & Sons Inc., 1934).

3 Theodore W. Schultz: "Investment in Man: An Economist's View", *Social Service Review*, 33 (June 1959), 110–17; see also "Capital Formation by Education" and "Investment in Human Capital," reproduced above in Part II, Nos. 1 and 2.

4 Harry G. Johnson, "The Economic Approach to Social Questions," *Economica*, 36 (Feb. 1968), 1–21.

5 Gary S. Becker, "A Theory of the Allocation of Time," *Economic Journal*, 75 (Sept. 1965), 493–517.
6 Reid, *Economics of Household Production*.
7 George J. Stigler, "The Economics of Information," *Journal of Political Economy*, 79 (1961).
8 *Rapid Population Growth*, National Academy of Sciences (Johns Hopkins University Press, 1971).
9 See above, Part II, No. 6, "Equity and Efficiency in College Instruction."

4

Children: An Economic Perspective*

In bringing economics to bear on procreation and children, a new dialogue between data and theory has begun. The studies that follow are a part of that dialogue. Whereas Malthus assumed that the price of children would remain constant, these studies argue that the cost of children increases with the rise in price of human time. We now see that fertility is affected by prices as well as by income and by the formation of human capital in children. We also see that the human capital embodied in adults, especially in women, affects fertility and the supply of labor. Recent developments in economic analysis provide some testable hypotheses. The empirical endeavors, as expected, disclose important new unsettled questions underscoring the fact that the work has just begun in understanding the mechanisms that account for changes over time.

In assessing the contributions of these studies, it would be premature to look for policy implications. The implications that matter at this stage of this work are primarily analytical. To see the setting of the problems that are on the agenda calls for an economic perspective which entails some elementary, albeit fundamental considerations. Although these considerations might be taken for granted, I shall elaborate on them to make sure that they are not overlooked. Fertility means children, and children are an important part of the standard of living of most families. Most married couples want their own children, and they proceed to bear and rear them. What is not clear is that parents derive satisfactions and productive services from their children and that the sacrifices made by parents in bearing children and in the investment they make in the care, health, and education of their children are in substantial part deliberate family decisions.

I anticipate that many sensitive, thoughtful people will be offended by these studies of fertility because they may see them as debasing the family

* First published in *Journal of Political Economy*, 81, No. 2, Part II (Mar./April 1973) S2-S13. Reproduced by permission of University of Chicago Press. I am indebted to Gary S. Becker, Yoram Ben-Porath, Dennis De Tray, Gregg Lewis, Marc Nerlove, Margaret Reid, T. Paul Schultz, and Robert Willis for their helpful suggestions to gain clarity and cogency.

and motherhood. These highly personal activities and purposes of parents may seem to be far beyond the realm of the economic calculus. I repeatedly expressed the same concern about this sensitive issue when I began to apply the concept of human capital to education. It, too, could be viewed as debasing the cultural purposes of education. I pointed out with care and at length that investment in education is fully consistent in serving cultural purposes in acquiring future cultural satisfactions along with the earnings associated with schooling and higher education. The same basic logic is applicable in this endeavor in explaining the sacrifices that parents make in acquiring the personal satisfactions and productive services that they derive from their children.

The analytical core of these studies rests on the economic postulate that the reproductive behavior of parents is in large part a response to the underlying preferences of parents for children. Given the state of birth control technology and the various classes of uncertainty associated with contraception, infant mortality, health and fecundity of the parents, and the income and wage rates parents expect to realize over their life cycles, these preferences are constrained by the parents' resources and the associated alternative economic opportunities in using their resources. In turn, these resources imply sacrifices, measured in terms of opportunity costs that parents must be prepared to make in acquiring the future satisfactions and productive service they expect to realize from children.

It could, of course, be argued that parents are nevertheless indifferent to these and all other economic considerations when it comes to having children, on the grounds that children are in considerable part the unintended outcome of sexual activity, that parents in general do not engage in any practical family planning, and that lifetime resource constraints are not known to parents with enough certainty to influence their decisions at the time they bear their children. I shall not, at this point, enter upon the reasons for not accepting this line of argument because of the evidence to the contrary that emerges from these studies. I shall instead proceed on the postulate that parents respond to economic considerations in the children they bear and rear and that parents equate the marginal sacrifices and satisfactions, including the productive services they expect from children, in arriving at the value of children to them. Thus, in thinking about the economics of fertility, social cost and benefits aside, the analytical key in determining the value of children to their parents is in the interactions between the supply and demand factors that influence these family decisions.

Growth economists, to the extent that they have dealt with fertility, have featured the gross economic *effects* of population growth, leaving to biologists, sociologists, and demographers the task of explaining the increases in the size of the human population. This concentration on such gross effects is understandable in view of the fact that the factors determining population growth have been a major unsettled part of economic theory. The concept of an optimum population has not been fruitful. Modern growth theory, with some notable exceptions, treats increases in the size of the population as an exogenous variable, although in classical economics it was (following Malthus) an endogenous variable. The Malthusian assumption about bearing and rearing children in response to economic growth led, of course, to the long-standing dismal economic perspective with respect to the population consequences of the accumulation of capital and of any advances in the techniques of production. Economists no longer accept the subsistence standard of living as invariant over time, in view of the widely observed rise in standards of living that has occurred with the rise in real family income associated with economic growth. The recent proliferation of doomsday literature featuring the population bomb, produced mainly by a few biologists, rests basically on the early Malthusian notions of reproductive behavior.

Meanwhile, demographers have done much in clarifying the complexity of population data and in examining in depth particular differences among classes of parents in their fertility behavior.[1] Moreover, demographers know that population projections, even though they are based on well-standardized data, are tenuous projections even for the short run. Demographers are asking key questions, however, on which the economist would be well advised to ponder: What is the explanation of the rapid adoption of the pill? What accounts for the fluctuations in the birth rates in countries in which the economy is highly developed?[2] In my view, the most important question they are asking is: What is the explanation of the *demographic transition*, that is, how do we explain the economic and social processes and family behavior that accounts for the marked decline from very high birth and death rates to modern very low birth and death rates? It is obvious that a theory which treats population growth as an exogenous variable is of no help in answering these questions.

I shall restrict the rest of my paper first to considering recent advances in economic analyses that have made these new approaches possible. The economic picture that emerges will then be sketched briefly, and finally, I consider some of the implications of these studies for future economic thinking and work.

1   Advances in Economic Analysis

There are four developments in economic analysis that are relevant here: the investment in human capital; the theory to treat a heretofore neglected basic attribute in the allocation of human time; the household production function; and a view of the family that encompasses both consumer choice and household production decisions, including the bearing and rearing of children.

Investment in human capital rests on the proposition that there are certain expenditures (sacrifices) that are made deliberately to create productive stocks, embodied in human beings, that provide services over future periods. These services consist of producer services revealed in future earnings and of consumer services that accrue to the individual as satisfactions over his lifetime.

Harry Johnson[3] summarized the producer attributes of human capital succinctly as follows:

> The contribution of human capital to the productive process is developed by a process of investment (which means simply the sacrifice of current resources for future returns) incurred in the formal education system and through on-the-job training, and that this investment yields its returns over the life-time of the individual concerned . . . The concept of human capital has tremendous integrative power, in that it provides a unifying principle for the consistent explanation of many phenomena of the labour market. Perhaps its most fundamental implication, from the point of view of social thought, is that the worker in an advanced industrial economy is typically a very considerable capitalist . . . . A second implication, which is extremely relevant to the broad question of social and economic inequality, is that the economic rewards for alternative occupations and careers need to be compared in terms of lifetime income profiles, and not in terms of the highest annual income earned in the course of the career . . . . A third implication, also relevant to the question of inequality, is that in their choices among alternative possible careers, new entrants to the labor force face the same problems of assembling information, assessing risks, evaluating returns, and obtaining the resources for investment, as do prospective investors in material capital equipment or in stocks and shares". (Johnson, p. 7–8).

Children are here viewed as forms of human capital. From the point of view of the sacrifices that are made in bearing and rearing them, parents in rich countries acquire mainly future personal satisfactions from them, while in poor countries children also contribute substantially to the future real income of their parents by the work that they do in the household and on the farm and by the food and shelter they provide for their parents when their parents are no longer able to provide these necessities for themselves. Children are in a very important sense the *poor man's capital*. It is becoming clear that the investment in children is in many ways akin to the investment in home-grown trees for their beauty and fruit. A very young child is highly labor-intensive in terms of cost, and the rewards are wholly psychic in terms of utility. As a child becomes a teenager the additional cost borne by the parents involves less labor intensiveness, and the rewards, especially in poor countries, consist in an increasing part of useful work that the teenager performs.

The second important advance in economic analysis is in the treatment of human time in allocative decisions with respect to both market and non-market activities.[4] The linkage between human capital and this concept of time allocation is strong and clear. The usefulness of the new concept of human time is not restricted to work in the labor market for it is also applicable to work in the household. With respect to the household, the individual, predominantly the housewife, allocates her time in part in choosing and shopping for consumer goods and in part in using them in household production leading to consumption. Then, too, consumption per se also requires time. The central principle of this advance in analysis is that in reality each consumer service has two prices attached to it: (1) a money price, as in traditional theory of consumer choice, and (2) a time cost of acquiring the consumer goods and processing them in the household; and the time cost that is involved in consuming the services obtained from this household activity.

It is obvious that bearing a child and caring for the infant child are normally highly labor-intensive activities on the part of the mother. What has not been clear is the difference in the value of time of mothers in bearing and rearing children associated with the difference in the human capital of the mothers.

There is, then, the treatment of the economics of household production. This household production function is an outgrowth of the concepts of human capital and of the value of human time. It provides a comprehensive approach to the nonmarket activities of the household, an approach that was foreshadowed by the much earlier work of Margaret Reid.[5] The distinctive merit of Becker's 1965 formulation of a theory of the allocation of time is in accounting for the use of the time of individuals in household production activities. Clearly, the housewife is not only allocating her time in choosing among consumer goods and in acquiring them, but she also engages in altering these goods as she processes and prepares them for consumption. The household production function is for this purpose a useful tool.[6] A further development of the household production function is now called for. Empirical analysis indicates that the production of a child (children) differs importantly in terms of inputs of time and of the services of purchased goods depending upon the age of the child (children).

The fourth advance is envisioning the family as a decision making unit not only in maximizing its utility in consumption but also in determining the allocation of human time and of goods in the production activities of the household. In terms of economic analysis, the family as a decision making unit with respect to household production is here viewed as an application of theory of the firm in traditional economic theory. In this view of the family, the assumption is made that the welfare of each member of the family is normally integrated into a unified family welfare function.

2   The Emerging Economic Picture

A theory restricted by its static economic assumptions is now on hand, from which one derives a good deal of analytical power; it cannot as yet, however, cope adequately with the lifetime behavior of parents with respect to the many diverse investments they make in the health, education, on-the-job training, travel, and marriage of their children and with respect to the transfer of property via inheritance. The core of the theory is designed primarily to analyze the effects of the differences in the price of the time of parents that enter directly and indirectly into the production of children. The static theory at hand still lumps together first all expenditures on children and then all satisfactions from children that occur over the life cycle. It does not disentangle the early and later parts of this cycle in determining the relative importance of the two parts. In my thinking, important parts of the changes in fertility over time, changes that are related to the rise in the expenditures on children, are consequences of long-term developments with respect to the economic value of education, job opportunities, incentives to migrate toward better economic locations, opportunities to reduce infant mortality, and improvements in contraceptive techniques and the decline in their cost, along with the secular rise in family income. The treatment of these and other secular developments, including the rates at which families adjust their fertility to these various types of disequilibria, is as yet beyond the scope of this theory.

Admittedly, also, the empirical analysis is subject to serious data limitations and to some econometric complexities that remain unsolved. Data are always hard to come by when it comes to testing economic hypotheses. Better data, however, for these purposes can undoubtedly be "made." Then, too, although there have been major advances in the development of econometric techniques, some of them are not as yet common property among economists; meanwhile new unsolved econometric problems keep cropping up.

Turning to the empirical part, the responses of parents to differences in relative prices inducing substitution are evident. Specifically, the negative effects of increases in price of the mother's time on the number of children leaves little room for doubt that there is a role for economics in analyzing fertility. When education is used as a measure of the price of her time, the task of untangling the several different influences of education presents difficulties which I shall consider presently.

The responses of parents to differences in income and to changes in income over time are very difficult to get at. There is, however, an unwarranted tendency to treat the estimates at hand as weak and ambiguous for the wrong reason. These income effects are not for theory to resolve any more than in the case of the income elasticity of the demand, say, for food. The wrong reason is in the belief that the partial effect of income must be to increase fertility.

In my view, the determination of these income effects will depend ultimately on data. But it is exceedingly difficult to determine empirically the effects of income while holding the price of time and goods constant. It is even more difficult to measure correctly true family wealth over the family life-cycle. What are needed are the ex ante expectations of the time path of the family income streams over the life-cycle, with the appropriate weights of these expectations at different stages in the life cycle with due regard for risk and discounting. Static models are unable to account for revisions of these expectations and for the adjustments that parents make to unexpected income changes along the life-cycle path. Furthermore, the effect of changes in the ratio of quality per child to the number of children may cause the relative price of numbers of children to rise as income rises even when the price of time is held constant.[7]

More generally and fundamentally, with respect to the interaction between quality per child and number of children, is the overall constraint of family resources in the sense that additional numbers of children necessarily imply fewer resources to draw upon to invest in quality per child.

The ongoing research here under consideration faces a major challenge in untangling and isolating the various functions that the education of parents performs in household family behavior as it influences fertility. The education of parents, notably that of the mother, appears to be an omnibus. It affects the choice of mates in marriage. It may affect the parents' preferences for children. It assuredly affects the earnings of women who enter the labor force. It evidently affects the productivity of mothers in the work they perform in the household, including the rearing of their children. It probably affects the incidence of child mortality, and it undoubtedly affects the ability of parents to control the number of births. The task of specifying and identifying each of these attributes of the parents' education in the family context is beset with analytical difficulties on a par with the difficulties that continue to plague the economic analysis of growth in coping with the advances in technology.

I am impressed by the evidence that the relationship between additional schooling of mothers and the number of children is strongly negative for the early years of schooling of mothers. But why this relationship should not continue for additional education at the higher levels is a puzzle.[8] In view of the importance of this relationship in determining public policy in support of elementary schooling, a special effort is called for, both in making sure of the empirical inferences and in resolving the apparent puzzle.

Analytically, I deem it to be a real advance to treat children as a heterogeneous stock of human capital. Clearly, a child less than age 3 is a very different component of human capital, both in terms of costs which consist largely of the value of the mother's time and in terms of psychic satisfactions that parents derive from so young a child, compared with an older child who has become a teenager. As I noted at the outset, a very young child is highly labor-intensive measured in terms of the input of the mother's time. As the child becomes older, he becomes less and less labor-intensive and more costly in terms of other family resources that are required for the schooling and other activities that enhance his acquired abilities.

The problem of determining the allocation of family resources as between quality per child and numbers of children looms large. It deservedly is high on the agenda.

There is all too little explicit analysis of the investments by parents in the abilities that children acquire from education (except by De Tray[9]), on-the-job experience, travel, and other activities that enhance the capacities of children; these are investments from which the family benefits and which it can afford by drawing on family resources, in addition to the mother's time, through dissaving during the early stage of the family life cycle, especially so in the advanced, modern economies such as Israel[10] and the United States.

The rate of child mortality in the United States is not only low, but the difference in this rate among the white families has become sufficiently small so that variation in their child mortality is no longer a significant factor in fertility behavior. But the decline in child mortality currently underway in most poor countries is in all probability an important variable to which parents are responding with lags as they become informed and are prepared to act, given the state of the information that appears relevant to their fertility decisions.

Last, one of the more important new insights pertains to the economics of the supply of and demand for contraception techniques. Would that we had estimates of the rates at which the superior and cheaper contraceptive techniques are adopted. The indications are that this information will tell a story that is in many respects comparable to that of farmers in a number of poor countries in their adoption of new, superior varieties of wheat, rice, and other crops that has set into motion the so-called Green Revolution. The responses of parents in adopting these contraceptive techniques is also further support of the economic postulate that parents are not indifferent in their fertility behavior to changes in economic conditions.

3 Prospects

Are we, as Norman Ryder suggests, destroying the idea of a family? On the contrary, we are enlarging and enriching the role of the family as it is envisioned in the new home economics. The assumption that the family integrates the welfare of its members into an internally consistent family utility function attributes a role to the family that undoubtedly exceeds its capacity as a social institution. Thus, one of the unsettled issues for future work is an approach for treating the individual utility functions of the husband, wife, and older children.

The family is indeed one of the basic social institutions that has been fortified legally as it has evolved culturally. Ryder is correct in noting that "society intervenes, in obvious and in subtle ways." With regard to the family's social functions, there has been a persistent concern with respect to marriage, procreation, and children. The family is for three reasons a concept that is basically in the domain of anthropologists, sociologists, and legal scholars, and all of them contribute to demographic studies. Can economists also contribute, in view of the advances in economic analysis made possible by concepts of human capital, the value of human time, the household production function, and the family as a decision-making unit in consumption and in household production? What are the prospects that these new approaches will contribute significantly in explaining marriage, fertility, and the investment in children?

The prospects would not be promising if it were true that virtually all that has been and could be learned using these economic approaches is already known by scholars in other disciplines. While it would be presumptuous to proclaim that an economic theory of population is in prospect, it is not to be ruled out at this stage. The more modest prospects, which are nevertheless important, are of two parts: (1) the substantive contributions already at hand, and (2) the potentially rewarding research opportunities that these approaches afford.

The substantive contributions featured in the preceding section are new and important. We see that the household family unit responds to changes in relative prices in the manner implied by the economic theory, that the most important price in the production of children during the early years of each child is the price of the mother's time, that there is substitution in the family context between the quality embodied in children and the quantity (number) of children, that the investment in the quality of children looms large as family income rises, that additional schooling at the lower level of education of mothers has a strong negative effect on family fertility, and that the response to superior and cheap contraceptive techniques is clearly subject to economic analysis.

Furthermore, these studies are a rich source of economic hypotheses that have as yet not been tested and of ideas and speculations worthy of much more economic thinking. Most of the research opportunities that I see are mentioned in the preceding section. I shall restrict my closing comments to several specific ways of getting at some of the unexplored issues and at some of the long-term economic developments that may have substantial explanatory power in accounting for the observed changes in fertility over periods of two and more family cycles.

The static household family models can be extended to take account explicitly of the array of consumer durables that enter into the household production and of the ready-made consumer items that save on the time of housewives. The acquisition of consumer durables by borrowing funds during the childbearing and rearing stage of the family cycle can also be made an integral part of these models. I would expect that as the education of the parents increases, we will observe a significant positive effect in acquiring borrowed funds more cheaply and in the effectiveness with which parents manage their investment portfolio, including their investment in children. Hired household help is included in some of these studies but it probably requires substantially more attention in analyzing empirically the economic behavior of parents in allocating their own time to children who are no longer infants.

Important parts of these models patently call for cross-sectional data covering in sequence several dates encompassing the family life-cycle from marriage and presumably until the children are really on their own, inasmuch as most of the investment in children made by parents occurs after the childbearing period is over. In this endeavor, it will be necessary to account for the savings and the accumulation of assets by the household family along with the borrowed funds that the family acquires, thereby enhancing the current resources it has available, resources that are used in part to purchase labor-saving consumer items and in part to finance investments in the quality of the children.

As we proceed beyond the stationary economic state, we enter an uncharted frontier. Our analytical maps do not tell us how to proceed. The typical family that we observe, especially in rich countries, lives and has lived in an economy in which economic conditions are and have been changing substantially over time. As these changes occur, thinking in terms of economics, there presumably are responses – responses in the age at which marriage occurs, responses in spacing and numbers of children, and responses in the amount of family resources devoted to investment in children. Furthermore, before these families have fully adjusted and have arrived at an equilibrium with respect to any given economic change, additional unexpected changes will have occurred. Thus, the families we observe are seldom, if ever, in a state of economic equilibrium. This uncharted frontier is beset with all manner of disequilibria. Economic theory, capable of coping with them in the family context, is still in its infancy.

It is, of course, possible to improvise by endeavoring to analyze each of these major changes one at a time and, in doing so, abstract from the other changes. Admittedly, there are severe limitations to this procedure; it may, however, provide enough additional information to apply a comprehensive simultaneous economic model encompassing family decisions over the life-cycle under changing economic conditions.

In my thinking, research priority should be given to the economic attributes of the following changes to determine the extent to which they influence marriage, fertility, and investment in children:

1   improvements in the technology of contraceptive goods and services reckoned in terms of their effectiveness and their cost to the family:
2   improvements and the declines in the price of labor-saving consumer items;
3   changes in the economic opportunities of investing in the education of children;
4   changes in the labor market opportunities (*a*) for women and (*b*) for teenagers;
5   changes in the reduction in labor market earnings that are a consequence of the curtailment of on-the-job training during the period when women leave the labor force to bear and to take care of a child (children);

6 the decline in the cost of reducing infant mortality, a change that currently characterizes mainly the developments underway in poor countries;

7 the changes in the location of job opportunities associated with economic growth that require geographical migration of youth and of established families.[11]

As a framework to guide one's thinking in accounting for these various economic changes over time and the economic interactions among them, a model of the type developed by Marc Nerlove and T. Paul Schultz is an appropriate instrument in charting this frontier.[12] In my view, the empirical usefulness of this model, however, is dependent upon our acquiring a substantial amount of new information with respect to each of these major changes.

In conclusion, the stage is set for analyzing the economic attributes of marriage, of procreation, and of children. The research opportunities are abundant and the prospects are good that real contributions can be made. As of now, however, the dialogue between data and theory has just begun.

Notes and References

1 See, for example, Norman B. Ryder and Charles F. Westoff, *Reproduction in the United States, 1965* (Princeton University Press, Princeton, NJ, 1971).

2 This question has been mainly on Richard A. Easterlin's agenda: see *Population, Labor Force, and Long Swings in Economic Growth: The American Experience* (National Bureau of Economic Research, General Series 86, New York, 1968); and "Towards a Socio-Economic Theory of Fertility: A Survey of Recent Research on Economic Factors in American Fertility," in S. J. Behrman, Leslie Corsa Jr, and Ronald Freedman (eds), *Fertility and Family Planning: A World View* (University of Michigan Press, Ann Arbor, Michigan, 1969).

3 Harry G. Johnson, "The Economic Approach to Social Questions," *Economica*, 36 (Feb. 1968), 1–21.

4 See Gary S. Becker, "A Theory of the Allocation of Time," *Economic Journal*, 75 (Sept. 1965), 493–517.

5 Margaret G. Reid, *Economics of Household Production* (John Wiley & Sons Inc., New York, 1934).

6 Its usefulness is suggested by its applications in analyzing the derived demand for health, leisure, durable goods, transportation, and here in ascertaining the derived demand for children.

7 The latter part of this paragraph owes much to clarifying comment from Robert Willis.

8   Some possible explanations of this puzzle are provided by Yoram Ben Porath, "The Production of Human Capital and the Life Cycle of Earnings," *Journal of Political Economy*, 75 (Aug. 1967), 352–65; and by Robert J. Willis, "A New Approach to the Economic Theory of Fertility Behavior", mimeographed (National Bureau of Economic Research, New York, 1969, rev. 1971); see also his PhD Dissertation, "The Economic Determinants of Fertility Behavior" (University of Washington, 1971).

9   See Dennis N. De Tray, "The Interaction between Parent Investment in Children and Family Size: An Economic Analysis" (Rand Corporation, R-1003-RF, Santa Monica, Ca., May 1972); and his PhD dissertation, "The Substitution between Quantity and Quality of Children in the Household" (University of Chicago, 1972).

10 See Yoram Ben-Porath, *Fertility in Israel, an Economist's Interpretation: Differentials and Trends, 1930–1970* (Rand Corporation, RM-5981-FF, Santa Monica, Ca., Aug. 1970; reprinted in Charles A. Cooper and Sidney S. Alexander (eds), *Economic Development and Population Growth in the Middle East* (American Elsevier, New York, 1972).

11 Theodore W. Schultz, *Human Resources*, Fiftieth Anniversary Colloquium VI (National Bureau of Economic Research, New York, 1972).

12 Marc Nerlove and T. Paul Schultz, *Love and Life between the Censuses: A Model of Family Decision Making in Puerto Rico, 1950–1960* (Rand Corporation, RM-6322-AID, Santa Monica, Ca., Sept. 1970).

5

*High Value of Human Time Population Equilibrium**

Two decidedly different population equilibria can now be formulated. They may be viewed as two extreme types with respect to the state of economy. The foundation of the first equilibrium is a consequence of increases in the price of the services of natural resources relative to the services of labor (wages). The foundation of the second equilibrium is determined by increases in the price of human time relative to that of materials. The supply of time for consumption becomes the limiting factor. The per capita income implication of the first is subsistence and that of the second a high standard of living.

The first type, as it was envisaged by early English economists, has long been a standard part of economics. It assumes that the supply of land is fixed and that diminishing returns increase the price of food as a consequence of population growth. Gains in productivity from capital are exhausted by this process. This concept can, of course, be extended to encompass the results of the recent macrosystem models that purport to show the limits of the earth in accommodating population growth. These models are not restricted solely by the availability of land to produce food, since they also include the physical limits set by the availability of minerals, energy, and space for people. The fertility behavior of people in these models is crudely Malthusian; population growth stops as a consequence of the inevitable food, energy, and space limitation. Within the Ricardian framework, this concept is a logical conception of a population equilibrium. It is a dismal view of human behavior that has long been important in social thought.

The foundation of the second concept is the high price of human time relative to the price of the services of material factors and goods. This concept rests on the proposition that the state of the economy is such that the value of services of natural resources and of intermediate material

* First published in *Journal of Political Economy*, 82, No. 2 (2) (Mar./April 1974), S2–S10, and reproduced by permission of University of Chicago Press. I am indebted to Gary S. Becker, Marc Nerlove, and T. Paul Schultz for their helpful comments on my early draft.

products is small relative to the value of services of human agents. Accordingly, the contribution of materials to human satisfactions is small compared to that of human agents. In such an economy, the opportunity cost of bearing children is high and the investment in their human capital is large. The welfare implications of this concept are unmistakably optimistic because the gains in productivity from the accumulation of human and nonhuman capital are transformed into high standards of living supported by high per capita income. Advances in useful knowledge, embodied in human and nonhuman capital, have gradually destroyed the assumption of the fixed supply of the "original properties of the soil." In the process, it is the scarcity of human time and its high value that dominate, and it is the "fixed supply of human time" consisting of 24 hours per day and of a man's lifetime that become the critical factor in analyzing the economic behavior of people, including their fertility.

There is an abundance of evidence which shows that the price of human time accounts for most of the costs in a modern economy. The upward tendency of real wages and salaries, including fringe benefits, of earnings foregone by mature students, and of the value of the time of housewives relative to the price of materials is well documented.[1] Economic theory implies, and we observe, that material goods are substituted for human time by firms and by households. Received theory, however, is silent on the effects of the high and rising price of human time on pure consumption, although consumption obviously entails time. The ultimate economic limit of affluence (economic growth) is not in the scarcity of material goods but in the scarcity of human time for consumption.[2]

The critical postulate assumes that there is a dynamic process that determines the increases in the price of human time relative to the price of services of the nonhuman factors and that this process tends toward an equilibrium. The dynamic part is the economic key to the following four issues:

1 the relative increase in investment in human capital augmenting the quality of human beings;
2 the relatively high price of all labor time-intensive goods and other sources of labor-intensive satisfactions, including children, thus leading to the substitution of quality for numbers of children;
3 the relatively cheap material goods that are not labor-intensive;
4 the scarcity of the time for consumption, setting the ultimate limit to the satisfactions that can be derived from materials provided by economic growth.

Although it is obvious that the economic value of human time is high in affluent countries that have a modern economy, it is not obvious why these economies have developed the demand for and supply of human abilities that have such a high value, in terms of earnings and satisfactions that people derive from them.

My approach to a persistent secular increase in the economic value of human time consists of supply and demand developments that determine the rise of the price of human time in the context of the modernizing processes. The developments explaining the increases in the supply of the quality attributes of human agents are fairly clear, whereas the developments underlying the increases in the demand for these quality attributes are less clear. Recent advances in economic analysis[3] provide parts of the theory for determining the supply of these quality attributes. They treat the useful abilities that people acquire as forms of human capital. The investment in these abilities is taken to be in response to favorable investment opportunities, and thus the increases in the supply depend on current expenditures (sacrifices) made by individuals, families, and public bodies on education, health, job training, as well as for information, and geographical migration to take advantage of better jobs or of better consumption opportunities. These expenditures (sacrifices) are presumably made deliberately with an eye to future satisfactions and earnings. The theories of the allocation of time and household production are of special importance in analyzing the incentives and responses of people in acquiring education and job training, in enhancing their health, in searching for information, and in altering their fertility, including the substitution of quality for numbers of children. Thus, these supply responses to the increases in the economic incentives associated with modernization are not hard to comprehend. The human capital literature abounds with studies dealing with aspects of these supply responses.

But these human capital studies have not explained the secular increases in the demand for these quality attributes of human agents. The clue to this unresolved puzzle is concealed in two basic factual issues. The first is that diminishing returns to capital have not occurred generally, despite the vast accumulation of capital in the advanced economies. The second issue is the relatively high rate at which the formation of human capital has occurred. Of the two concerns the first is fundamental, and the resolution of it provides a solution for the second. The key to both is in that part of the economic process that increases the stock of useful knowledge.[4] It is the acquisition, adoption, and efficient utilization of this knowledge that has provided *decisive new sources of investment opportunities* that have maintained the growth process and have kept the returns to capital from diminishing over time. Furthermore, these additions to the stock of knowledge have been relatively more favorable in increasing the investment opportunities in the quality attributes of human agents than in the quality components of material agents of production. The investment incentives that are revealed by the inequalities in these investment opportunities, as they occur over time, are the mainspring in this process.

In an all-inclusive view of these investment opportunities, the knowledge-producing sector must be included. It is not a trivial sector in modern countries, nor is it exogenous. Research is an organized activity that requires specific, expensive, scarce resources. Although research is costly, recent studies, many of them devoted to analyzing the rates of return to investment in organized agricultural research, show high rates of return.

With respect to this investment process, economists could have been spared much aimless wandering had they perceived the implications of the concept of capital as Marshall saw it. His predecessors had formulated the concept of the "state of the productive arts," and they then proceeded to develop the core of economic theory under the assumption that these arts remained constant. It was an ingenious simplification, and their theory was in general relevant to a wide array of problems of their day. But industrialization undermined this simplifying assumption, and Marshall saw it clearly and cogently. In his treatment of the agents of production, he extended the concept of labor to include work with our heads. It should be noted with care that his concept of capital:

> consists in great part of knowledge and organization; and of this some part is private property and the other part is not. *Knowledge is our most powerful engine of production* . . . Organization aids knowledge . . . The distinction between public and private property in knowledge and organization is of great and growing importance: in some respects of more importance than that between public and private property in material things.[5]

In not seeing the implications of Marshall's remarkable insights, economists have wandered for years in the wilderness of capital confined to material goods.

Thus, in a nutshell, the persistent increase in the demand for the high-quality services of human agents is a function of the additions to the stock of useful knowledge.[6] The complexities of the additions to this knowledge have been much greater in recent, modern economic growth than during early, relatively simple industrialization. The rate at which the stock of useful knowledge has increased has also been higher than the rate at which it grew during the early stages of industrialization.

This approach has broad integrative power in that it provides a unifying principle for a consistent explanation of the allocation of investment resources encompassing both human and nonhuman capital as modernization proceeds. From it we derive important empirical implications that can be tested. It implies that the value of human time increases relative to the cost of investment resources.[7] It implies that the relative share of national income accruing to labor increases over time.[8] It implies that there is a special premium for the allocative ability of both males and females in managing firms[9] and households, and in allocating their own time, including investments in themselves. It also implies that as the value of the time of mothers increases, fertility declines.[10] These implications are derived from the process, as the economy arrives at this equilibrium.

The concept of a general economic equilibrium in this context is useful, however, as an analytical guide. It is an assumed economic state toward which this modernization process tends. Given this state, there are no inequalities among investment opportunities. The high price of human time is stable in the sense that it is no longer increasing relative to other factor service prices. There is no incentive to make additional investments in human capital or in the knowledge-producing sector, as a consequence of the completion of the modernization process, and advances in knowledge no longer augment the productivity of human time within firms and households; presumably, virtually all of the value added in production is contributed by the input of human time. The basic economic constraint that determines this equilibrium is the increasing scarcity of human time for consumption. The underlying logic can be put simply: modernization increases the consumption stream; consumption requires human time; advances in knowledge, whether they are embodied in material capital or in human capital, are ultimately severely limited in the extent to which they can alleviate the scarcity of human time for consumption.

Notes and References

1   Evidence, for example, on long-term changes in wages and salaries relative to rent paid for the services of farmland in the United States shows that the total real compensation per hour at work of all manufacturing-production workers increased between 1929 and 1970 more than four times as much as did the rent on farm real estate per acre, similarly adjusted (see above, Part III, No. 2, "The Increasing Value of Human Time").

2   The approach outlined in this paragraph and a considerable part of the argument that follows appear in Theodore W. Schultz, "Explanation and Interpretations of the Increasing Value of Human Time (Woody Thompson lecture to the Midwest Economics Association, Chicago, April 5, 1973).

3   Ibid; see also Theodore W. Schultz, *Human Resources*, Fiftieth Anniversary Colloquium VI (National Bureau of Economic Research, New York, 1972).

4   Simon Kuznets, in his Nobel Prize lecture, which appeared in the June 1973 *American Economic Review* under the title "Modern Economic Growth: Findings and Reflections," also attributed a major role to the additions in knowledge in this context. He argued that the last two centuries have been periods during which there has occurred "enormous accumulation in the contribution to the stock of useful knowledge by basic and applied research" (p. 251).

5   Alfred Marshall, *Principles of Economics* (8th edn, Macmillan & Co. Ltd., 1930), book 4, chapter 1, pp. 138–9; the italics are mine.

6   The argument in support of this summary statement appears above in Part III, No. 2, and in Schultz, "Explanation and Interpretations of the Increasing Value of Human Time." It is anticipated in Theodore W. Schultz, *Investment in Human Capital: The Role of Education and Research* (Free Press, New York, 1971), chapters 1 and 2. Chapter 12 treats the "Allocation of Resources to Research."

7   A simplified approach to this implication is to treat the cost of investment resources as constant under the assumptions that the "normal" long-term real rate of interest remains constant and that, from an increasing amount of capital embodied in human beings, people derive earnings and satisfactions commensurate with the going rate of interest.

8   As the earnings from the increasing stock of human capital rise relative to income acquired from property assets.

9   Finis Welch, "Education in Production," *Journal of Political Economy*, 78 (Feb. 1970), 35–59.

10 See Marc Nerlove, "Household and Economy: Toward a New Theory of Population and Economic Growth," *Journal of Political Economy*, 82, No. 2, Part II (Mar.–April 1974), S200–S218.

6

*Investment in Entrepreneurial Ability**

1 Introduction

In large measure economic theory either omits the entrepreneur or it burdens him with esoteric niceties the implications of which are rarely observable. The entrepreneur is not required in equilibrium theory in solving the problems for which that theory is appropriate. In nearly all of the production function literature the entrepreneur does not appear as an explicit economic agent. In the part of theory that deals with "pure profit" the entrepreneur is indentured to risk and uncertainty. The argument of this paper is that the abilities of entrepreneurs to deal with the disequilibria that are pervasive in a dynamic economy are part of the stock of human capital. It is well documented that experience, health and especially schooling enhance the acquired abilities of entrepreneurs. Most of the relevant studies pertain to the effects of schooling of farmers on their ability to perceive and to interpret new information and to decide to reallocate their resources to take advantage of new and better opportunities. In this human capital approach schooling is treated as an investment. Thus the argument of this paper features investment in entrepreneurial ability.

Entrepreneurs have not received their due in economics; they are not given adequate credit for the contributions they make in a dynamic economy. It is not sufficient merely to attribute some innovations to business enterprises, or to treat entrepreneurs as doing no more than collecting windfalls and bearing losses that occur as a consequence of surprises. Although it is obvious that the economic behavior of many people in a dynamic economy is neither repetitive nor routine, what is not obvious is that in addition to businessmen, there are many other people who at different junctures during their life-cycle are entrepreneurs, that the demand for what they do depends on the changes that

* First published in *Scandinavian Journal of Economics* (1980), 437–48. Reproduced by permission of Blackwell Publishers. I am indebted to Gary S. Becker and Robert E. Lucas, Jr. for their helpful comments.

characterize the particular economic dynamics, that the supply depends on their number and ability and that the economic value of their services (inputs) is substantial. The contribution of entrepreneurs to economic growth is of major importance, although it is concealed in national income accounting. The economics of the acquisition of entrepreneurial ability is still in its infancy. The puzzle of the emergence of firms may also be explained in terms of organizational human capital.[1]

For there to be a "rent" that accrues to the "scarce" entrepreneurial ability, what entrepreneurs do must have some economic value. They are innovators in Schumpeter's theory; in Dahmén's phrase, Schumpeter succeeded in integrating the dynamics of technology and business enterprise.[2] What Schumpeter could not have anticipated is the growth of research and development (R and D) in the public sector. In the United States, for example, 70 percent of all basic research is funded by the federal government[3] and in the case of agricultural research only 25 percent is being done by private firms.[4] Schumpeter's innovators have become a decreasing part of the technological story.

Knightian uncertainty bedevils many economists in analyzing entrepreneurship. Knight's modest preface in *Risk, Uncertainty, and Profit* states simply that, "The particular technical contribution to the theory of free enterprise which this essay purports to make is a fuller and more careful examination of the role of the *entrepreneur . . .*" Although much of Knight's treatise is devoted to the function of entrepreneurs in a dynamic market economy, this part has received all too little attention. It is perceptive and relevant to my approach, and I shall turn to it presently. It is noteworthy that economists who draw on Knight rarely consider Knight's entrepreneurs in a dynamic economy nor are they aware, so it would appear, of Knight's remarkable 23 page preface to the London School of Economics 1933 reissue of his treatise.[5]

As already noted, it is not sufficient to treat entrepreneurs solely as economic agents who only collect windfalls and bear losses that are unanticipated. If this is all they do, the much vaunted free enterprise system merely distributes in some unspecified manner the windfalls and losses that come as surprises. If entrepreneurship has some economic value it must perform a useful function which is constrained by scarcity, which implies that there is a supply and a demand for their services.

Entrepreneurial ability continues to be an elusive concept in economics. The dialogue between theory and observable entrepreneurial behavior is not one of the more cogent and useful parts of economics. The supply of this ability is rarely considered; nor is the demand for it an integral part of economic analysis. The entrepreneur seldom appears in our theoretical literature. Baumol[6] put its neatly: "The references are scanty and more often they are totally absent. The theoretical firm is entrepreneurless – the Prince of Denmark has been expunged from the discussion of *Hamlet*." There are of course well-defined problems that equilibrium theory deals with which require no entrepreneur for their solution. If there were competition with no contrived scarcity and if the economy had arrived at an equilibrium, and if there were no changes that would disturb that equilibrium, entrepreneurial ability would have no economic value.

Kirzner[7] approaches the entrepreneur in the tradition of the Austrian School. He also argues that there is no room for the entrepreneur in equilibrium theory. He presents a theory of the market and prices in which the entrepreneur is a necessary active agent. Nevertheless, all of his analysis comes to naught for he concludes ". . . that at the market level . . . entrepreneurship is not to be treated as a resource . . . The market never recognizes entrepreneurial ability in the sense of an available useful resource." What went wrong in arriving at this conclusion? Whether or not there are returns to entrepreneurship that are not "profits" is not made explicit. Accordingly, the returns that accrue to economic agents who bring about the equilibrating process as changes occur that give rise to disequilibria do not surface. This means that the essential and rewarding activities of entrepreneurs in dealing with disequilibria that are inevitable in the dynamics of modernization and economic growth are omitted.

Knight, however, faces up to the contributions of entrepreneurs in a dynamic market economy. He deals at length with the risk-uncertainty problem inherent in Nature, i.e. natural resources, in technological changes and in the instability of prices. He sees factor prices as more amenable to contracts than output prices. Thus the interval of time between production based on contracted factors and the sale of the output is a special source of risk. He also sees advances in knowledge as the most pervasive and important part of the risk problem. The treatise is rich with insights on the limitations of information and of expectations as change and progress occur under actual market conditions. He is indeed much concerned with the contributions of entrepreneurs to the equilibrating process, despite all manner of risk and uncertainty.

Knight devotes a long chapter (chapter V) to the theory of change and progress with uncertainty absent. In chapter XI he returns to this *"unchanging property of changing"*, noting that it would require a completely knowable world which is in his view a pure artifact of our minds, a refuge to which we flee from an unknowable world. It should also be noted that whereas windfalls and losses that are not anticipated have no effect on current production, *ex post*, however, they can affect the distribution of income and the subsequent allocative behavior of entrepreneurs. But there is a critical, unsettled issue. It pertains to Knight's "distinction between *risk*, as referring to events subject to a known or knowable probability distribution, and *uncertainty*, as referring to events for which it was not possible to specify numerical probabilities".[8] Friedman does not believe that this is a valid distinction. He follows, as I do, L. J. Savage in his view of personal probability, which denies any valid distinction along these lines. But to argue that this distinction is not valid for the decision of the entrepreneur, does not solve the problem of the observer, i.e., the economist, because he is not privy to what the entrepreneur subjectively thinks is probable.

2 Attributes of Entrepreneurs

While it is permissible to use "ability" and "capacity" of people interchangeably,[9] it is better to think of people as having abilities and of nonhuman factors as having capacities. The capacity of cropland can be increased by irrigation, drainage, lime to neutralize the acidity of the soil and by the application of fertilizers. The productive capacity of high yielding new varieties of wheat exceeds that of some traditional varieties. Capacity, but not ability, is applicable to all nonhuman factors, including machines, equipment, and structures. People, however, have abilities both innate and acquired. It is the acquired abilities of entrepreneurs that are enhanced by schooling, health and experience.

What are the attributes that distinguish the entrepreneur from people who are also active economic agents but who are not entrepreneurs? Schumpeter's concept has merit but it excludes most of the worthwhile services that entrepreneurs render. It is useful to treat entrepreneurs as providing firm specific human capital, or as organizational human capital within firms. The treatment of what entrepreneurs in large corporations do is ambiguous. It is noteworthy that this vast literature is silent on the much larger numbers of small entrepreneurs. The survey of Marris and Mueller is committed to the failure of competition whereas Fama provides support for the efficiency of large corporations.[10] Small firms, however, have not become extinct. I am especially mindful of agriculture throughout the world; there are literally many millions of small farmers who are entrepreneurs. The entrepreneurial domain of many other people is also small as they reallocate their resources in response to changes in economic conditions. People who supply labor services for hire or who are self-employed reallocate their services in response to changes in the value of the work they do. Students likewise are entrepreneurs when they reallocate their own time along with the educational services they purchase as they respond to changes in expected earnings and to changes in the personal satisfactions they expect to derive from their education. Housewives are also entrepreneurs in dealing with changes in the value of their own time and of the purchased goods and services they devote to household production. Consumption opportunities also change in a dynamic economy and inasmuch as pure consumption entails time, here, too, consumers act as entrepreneurs in responding to such changes. [11] By all odds, the economic domain of most entrepreneurs is indeed small.

The bearing of risk is not a unique attribute of entrepreneurs. Whereas entrepreneurs assume risk, there also are people who are not entrepreneurs who assume risk. Conceptually, in a dynamic economy there are entrepreneurs and there is a risk; in a stationary (static) economy there are no entrepreneurs and there is risk, and human agents in such an economy who engage in economic activities also assume and bear risk. The implication is that no economy whether it be stationary or dynamic is riskless, whereas entrepreneurs are dynamic specific. Empirically, it is highly implausible that there ever was or will be a riskless economy. Any observable stationary economy that has arrived at economic equilibrium, and as long as the equilibrium persists, does not need and does not have entrepreneurs, but such an economy is not free of risk. Accordingly, the bearing of risk does not distinguish between people who are entrepreneurs and those who are not entrepreneurs.

Some elaboration of this issue is warranted. In traditional agriculture that has arrived over many generations at what is a close approximation of a (stationary) economic equilibrium, [12] farmers are bearing risk. Since they do what their forebears have done for generations, their production activities are routine and repetitive; there is no need for, or demand for, entrepreneurial ability. Although traditional agriculture is not riskless, no new economic decisions are required. There are no incentives to alter the prevailing routine. What is known from past experience is optimal in allocating the available resources efficiently. No new skills are called for. There are no changes in expectations. The rational thing to do under these conditions is to repeat doing what is being done. Although people may be very poor, they may be illiterate, their economic life may be harsh, they are routinely equating their marginal utility and their marginal cost to a fine degree. It bears repeating: the bearing of risk is not a unique attribute of entrepreneurship.

Before I leave the routine, repetitive economic state, it is evident that highly sophisticated decision rules can evolve over time that are routinely applied. In thinking about the non-repetitive activities of human agents, my concept of a disequilibrium state calls for entrepreneurship which entails making decisions that are neither routine nor repetitive.

The economic behavior implications of risk aversion in a dynamic economy are not pursued in this paper. They have received much attention whereas the acquired abilities of entrepreneurs have been neglected. Kihlstrom and Laffront[13] provide a useful brief review of part of the literature bearing on risk aversion and they have a model to determine who chooses to be or not to be an entrepreneur. It is not obvious, however, that when one's own time needs to be reallocated the individual has this choice.

A more general analytical problem in economics is that economic disequilibria are not at home in equilibrium theory. It is plausible to argue that what economic agents do today given their information and expectations is consistent with the implication of equilibrium theory. But this approach does not deal with the effects of the shortcomings of yesterday's information and expectations on the situation in which economic agents find themselves today. Nor does it deal with tomorrow's problem when corresponding limitations of today's information and expectations become evident. Substantial advances have been made in treating aspects of this problem in terms of the costs of searching for information and the returns on this search process and in developing "more" rational expectations to deal with this problem. For the purpose at hand, the assumption is that increases in the ability of entrepreneurs contribute to their efficiency in acquiring information and in formulating and acting upon their expectations.

The substance of my argument is that disequilibria are inevitable in dynamic economy. These disequilibria cannot be eliminated by law, by public policy, and surely not by rhetoric. A modern dynamic economy would fall apart were it not for the entrepreneurial actions of a wide array of human agents who reallocate their resources and thereby bring their part of the economy back into equilibrium. Every entrepreneurial decision to reallocate resources entails risk. What entrepreneurs do has an economic value. This value accrues to them as a rent, i.e., a rent which is a reward for their entrepreneurial performance. This reward is *earned*. Although this reward for the entrepreneurship of most human agents is small, in the aggregate in a dynamic economy it accounts for a substantial part of the increases in national income. The concealment of this part in the growth of national income implies that entrepreneurs have not received their due in economics.

3   Demand for Entrepreneurship

This demand is a function of economic disequilibria. Human agents who perceive and evaluate such disequilibria with a view of deciding whether or not it is worthwhile for them to reallocate their resources, including the allocation of their own time, are entrepreneurs. The analytical problem is made difficult by virtue of the fact that economic disequilibria are exceedingly heterogeneous. They differ depending on the source (cause) of the disequilibria. In the event of war, all manner of economic disequilibria as a rule occur abruptly. One of the effects of political instability on the economy is that it becomes disorganized and beset with economic disequilibria. Economic activities are altered by various government interventions that nationalize parts of the private sector, impose regulations on other parts and pursue policies designed to redistribute personal income. In dealing with changes in economic events, economists tend to concentrate on the process of economic growth and modernization, treating this process as an integral part of economic dynamics. This process, however, also gives rise to a wide array of different classes of economic disequilibria. Thus, no matter where one turns in investigating what entrepreneurs actually do, the disequilibria that are observed are characterized by much heterogeneity.

Many of the disequilibria that are associated with economic growth are endogenous. An innovation by a business enterprise (Schumpeter's innovator) is an endogenous event. Individual economic agents – laborers, students, housewives, consumers, and small farmers – are rarely innovators of anything of measurable importance. Publically financed and organized research has become an increasing source of technological advances. The results of research are a major source of economic disequilibria. This set of disequilibria is pervasive in modern economic growth. Much of the demand for entrepreneurship is a consequence of this set.

It is helpful to approach the demand for entrepreneurship as having the attributes of a schedule. When a disequilibrium occurs, the particular entrepreneur faces a schedule where the incentive to act is relatively high at the outset and as he proceeds to reallocate his resources, the incentive to make further adjustments declines. The part of this demand schedule that matters in analyzing the observable behavior lies substantially above that of a zero gain. When the additional gain has become sufficiently small, the incentive becomes too weak to warrant proceeding to the perfect equilibrium point.

Under competition the demand for entrepreneurship occasioned by a particular technological advance is transitory. Once the technique has been adopted, a new equilibrium will have been attained[14] and the demand for entrepreneurship from this event will no longer exist. A sequence of technological advances over time, however, maintains this demand. The implications for the supply of entrepreneurship for the transitory case, which entails a once for all adoption, differs importantly from that of the steady sequence of technological advances, which has come to characterize the modernization of agriculture. This difference will be considered presently.

4 Supply of Entrepreneurship

The supply is not restricted to a small part of the adult population. One observes that many people, if not all, have some ability to supply entrepreneurship when there is a demand for it. It is also documented that this particular ability is enhanced by experience, education, and health. When it is worthwhile, people invest in education and also in health and one of the effects of doing so is revealed in their additional entrepreneurial ability.

It is clearly evident that millions of farmers in low income countries have substantial ability to alter the use that they make of their land, labor and their stock of reproducible physical capital in response to better technical and price opportunities.[15] Their responses demonstrate that they are not bound to what had been routine traditional farming and that they are not indifferent to opportunities to improve their economic lot.

Learning from Experience

The necessity of dealing with disequilibria is a good teacher. Although most farmers in low income countries have little or no schooling, their recent performance reveals considerable ability to learn; to wit, in their success in the adoptions of new high yielding varieties of food grains. In view of the contributions of agricultural research oriented to the requirements of low-income countries and the large amounts of additional capital being committed to agricultural development in these countries, the observed ability of this new breed of farmers to transform these research contributions and the additional capital into increases in food production is clear and substantial.

One measure of the entrepreneurial ability of farmers in low-income countries is the high rate at which high yielding varieties of wheat and rice are adopted. Such high yielding varieties became variable to these farmers less than two decades ago. The suitability of these varieties differed by countries; new complementary inputs had to be purchased, notably fertilizer, and the appropriate changes in farm practices had to be learned. There were new risks. By 1976–77, throughout South and East Asia, of all the cropland used to grow wheat 74 percent was devoted to high yielding varieties; in the case of rice, this achievement was 30 percent of the cropland used to grow rice.[16]

In turning to the comparative advantage of the schoolroom in acquiring entrepreneurial ability, the limitations of on-farm experiences need to be considered. As the technology becomes more complex the comparative advantage of schooling increases. The economic value of learning from experience and so too from schooling in dealing with a once for all improved technology is exhausted when the farmer attains his new equilibrium. Although steady technical changes render both experience and schooling time dependent, the ability acquired from schooling is more useful in dealing with changes in a complex technology and also more durable than that acquired from experience. The implications of a sequence of steady technical changes are succinctly put by Welch.[17] "A rapid rate of technical change renders past experience obsolete and it increases the informational content of today's experience. But, just as more rapid technical change renders yesterday less relevant from today's perspective, it renders today less relevant from tomorrow's perspective." One implication is that no general statements are possible about the value of the entrepreneurial ability acquired from experiences unless the attributes of the technical changes are specified. Another implication is that the comparative advantage of schooling rises relative to that of learning from experience as technology becomes more complex.

Education and Entrepreneurship

The complexity and dynamics of US agriculture provide strong evidence that education enhances the entrepreneurial ability of farmers. The empirical issue is not restricted to difference in the effects between 8 and 12 years of schooling on the allocative ability of farmers. The evidence also resolves the puzzle why the proportion of US farmers with one or more years of college education increased between 1940 and 1960 (white males, aged 35 to 54) by 83 percent, which exceeded by a wide margin that of the non-farm occupations. Farmers are normally both self-employed workers and entrepreneurs. Thus, in the case of farmers, the productivity effects of education are of two parts, namely, on work skills and on entrepreneurship in dealing with the disequilibria that occur as a consequence of changes in the economy. In my *Transforming Traditional Agriculture*, I advanced the hypothesis that traditional farmers are more efficient in allocating their resources than modern farmers are because modern farmers do not fully regain an economic equilibrium before they face new technical advances. This hypothesis has lead to many studies to determine the rate of adjustment with special attention to the effects of education. Chandhri[18] was among the vanguard in showing that the input composition in agriculture is sensitive to the education of farmers. Research in this area owes much to Welch[19] who built on the work of Griliches[20] and Evenson.[21] In Welch's approach, the demand for entrepreneurship is determined by the level of agricultural research activity: the higher the level the more rapid the changes in production opportunities and the larger the advantages of the entrepreneurial ability acquired from education. Although the increases in productivity from the new technologies called for more work skills, it was not plausible that the additional skills of college graduates could account for all of the very considerable increases in their earnings which in Welch's study came to 62 percent more for the college graduates than for those who had completed high school. He found that the advances in agricultural research explained roughly one-third of this difference between college and high school graduates.[22]

Huffman's studies[23] get at the heart of allocation issue. He focused on the use of a single input, nitrogen fertilizer, in the production of corn. His rationale is that where a major change occurs with various lesser changes in its wake, the education of farmers should speed the adjustments. The major change was the 22 to 25 percent decline in the prices of nitrogen relative to that of corn. Using a sample of county data drawn from five key corn belt states for the period 1950–54 to 1964, he found that one additional year of education resulted in the farmers earning $52 more from this one dimension of improved allocative efficiency in one farmer activity, i.e., in using nitrogen in corn production.

Petzel's study[24] deals with the relationships between farmer education and the dynamics of acreage allocations to soybean production in the United States. He uses an implicit optimizing model based on farmers' expected prices. His study focuses on a period of rapid growth in the acreage devoted to soybeans in nine states from 1948 to 1973. Petzel found that the adjustments made by farmers occurred more rapidly in the counties where average education levels are highest. He also found more rapid adjustments with respect to two dimensions of scale, namely the total crop area devoted to soybeans and the unit scale per farm.[25]

It is clear from these studies along with the results from various other studies that in US agriculture, which has been remarkably dynamic during recent decades, the entrepreneurial ability of farmers is measurably enhanced by their education.[26]

Rare is the entrepreneur who is only an entrepreneur. Most people who perform entrepreneurial functions also do routine work which may be unskilled or at the other extreme highly skilled, technical work. Whereas students make entrepreneurial decisions their program of studies is essentially routine work; the activities of housewives in household production have the same attributes, and it is also true for consumers. Schooling and higher education and also health, on which the empirical evidence is still very sparse, are investments in acquired abilities. They enhance not only the skills that people use routinely but they also increase the entrepreneurial ability of individuals. While much progress has been made in analyzing the return to investment in human capital, these returns to education undervalue both the private and social return because of the omission of the contribution to entrepreneurial ability.

5   Closing Remark

Entrepreneurship is a pervasive activity in a dynamic economy. At various points over the life-cycle, every person is an entrepreneur if for no other reason than the increases in the value of human time over time. Since 1900, the real value of an hour of work of the normal labor force in the United States has increased five fold.[27] The processes of a dynamic economy make disequilibria inevitable. Not only businessmen but also laborers, students, housewives, consumers and farmers perceive, assess and, when they deem it to be worthwhile, act to regain equilibrium. Every entrepreneurial action entails a risk. But risk is not a unique attribute of a dynamic economy. Experience, education and health enhance entrepreneurial ability. The return to investment in education is well documented. In agriculture, a substantial part of this return to investment in education accrues from its contribution to the entrepreneurial ability of farmers.

Notes and References

1   Edward C. Prescott and Michael Vincher, "Organizational Capital," *Journal of Political Economy*, 88 (June 1980), 446–61.
2   Erik Dahmen, *Entrepreneurial Activity and the Development of Swedish Industry, 1919–1939* (translated into English by Axel Leijonhufvud and

published for the American Economic Association by Richard D. Irwin, Inc., 1970). See preface by Theodore W. Schultz, dated Nov. 1969.

3   Theodore W. Schultz, "The Politics and Economics of Research", Museum of Science and Industry Nobel Hall of Science Induction Program, Chicago, Illinois (April 23, 1980).

4   Theodore W. Schultz, "The Politics and Economics of Research and Agricultural Productivity", International Agricultural Development Service Occasional Paper (New York, 1979).

5   Frank H. Knight, *Risk, Uncertainty, and Profit* (London School of Economics and Political Science, Reprint No. 16, 1933).

6   I find William J. Baumol's very brief paper "Entrepreneurship and Economic Theory", *American Economic Review*, Papers and Proceedings, 68 (May 1968), 68–71, exceedingly perceptive in seeing that the entrepreneurial function is an essential part of the process of economic growth.

7   Israel M. Kirzner, *Competition and Entrepreneurship* (University of Chicago Press, Chicago, Ill., 1973), contains many cogent economic insights. His counterproductive conclusion is clearly set forth in his paper "Alertness, Luck, and Entrepreneurial Profit", presented at the American Economic Association meetings, Aug. 31, 1978. To the best of my knowledge, this paper has not been published.

8   Milton Friedman, *Price Theory* (Aldine Publishing Co., Chicago, Ill., 1976), p. 282.

9   Friedman, ibid., uses these two terms interchangeably; the "capacity of entrepreneurs" predominates.

10 Robin Marris and Dennis C. Mueller, "The Corporation, Competition, and the Invisible Hand," *Journal of Economic Literature*, 28 (March. 1980), 32–63; see also Eugene Fama, "Agency Problems and the Theory of the Firm", *Journal of Political Economy*, 88 (April 1980), 288–307.

11 Theodore W. Schultz, "The Value of the Ability to Deal with Disequilibria," *Journal of Economic Literature*, 13 (Sept. 1975), 827–46.

12 The economics of traditional agriculture is featured in Theodore W. Schultz, *Transforming Traditional Agriculture* (Yale University Press, New Haven, Conn., 1964, reprinted Arno Press, 1976).

13 Richard E. Kihlstrom and Jean-Jacques Laffront, in "A General Equilibrium Entrepreneurial Theory of Firm Formation Based on Risk Aversion," *Journal of Political Economy*, 89 (Aug. 1979), 719–48, present a model on the assumption that "individuals decide whether to become entrepreneurs or workers by comparing the risky returns of entrepreneurship with the non-risky wages determined in a competitive labor market". This model omits any consideration of the entrepreneur's contribution to the production process. They "assume that all individuals are equal in their ability to perform entrepreneurial as well as normal labor functions". They state that their model is a special case of Knight's view while acknowledging that Knight emphasizes differences in ability.

14 Both production and consumption are altered by the new equilibrium. The even ot hybrid corn is illustrative of what such a new equilibrium entails.

The costs of producing corn are reduced. When the hybrid corn is widely adopted the benefits from the reduction in costs are transferred to consumers. The gain in real consumer income alters consumer behavior. As a consequence of the increase in productivity occasioned by hybrid corn and the associated complementary inputs that followed in its wake, in the United States, although the corn acreage harvested in 1979 was 33 million acres less than in 1932, the production in 1979 was three times the amount produced in 1932. There were also marked scale and location effects: farms became larger and the number of farms declined very substantially. The comparative advantage of the heart of the corn belt increased and more of the production shifted into the better parts of this corn producing area.

15   An extended analysis of this behavior is presented in Theodore W. Schultz, "Investment in Population Quality Throughout Low-Income Countries", in Philip M. Hauser (ed.), *World Population and Development: Challenges and Prospects* (Syracuse University Press, 1979), pp. 339–60.

16   Dana G. Darymple, *Development and Spread of High Yielding Varieties of Wheat and Rice in Less Developed Nations* (USDA, Foreign Agricultural Economic Report No. 95, 1978).

17   Finis Welch, "The Role of Investment in Human Capital in Agriculture," in Theodore W. Schultz (ed.), *Distortions of Agricultural Incentive* (Indiana University Press, Bloomington, Indiana, 1978), pp. 259–81.

18   D. P. Chaudhri, "Education and Agricultural Productivity in India", PhD dissertation (University of Delhi, India, 1968).

19   Finis Welch, "Education in Production," *Journal of Political Economy*, 78 (Jan.–Feb. 1970), 35–59.

20   Zvi Griliches, "The Sources of Measured Productivity Growth: United States Agriculture, 1940–1960", *Journal of Political Economy*, 71 (1963), 331–46; also "Research Expenditures, Education, and the Aggregate Agricultural Production Function", *American Economic Review*, 54 (1964), 961–74.

21   Robert Evenson, "The Contribution of Agricultural Research and Extension to Agricultural Production" (PhD dissertation, University of Chicago, 1968).

22   Research expenditure per farm was $4.30 in 1940 and $28.40 in 1959. The implication of Welch's analysis is that if research were to fall from $28.40 to $4.30 per farm, about one-third of the differential would disappear. In my view, if there were no agriculture research for a decade, the technology of US agriculture would arrive at an economic equilibrium and the complexity of agricultural production would require the skills of less than that of a high school education.

23   Wallace E. Huffman: "Contributions of Education and Extension in Differential Rates of Change", PhD dissertation (University of Chicago, 1972); "Decision Making: The Role of Education," *American Journal of Agricultural Economics*, 46 (1974), 85–97; "Allocative Efficiency: The Role of Human Capital," *Quarterly Journal of Economics*, 91 (1977), 59–77. It is

noteworthy that the decline in the price of nitrogen fertilizer was a consequence of a major technological advance. The development of the "Kellogg" process reduced sharply the real costs of producing nitrogen.

24 Todd Petzel, "Education and the Dynamics of Supply", PhD dissertation (University of Chicago, 1976).

25 See Finis Welch, "The Role of Investment in Human Capital in Agriculture", 273–74, for a fuller account of Petzel's contribution.

26 Other studies on education and allocative ability are reviewed by Welch, ibid., and in Theodore W. Schultz, "The Value of the Ability to Deal with Disequilibria".

27 See below, Part III, No. 7, "A Long View of the Value of Human Time."

7

A Long View of Increases in the Value of Human Time*

1 Introduction

In Ricardo's day '. . . English laborers' weekly wages were often less than the price of half a bushel of good wheat'.[1] By the time that Ricardo published his classic work (1817), the weekly wage of unskilled workers in the United States was equal to the price of two bushels of good wheat.[2] In 1890, when Marshall's *Principles* appeared, US unskilled workers could buy close to nine bushels of wheat with their weekly wage. In as much as my story pertains largely to changes since then, let me continue for a moment with wages and wheat in the United States. By 1970 the weekly compensation of manufacturing production workers was sufficient to buy 96 bushels of high-quality wheat.[3] The economics of the decline by half between 1900 and 1970 in the deflated price of wheat is well known. But the economics of the rise in real wages for time spent at work by labor, which is vastly more important, is still in large part unsettled.

Although it is obvious that the real price of the services rendered by people is very high in countries that have the most modern economies, it is not obvious that this price has risen markedly relative to the price of the services of material resources; that this rise in the price of human time has been in large part a consequence of the formation of new forms of both human and nonhuman capital, and that human agents in these countries have been responding to strong economic incentives in the formation of such capital. It is undoubtedly true that the most important achievement of modern economic growth is the rise in the value of human time.

In analyzing changes in the supply and demand for human time there have been advances in economics starting with concepts of human capital

*First published as "On the Economics of the Increases in the Value of Human Time over Time," in R.C.O. Matthews (ed.), *Economic Growth and Resources*, vol. 2 (Macmillan Press Ltd, London, 1980), pp. 107–29. Reproduced by permission of Macmillan Academic and Professional Ltd.

and of the earnings foregone that are a part of the costs of acquiring human capital. These concepts lead to the theory of the allocation of time, to the household production function and to models for analyzing the price and income effects of the value of the time of women in household activities, including the bearing and rearing of children. These advances have made possible a wide array of empirical studies. Of the factors that determine the price of human time, a good deal is now known about those that determine the supply, but the state of knowledge about the demand is still fragmentary. Measurement for the purpose at hand of secular real changes in the value of time has received all too little attention. My plan is to start with measurement, then turn to explanations, and from there proceed to implications.

2 Measurement

We need some measures of the value of human time and of the changes in it over time to know what it is that requires explanation. Measures of the price of wheat come easily. The market specification of the attributes of hard red winter wheat are well established; Kansas City is the major market; and the price per bushel is readily available. But the attributes of the services of labor differ widely by occupation in any year, and they change over time. For the rank and file of people in the labor market, total compensation for time spent at work is presently of two parts: money paid as wages and various wage supplements.[4] In the United States prior to 1936, wage supplements were less than one cent per hour at work. By 1957 these supplements had risen to 16 cents, and by the seventies our estimate is that they added 13 percent to the wages paid.

Actual time spent at work is a significant variable. Official statistics of hourly earnings overstate the time spent at work because they do not adjust for increases in paid vacations, holidays or sick leave. Nor do they exclude time that is devoted to lunch periods, coffee breaks, wash up time, call in time, and jury duty.[5]

Estimates of changes in actual real hourly wages are not precise when one uses the Consumer Price Index. Consumer prices have various limitations for the purpose at hand. But even if the CPI were a perfect measure of purchasing power of dollar wages, it is incorrect to apply this index to wage supplements invested in pensions and other future benefits, the real value of which depends on the price level when these future benefits are received. As Rees has noted,[6] there is currently no satisfactory solution of this problem. Obviously the same problem arises in adjusting the wages paid to workers by this index to the extent that their wages are added to savings.

We shall use Rees's estimates because they account for most of the more important wage supplements and because they get fairly close to the actual time spent at work. We have brought his estimates up to date, and we have adjusted his estimates and our own to 1967 dollars using the official CPI, mindful as we do this of the unsolved problems that this adjustment entails. How to deal with the changes in the attributes of labor is our next problem. Clearly the composition of the labor force does not remain constant in terms of age and sex distribution; health has become better, life span has increased, youth spends more years in school and thus enters the labor market older, and the aged can afford to retire earlier than formerly. The years of education of workers have been increasing at a high rate. It follows that the attributes of the people working for wages or salaries since 1900 differ substantially from decade to decade.

We could use either of two approaches in dealing with the problem of the changing attributes of the labor force in estimating the price paid for the services of an hour of a worker's time. We could construct an index of wages and salaries comparable to the Consumer Price Index. It would be a labor price index which would indicate the changes in the level of wages and salaries over time. The other approach, the one we shall use in coping with this problem, is to assume that there is a pattern of normal wages and that this pattern of normal wages may change from one sub-period to the next. This approach rests on the assumption that the wages of the various major subsets of workers stay approximately the same relative to one another during the sub-period. This approach has the advantage that the array of such wages, for the purpose of functional, allocative economics, may be treated as if there were a normal wage.

We shall treat the hourly total compensation of production workers in manufacturing for the actual time spent at work at the normal wage. Manufacturing workers are the largest part of the labor force. Retail trade workers are the second largest, and although they have been increasing very much relative to manufacturing workers, the level of their hourly wages has stayed at about 70 percent of that of manufacturing workers.[7] Furthermore, it will become evident presently that the real earnings of educated people, when due allowance is made for the cost of their education, are determined in the long run by normal wages, that is, by what the labor market pays for the services of the rank and file of labor. This means that over any long period the real earnings, for example, of elementary and secondary school teachers, of academic faculties, and of other college educated people are the sum of normal wages and of the additional compensation that is required to have made their education worthwhile. It may be easier to see the dependency on normal wages in the case of real wages in agriculture. They too are determined primarily by the secular rise in normal wages throughout the economy and not by particular agricultural events.

In our endeavour at measurement, we are mainly concerned about the price of human time, that is, the price that is paid for an hour of that time. It is well to be explicit on this point of concern. Economic growth theories tend to omit the changes that occur over time in relative prices of the services of the factors of production. The price of human time, as will be shown, has been increasing relatively. Thus the omission of this change in relative prices means that there is no reckoning of such price effects on incentives in allocating currently available resources and in investing to enhance the future stock of capital. Price effects matter; the resulting income effects follow.

In the United States, hourly compensation for time spent at work in 1967 dollars for the part of the labor force to which we turn for our normal wages increased from 1900 to 1970 from about $0.60 to $3.27, well over fivefold (table 3.7.1). When we partition this long upward trend into four sub-periods, each beginning and ending when the economy was performing well, the annual rates for each sub-period are as follows:[8]

Annual Rates Increases

1900–15	1.4
1915–30	2.4
1930–50	3.7
1950–70	2.12

We now turn to the hourly earnings of unskilled workers, teachers, and associate professors (table 3.7.2). It should be borne in mind that wage supplements are not included for the unskilled. An adjustment for such supplements is included in the hourly earnings of teachers and associate professors.[9]

The change in the absolute differences holds the key to the economic incentive (disincentive) whether or not it is worthwhile to invest in human capital, mainly in education, for the purpose of increasing (future) earnings. Manufacturing workers in 1900 received only $0.02 more per hour (1967 dollars) than the unskilled, teachers $0.24 more, and associate professors $2.02 more. By 1970 these absolute differences were $0.79, $1.91, and $3.70 respectively. The difference in favour of associate professors is the largest although it had increased much less relatively than each of the other three groups over this long period.

Table 3.7.1 Total compensation per hour at work of manufacturing production workers in the United States, 1900–75

Year	Consumer prices 1967 = 100	Hourly wages 1967 dollars	Hourly wage index 1900 = 100
1900	25	0.60	100
1910	29	0.70	117
1920	60	0.92	153
1930	50	1.06	177
1940	42	1.60	267
1950	72	2.15	358
1960	89	2.85	475
1970	116	3.27	545
1972	125	3.44	573
1975	161	3.37	562

Source: The hourly wages are Albert Rees's estimates of total compensation per hour of work of manufacturing production workers appearing in *Long-Term Economic Growth, 1860–1970* (US Bureau of Economic Analysis, Washington, DC, 1973) Appendix 2, B70, pp. 223–23. They are up-dated and adjusted from 1957 to 1967 dollars.

Table 3.7.2

	Earnings per hour (in 1967 dollars)		Relative increase in per cent 1900 = 100	Absolute increase 1900 over 1970 (in 1967 dollars)
	1900	1970		
Normal wages (mfg. workers)	0.60	3.27	545	2.67
Unskilled workers	0.58	2.48	427	1.90
Teachers	0.82	4.39	535	3.57
Associate professors	2.60	6.18	238	3.58

Source: Appendix, Table 3.7.A2.

We have already noted that we have partitioned this seventy year period into four sub-periods and that each sub-period begins and ends in years when the economy was doing well. The first two sub-periods cover 15 years each, and the latter two 20 years each. From 1900 to 1915, the US labor force increased by 37 per cent, during the next 15 years by 26 per cent, and it increased by 35 percent during each of the two subsequent sub-periods[10] The unemployment rate was 5 percent in 1900 and 4.9 in 1970. In 1950 it was 5.3. On this score, 1913 would have been a better date than 1915 and 1929 better than 1930 because the unemployment rate was 4.3 in 1913 and 3.2 in 1929. Table 3.7.3 gives the increases in real hourly earnings for each of these four sub-periods.

In analyzing the allocation of resources as of any given year when stocks of such resources are given, employees and employers respond to the relative prices of the productive services of these resources. Seeing the prices for work time during each of the five dates encompassing our four sub-periods, table 3.7.4 indicates that our measure of normal wages (manufacturing workers) rose relative to that of unskilled wages gradually by about a third over the 1900 to 1970 period. Recall, however, that no wage supplements are here reckoned for the unskilled. The hourly salary of teachers tended for each of these dates to be about 50 percent above that of the unskilled. But the relative price of the time of associate professors declined markedly.

To the best of my knowledge, there are no complete time-series estimates of hourly earnings for other countries where earnings are high that are comparable to those presented for the United States. Phelps Brown's real annual wages in industry, however, are useful in this connection.[11] The upward trends in real wages in industry in France, Germany, Sweden and the United Kingdom, shown in table 3.7.5, are in general much like that of the United States. They differ somewhat, however, in that the rate of increase is higher in Sweden and the United States than it is in the other three up to about 1960, except for the United Kingdom which did not stay abreast of the rest. There are also other country differences in the movement in real wages that are noteworthy. France and the United Kingdom show no increase between 1900 and

Table 3.7.3 Increase in hourly earnings

	1915 over 1900	1930 over 1915	1950 over 1930	1970 over 1950
		(increase in percent)		
Mfg. workers	23	43	103	52
Unskilled workers	21	337	72	50
Teachers	32	38	54	91
Associate professors	20	8	7	72

Source: These estimates are derived from Appendix, Table 3.7.A2

Table 3.7.4 Relative real hourly earnings: unskilled = 100

	1900	1915	1930	1950	1970
Unskilled workers	100	100	100	100	100
Rees's mfg. workers	103	106	110	130	132
Teachers	141	154	155	139	155
Associate professors	448	444	350	218	249

Source: Appendix, table 3.7.A2.

Table 3.7.5 Indexes of real wages in industry in France, Germany, Sweden, United Kingdom and the United States, 1900–70 (1890–99 = 100)

	France	Germany	Sweden	United Kingdom	United States
1900	112	108	110	104	110
1910	112	116	131	104	121
1925	135	127	158	113	160
1930	138	156	183	124	160
1938	142	155	190	133	203
1950	168	174	252	169	292
1960	290	282	343	219	381
1970	442	482	473	301	446

Source: Phelps Brown, "Levels and Movements of Industrial Productivity and Real Wages Internationally Compared, 1860–1970". Based on tables III and V of the Appendix. See p. 112, n. 1, for a comment on the lack of comparability between these wages indexes and the hourly wages presented for the United States in the preceding tables.

1910. As of 1925, the increases show Sweden and the United States substantially ahead of the other three countries (was this a consequence mainly of differences in the effects of the aftermath of the war?). Sweden and the United States maintain their advantage over the others up to 1960 with the United Kingdom losing ground in relative terms. Lastly, at the end of the decade of the sixties, France and Germany joined Sweden and the United States in showing a fourfold and more relative increase in real annual wages in industry over the period from 1900 to 1970, whereas the relative increase for the United Kingdom is slightly less than threefold.

This endeavor at measurement supports five observations pertaining to increases in the value of human time:

1   In the United States the interaction between the preferences of people to engage in work for pay and the availability of work opportunities

has resulted in a very large secular increase in the real hourly compensation for time spent at work.

2   While the evidence presented is fragmentary, it is consistent with the findings from recent human capital studies in showing that the relative difference between the real hourly earnings of wage workers and of highly educated workers in the labor market has become smaller over time.

3   The absolute difference, however, between these two classes of workers has become larger, and it is presumed sufficiently so to have provided compensation for the rising cost of the additional education and to have induced relatively more people to acquire the additional (college) education.

4   The secular rise in real earnings of labor in industry in the four selected European countries suggests a secular process since 1900 that may be similar in terms of increases in the value of human time to that described for the United States.

5   When it comes to explaining this historical behavior of value and prices, it may be presumed that the observed behavior is a consequence of a particular type of economic growth.

Before entering upon explanations, however, there is one additional set of special prices to bear in mind, namely the prices of the commodities that are most closely identified with natural resources. It is useful to see these prices over time because of the widely held belief that natural resources are the critical limiting factor available to the economy. We present them for renewable natural resources – agriculture and forestry – and for non-renewable natural resources – mining, including mineral fuels. The commodity prices that we present are of course not pure natural resource service prices; far from it, for they embody in various combinations the productive services for labor, the price of which has been rising, and of reproducible material capital along with the productive services derived from natural resources.

Most of the natural resource commodities tend to remain fairly constant over time in their physical, chemical, or biological attributes. A bushel of wheat, as already noted, produced in 1900, differed very little from a bushel produced in 1970; similarly, in the case of a ton of lead, copper, or sulphur. Quality changes occur, however, for example, in milk and in other livestock products. The historical records of these commodity prices are in general more reliable than that of intermediate goods. For the United States, we have the excellent study by Potter and Christy of commodities produced by extractive industries.[12] The Potter–Christy estimates have been updated by Manthy.[13]

What table 3.7.6 shows is that the trend of the deflated natural resource commodity prices over this period was not upward but slightly downward,[14] compared to the more than fivefold rise in real hourly "wages" shown in table 3.7.1. Within agriculture, the deflated prices of all crops declined about a third despite various government price supports during parts of this period; the index for all livestock closed out this period at the level where it began (Appendix, table 3.7.A.3). In general, the costs of producing livestock products have been affected more by the increase in the price of human time than have the costs of producing crops. The deflated prices of mineral fuels (Appendix, table 3.7.A.4) indicate that whereas the deflated price index for all mineral fuels was about a fourth less at the end of this period compared to 1900, the price of bituminous coal rose and that of petroleum fell. It is undoubtedly true that the rise in real wages accounts for a good deal of the increase in coal prices.[15]

Table 3.7.6 Indexes of deflated natural resource commodity prices, United States, 1900–72 (1900 = 100)

Year	All commodities	All agriculture	All forestry	All metals
1900	100	100	100	100
1910	99	126	99	76
1920	109	111	97	66
1930	76	90	56	45
1940	77	86	87	60
1950	108	131	99	68
1960	87	95	90	75
1970	79	88	74	76
1972	83	92	84	71

Source: N. Potter and F. T. Christy, Jr., *Trends in Natural Resource Commodities* (Johns Hopkins Press, Baltimore, for Resources for the Future, 1962). Actual prices are weighted by the values of output, updated using 1967 weights by Robert S. Manthy, Michigan State University. The indexes of actual prices are deflated by the Consumer Price Index, 1967 = 100.

3 Explanation

Without a useful theory there can be no satisfactory analysis of the determinants that account for the changes in relative prices that have been presented. The determinants presumably are an integral part of the particular historical process covered in the preceding section. Since "growth" implies changes over time, the theory that is required could be referred to as a theory of economic growth. But it is fair to say that as yet there is no growth theory that is sufficiently comprehensive in specifying the factors and events that determine the changes in relative prices and in the stocks of resources that occur as a consequence of observable economic behavior and that in turn are consistent with that behavior. Early classical economics was much concerned about prices but not about the turn that the prices of the services of the factors of production have taken in the countries here under consideration. Meanwhile, modern macro growth theory has tended to concentrate on changes in resource quantities.

There is little that is analytically useful in the various classical controversies that bears on the prices before us. The history of the price effects of natural resource rents on growth and income shares is not at home in Ricardian Rent. In fact, the rent share and the economic and associated social and political importance of landlords have declined markedly over time in high income countries. Why has Ricardian Rent lost its economic sting in these countries? The controversy on the Malthusian tendency toward subsistence wages provides no real clues to the factors and the process that may have accounted for the present high levels of living of the rank and file of people who work for a living in the countries at hand. What is called for instead is a population equilibrium theory that is determined by the high value of human time.[16] Nor do exploitation of labor polemics, coupled with the argument of Marx that wages tend to a subsistence level because of the industrial reserve army of unemployed workers, throw any light on the reasons for the large increases in real wages which require illumination. Although the magnificent classical dynamics gives much attention to prices and wages, it is not oriented to deal with our problem.

Before venturing on propositions for theorizing about growth, a simple supply and demand approach helps to clarify the unsolved problem. It is the intercept of the supply of and the demand for human time that presumably reveals the price we observe. An appeal to shifts in these schedules then accounts for the recorded increases in this price over time. Proceeding thus we see clearly that the key to this pricing problem is in the factors that determine the shifts in these schedules. We know a good deal about the factors that shift (increase) the supply both in terms of the size of the labor force and of the quality attributes of the workers. While this knowledge is useful, it is at best a partial picture of the supply changes that occur. The nub of the unresolved problem, however, arises out of the fact that we know very little about the factors that shift the demand upward over time and strongly so. But economic thinking along these lines does not take us beyond the point of seeing that these shifts in schedules are an important part of the story of economic growth.

In devising an approach to get at the factors that explain the shifts in these two schedules, an all-inclusive concept of capital formation is necessary. In using this concept it is essential to see the heterogeneity of the various old and new forms of capital and to specify each of these forms of capital in sufficient detail to determine not only substitution between them but also the interacting complementarity between them. In as much as capital formation entails investment, it is important not to conceal the changes over time in incentives, the anticipated rates of return to be had from alternative investment opportunities.

Changes in investment opportunities, events, and human behaviour alter the scale of value and the composition of the stock of capital. Alterations that enhance the scope of choices are favourable developments. The various forms of capital differ significantly in their attributes. Natural resources are not reproducible; structures, equipment, and inventories of commodities and goods are physical entities that are reproducible; and human beings are productive agents with the attributes of human capital. Human beings are also the optimizing agents, and in a fundamental sense it is their preferences that matter in the use that is made of the various forms of capital. The concept of human capital, its development and its usefulness, is a recent innovation. It is noteworthy that in high-income countries, the rate at which human capital increases exceeds that of nonhuman capital.

In specifying the heterogeneity of capital, it is not sufficient to classify the capital forms as natural resources, reproducible material forms and human capital, because of the important role that new forms of capital within each of these classes play in altering relative prices (returns) and in shifting supply and demand schedules. An all-inclusive concept of capital that accounts fully for its heterogeneity is the core of the analytical model that is required.[17]

It will be necessary to make room in this approach to growth and changes in relative prices for the following three propositions:

(1)   The Ricardian principle that an increasing share of national income accrues to land (natural resources) rent needs to be replaced by the proposition that this share tends to decline as a consequence of man-made substitutes for land. The creation of hybrid corn is a notable example which may be viewed as a substitute or alternatively as a new input augmenting the yield from land. Plastics and aluminium become substitutes for various metals and wood; and nuclear energy becomes a substitute for fossil fuels. The economics of producing such substitutes (research and development) is still in its infancy, and the prospective

output of this sector is subject to the same uncertainty as are the advances in useful nowledge.

(2)   Some new forms of capital are complementary to other forms of capital in production. A consequence of such complementarity is that particular new forms of material capital increase the demand for particular human skills (a subclass of human capital). A recent example of this is the computer. In turn particular new forms of human capital increase the demand for additional material capital of a particular sort. The development of an intricate bacteriological method for controlling airborne fungi while introducing desired flavor augmenting bacteria in producing cheeses and other milk products – a method that required the skill of a PhD in a branch of bacteriology – increased the demand for PhDs qualified to use this method and the demand for new types of equipment on the part of dairy industry. These complementary forms of capital need to be identified and included in the analytical model.

(3)   Changes in relative prices over time matter. Making room in economic growth models for this role of prices is a return to the approach of early classical economics. Since modern macro growth models tend to take prices as given (usually fixed), the inclusion of relative prices and their function is a radical analytical proposition. Be that as it may, relative prices, which include the alternative rates of return on investment, are the mainspring that drives the economic system. If this mainspring were not to exist, we would have to invent it by appealing to shadow prices.

The shifts in demand in favour of productive services of labor, which we need most of all in explaining the increases in the price of human time, are in large part a consequence of the complementarity advanced in the second of these propositions. But the state of the art of economics does not as yet permit us to identify and determine the effects of this complementarity on the demand for labor.

4   Implications

The implications to which we turn in closing are primarily the price and income effects of the increases in the value of human time. These effects include the enlargement of institutional protection of the rights of workers favoring human capital relative to property rights, the increases in the value added by labor relative to that added by materials in production, the decline in hours worked, the increases in labor's share of national income, the decline in fertility, and the high rate at which human capital increases. The human agent becomes ever more a capitalist by virtue of his personal human capital, and he seeks political support to protect the value of that capital. These are some of the major implications that call for brief comments.

(a)   Institutions

The rise in the value of human time makes new demands on institutions. Some political and legal institutions are especially subject to these demands. What we observe is that these institutions respond in many ways. The legal rights of labor are enlarged and in doing so some of the private rights of property are curtailed. The legal rights of tenants are also enhanced. Seniority and safety at work receive increasing protection and discrimination in employment is curtailed. I have dealt with these institutional issues and with ways of bringing the analytical tools of economics to bear on them elsewhere.[18]

(b)   Value Added to National Income

The history of national income by type indicates clearly that large changes have occurred over time that parallel and are associated with a rise in the real earnings of workers. The interactions between the labor force at work and hourly wages on the one hand and the amount of nonhuman capital and the price of the services of that capital on the other, are exceedingly complex. Kuznets[19] gives us an analysis of these interactions in which he takes account of the increases in the stock of wealth represented by 'land' and of the stock of reproducible producer capital and the changes in the prices of the services of these forms of capital along with the increases in man-hours worked and the rise in the price per man-hour worked. His analysis implies a large relative increase in the value added by labor.

The obverse of the increase in labor's contribution to national income is the decline in the share contributed by property assets. I appeal once again to the studies of Kuznets,[20] where he takes a fairly long view of the development in Western countries and finds that the share of national income attributed to property assets declined from about 45 to 25 percent, while labor's part rose from about 55 to 75 percent.

By 1970, about three-fourths of the official US national income by type consisted of employee compensation.[21] The remaining fourth is classified as proprietors' income, rental income, net interest and corporate profits. These four classes of 'property' income include considerable amounts of earnings[22] that accrue to human agents for the productive time they devote to self-employed work and to the management of their property assets. A conservative estimate of the aggregate contribution to human agents in 1970, measured by employee compensation plus self-employment earnings, and for management of assets, within the domain of the market sector, was fully four-fifths of the value of the production that is accounted for in national income.

Measured national income, however, is substantially less than the full income that people realize from the services of their property and from their time, inasmuch as the concept of national income is restricted to the economic activities of the market sector. It excludes the economic value of all household production. The additional income that is realized from household production is in large part contributed by the value of the time of housewives. Also omitted is the value of time that adult students invest in their education, and the time that is not paid for fully that (younger) members of the labor force invest in on-the-job training. These and still other income producing activities are not included in the accounting of national income.

(c) Time Allocated to Work

Price and income effects of hourly earnings explain a wide array of changes in the allocation of time. When expected future earnings from more education rise, the response of youth is to postpone entering upon work for pay in order to devote more years to education. The advantage of youth in acquiring the additional education is of two parts, namely the wages that youth forgo are lower than they are at older ages and there are more years on ahead for youth to cash in on the expected higher earnings from the additional education. As wages increase, people who earn their income by working can afford to retire at an earlier age because of the larger retirement income that they are able to accumulate during their prime working years. A counter-effect of increases in earnings is in the improvement in health that is purchased, which extends the years that individuals may opt for work. The rise in the value of time of women is an incentive to substitute various forms of physical capital for their time in household production, and in as much as children are for women labor-intensive, the demand for children is reduced, and an increasing part of the time of women is allocated to the market for labor.

The increases in earnings also explain the decline in hours of work or the increase in 'leisure' during this century. For the US civilian economy the average weekly hours declined from about 53 to 37 hours over the period from 1900 to 1970, and the average annual hours per employee decreased from 2766 to 1929 hours. The interaction between annual hours allocated to work and earnings shows a decline of 7 percent in hours and a 43 percent increase in annual earnings between 1900 and 1920, for the 1920 to 1940 period these changes were 12 percent and 53 percent respectively; and for 1940 to 1970 there occurred a 13 percent decline in annual hours while real annual earnings increased by 73 per cent.[23]

(d) Labor's Income Share

Most of the story on the changes in labor's share can be inferred from relative increases in the value added by labor to national income already presented. There is, however, another set of estimates that tend to confirm the inferences from the value added by labor. The US employed civilian labor was 26.96 million in 1900 and 78.63 million in 1970, a 2.9-fold increase. When the adjustment is made for the 30 per cent decline in annual hours worked, the increase in total employed hours in 1970 is only twice that of 1900. Despite the decline in annual hours, the 1970 aggregate labor earnings in 1967 dollars was slightly more than eleven times as large as it was in 1900. Since the distribution of US national income by type implies a somewhat larger aggregate for the earnings of labor in 1970, the plausible explanation for the difference is that the real wage of manufacturing workers understates somewhat the average annual earnings of the employed labor force as would be expected in view of relatively large increases in the number of more educated, mostly salaried, workers.

Another confirming approach to labor's share is to examine the changes in the functional shares of the various types of national income. During 1900–9, using the official concept of national income, employee compensation accounted for about 55 per cent of national income compared to 75 percent in 1970. Between 1900–9 and 1970, the changes in the shares of income other than employee compensation were as follows: proprietors' income declined from about 24 to 8 percent, rental income from 9 to 3 percent and net interest from 5.5 to 4.1 percent of national income, whereas corporate profits rose from 7 to 9 percent. The latter two income components fluctuated widely over this period as would be expected in view of the uneven performance of the economy over time.

(e)   Increases in Labor's Stock of Human Capital

Lastly we turn to the investment in human capital.[25] Economic theory has been extended to explain the accumulation of human capital and even more so to an analysis of the price and income effects of this form of capital, which has led to important new approaches in bringing economics to bear on human behaviour.[26] The absolute difference in the earnings between the less and more educated workers is an important incentive (disincentive). A part of the increases in the price of human time is a consequence of investments in education.

As already noted, although the US labor force virtually tripled between 1900 and 1970, the aggregate hours devoted to market work increased much less as a consequence of the decreases in annual hours that employed labor worked. During this same period, however, the aggregate stock of education embodied in the US labor force, measured in terms of 1956 unit costs of education, increased from 63 billion to 815 billion dollars, a thirteen-fold increase. Estimates of these costs of education for selected years from 1900 to 1967 were published in 1961.[27]

The first important calculation in these estimates of the costs of education is the adjustment for changes in the level of prices. For the base price year, 1956, the costs come to $280 per year for the elementary schooling, $1420 per year for high school and $3300 per year for college and university education. The second entails adjusting the elementary schooling to an *equivalent school year* of 152 days of school attendance to cope with the fact that starting with 1900 the average attendance of enrolled pupils, ages 5 to 15, was only 99 days. Table 3.2.7 shows the years of schooling and all the costs of this schooling per member of the labor force for 1900, 1940, 1957, and 1970.

Whereas human capital accounting includes investment in on-the-job training, which is large as Mincer has shown,[28] the costs and returns to migration[29] and investments made to improve health, education is probably the most important in this context. The increases in the value of education in the US labor force, based on the costs of acquiring the education, add to the stock of human capital relative to the stock of reproducible non-human capital, which is shown for selected years from 1900 to 1970 in table 3.7.8.

Throughout most of the world, labor earns a pittance. Work is hard and life is harsh. Countries with low earnings cover most of the world's map. In a few countries, however, the value of the time of the rank and file of people is exceedingly high. In these countries the secular increases in real wages and salaries represent gains in economic welfare, which are

Table 3.7.7 United States labor force years of schooling adjusted for school attendance and costs of education adjusted to 1956 prices, 1900, 1940, 1957 and 1970

Level of schooling (1)	Years of school per member (2)	Cost per year in 1956 prices (3)	Cost per member of labor force col. (2) × col. (3) (4)	percentage distribution of col. (4) (5)
1900				
Elementary	3.437	$ 280	$ 962	43
High school	0.556	1420	790	35
College and university	0.147	3300	485	22
TOTAL	4.140		2237	100
1940				
Elementary	6.85	280	1918	33
High school	1.71	1420	2428	41
College and university	0.46	3300	1518	26
TOTAL	9.02		5864	100
1957				
Elementary	7.52	280	2106	28
High school	2.44	1420	3458	45
College and university	0.64	3300	2099	27
TOTAL	10.60		7663	100
1970				
Elementary	7.75	280	2170	23
High school	3.04	1420	4317	45
College and university	0.91	3300	3003	32
TOTAL	11.70		9490	100

Sources: The estimates for 1900, 1940 and 1957 appears in Theodore W. Schultz, 'Education and Economic Growth', tables 11, 12, and 13. Those for 1970 were undertaken for this paper. The official data on median years of schooling overstate the actual years as shown in this table. No upward adjustment has been made for the fact that the average days of school attendance had risen to 163 days by 1970.

Table 3.7.8 Stock of education in the labor force and the stock of two classes of reproducible non-human capital compared for selected years, 1900 to 1970, United States (billion dollars)

Year (1)	Educational stock in labor force (2)	Stock of reproducible non-human wealth (3)	Percentage col. (2) of col. (3) (4)	Stock of business capital (5)	Percentage col. (2) of col. (5) (6)
1900	63	282	22		
1910	94	463	23		
1920	127	526	24		
1930	180	735	24	491	37
1940	248	756	33	475	52
1950	359	969	37	557	64
1957	535	1270	42	700	76
1970	815			1089	75

Sources: cols (2) and (3) for 1900 and up through 1957 are from Theodore W. Schultz, 'Education and Economic Growth', table 14. Col. (3) is from Raymond W. Goldsmith, *The National Wealth of the United States in the Postwar Period*, (Princeton University Press, Princeton, N.J., 1962). See the note on these estimates that is part of table 14 in 'Education and Economic Growth'. Col. (5) is from series A 151 in *Long Term Economic Growth, 1860–1970*, pp. 206–7. In estimating the educational stock in the labor force for 1970 the labor force aged 16 and over is used, whereas for early years the reported labor force is for ages 12 and over.

the most significant achievement of their economic growth. Much less time is allocated to work for pay. Most of the work is no longer hard physically. Ever more skills are demanded, and the supply response of skills is strong and clear. But the increases in demand are still concealed in the complementarity between the various new forms of capital. On human capital formation, Kuznets' telling remarks open the door.

> . . . [Some] components now included under consumption could be viewed as capital investment, not because the expenditure is on durable goods . . . but because the use of the good is closely related to the efficiency of the consumer as a producer. The main item in question is the outlays on education (formal and on-the-job training) and there are some outlays on health care and recreation. . . . These components are far from negligible. . . . If direct costs of formal education alone are over 20 percent of gross capital formation, outlays on education, health, and recreation, treatable as investment in man, may well be as high as four-tenths of capital formation.[30]

Seeing the historical fact that despite the vast accumulation of capital the real rate of return to investment has not diminished over time, Knight in one of his classic papers perceived the role of improvements in the quality of the labor force and of the advances in the sciences as they affect, over time, the rate of return on investment.[31] There has been much aimless wandering in analyzing growth that could have been avoided had the perceptions of Marshall been heeded.

> Capital consists in a great part of knowledge and organization: knowledge is the most powerful engine of production; . . . The distinction between public and private property in knowledge and organization is of great and growing importance: in some respects of more importance than that between public and private property in material things. (Marshall Principles of Economics, book iv, pp. 138–9.)

Public and private investment in human capital and in useful knowledge are a large part of the story in accounting for the increases in the value of human time over time.

Appendix

Table 3.7A.1 Wages and the price of wheat for selected years 1817 to 1970 and October 1976

	Wheat (bushel) (1)	Wages (weekly) (2)	Weekly wages in bushels (3)
1817	$2.41[aa]	$ 5.04[d]	2.1
1890	0.97[b]	8.40[d]	8.7
1900	0.67[b]	8.64[d]	12.9
1970	1.58[c]	151.60[e]	95.9
1977 (August)	2.31[c]	255.38	110.6

Sources:
[a]*Historical Statistics of United States* (US Department of Commerce, 1960) Wholesale Price, Series E-101, Wheat.
[b]Neal Potter and Francis T. Christy, Jr., *Trends in Natural Resource Commodities*, published for Resources for the Future (Johns Hopkins Press, Baltimore, 1962), table Ap-3, p. 93, Kansas City average.
[c]Hard winter wheat, Kansas City, from current USDA reports.
[d]Hourly current wages of unskilled workers working 60 hours per week.
[e]Hourly current wages of manufacturing production workers working 40 hours per week including non-wage compensation, which adds 13 per cent to the money wages paid. From current reports of the Bureau of Labor Statistics.

Table 3.7A.2 Hourly wages or earnings and in 1967 dollars of unskilled workers, public school teachers, associate professors, and Rees's manufacturing production workers, US, selected dates since 1900

Year	Consumer price index 1967 = 100 (1)	Unskilled workers		Public school teachers in 1967 dollars (4)	Associate professors in 1967 dollars (5)	Rees's mfg. workers' wages in 1967 dollars (6)
		Hourly wage current dollars (2)	In 1967 dollars (3)			
1900	25	$0.144	$0.58	$0.82	$2.60	$0.60
1908	28	0.182	0.65	0.95	2.94	0.67
1910	29	0.181	0.62	0.96	2.98	0.70
1913	29.7	0.198	0.67	1.05	3.05	0.74
1915	30.4	0.212	0.70	1.08	3.11	0.74
1918	45.1	0.426	0.94	0.85	2.22	0.92
1919	51.8	0.513	0.99		2.11	0.92
1920	60	0.529	0.88	0.86	2.03	0.92
1922	50.2	0.402	0.80	1.30	2.99	0.90
1924	51.2	0.458	0.89	1.30	3.00	1.01
1926	53.0	0.461	0.87	1.28	2.98	0.96
1930	50	0.478	0.96	1.49	3.36	1.06
1932	40.9	0.400	0.98	1.82	4.17	1.09
1934	40.1	0.479	1.19	1.61		1.32
1935	41.1	0.495	1.20	1.62	3.56	1.32
1940	42.0	0.611	1.45	1.85	4.20	1.60
1942	48.8	0.773	1.58	1.66	3.49	1.77
1950	72.1	1.19	1.65	2.30	3.60	2.15

1955	80.2	1.52	1.90	2.72	n.a.	2.55
1960	88.7	1.83	2.06	3.28	4.57	2.85
1965	94.5	2.15	2.28	3.91	5.61	3.13
1969	109.8	2.69	2.45	4.31	6.12	3.29
1970	116.3	2.88	2.48	4.39	6.18	3.27
1972	125.3	3.30	2.63	4.65	6.15	3.44
1975	161.2	4.24	2.63	4.32	5.75	3.37

Sources: The hourly wages in column (6) are Albert Rees's estimates of total compensation per hour of work of manufacturing production workers appearing in *Long Term Economic Growth, 1860–1970* (US Bureau of Economic Analysis, Washington, DC, 1973) Appendix 2, B70, pp. 222–23. They are up-dated and adjusted from 1957 to 1967 dollars. The estimates for unskilled workers, teachers and associate professors are from a paper by Peter H. Lindert and Jeffrey G. Williamson, "Three Centuries of American Inequality", in Paul Uselding (ed.), *Research in Economic History*, vol. I (1976), table A-1, pp. 118–19. Beginning with 1930, the salaries of teachers are from the *Digest of Educational Statistics, 1975 Edition*, table 53, and the salaries of associate professors are from Beardsley Rumle and Sidney G. Tickon, *Teachers' Salaries Then and Now*, Bul. No. 1, (Ford Foundation, 1955) table 3, p. 55 up through 1953. Beginning in 1960, they are from the *Digest of Educational Statistics 1975 Edition*, table 99. Beginning with 1940 the salaries of teachers and associate professors are adjusted for fringe benefits as follows: 1940 and 1942, by 2½ percent; 1950 and 1955, by 5 percent; teachers' salaries are increased by 7½ percent for 1960 and 1965 and from then on by 10 percent. Associate professors are raised by 10 percent beginning in 1960 and on. The 1900 estimate for associate professors was derived from supplementary data.

Table 3.7A.3 Indexes of deflated agricultural commodity prices, United States, 1900–72 (1900 = 100)

Year	All agriculture	All livestock	All crops
1900	100	100	100
1910	126	127	118
1920	111	118	87
1930	90	99	73
1940	86	95	73
1950	131	141	110
1960	95	101	75
1970	88	100	66
1972	92	104	69

Sources: The same as those cited in table 3.7.6 of the text.

Table 3.7A.4 Indexes of deflated commodity prices of metals and mineral fuels (1900 = 100)

Year	All metals	All mineral fuels	Petroleum	Natural gas	Bituminous coal
1900	100	100	100	(100)	100
1910	76	48	42	–	93
1920	66	118	131	118	146
1930	45	61	59	111	79
1940	60	59	57	80	104
1950	68	81	84	68	156
1960	75	79	79	119	125
1970	76	72	68	111	125
1972	71	73	67	112	143

Sources: The same as those cited for table 3.7.6 in the text.

Table 3.7A.5 Weekly hours, annual hours, hourly wages and annual earnings in 1967 dollars, selected years 1900 to 1970 for the United States economy

	Average weekly hours civilian economy (1)	Average annual hours per employee (2)	Hourly wages in 1967 dollars (3)	Annual earnings in 1967 dollras (col. 2 × col. 3) (4)
1900	53.2	2766	0.60	1660
1910	52.1	2705	0.70	1894
1920	49.8	2584	0.92	2377
1930	47.7	2477	1.06	2626
1935	42.6	2210	1.32	2917
1940	43.9	2278	1.60	3645
1945	45.7	2331	1.97	4592
1950	41.4	2141	2.15	4603
1960	40.0	2068	2.85	5894
1970	37.1	1929	3.27	6308

Sources: cols (1) and (2) are from *Long Term Economic Growth, 1860–1970*, (Bureau of Economic Analysis, USDA, Washington, DC), Series B4 and B5, p. 212; col. (3) is from table 3.7A.2 above.

Notes and References

1 Alfred Marshall, *Principles of Economics* (8th edn, Macmillan and Co., 1930), preface, p. xv.
2 In 1975 the weekly wage of the ploughman in India was somewhat less than the price of two bushels of wheat.
3 See Appendix, table 3.7 A.1. It may be said that the 1970 price of wheat was an unrealistic low price in view of events that occurred in the early 1970s. It is true that wheat prices soared but then declined sharply as production increased. By August 1977, a week of wages was equal to the price of 110 bushels of wheat.
4 See Albert Rees, "Pattern of Wages, Prices and Productivity," in *Wages, Prices, Profits, and Productivity*, Proceedings of the American Assembly (Columbia University Press, New York, June 1959), pp. 11–35 for the components that account for these wage supplements and his estimates of them from 1929 to 1957 which appear in table 1, p. 15.
5 Ibid., p. 12.
6 Ibid., p. 13.
7 See *Economic Report of the President*, 1976, tables B-27 and B-28.
8 Another way of describing these changes is to note that real hourly wages

rose weakly from 1900 to the middle of the next decade, they then rose sharply during the First World War, after which they rose weakly throughout the 1920s and early 1930s. There then follows a strong upward trend for two and a half decades, after which they rose less strongly once again from the late 1950s to 1970. The years which show a decline are 1904, 1907, and 1908, and then 1914, 1919, 1921, 1922, 1925, 1932, 1945, and 1946.

9 The academic market for associate professors is a more active market than it is for professors; it is therefore subject to shorter lags in adjusting to changes in normal wages and in the costs of acquiring the required professional skills than it is for those who attained the rank of professor.

10 The projected labor force for 1990 was 112.6 million, an increase of 31 percent over that of 1970. From *Manpower Report of the President*, 1975, table E-3, p. 309.

11 In interpreting the increases in real wages shown in table 3.7.5, it should be borne in mind that we are now dealing with real annual wages in industry. They are not hourly wages. They are less complete in getting at the total compensation of employees than the estimates by Rees. Accordingly, Rees's estimates show a higher rate of increase than those in E. H. Phelps-Brown, "Levels and Movements of Industrial Productivity and Real Wages Internationally Compared, 1860–1970," *Economic Journal*, 83, 58–71. Thus, for the United States during the period from 1900 to 1970, Brown's real wages show a fourfold increase and Rees's real hourly "wages" a strong fivefold rise.

12 N. Potter and F. T. Christy Jr., *Trends in Natural Resource Commodities* (Johns Hopkins Press for Resources for the Future, Baltimore, 1962).

13 Professor Robert S. Manthy, Michigan State University, has been most generous in making offsets of his numerous tables available to me. I am much indebted to him.

14 The reader may believe that the 1973–75 rise in prices of the services most dependent on natural resources was the beginning of a new era. But the upsurge in prices was in large part transitory. The economic processes that accounted for the observed prices, say from 1960 to 1972, were approximately the more permanent relative prices that are in general likely to prevail instead of the very high transitory prices of 1973–75.

15 For a more complete analysis of these commodity prices and of natural resource rents, see Theodore W. Schultz, *The Economic Value of Human Time* (Economic Research Service, USDA, Washington, DC, 1977, pp. 1–24). See also John V. Krutilla and Anthony C. Fisher, *The Economics of the Natural Environments* (Johns Hopkins Press for Resources of the Future, Baltimore, 1975); and Peter H. Lindert, "Land Scarcity and American Growth," *Journal of Economic History*, 34 (1974), 851–84.

16 Theodore W. Schultz, "Fertility and Economic Values, II: The High Value of Human Time: Population Equilibrium," and Marc Nerlove, "Toward a New Theory of Population and Economic Growth," both in Theodore W. Schultz (ed.), *Economics of the Family: Marriage, Children, and Human*

Capital (University of Chicago Press, Chicago, Ill., 1975), pp. 14–22 and 527–45 respectively.

17 Harry G. Johnson, "Toward a Generalized Capital Accumulation Approach to Economic Development," in *The Residual Factor and Economic Growth* (OECD, Paris, 1964), pp. 219–27.

18 See Theodore W. Schultz, "Institutions and the Rising Economic Value of Man," *American Journal of Agricultural Economics*, 50 (Dec. 1968), (113–22). See also the useful paper by Vernon W. Ruttan, *Integrated Rural Development Programs: A Skeptical Perspective* (Agricultural Development Council, New York, 1975, reprinted from *International Development Review*, 17, No. 4, 1975).

19 Simon Kuznets, *Modern Economic Growth* (Yale University Press, New Haven, Conn., 1966), chapter 4, pp. 181–83, bears directly on this analytical issue. This part of the analysis is restricted to the US and to the period from 1909–14 to 1955–57.

20 Simon Kuznets' studies of economic growth and the distribution of income are classic contributions to this subject. See: (1) "Economic Growth and Income Inequality," *American Economic Review*, 45 (Mar. 1955), 1–28; (2) "Quantitative Aspects of the Economic Growth of Nations, VIII: Distribution of Income by Size," *Economic Development and Cultural Change*, 11(II) (Jan. 1963), 1–80; (3) *Modern Economic Growth*, and (4) *Economic Growth and Nations* (Harvard Unviersity Press, Cambridge, Mass., 1971).

21 US Bureau of Economic Analysis, *Long Term Economic Growth, 1860–1970* (Washington, DC, 1973), p. 22. Compensation of employees includes income accruing to persons in an employee status as wages and salaries, tips, bonuses, commissions, vacation pay, and payments in kind. Also included are supplements and fringe benefits such as employers' contributions to private pension, health, and welfare funds.

22 We shall restrict the concept of *earnings* to the income that accrues to human agents as compensation for their productive services. The income accruing to the owners of property assets for the productive services of their property will be referred to as *property income*.

23 See Appendix, table 3.7A.5, for the data on which the figures in this paragraph are based.

24 *Long Term Economic Growth*, p. 22, percentage distribution of national income by type.

25 For a generalized approach to this type of investment, see above, Part II, No. 1. See also Theodore W. Schultz, *Human Resources*, Fiftieth Anniversary Colloquium VI (National Bureau of Economic Research, New York, 1972); *The Economic Value of Education* (Columbia University Press, New York, 1963); and *Investment in Human Capital: The Role of Education and Research* (Free Press, New York, 1971).

26 See especially the seminal contributions of Gary S. Becker, which include his *Human Capital: A Theoretical and Empirical Analysis with Special Reference to Education* (National Bureau of Economic Research, New York,

1964); "A Theory of the Allocation of Time," *Economic Journal*, 75 (Sept. 1965), 493–517; "A Theory of Marriage," in Schultz (ed.), *Economics of the Family*; and *The Economic Approach to Human Behavior* (University of Chicago Press, Chicago, Ill., 1976). See also Jacob Mincer, *Schooling, Experience and Earnings* Columbia University Press for National Bureau of Economic Research, New York, 1974).

27 See Theodore W. Schultz, "Education and Economic Growth," in Nelson B. Henry (ed.), *Social Forces Influencing American Education* (University of Chicago Press, Chicago, Ill., 1961), pp. 46–88.

28 Jacob Mincer, "On-the-Job Training; Costs, Returns, and Some Implications," in Theodore W. Schultz (ed.), *Investment in Human Beings, Journal of Political Economy*, part 2, Supplement (Oct. 1962), pp. 50–79.

29 See Larry A. Sjaastad, ibid., pp. 80–93.

30 Kuznets, *Modern Economic Growth*, p. 228.

31 Frank Knight, "Diminishing Returns from Investment," *Journal of Political Economy*, 52 (Mar. 1944), 26–47.

Index

Printed and bound by CPI Group (UK) Ltd, Croydon, CR0 4YY

16/04/2025

14658825-0003